T0314306

WHAT WORKS, WHAT DOESN'T (AND WHEN)

Behaviourally Informed
Organizations

**BEHAVIOURALLY INFORMED
ORGANIZATIONS**

To date, there has been a lack of practical advice for organizations based on behavioral research. The Behaviourally Informed Organizations series fills this knowledge gap with a strategic perspective on how governments, businesses, and other organizations have embedded behavioral insights into their operations. The series is rooted in work by academics and practitioners cocreating knowledge via the Behaviourally Informed Organizations Partnership (www.biorgpartnership. com), and is written in a highly accessible style to highlight key ideas, pragmatic frameworks, and prescriptive outcomes based on illustrative case studies.

Also in the series:

What Works,
What Doesn't (and When)

Case Studies in Applied
Behavioral Science

EDITED BY DILIP SOMAN

UNIVERSITY OF TORONTO PRESS
Toronto Buffalo London

© University of Toronto Press 2024
Rotman-UTP Publishing
An imprint of University of Toronto Press
Toronto Buffalo London
utorontopress.com

ISBN 978-1-4875-4873-5 (cloth)   ISBN 978-1-4875-5106-3 (EPUB)
                                   ISBN 978-1-4875-5050-9 (PDF)

Library and Archives Canada Cataloguing in Publication

Title: What works, what doesn't (and when) : case studies in applied
    behavioral science / edited by Dilip Soman.
Names: Soman, Dilip, editor.
Description: Series statement: Behaviorally informed organizations |
    Includes bibliographical references.
Identifiers: Canadiana (print) 20240280989 | Canadiana (ebook)
    20240281047 | ISBN 9781487548735 (cloth) | ISBN 9781487551063
    (EPUB) | ISBN 9781487550509 (PDF)
Subjects: LCSH: Psychology – Research – Case studies. | LCSH: Human
    behavior – Research – Case studies.
Classification: LCC BF76.5 .W43 2024 | DDC 150.72 – dc23

Cover design: Regina Starace

We wish to acknowledge the land on which the University of Toronto Press
operates. This land is the traditional territory of the Wendat, the Anishnaabeg,
the Haudenosaunee, the Métis, and the Mississaugas of the Credit First Nation.

University of Toronto Press acknowledges the financial support of the
Government of Canada and the Ontario Arts Council, an agency of the
Government of Ontario, for its publishing activities.

Funded by the   Financé par le
Government   gouvernement
of Canada   du Canada

ONTARIO ARTS COUNCIL
CONSEIL DES ARTS DE L'ONTARIO
an Ontario government agency
un organisme du gouvernement de l'Ontario

Contents

Supplemental figures and tables for chapters 3, 7, 11, 14, and 15 are provided in an online appendix that can be viewed at https://www.biorgpartnership.com/what-works.

Acknowledgments

This book was made possible due to the support of the Behaviourally Informed Organizations Partnership (biorgpartnership.com) housed at the Behavioural Economics in Action at Rotman (BEAR) research center at the University of Toronto. The partnership is financially supported by a grant from the Social Sciences and Humanities Council of Canada (SSHRC). We thank all the members of the partnership for their comments, suggestions, and discussions on the materials in this book. Special thanks are due to Karrie Chou and Cindy Luo for managing the book project, to Bing Feng for managing the partnership, and to Nina Mažar for serving as a guest editor (for chapter 3) and providing feedback. We also thank the members of the partnership steering committee and our internal review board – Abigail Dalton, Dale Griffin, Melanie Kim, Katy Milkman, Kyle Murray, Sasha Tregebov, Melaina Vinski, and Min Zhao.

Joonkyung Kim and Dilip Soman (chapter 3) acknowledge that their project was made possible through the support of the New Paths to Purpose Project at the University of Chicago's Center for Decision Research, funded by a grant from the John Templeton Foundation (FP049739-F). The opinions expressed in this publication are those of the author(s) and do not necessarily reflect the views of the John Templeton Foundation. They also thank Dan Tao, Zohra Ilhom, Yue Zhuo, Christine Lim, and Liz Kang for managing the project, and Julie Lee and colleagues at MultiMension for developing the Purpose App. This project was completed when Kim was a graduate student at the University of Toronto.

Ulf J.J. Hahnel, Christian Mumenthaler, Tessa Dent Ferrel, and Tobias Brosch (chapter 5) would like to thank the Services Industrials de Genève (SIG) for enabling and supporting this project and the

Behaviour Change Lab (BCLab) for their valuable contributions to the implementation of the experimental design in the field.

Anisha Singh and Steve Wendel (chapter 6) thank the Busara Center of Behavioral Economics and Centre for Social and Behavior Change (CSBC). Their chapter is based on a study conducted by the Busara Center.

Alex Gyani (chapter 12) thanks the large team of people who were involved in the project in ANZ, especially Janice Wilson, Catherine Gerard, Richard Hamblin, Carl Shuker, Janet Mackay, Rawiri McKree Jansen, Richard Medlicott, Aniva Lawrence, Sally Roberts, Jan White, Sarah Hayward, and Leanne Te Karu. He would especially like to acknowledge all the work that Nathan Chappell put into the trial in ANZ; the trial would not have happened without Nathan. He would also like to acknowledge all the work undertaken by the teams in the UK that developed the original interventions and the replications undertaken in Australia by the Behavioural Economics Research Team in the Australian Department of Health (BERT) and the Behavioural Economics Team of the Australian government (BETA). Finally, he would like to thank Michael Hallsworth for his helpful comments on the manuscript.

Wing Hsieh, Nicholas Faulkner, and Rebecca Wickes (chapter 14) acknowledge that their chapter is derived in part from an article published in *Basic and Applied Social Psychology* – Hsieh, W., Faulkner, N., Wickes, R. (2022). Perceived variability as a video-media prejudice reduction intervention. *Basic and Applied Social Psychology*, 44(2), 66–83. https://doi.org/10.1080/01973533.2022.2069025. This research was completed as part of a PhD undertaken at Monash University, supported by the Australian Government Research Training Program and Australia Post. They would also like to thank Gilda Good for the filming and editing of the intervention videos.

Andris Saulītis (chapter 15) would like to thank Eva Juhņēviča, Zaiga Barvida and Ģirts Slaviņš for their support throughout the project, and Ivars Austers, Anda Ķīvīte-Urtāne and Vineta Silkāne for their comments on the initial experimental design, as well as Ņikita Trojanskis and Signe Širova for their assistance during the data collection. The study has been supported by the European Regional Development Fund under the activity "Post-doctoral Research Aid", project Nr. 1.1.1.2/VIAA/4/20/612.

Todd Rogers (chief scientist [unpaid], cofounder, board member, and equity holder) and Avi Feller (cofounder and equity holder of Every-Day Labs), authors of chapter 16, would like to thank the dozens of people involved in conducting the research described in this chapter and in building EveryDay Labs. Special thanks to funders, including

The Laura and John Arnold Foundation, Chan Zuckerberg Initiative, Institute of Education Sciences (US Department of Education), Heising-Simons Foundation, Silicon Valley Community Foundation, and Pershing Square Venture Fund for Research on the Foundations of Human Behavior; district leaders, including Bill Hite (School District of Philadelphia) and Nancy Magee (San Mateo County Office of Education); and previous members of the S3 R&D Lab.

Behavioral Science and "What Works" – Inseparable but in Tension? A Foreword

Michael Hallsworth

Over the last fifteen years, the application of behavioral science to practical issues has become intertwined with the question of "what works." Attempts to answer this question have usually prioritized several principles or assumptions that sometimes remain implicit. These include the following: an intervention should be evaluated (rather than just implemented on the basis of existing evidence); the evaluation should mainly use quantitative methods; establishing a causal link between intervention and outcome is extremely important, and therefore randomized approaches are valuable; and measurements of revealed behavior in real-world settings are particularly meaningful. Most guides to applying behavioral science emphasize some or all of these principles. Arguably, the paradigmatic behavioral insights project involves a randomized controlled trial (RCT) in a real-world setting: one of the first (and most high-profile) publications from the UK's Behavioural Insights Team (BIT) was called "Test, Learn, Adapt."[1]

The pairing of "what works?" with behavioral science had enduring and important consequences, as I explain below, but we should not see it as inevitable. It could have been that the pioneers of the latest wave of applied behavioral science decided that their standard approach would be to take findings and simply apply them to major policy questions with no testing or focus on outcomes. Or there could have been another surge of interest in the use of experimental and quasi-experimental policy evaluations that had little or nothing to do with the findings from behavioral science. In fact, some offshoots of the behavioral insights movement have been explicitly focused on promoting policy evaluation, with only a light application of behavioral science.[2]

Many readers will be familiar with the concept of hindsight bias – what happens when people feel "I knew it all along," even if they did not.[3] We think that an outcome was more predictable than it was, just because it happened. And so it's worth pausing to consider why you are reading a book titled simply "What Works, What Doesn't (and When)" that is actually all about applied behavioral science. I can offer reflections based on my direct experience in the UK context, as well as some broader speculations.

One set of drivers came from practitioners and public officials. Certainly, in the UK, there was continuity between (a) explicit attempts to establish better use of evidence and evaluation and (b) the growth of the behavioral insights movement. Back in 1999, the UK Cabinet Office launched its model of "professional policymaking," presenting policymaking as an activity that "uses best available evidence from a wide range of sources and involves key stakeholders at an early stage," "builds systemic evaluation of early outcomes into the policy process," and "learns from experience of what works and what does not."[4] These attempts were closely associated with a team called the Performance and Innovation Unit, which, in 2002, was merged with a couple of others to create the Prime Minister's Strategy Unit (PMSU).[5]

Unsurprisingly, the PMSU had an explicit commitment to empirical and evidence-based policymaking. As part of this agenda, in 2004 it published a lengthy position paper that ran through current findings from behavioral science and how they might be applied to policy (including ideas that were indeed applied later, such as opt-out pensions schemes).[6] Moreover, when the BIT was created in 2010, a substantial number of its staff were taken from the newly-deceased PMSU – including its chief executive, David Halpern, who was also to serve as the UK's National What Works advisor between 2012 and 2022.[7]

In addition to this overlap of personnel and institutions between the "what works" and behavioral science agendas, there were also similarities from a conceptual perspective. Kahneman and Tversky's studies from the 1970s onwards were a core intellectual foundation of the new wave of applied behavioral science. They supplied experimental results that challenged the accepted principles of neoclassical economics. In other words, they offered empirical evidence of behavioral drivers and influences that did not fit with the dominant intellectual system or ideology.

Kahneman and Tversky's studies therefore offered a clear and salient example of how the experimental paradigm could disrupt existing thinking with new evidence of "what works." For those trying to apply behavioral science to public policy in the late 2000s and early 2010s, the "existing thinking" about behavior often seemed to be qualitative research that overemphasized the role of attitudes and intentions, and underemphasized the role of non-conscious processes. In this context, skepticism about existing claims encouraged the use of experimental methods to evaluate them.

Such skepticism was not partisan; it extended to findings from the heuristics and biases literature as well. At this point in time, there were widespread concerns that findings obtained in laboratory settings would not hold true in the real world – or, if they did, they would not have a meaningful effect on behavior.[8] Practitioners were genuinely uncertain about what effect they might be having. Hence the fact that the UK Behavioural Insights Team was set up with a "sunset clause": if it failed to demonstrate a tenfold financial return on the cost of the team within two years, it would be shut down.[9]

Taking this skeptical approach has many commendable results. The practitioner's expectations and desires become secondary to the reality of "what works" (and what does not) according to the outcome data. On many occasions, I have had to stand in front of partners and tell them that we did not find any effects (interestingly, these conversations often go better than one may expect). Real-world testing can also provide early warnings about unsound results. Famously, a 2012 study found evidence that "signing at the beginning" of forms reduced dishonest self-reports.[10] I and others at BIT failed to replicate this study, sometimes at considerable cost. Two of these studies were subsequently cited in the 2020 paper (coauthored by the original authors) that found that "signing at the beginning versus at the end does not decrease dishonesty."[11]

However, applied behavioral science's focus on "what works" has also produced complications. Let us note that the approach may place strong emphasis on the result of an evaluation as a judgment on whether it "works" or not (often using this binary distinction implicitly or explicitly). Sometimes the act of setting up an RCT has required effort and sacrifice from both the behavioral scientist and the partner organization; arguably, this can mean that they privilege the results in order to reduce cognitive dissonance.[12]

Regardless of the exact mechanism, the outcome can be that the trial results are treated as definitive, frozen, and reified. "Now we know what works." The principles of the approach that produced such a result – the importance of skeptical testing – may fade in people's minds, leaving only the finding behind. I know of several messages that I tested in public-sector organizations over a decade ago that are still being used, word-for-word. The good news is that I have heard they still "work," but they were created with the expectation that they (and others) would be re-evaluated, rather than petrified.

This may be a naive view. Quite apart from the fact that humans are usually effort minimizers, it may be that the "what works" approach faces a more specific conundrum. If running an RCT in a real-world setting produces a convincing result, there may be an appetite to try this approach on other issues and produce other results. But – at least in my experience – there is often little appetite to run the *same* trial again in a different place or a different time (in other words, to complicate the question of "what works" again).

I don't want to overemphasize this point. I've been involved in many studies that explicitly retested an intervention in a different time or place.[13] But, in a world where RCTs evaluating policy and administrative practices are still relatively rare, it can seem almost unreasonable to push for more when you *have* managed to conduct an RCT on a meaningful issue. The evidence you have here is still more convincing than that for all the other decisions where organizations are operating on chance, habit, or instinct.

Therefore, in practice, emphasizing the question of "what works" may cut against answering the broader question of "what works for whom, where, and when." Building anticipation for a trial result may obscure the fact that "what works" should be seen as an insistent question linked to a continual process. The hard part is that such anticipation and enthusiasm may be unavoidable in the first place.

Other aspects of the "what works" agenda are worth digging into. Fairly obviously, "what works" offers a technocratic perspective on government.[14] Beliefs, convictions, political positions, and ideology are placed in opposition to evidence of "what works" produced by experts. This opposition can be seen clearly in statements from the UK government in the period leading up to the creation of BIT in 2010:

> This Government has given a clear commitment that we will be guided not by dogma but by an open-minded approach to understanding what works and why.[15] (2000)
>
> While not a new concept, the current emphasis on evidence-based policy making has its roots in Government's commitment to "what works" over ideologically driven policy.[16] (2006)

This contrast is not always drawn so explicitly, but it is often present in some way. There are definitely benefits to this technocratic frame. It can bridge partisan divides, for example: testing and trialing government activities as part of a commitment to evaluation can attract support across the political spectrum. From the left, it can represent a commitment to evidence and expertise; from the right, it can represent a skeptical commitment to making sure tax revenues are spent effectively. For example, the US federal government's Office of Evaluation Sciences applied behavioral science on this basis throughout the Trump administration (the same administration that signed the 2018 Foundations for Evidence-Based Policymaking Act). The Bloomberg Philanthropies "What Works Cities" program, which BIT supports as a core partner, manages to engage mayors from both major US parties for precisely this reason.

Attempts to apply scientific or technical knowledge to resolve or obviate political questions have a long history, going back to the Positivism of the nineteenth century. Back then, Henri de Saint-Simon dreamed of a world where technical skill had allowed policy to rise above the realm of politics: "All the questions which have to be debated in such a political system ... are eminently positive and answerable; the correct decisions can only be the result of scientific demonstrations."[17]

The more modern version of this worldview has been termed "scientism": the idea that "all the important problems facing human civilization are technical, and that therefore they are all soluble on the basis of existing knowledge or readily attainable knowledge" (Crick, 1962, p. 71).[18]

I am not saying that scientism is a fair characterization of the behavioral science / "what works" agenda; instead, I want to highlight temptations that proponents need to recognize and resist. The truth is that every attempt to move beyond ideology risks creating its own ideology, even if it's less explicit. In the case of the "what works" agenda, the seductive ideology is that certain kinds of evidence and techniques are superior to others (and certainly to political considerations) and self-evidently require us to have confidence in them.

I have argued elsewhere at length that politics cannot be excised from policymaking – and nor should it, for it provides a means for choosing between incommensurate values or value systems in a way that technology never can.[19] But the point about privileging certain kinds of evidence and techniques is more specific to this book and therefore requires more comment.

My first few paragraphs set out the main features that the "what works" agenda usually privileges: quantitative analyses, randomized experiments, and observations of revealed behavior in real-world settings. While this focus has undeniable strengths and has led to many successes, it's worth asking what it misses and how it can be broadened.[20] I've already noted that it can create a strong focus on individual trials that can reduce the perceived need or desire to run follow-up studies. Similarly, the desire to prioritize tightly framed outcome measures as meaningful representations of a policy issue may obscure (a) the importance of unmeasured contextual factors and (b) how that policy issue is made up of a collection of networked challenges. In other words, we may have the impression that we are identifying "what works," while only dealing with a sliver of the true issue.

These two factors have been termed "contextual brittleness" and "systemic brittleness" in an excellent paper by Ruth Schmidt and Kaetlyn Stenger.[21] "Contextual brittleness" occurs "when interventions are insufficiently situated within the particulars of their context or are conceived with the assumption of 'normal' or universal values that ignore the pluralistic and heterogeneous nature of values, contexts, resources, or perceptions."

The idea would be that a simplistic approach to "what works" may not appreciate to what extent a particular result is actually the result of contingent factors. What looks like a subsequent failure to "replicate" may actually be owing to an unnoticed shift in the composition of the recipients or the specific way that the intervention was realized. Prioritizing experiments that are rapid and low-cost may have made it more likely that such factors go unnoticed, since it made it less likely that they were recorded – the "why" aspect of "what works" may have been neglected. This is the characterization of RCTs as a "black box."[22] Again, there may have been good reasons to make this trade-off; my point is that we need to recognize that it took place and see the tensions in the "what works" agenda clearly.

There is an irony here, since the last century of social psychology has emphasized just how strongly contextual factors can influence behavior.[23] Arguably, the "what works" aspect of applied behavioral science has meant it has not pursued the implications of this insight as far as it could have. Behavioral scientists work hard to design interventions and environments with care, in the knowledge that "supposedly irrelevant factors" (SIFs) can significantly influence behavior. However, even though we cannot predict or control all these factors in all contexts, the ideology of the "what works" agenda may lead us to think that RCT evidence is strong enough to transcend these concerns. In other words, we may not always follow the advice of Nicole Robitaille, Julian House, and Nina Mažar in chapter 13: "It is very important, before simply applying any intervention, that practitioners do careful background research on the domain they are working in to try to identify if there are reasons why their intervention may or may not be effective." Similarly, in chapter 6 Anisha Singh and Steve Wendel offer an excellent discussion of the difficulty of identifying what SIFs are actually irrelevant.

On the other hand, "systemic brittleness" occurs when "solution development fails to consider critical system interactions, such as competing policies or trends, that cause interventions to function differently or in more limited ways than expected."[24] The concern here is that the admirable desire to get "uncomfortably specific"[25] about zeroing in on a particular behavioral outcome – and, in line with best practices, preregistering that outcome – may produce only an artificially narrow answer to the question of "what works." Of course, this is not a given: there are many instances where behavioral scientists have anticipated wider possible outcomes and used methods that can be adapted to emerging issues.[26] But it is fair to say that a commitment to "what works" may have impeded behavioral scientists from realizing when systemic change has meant that the problem that originally existed, and for which an intervention was created, may exist in a very different form now – and may require a new approach.

What can and should we do in response to these concerns? More work is needed, but we can start to see what questions may be important.[27]

First, as Dilip Soman indicates in his preamble, we may have to recalibrate and move away from the idea that we can provide definitive answers to the question of "what works." The role of heterogeneity and "supposedly irrelevant factors" may mean that some claims about behavior cannot attain much generalizability. One analysis of 8,000 studies found that heterogeneity means that "there will always be a sizable chance of unsuccessful replication, no matter how well conducted or how large any of the studies are."[28] The practical implication is that we need to be more conservative in our claims and caveat them when we do not adequately understand how heterogeneity affects them. As noted in the previous book from the BI-Org partnership, we may need to treat interventions as *hypotheses* that were true in one place, and which may need adapting in order for them to be true elsewhere also.[29]

A second priority therefore is to understand this heterogeneity better – that is, the ways in which "what works" varies. Experiments would aim to answer for whom the effect appears, and in what contexts. One way of doing this is to systematically test the impact of different designs to investigate the same question. That's what has been done by "crowdsourcing" studies that enlist different research teams to develop an approach to testing a hypothesis, and then randomly assign people to each approach.[30] This setup allows researchers to measure the effect of different design choices on behavior, and then run a meta-analysis across the studies to establish which hypotheses survive the varying attempts to test them.

The obvious complement to measuring the impact of contextual and design choices is to broaden the range of participants in studies. We're seeing an increasing number of studies that, for example, test whether prospect theory holds across multiple countries and cultures.[31] But we shouldn't pretend that collecting more varied data is easy. There are multiple barriers to coordination and standardized data collection, including the limited nature of public administration data sets. A big question is whether large institutional funders will see the value in putting up the sums required to set up the necessary infrastructure.

As well as expanding the range of contexts and participants, we may also need to broaden the types of evidence involved – to expand away from the standard "what works" formula I outlined above. This expansion would cover both new sources of evidence and new methods, including qualitative and ethnographic ones, so that we are "supplementing informational, evaluative, and analytic problem-solving methods with inspirational, generative, and synthetic approaches."[32]

Finally, we need to focus more closely on how to successfully adapt interventions to new contexts. We need to move away from the perception that behavioral science mainly concerns knowing about findings, rather than possessing the ability to understand context and make choices sensitive to that context. That ability, after all, is at the core of successfully developing an intervention in the first place. Making this change means paying more attention to what has already been documented by implementation science. The Consolidated Framework for Implementation Research (CFIR) seems like a good place to start, since it maps the factors involved with moving an intervention from one context to another.[33]

Learning from practitioners will be key to achieving this deeper understanding of adaptation. And that's why this book, with its in-depth examples of how people have confronted these issues, is particularly valuable. I think it's especially significant that the chapters have been asked to adopt a standardized format (situation and context, the original study, differences between old and new study, procedure, results, reflections, and practical advice). This requirement ensures the studies are comparable and complete, and it signals a commitment to a more serious engagement with the deceptively simple question: "What works?"

NOTES

1 Haynes, L., Goldacre, B., & Torgerson, D. (2012). *Test, learn, adapt: Developing public policy with randomised controlled trials*. Cabinet Office Behavioural Insights Team. https://www.gov.uk/government/publications/test-learn-adapt-developing-public-policy-with-randomised-controlled-trials.

2 See Markovits, Z., et al. (2023). Nudging United States local government to what works. In M. Sanders, S. Bhanot, & S. O'Flaherty (Eds.), *Behavioral public policy in a global context – Practical lessons from outside the nudge unit*. Palgrave Macmillan.

3 Roese, N.J., & Vohs, K.D. (2012). Hindsight bias. *Perspectives on psychological science, 7*(5), 411–26. https://doi.org/10.1177/1745691612454303.

4 Strategic Policy Making Team. (1999). *Professional policy making for the twenty first century*. Cabinet Office. https://dera.ioe.ac.uk/id/eprint/6320/1/profpolicymaking.pdf.

5 Hallsworth, M. (2011). *Policy making in the real world*. Institute for Government. https://doi.org/10.1111/j.2041-9066.2011.00051.x.

6 Halpern, D., Bates, C., Mulgan, G., Aldridge, S., Beales, G., & Heathfield, A. (2004). *Personal responsibility and changing behaviour: The state of knowledge and its implications for public policy*. Prime Minister's Strategy Unit, Cabinet Office. https://ia800703.us.archive.org/13/items/PersonalResponsibilityandChangingBehaviour/UKCabinetOfficeNannyStateStatus.pdf.

7 Halpern, D. (2015). *Inside the nudge unit: How small changes can make a big difference*. W.H. Allen; and Institute for Government. (2022, October 24). *"What works" in government: 10 years of using evidence to make better policy and what comes next*. https://www.instituteforgovernment.org.uk/event/online-event/what-works-government-10-years-using-evidence-make-better-policy-and-what-comes.

8 Levitt, S.D. & List, J.A. (2007). What do laboratory experiments measuring social preferences reveal about the real world? *Journal of Economic Perspectives, 21*(2), 153–74. https://doi.org/10.1257/jep.21.2.153.

9 Hallsworth, M., & Kirkman, E. (2020). *Behavioral insights*. MIT Press.

10 Shu, L.L., Mazar, N., Gino, F., Ariely, D., & Bazerman, M.H. (2012). Signing at the beginning makes ethics salient and decreases dishonest self-reports in comparison to signing at the end. *Proceedings of the National Academy of Sciences, 109*(38), 15197–200. https://doi.org/10.1073/pnas.1209746109.

11 Kristal, A.S., Whillans, A.V., Bazerman, M.H., Gino, F., Shu, L.L., Mazar, N., & Ariely, D. (2020). Signing at the beginning versus at the end does not decrease dishonesty. *Proceedings of the National Academy of Sciences, 117*(13), 7103–7. https://doi.org/10.1073/pnas.1911695117.

12 Aronson, E., & Mills, J. (1959). The effect of severity of initiation on liking for a group. *The Journal of Abnormal and Social Psychology, 59*(2), 177–81. https://psycnet.apa.org/doi/10.1037/h0047195.

13 See The Behavioural Insights Team. (2018, April 20). *Green means go: How to help patients make informed choices about their healthcare.* https://www .bi.team/blogs/green-means-go-how-to-help-patients-make-informed -choices-about-their-healthcare/; Hallsworth, M., List, J.A., Metcalfe, R.D., & Vlaev, I. (2017). The behavioralist as tax collector: Using natural field experiments to enhance tax compliance. *Journal of Public Economics, 148*, 14–31. http://www.nber.org/papers/w20007.

14 Clarence, E. (2002). Technocracy reinvented: The new evidence based policy movement. *Public policy and administration, 17*(3), 1–11. https:// doi.org/10.1177/095207670201700301.

15 Hodgkinson, P. (2000). Who wants to be a social engineer? A commentary on David Blunkett's speech to the ESRC. *Sociological Research Online, 5*(1), 74–84. https://doi.org/10.5153/sro.433.

16 Select Committee on Science and Technology. (2006, November 8). *Written evidence, appendix 1, memorandum from government.* UK Parliament. https:// publications.parliament.uk/pa/cm200506/cmselect/cmsctech/900/900we02 .htm.

17 Saint-Simon, H. (1975). On the replacement of government by administration. In Keith Taylor (Trans.), *Selected Writings on Science, Industry, and Social Organisation* (pp. 207–10). Croom Helm. (Original work published 1820).

18 Crick, B. (1962). *In defence of politics.* University of Chicago Press.

19 Hallsworth, M. (2011). *Policy making in the real world.* Institute for Government.

20 I'm aware that there are many existing critiques of the use of RCTs in policymaking. Here I am trying to shape my comments specifically to the fusion of behavioral science and evaluation that is represented in the following volume. Deaton, A., & Cartwright, N. (2018). Understanding and misunderstanding randomized controlled trials. *Social Science & Medicine, 210*, 2–21. https://doi.org/10.1016/j.socscimed.2017.12.005.

21 Schmidt, R., & Stenger, K. (2021). Behavioral brittleness: The case for strategic behavioral public policy. *Behavioural Public Policy*, 1–26. http:// dx.doi.org/10.1017/bpp.2021.16.

22 Grimshaw, J.M., Presseau, J., Tetroe, J., Eccles, M.P., Francis, J.J., Godin, G., Graham, I.D., Hux, J.E., Johnston, M., Légaré, F., Lemyre, L., Robinson, N., & Zwarenstein, M. (2007). Looking inside the black box: A theory-based process evaluation alongside a randomised controlled trial of printed educational materials (the Ontario printed educational message, OPEM) to improve referral and prescribing practices in primary care in Ontario, Canada. *Implementation Science, 2*(1), 1–8. https://doi.org/10.1186/1748-5908-9-86.

23 Lewin, K. (1936). *Principles of topological psychology* (F. Heider and G. Heider, Trans.). McGraw-Hill; Camerer, C.F., Loewenstein, G., Rabin, M., (Eds.) (2011). *Advances in behavioral economics*. Princeton University Press.

24 Schmidt, R., & Stenger, K. (2021). Behavioral brittleness: The case for strategic behavioral public policy. *Behavioural Public Policy*, 1–26. http://dx.doi.org/10.1017/bpp.2021.16.

25 Irrational Labs. (2022). *The 3B framework*. https://irrationallabs.com/content/uploads/2022/07/3B-Framework-2022.pdf.

26 Heal, J., Groot, B., Sanders, M., & Anders, J. (2017, November 1). *Running RCTs with complex interventions*. https://www.bi.team/blogs/running-rcts-with-complex-interventions/; Berry, D.A. (2006). Bayesian clinical trials. *Nature Reviews Drug Discovery*, 5(1), 27–36. https://doi.org/10.1038/nrd1927.

27 Many of the following ideas are taken from Hallsworth, M. (2023). *A new "manifesto" for the future of applied behavioral science*. Behavioural Insights Team.

28 Stanley, T.D., Carter, E.C., & Doucouliagos, H. (2018). What meta-analyses reveal about the replicability of psychological research. *Psychological Bulletin*, 144(12), 1325–46. https://doi.org/10.1037/bul0000169.

29 Soman, D. & Mazar, N. (2022). The science of translation and scaling. In N. Mažar and D. Soman (Eds.), *Behavioral science in the wild* (pp. 5–19). University of Toronto Press.

30 Landy, J.F., Jia, M.L., Ding, I.L., Viganola, D., Tierney, W., Dreber, A., Johannesson, M., Pfeiffer, T., Ebersole, C.R., Gronau, Q.F., Ly, A., Bergh, D. van den, Marsman, M., Derks, K., Wagenmakers, E.-J., Proctor, A., Bartels, D.M., Bauman, C.W., Brady, W.J., & Crowdsourcing Hypothesis Tests Collaboration. (2020). Crowdsourcing hypothesis tests: Making transparent how design choices shape research results. *Psychological Bulletin*, 146(5), 451–79. https://psycnet.apa.org/doi/10.1037/bul0000220.

31 Ruggeri, K., Alí, S., Berge, M.L., Bertoldo, G., Bjørndal, L.D., Cortijos-Bernabeu, A., Davison, C., Demić, E., Esteban-Serna, C., Friedemann, M., Gibson, S.P., Jarke, H., Karakasheva, R., Khorrami, P.R., Kveder, J., Andersen, T.L., Lofthus, I.S., McGill, L., Nieto, A.E., ... Pérez, J. (2020). Replicating patterns of prospect theory for decision under risk. *Nature Human Behaviour*, 4(6), 622–33. https://doi.org/10.1038/s41562-020-0886-x.

32 Schmidt, R., & Stenger, K. (2021). Behavioral brittleness: The case for strategic behavioral public policy. *Behavioural Public Policy*, 1–26. http://dx.doi.org/10.1017/bpp.2021.16.

33 Damschroder, L.J., Aron, D.C., Keith, R.E., Kirsh, S.R., Alexander, J.A., & Lowery, J.C. (2009). Fostering implementation of health services research findings into practice: A consolidated framework for advancing implementation science. *Implementation Science*, 4(1), 1–15. https://doi.org/10.1186/1748-5908-4-50.

What Works, What Doesn't (and When): A Preamble

Dilip Soman

Over the past many decades, several academic disciplines have studied the decision-making process of humans and other agents. However, it is perhaps uncontroversial to say that this field really only became a popular applied discipline recently, in 2008. The transition from academia to an applied science was catalyzed by the publication of the book *Nudge*, by Richard Thaler and Cass Sunstein.[1] The book used a number of examples that the average reader could relate to, and made the provocative claim that human decision-making is driven significantly by the situation or context in which the decision is made and not just by the merits or demerits of the choice options themselves. Furthermore, it made the case that because changing the situation in which a particular choice is made (i.e., the context) can change the outcome of the choice process, it might be possible to create situations to steer people toward an appropriate choice. This process is called choice architecture.[2]

The Advent and Growth of Applied Behavioral Science

The field of applied behavioral science subsequently took wings with the formation of several behavioral units within governments, followed by a number of private enterprises and not-for-profits. These organizations created centers of excellence or internal consulting and implementation units. Indeed, in 2017, the Organization for Economic Development and Cooperation (OECD) estimated that there were upward of two hundred units that applied behavioral science to government policy and programs,[3] and a more recent report suggests that there are almost six hundred behavioral units across for-profit enterprises, governments, academic institutions, and not-for-profit organizations.[4]

In the decade since the publication of *Nudge*, behavioral science had evolved from an academic discipline into an applied discipline that had caught the eye and the fancy of organizations.[5]

Not surprisingly, as is the case with any new applied discipline, the early efforts in this field were best characterized by the term cheerleading. Academic researchers and practitioners alike touted the relative ease (cost) with which these interventions could be deployed, and the breadth of problems they could be used to solve as key benefits of choice architecture.[6] Behavioral science was "marketed" as a low-cost high-impact and low-touch approach to changing the behavior of stakeholders, be they citizens interacting with a government and its programs or customers of a for-profit enterprise.

After the initial enthusiasm with choice architecture and applied behavioral science, I believe that the field has reached a stage where the benefits of effectively using behavioral science are apparent to most organizations. The key questions that organizations now struggle with are the when, the where, and the how of using the science. In addition, a number of other troubling questions have started cropping up. Why don't low-touch interventions always work, and why are their effects smaller than in published work? Is it ethical to use behavioral science to influence the behavior of citizens and customers? What is the process by which a behavioral insight can be converted into an actionable intervention? What is the actual impact of behavior interventions on consumer welfare? How does the behavioral approach compare to other approaches to change human behavior? What should a practitioner keep in mind as they look through the basic science as an inspiration into developing interventions, products, or services?

In the backdrop of questions like these, a group of behavioral science academics and practitioners worldwide put together an international consortium known as the Behaviourally Informed Organizations (BI-Org) partnership, housed at the BEAR Research Center at the University of Toronto.[7] The key paradox motivating this partnership's work is that while behavioral science is clearly applicable to organizations, it has not been harnessed anywhere close to its full potential. The partnership believes that one reason why we have much work to do in realizing the full potential of the science is that we do not have a good science of using behavioral science. Two recent books from the partnership have highlighted important dimensions that underlie the friction. The first book, *The Behaviorally Informed Organization* (edited by Dilip Soman and Catherine Yeung),[8] made the point that for organizations to harness behavioral science successfully, they need to develop appropriate resources as well as an appreciation of the scientific method and take active steps at pushing down the cost of experimentation. A second book, *Behavioral Science in the Wild* (edited by Nina Mažar and Dilip Soman),[9] picked on the notion of knowledge translation and scaling. This book highlighted the fact that an intervention based on success in a particular situation, and with a specific type of target audience, might not work well in a different situation, a different substantive domain, or with a different audience. As the editors wrote, "As the imprint of behavioral science began to spread from simple laboratory and pilot demonstrations into a) more scaled-up versions and b) newer domains that had not been the topic of inquiry in the past, these context dependencies started to show up in starker form."[10]

Going Beyond the Nudge Store

In one of the chapters of *Behavioral Science in the Wild*, my coauthors and I introduced a metaphorical "nudge store" – a repository of past demonstrations of attempts by researchers to change human behavior successfully.[11] While it is tempting for a practitioner to simply visit the "nudge store," identify things that have worked well for others, and deploy those interventions to solve their own behavior change challenge, we caution against doing this. This approach might only result in success if the situation and the participants in the earlier demonstration are identical to the present situation and the present participants. Ideally, it would help to know what intervention works, what doesn't work, and when (under what conditions) does it work, but this may not be easy to comprehensively document.[12] Instead, a better strategy can be summarized in a quote that has often been used by former US President Ronald Reagan – "Trust but verify."[13] Specifically, it is helpful for practitioners to use previous demonstrations as a starting point for their own efforts, but then to ensure that the interventions are suitably customized to their target audience, take into account the nuances of their specific situations, and are then tested to ensure that they will work. This process of customization is often iterative and relies on research that might include the methodologies of surveys, interviews, user research, lab experiments, and ethnographic research.

Just as in *Behavioral Science in the Wild*, we will use the term "practitioner" here to refer to any entity that is conducting applied behavioral work outside the well-controlled environment of the laboratory. Thus, practitioners could include employees of either the academic or the nonacademic sectors who are working to create real behavior change to meet some organizational goal, not working solely for the sake of knowledge creation.

Consider a practitioner who is looking to create behavior change through an intervention. This behavior change might be central to their organizational goals – perhaps it involves getting people to conserve energy, increase compliance with a medication regime, help people achieve goals, reduce misinformation, improve tax collection, or increase the take-up of various products and services. The behavioral science practitioner will typically draw inspiration from a previous paper or study (hereafter, "the original study") in developing their own intervention (hereafter, "the new study"). There are four different ways in which the practitioner might take the knowledge from the original study and transfer it to the field.

1) **Replication:** In this case, the practitioner might use an intervention as is from an original study done in a similar situation, on roughly a similar sample of participants, and with a similar procedure.
2) **Translation:** In this case, a practitioner might draw inspiration from previously published laboratory or pilot studies to develop an intervention that they can embed into their field setting. Translations could take the form of one-to-one (the new intervention mimics an intervention from one specific original study) or many-to-one (the new intervention incorporates different interventions from a number of original studies), and they often have to be adapted for delivery in the field. In particular, interventions that might be easy to deliver in the lab might not be as easy in the field, and hence the translation process usually requires significant adaptation of the procedures from the original study / studies.
3) **Horizontal scaling:** In this case, the practitioner identifies an intervention that was used in a different domain and adapts it for use in their own domain. For example, a practitioner that is looking to increase compliance with tax filing deadlines might use a similar intervention done by the health ministry to improve adherence to medication regimens.
4) **Vertical scaling:** In this case, the practitioner starts with a laboratory experiment or a pilot field test and runs a larger version of the same intervention. This larger version essentially means that the same intervention might now reach a significantly greater number of people. Examples include taking a pilot study done in one province and scaling it nationally or taking a small experiment done in one regional office of an organization and adopting it globally.

A number of writers in the applied behavioral science area have recently started to document and theorize on what happens when translation and scaling is attempted. In addition to *Behavioral Science in the Wild*, a recent book also documents the so-called "voltage effect" – that when interventions are scaled, they appear to be less effective.[14] Similarly, there is an acknowledgment of brittleness (or, lack of portability) of the results in our field.[15]

Seventeen Chapters, Seventeen Case Studies

In this volume, each of the seventeen chapters reports a case study of replication, translation, horizontal scaling, or vertical scaling. In each chapter, authors report the results of a field intervention that was inspired by previous work. The goal of this volume is to illustrate the current discourse about translation and scaling challenges concretely and vividly through examples. Each chapter begins with a concise "At a Glance" summary so that the reader gets a quick taste of the chapter. Table P.1 provides a snapshot of the seventeen cases.

As the table indicates, these case studies come from a diverse set of domains of inquiry, types of project, and geographic areas where the projects were implemented. In particular, we have cases of behavior change interventions in healthcare, development, productivity, wellness, misinformation, diversity and inclusion, education, and law and order. Projects have been implemented from all of the continents in the world except Antarctica and have been run in both the Global North and the Global South, in the physical Northern Hemisphere and the physical Southern Hemisphere, and in a wide variety of languages, cultures, and settings.

The chapters are arranged in an order of increasing complexity in the translation process. We start with (a) chapters that simply translate interventions from the lab to the field, then go to (b) chapters that develop field interventions based on lab studies, (c) horizontally scale from one domain to another, (d) translate and significantly scale to larger populations, and we finally end with a chapter that describes iterative and successive translation, adaptation, and scaling across multiple geographic locations.

In addition to the diversity that is apparent in this table, there is also diversity in terms of the outcomes of the studies. In some cases, the reported intervention worked exactly the way it did in the original study, in some cases it worked but not in exactly the same way (or with a voltage drop), in some, the results were a mixed bag, and in yet other cases the intervention had no effect on the intended behavior change.

Table P.1. Summary of the case studies

Case	Domain of Inquiry / Outcome Variables	Nature of Project	Country
1	Healthcare: Conflict of interest (COI) disclosures in a healthcare setting	Translation of laboratory research in a field setting to study effect of COI disclosures	USA
2	Development/Welfare: Unconditional cash transfer and provision of time-saving services	Translation – earlier research on cash-transfer programs and time-saving services built into the design of a welfare program	Kenya
3	Productivity/Goal Striving: Helping people achieve goals and targets with a smartphone app	Translation – using laboratory research on implementation mindsets to design an app that delivered "behaviorally informed reminders"	Canada
4	Financial Well-Being: Helping people achieve financial savings goals	Conceptual replication of a previous study showing that gamification of a financial web-app impacts savings	UK
5	Conservation: Conservation of heating energy in buildings	Translating past research using the EAST framework to help households make optimal choices	Switzerland
6	Healthcare: Anemia prevention in rural India by encouraging consumption of iron folic acid (IFA) pills	Translating lab research on the intention-action gap into a field trial to help rural women actually consume IFA pills	India
7	Wellness: Improving well-being of social workers	Translating laboratory research on goal setting to develop wellness interventions	UK
8	Misinformation: Understanding and reducing COVID-related misinformation	Translating past research on the role of inattention to accuracy as a basis for spreading misinformation	Canada
9	Conservation: Encouraging water conservation by messages in water bills	Translating and scaling past laboratory research on social norms to develop an intervention in a field trial	Israel
10	Law and Order: Reducing fare evasion in a public transit system	Translation and replication – using previous research on (a) effects of making payment easy and (b) increasing empathy to develop interventions tested in a field trial	Chile

11	Diversity and Inclusion: Self-identification as underrepresented groups	Translation – Using the results of past research to develop interventions encouraging federal employees to self-identify as members of underrepresented groups	Canada
12	Healthcare: Reducing over-prescription of antibiotics by physicians	Translation and Scaling of past research on using social norms to reduce antibiotic prescription	New Zealand
13	Government: Improving tax collections	Horizontal scaling – Adapting the use of planning prompts from studies in other domains to help improve tax collection	Canada
14	Diversity and Inclusion: Reducing prejudice against immigrants	Horizontal scaling – Adapting the perceived variability interventions from studies in other domains to help reduce prejudice	Australia
15	Healthcare: Encouraging the take-up of COVID-19 vaccinations	Horizontal scaling – Adapting reminders that have been used in previous vaccination studies to encourage people to take COVID vaccines	Latvia
16	Education: Reducing student absenteeism in schools	Translation and scaling of research on social norms to develop interventions to reduce student absenteeism	USA
17	Development/Welfare: Encouraging female entrepreneurs in the Global South	Replicating, translating, and scaling iteratively previous research on heuristics-based training	Dominican Republic, India, Philippines, and Ethiopia

Each chapter has been written to go beyond the relatively sterile descriptions that one would find in published journal studies. In each case, the authors describe:

a) The situation and the context: What was the key problem or issue that the authors were trying to solve? Why was the behavior change essential or desired? What were the background variables of interest?
b) The original study that inspired their own intervention: What was the original study? What did those authors do and what were their results?
c) Differences between the original and the new study: In particular, authors highlight differences in this situation in which the original study was conducted relative to the current study, differences in the population, as well as differences in methodology and the way in which the intervention was delivered (the medium, the timing, the language, and other specific details).
d) The procedure: Each chapter reports a flow chart to illustrate exactly how the randomization was done. These charts were developed using templates developed by the Consolidated Standards of Reporting Trials (or CONSORT initiative),[16] and follow from a recommendation made in *Behavioral Science in the Wild* to standardize the nature of our reporting.
e) Results: Authors present their results and discuss how these relate to the original results. In other words, they answer the question: "What works, what doesn't (and when)?"
f) Reflections: How do the authors reconcile any differences between their results and the original? What might they have done differently? If they successfully replicated the original, why do they believe they were successful?
g) Practical advice: What did the practitioners learn from their experience of translating and scaling? If they had to do the process all over again, what would they do differently? What are things that they are likely to do more of, and what are they likely to avoid going forward? What practical advice do they have for others looking to take findings from the lab to the field?

This book is not intended to be a comprehensive response to the question of what works, what doesn't work, when it works, and when it does not. In fact, building on the growing discourse in the applied behavioral science field, I believe that we will probably never have a comprehensive understanding of this.[17] As Richard Thaler wrote in *Misbehaving*,[18] human behavior is significantly influenced by SIFs (supposedly irrelevant factors). What is a SIF? These are things that we do not expect to influence decision-making because they are not central to the value or the utility of the options to be chosen from, but that research has shown to have an effect on decision-making. One hallmark of a supposedly irrelevant factor is – unsurprisingly – that it is supposedly irrelevant. This means that it is only after running a study and finding that the results do not align with the original that the practitioner can infer that there was a SIF at play. SIFs are, by definition, difficult to forecast.

Instead, the value of this book is fourfold. First, this volume can be used as a set of case studies in education and training programs, or more generally to expose the reader to the breadth of what behavioral science can accomplish. There are other compilations of short use cases, but the accounts in this book are different. Rather than sterile descriptions of studies, each chapter provides a "behind the scenes" look at how their intervention was developed, and more importantly, what the authors learned from the process. The reader will also learn about the anxiety, excitement, disappointment, happiness, or regret that the practitioners experienced at different phases of their projects.

Second, the book contains a treasure trove of reflections and practical insights from leading practitioners (many of whom also happen to be academics). These pieces of advice span the spectrum – what sort of interventions are good candidates to scale? How important is it to test before translating? What form of testing should be used? What small but potentially consequential pitfalls might occur while translating? When (i.e., how long after the intervention) and how should the critical outcomes be measured? How should one analyze the context to make a judgment about possible translatability? Which subsegment of the target population might the intervention be most effective on?

Third, the seventeen chapters highlight the diversity of approaches in embedding past research into developing interventions. Some chapters report new studies that closely resemble the original, others have designed completely new interventions (websites, apps, mailers) that draw elements from the original studies. Some chapters moved from an original lab study to the field in one jump, others moved in multiple, iterative steps. Some represent work done by academics alone; others are work done by academics in partnership with non-academics. Some of the chapters report that they stopped working on their intervention because they had no hope that it would ever work; others found opportunities to iterate, refine, or change course and pressed on. Some of the case studies were one-off projects or were part of an organization's continued efforts, while others started as one-offs but morphed into larger initiatives and organizations. Clearly, there is no one best model of cocreating good, applied behavioral research.

Fourth, I have long believed (and previously argued)[19] that the published literature in our journals does not paint a representative picture of our field. Not only does a reader of our journals see only successful interventions, in addition, they have no exposure to any of the struggles the researchers had and the decisions they needed to make in getting the results that they did. By publishing successes as well as failures, and by encouraging authors to narrate how their interventions came to be, this volume will hopefully be a small but important first step toward being representative.

The authors of some of the chapters have provided additional materials that supplement the materials in this book. These materials could include (but are not restricted to) study materials, background information, weblinks, or technical manuals. These materials will be posted to https://www.biorgpartnership.com/ (please look for the "What Works" tab under "Projects").

Many management and policy thinkers have long advocated for the benefit of learning from failure. Some of these chapters provide some very concrete examples of how we might learn from failure. Learning from the mistakes of the interventions that didn't work very well and learning from the reflections of why those that worked well actually did so will provide the reader with a terrific checklist for them and their teams as they start looking at published research to try and create their own interventions.

NOTES

1 Thaler, R.H., and Sunstein, C.R. (2008). *Nudge: Improving decisions about health, wealth, and happiness.* Yale University Press.
2 See also Johnson, E.J. (2021). *The elements of choice: Why the way we decide matters.* Riverhead Books.
3 OECD. (n.d.). *Behavioural insights.* https://www.oecd.org/gov/regulatory-policy/behavioural-insights.htm.
4 Wendel, S. (2020). *Behavioural teams around the world.* Behavioral Teams. https://www.behavioralteams.com/wp-content/uploads/2020/10/Behavioral-Teams-Around-the-World_4Oct2020.pdf.
5 See also Soman, D., Yu, J., & Feng, B. (2023). The between times of applied behavioral science. In A. Samson (Ed.), *The Behavioral Economics Guide 2023* (pp. 2–15). Behavioral Science Solutions. https://www.behavioraleconomics.com/be-guide/.

6 See, for example, Halpern, D. (2015). *Inside the Nudge Unit: How small changes can make a big difference.* Random House; Soman, D. (2015). *The last mile: Creating social and economic value from behavioral insights.* University of Toronto Press.

7 See https://www.biorgpartnership.com/.

8 Soman, D., & Yeung, C. (2021). *The behaviorally informed organization.* University of Toronto Press.

9 Mažar, N., & Soman, D. (Eds.). (2022). *Behavioral science in the wild.* University of Toronto Press.

10 See p. x in Preface, Mažar & Soman (2022).

11 Goodyear, L., Hossain, T., & Soman, D. (2022). Prescriptions for successfully scaling behavioral interventions. In N. Mažar & D. Soman (Eds.), *Behavioral science in the wild* (pp. 28–41). University of Toronto Press.

12 For a rubric attempting to codify different dimensions or context, see Yang, S., Yeung, M., Barr, N., Lee, C.Y., Malik, W., Mažar, N., Soman, D., & Thomson, D. (2023). *The elements of context.* Behavioural Economics in Action at Rotman (BEAR) Report Series. https://www.rotman.utoronto.ca/FacultyAndResearch/ResearchCentres/BEAR/Our-Research/White-Papers-and-Reports.

13 Massie, S. (2013). *Trust but verify: Reagan, Russia and me, a personal memoir.* Maine Authors Publishing.

14 List, J.A. (2022). *The voltage effect: How to make good ideas great and great ideas scale.* Currency.

15 Schmidt, R., & Stenger, K. (2021). Behavioral brittleness: The case for strategic behavioral public policy. *Behavioural Public Policy*, 1–26. http://dx.doi.org/10.1017/bpp.2021.16.

16 CONSORT Group. (n.d.). *The CONSORT statement.* http://www.consort-statement.org/.

17 Some recent work has started examining well-established findings and determining when they work and when they might not. These projects might use either meta-analytical approaches, or series of experiments in which the original effect is tested with variations in the stimulus, levels of factors, procedures, or other experimental details. These efforts will be a good first step in assessing generalizability or portability of findings, but they will still not give us a comprehensive view.

18 Thaler, R.H. (2016). *Misbehaving: The making of behavioral economics.* W.W. Norton.

19 Mažar & Soman (2022).

WHAT WORKS, WHAT DOESN'T (AND WHEN)

Translating Laboratory Research on Conflict of Interest Disclosures to Understand the Psychological Effects in the Real World

Sunita Sah

AT A GLANCE

- **Our Goal:** To understand the psychological effects of real-world conflict of interest disclosures on both recipients and providers.
- **The Intervention:** Providing or receiving a conflict of interest disclosure in medical and financial contexts.
- **The Results:** For recipients, disclosure increased patients' knowledge of their physicians' financial conflicts of interest but did not change patients' trust in their physician or the hospital or their likelihood to keep their appointment. For providers, disclosure increased or decreased bias depending on the professional norms to place recipients or self-interest first.
- **Lessons Learned:** For recipients, conflict of interest disclosures would be better served if they are provided to patients *before* they choose their physicians so that they can act on any preferences to avoid physicians with large financial conflicts more easily. For providers, the salience of professional norms and responsibilities play an important role as to whether conflict of interest disclosures increase or decrease bias in advice.

Motivation and Objective

People who advise for a living, including physicians, lawyers, and financial advisers, face conflicts of interests (COIs) when their professional duty to give high-quality, unbiased counsel to their clients clashes with their self-interest. For instance, physicians sometimes receive incentives or gifts from pharmaceutical companies,[1] and financial advisers may receive greater commissions if their clients buy certain products from them.[2] Such COIs are common – an estimated 65 percent of patients in the United States see physicians who have financial relationships with the healthcare industry, including receiving compensation for consulting and honoraria.[3] Because such conflicts can lead advisers to give biased advice, they have been at the heart of many economic crises,[4] including the sudden demise of corporations like Enron[5] and skyrocketing healthcare costs in the United States.[6]

A common approach to managing such conflicts is disclosure – that is, informing the advisee of the adviser's COI.[7] The American Medical Association's 2005 Code of Ethics, for example, states that when a physician advises a patient to enter a clinical trial, they should disclose any referral fees they would receive if the patient enrolled. In addition, the 2010 Physician's Payment Sunshine Act requires to be disclosed any transfers valued at approximately $10 or more from industry to a health provider on a public website. Turning to finance, the US Securities and Exchange Commission requires registered investment advisers to disclose commissions received for referring clients to solicitors or brokers.[8] Similarly, the US Federal Trade Commission requires bloggers to disclose to their online readers any COIs, including incentives or payments received for recommending products or services.[9]

Disclosure is often viewed as an attractive solution to COIs because it preserves advisees' autonomy[10] while theoretically enabling them to assess the risk and extent of any influence on the quality of the advice they receive[11] and adjust for potential bias.[12] Advice recipients say they want the disclosures,[13] and policymakers continue to oblige with new and broader disclosure mandates.[14]

Unfortunately, however, research on the effectiveness of COI disclosures has been mixed.[15] For advisers, disclosure has been found to both increase and decrease bias, depending on the context.[16] Advisees tend to trust their advisers less after they disclose a COI,[17] which is arguably the intended purpose of disclosure when the quality of advice is uncertain.[18] But even when advice quality is demonstrably high, advisees still trust their advisers less and become more interested in changing advisers after such disclosures.[19] The mere knowledge of an adviser's COI yields negative assessments of their integrity and benevolence – a *disclosure penalty* that emerges whether or not the disclosure is voluntary or mandatory, and even when advice quality is high, and the adviser is honest.[20] As a result, advisees may ignore or reject valuable advice.

Even as disclosure reduces advisees' trust in their advisers, it can also put pressure on them to comply with the advice, due to two psychological mechanisms: the *panhandler effect* and *insinuation anxiety*.[21] The panhandler effect describes the tendency for advisees to feel pressured to help satisfy their advisers' personal interests once the COI disclosure is communicated.[22] Disclosure becomes, in effect, a favor request from the adviser that pressures the advisee to give in to the adviser's interests. Similarly, disclosure – whether voluntary or required by law – pressures advisees to take the advice for fear of signaling distrust to the adviser and insinuating that they believe their adviser is biased, incompetent, or corrupt.[23] These pressures can lead to a perverse consequence of disclosure: increased compliance with less trusted advice.

In other research, disclosure increased advisees' compliance with advice but also actually *increased* – rather than decreased – their trust in their adviser.[24] This tends to be the case when there is a lot of information to process, and advisees lack the resources or motivation needed to pay sufficient attention to the disclosure. In such cases, advisees process the COI disclosure automatically and interpret the COI as an indicator of prestige and competence, thus increasing trust in their advisers' expertise.[25] This phenomenon, known as *disclosure's expertise cue*, can be mitigated and sometimes reversed by asking advice recipients to deliberate on the disclosure.[26]

To date, much of the literature on COI disclosure has been conducted in the lab. Rather than studying real-world relationships between advisers and advisees, researchers have placed participants in the role of an adviser or advisee. Given the range of responses seen in the lab, it is unclear what effect COI disclosure would have in the real world.

Patient Responses to Real-World Conflict of Interest Disclosures

Motivation and Objective

Most patients in the United States put their health in the hands of physicians who have financial relationships with the healthcare industry. These relationships can bias physicians' clinical decisions toward their sponsors' products, with potentially harmful effects on their patients' health, not to mention their bank accounts.[27] Given that disclosure is the most commonly proposed and implemented solution for dealing with physicians' financial ties with industry,[28] we designed a preregistered, highly powered, randomized field study to explore patient responses to real-world COI disclosures.[29]

The study addresses a significant policy debate currently raging in the literature, statehouses, Congress, and every reputable hospital on how best to manage and disclose physicians' financial relationships with industry. In healthcare, two important aims of COI disclosure are to educate patients about their physicians' COIs and to improve their decision-making by providing information that allows them to more accurately assess the risks of different treatments. By decreasing the information gap, disclosure helps ensure patient autonomy[30] and is essential for a valid informed-consent process.[31]

Inspiration

Due to the potential adverse consequences of COI disclosures, it is important to understand when they perform as intended and when they backfire. Medical decisions can be extremely difficult, requiring patients to sift through a range of competing data. Information over-load could lead patients focused on diagnosis and treatment options to deliberate less on a COI disclosure, resulting in automatic processing of the disclosure and subsequently *disclosure's expertise cue*. In particular, they may view physicians' financial relationships with industry as indicators of prestige and expertise, thereby increasing trust and compliance.[32] Patients who do deliberate on the disclosure may trust their physician less as a result, yet they may simultaneously worry about rejecting their physicians' advice to avoid insinuating they believe their physician was biased by their COI. This *insinuation anxiety* can lead to increased pressure to comply with distrusted advice.[33] Finally, if the COI disclosure yields negative attributions regarding the physician's character, the *disclosure penalty* may lead patients to overcorrect.[34] For these reasons, there was a pressing need to determine whether the deleterious effects of COI disclosure found in these laboratory studies also appear in a highly powered, real-world clinical field setting.

Interventions and Method

Table 1.1 shows the differences and similarities between the main laboratory studies that inspired this research and our field study. Most notably, we had a much higher sample size (over 1,900 patients) than past lab studies on the topic. We also attempted to reduce some of the

Table 1.1. Similarities and differences between field and laboratory studies: Advisees

	Field Experiment (Rose et al., 2021)	Lab Experiments Investigating Insinuation Anxiety (Sah et al., 2019)	Lab Experiments Investigating Disclosure's Expertise Cue (Sah et al., 2018)
Experimental Design	Five randomized conditions: • No-disclosure (control) • COI disclosure • COI disclosure with risks • COI disclosure with benefits • COI disclosure with both risks and benefits	Relevant randomized conditions examined over three medical scenario studies • No-disclosure • COI disclosure (from adviser) • Third-party (external private) disclosure	Relevant randomized conditions examined over three blog post studies • No-disclosure (control) • COI disclosure • COI disclosure with deliberation
Setting	Mailing and survey to Cleveland Clinic patients	Online studies in the United States	Online studies in the United States
Participants	Patients at four outpatient clinics	University student alumni and MTurk participants	Undergraduate students and MTurk participants
Sample Size	1,903 (approx. 381 per condition)	1,382 (ranging from approx. 50 per condition to 200 per condition)	458 (approx. 50 per condition)
Main Outcome Measures	• Missed or canceled appointments • Knowledge of physicians' COI • Trust in physician (expertise, integrity, benevolence) • Trust in hospital	• Insinuation anxiety • Trust in physician • Likelihood to take the physician's advice	• Persuasiveness (e.g., intent to share post, likelihood of taking advice) • Trust in blogger (expertise, integrity, benevolence) • Recall of disclosure • Perceptions of bias
Key Results	• Disclosure increased knowledge of physicians' COIs, but there was no significant difference in trust or missed or canceled appointments.	• Disclosure decreased trust and increased insinuation anxiety. • Both trust and insinuation anxiety explained (mediated) the relationship between disclosure and the likelihood to take advice. • External disclosure mitigated but did not eliminate the effect.	• Disclosure increased knowledge (recall), trust (expertise), and persuasiveness, but with no effect on perceptions of bias. • Trust in the blogger's expertise explained (mediated) the relationship between disclosure and persuasiveness. • Disclosure with deliberation increased knowledge further (recall), and increased perceptions of bias which mitigated the effect on trust and persuasiveness.

unintended consequences of COI disclosure on advisees. First, we gave patients the disclosure in private – that is, not in the presence of their physician. In scenario studies, private COI disclosure has reduced insinuation anxiety by easing the social pressure on patients to accept their physician's advice.[35] Second, in an attempt to reduce the occurrence of disclosure's expertise cue, we mailed patients a COI disclosure letter in advance of their meeting with their physician. We hoped this method would give patients more time, motivation, and ability to deliberate on the meaning of the disclosure, in part by separating it from important competing information they might receive from their physician regarding diagnosis or treatment options.

We recruited physicians at Cleveland Clinic who had received $20,000 or more from industry sources in the past year. Twenty-seven physicians (68 percent) agreed to participate in our study; twenty-five of them had accessible appointment systems, which allowed their inclusion in the study (see Figure 1.1). We identified 1,903 of these physicians' patients who had appointments during the study period (September 2015 to April 2016) and met the inclusion criteria, which were the following: English-speaking, non-terminally ill, over age eighteen, able to consent to medical treatments, and having an outpatient appointment with a study physician.

All 1,903 patients were sent an appointment-reminder letter signed by a Cleveland Clinic professional staff member (not the physician themselves) approximately one week before their physician appointment (see Figure 1.2). The letters were randomly assigned with a stratified random assignment to balance approximate equal distribution among physicians across five conditions. Patients were blinded to the purpose of the study, and physicians were blinded as to which condition letter patients received.

The control group received only the appointment-reminder letter with no COI disclosures. In the four disclosure conditions, the appointment-reminder letter notified patients that their physician received $20,000 or more from named companies, identified the companies' products, and explained the typical uses of these products in clinical care. In addition, we tested if describing the potential risks and benefits of the physician's COI affected patients' knowledge of their physician's COI and their trust in their physician. A statement highlighting the risks of physician bias may amplify unintended effects of disclosure, such as the disclosure penalty or insinuation anxiety, whereas a statement that frames industry relationships positively – for example, highlighting how they can foster clinical and research innovations in medical care – may amplify disclosure's expertise cue. Thus, the four intervention

Figure 1.1. CONSORT diagram describing the identification, accrual, and randomization assignment of study participants

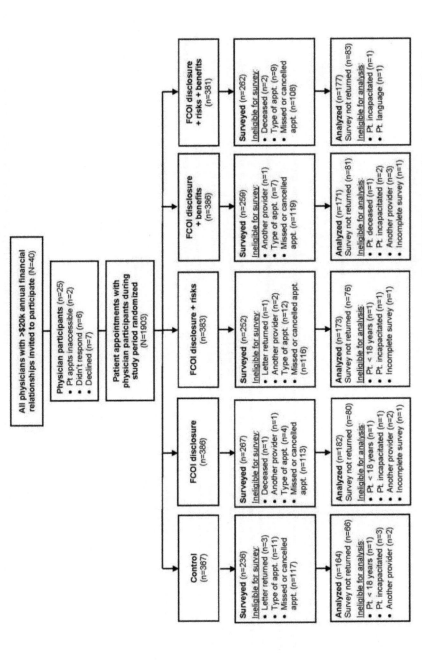

Note: FCOI = Financial conflict of interest. CONSORT stands for Consolidated Standards of Reporting Trials. Reprinted from Rose et al. (2021). Patient responses to physician disclosures of industry conflicts of interest: A randomized field experiment. *Organizational Behavior and Human Decision Processes*, 166, 27–38, with permission from Elsevier.

Figure 1.2. Appointment-reminder letter and disclosures

\<Date\>

\<FirstName\> \<LastName\>

\<Street Address\>

\<City\>, \<State\> \<ZIPCODE\>

Dear \<FirstName\> \<LastName\>,

You are scheduled for an appointment with Dr. \<PhysicianName\> on \<date\> at \<time\>, in \<building name\> of Cleveland Clinic, located at \<address\>. If you have questions about your appointment, including transportation or parking, please call \<number\> or visit our website.

[COI disclosure condition]

Cleveland Clinic wants you to know that your physician, Dr. \<PhysicianName\>, has a financial relationship with a company that makes products that may be prescribed or used in your care. These relationships are shown on the following page, and the Innovation Management and Conflict of Interest Program has reviewed Dr. \<PhysicianName\>'s relationships with drug and medical device companies. Physicians interact with the makers of drugs and devices in a number of ways. For example, a physician might receive compensation for inventing a drug or device, consulting, advising, providing education or other services.

[COI Risks condition]

Some research suggests that physicians who have financial relationships with companies may tend to favor products of those companies. The research suggests that physicians with such financial relationships may overestimate the benefits or underestimate the risks of the companies' products.

[COI Benefits condition]

The policy of the Cleveland Clinic permits physicians to engage in these financial relationships, because we believe that these collaborations are an important way to advance scientific and medical knowledge to develop life-saving technologies. Companies draw expertise from our physicians because they are leaders in their fields.

[COI disclosure condition]

We believe that it is important for patients to have this information, so that you can make fully-informed choices regarding which physician you see and your treatment options. Dr.

\<PhysicianName\> would be happy to respond to any questions or concerns you may have, or you may contact the Cleveland Clinic's Conflict of Interest Office, at \<email\>.

Please contact us if you have any questions.

\<Signature\>

Information about Dr. \<PhysicianName\>'s Financial Relationships

Dr. \<PhysicianName\> receives more than $20,000 per year for \<Activity1\> from \<CompanyName1\>.

Dr. \<PhysicianName\> receives more than $20,000 per year for \<Activity2\> from \<CompanyName2\>.

Dr. \<PhysicianName\> receives more than $20,000 per year for \<Activity3\> from \<CompanyName3\>.

[add/remove lines as necessary, to reflect number of relationships]

This table identifies products made by drug and device companies with which your physician has a financial relationship that may be used in your care and the typical uses of those products in your physician's practice.

This information was provided by your physician.

Company	Company's Products	Common Clinical Uses of Product

Reprinted from supplementary material from Rose et al. (2021). Patient responses to physician disclosures of industry conflicts of interest: A randomized field experiment. *Organizational Behavior and Human Decision Processes*, 166, 27–38, with permission from Elsevier.

conditions consisted of COI disclosure alone, COI disclosure with information on the risks of physician-industry relationships, COI disclosure with information on the benefits of such relationships, and COI disclosure with both risk and benefit information (see Figure 1.2).

Patients who saw their physician for a consultative appointment ($N = 1,276$) were mailed a cover letter and survey within a week after the appointment to assess their knowledge of their physician's COI and their trust in their physician. Nonresponders were sent a second survey two-to-three weeks later, were called if no response was received, and finally were sent a third mailing. Sixty-eight percent of patients ($N = 867$) completed the survey and received a $25 gift card. Finally, to assess if the intervention contributed to missed or canceled appointments, we tracked patients' appointment attendance via electronic hospital records.

Results

The disclosure intervention significantly increased patients' knowledge of their physicians' financial COI from 9 percent to 57 percent, with no significant differences in knowledge between the four disclosure conditions – a large effect size for a single mailed disclosure letter. The increase in patient knowledge to 57 percent was slightly larger than the immediate recall of the COI disclosure statement in past scenario-based research (see Table 1.1), which ranged from approximately 41 percent to 56 percent across studies.[36] Thus, the majority of patients received and read the disclosure letters. However, this still means that 43 percent of patients either did not receive the letter, did not understand it, ignored it, or forgot it. Future research could explore whether additional mailings or an interactive online disclosure message could further improve recipient knowledge. Approximately one-third (a usual percentage for Cleveland Clinic) missed or canceled their appointment in each condition. There were no significant differences in appointments canceled, missed, and completed among any of the conditions.

In line with the missed/canceled appointment results, there were also no significant differences in patient trust in their physician or the hospital due to the letter's COI disclosure. This finding is notable, given that our study was preregistered and sufficiently powered to detect modest differences in patients' trust and because we provided contextual information that highlighted the risks of financial COIs for some patients and the benefits of COIs for others. These results were also robust to various sensitivity analyses, such as excluding patients who reported their physicians disclosed their COI during their appointment, had established relationships with their physician, or had not recalled receiving the COI disclosure.

Discussion

Unlike past laboratory studies on COI disclosure, in our field study, actual patients responded to questions about their own physicians. Study participants who deliberate on COI disclosures from hypothetical physicians may naturally trust them less.[37] But there are reasons to believe advisees may react differently to disclosures from their own advisers.

People often mis-predict their own emotions and behavior, most often because they underestimate the effect of their feelings, external pressures, and other factors once they find themselves in a particular situation.[38] As such, patients may believe that disclosure of their physician's conflicting interests will be important to their evaluation of the physician; indeed, one national survey found that 74 percent of respondents believed that healthcare industry money influences how physicians treat patients, and half (51 percent) reported they would be less likely to choose a physician who received such money.[39] But when patients actually receive COI information about a physician they have already made an appointment with, they may feel unable to react adequately to it. Our survey data revealed as much: although nearly half of our patients (48 percent) reported wanting to receive COI information prior to making an appointment with a new physician, 75 percent subsequently reported that their physicians' COI had no or little impact on their medical decisions.

In this real-world setting, in which patients already had an appointment with their physician, patients were motivated to continue to trust that physician, as it would be costly not to trust them. That is, their dependence on their doctor may have overwhelmed any concern about the COI. Patients would have had to search for and switch physicians, a burdensome task that could delay their treatment. Past research has shown that trust in our *own* adviser increases with the cost of switching advisers,[40] demonstrating the strength of motivated reasoning[41] when we are dependent on an adviser.

Furthermore, the patients in our study reported very high levels of trust in their physicians and the hospital. Our sample of physicians, experts in their fields at Cleveland Clinic, represent typical recipients of substantial industry support, and thus a worthwhile population for study. However, the findings may not be generalizable to clinical settings where baseline levels of trust are lower. A high level of trust in one's physician, combined with a motivation to believe that one's *own* physician will not be affected by their COI, could lead patients to underreact to COI disclosures from physicians on whom they depend.[42]

COI disclosures provided at the time a patient chooses a physician (rather than before an appointment) might lead to different preferences. Patients typically don't have time to shop around for doctors when they are ill.[43] If patients could quickly and easily select unconflicted physicians – for example, if COI disclosure information were readily available at the time of appointment scheduling – they might not choose to make appointments with physicians with large financial conflicts. Thus, providing disclosures at the time patients choose physicians could encourage them to enact their preferences before they become too costly to change.

Although we did not observe any of the unintended consequences of disclosure that have been found in the lab, disclosure cannot be a panacea if its intended purpose is to allow patients to digest the information and account for potential physician bias.

Real-World Advisers' Responses to Conflict of Interest Disclosures

Motivation and Inspiration

Disclosing COIs affects advisers as well as advisees. My own research has shown that disclosure can be beneficial when providers can opt to avoid conflicts: Across a series of simple laboratory studies, my colleague and I reveal that mandatory and even voluntary disclosure can deter advisers with real monetary incentives from accepting COIs so that they have nothing to disclose but the absence of conflicts.[44] An elegant feature of this type of disclosure is its self-calibrating quality. Advisers who wish to appear unbiased and ethical will opt to reject COIs, thus protecting even naive consumers as the market for unconflicted advisers increases.

As these laboratory studies demonstrate, advisers, like most people, are averse to being viewed as biased. Thus, a salient disclosure revealing the *absence* of COIs at the time advice is offered should be effective at reducing the acceptance of COIs. Evidence from the financial services field, albeit limited, complements this finding: auditors provided fewer non-audit services like tax consulting, IT services, or due diligence and transaction support when disclosure of these services was mandated.[45]

While this type of disclosure seems promising, in our laboratory studies, advisers had to simultaneously decide whether to accept a COI and contemplate its immediate disclosure to the advisee. In the real world, there is often a temporal separation between an adviser accepting a COI, its disclosure to the advisee, and the provision of advice. And in many situations, it may not be possible for advisers to reject COIs as they are built into the system or institution. Financial advisers, for example, may have a limited ability to determine their incentive compensation structure.

When COIs are unavoidable, influential laboratory research revealed that disclosure can *increase* adviser bias,[46] possibly due to advisers strategically exaggerating their biased advice to compensate for anticipated discounting by advisees with COI disclosure or feeling morally licensed to provide biased advice once a COI has been disclosed.

However, several studies in the medical field show the opposite effect – namely, *decreased* physician bias in the presence of COI disclosure. A large body of evidence reveals that physicians who receive payments from industry are more likely to prescribe branded drugs from their sponsors (rather than generics).[47] In Massachusetts, after laws mandating public disclosure of industry payments to physicians were enacted, physicians prescribed fewer branded drugs than similar physicians in nondisclosure states.[48] This reduction occurred even when there was no change in how much physicians received from industry, suggesting the physicians were less biased due to self-monitoring rather than changes in how firms deliver payments.[49]

Other laboratory experiments have also documented that COI disclosure can decrease adviser bias in certain conditions, including when advisers have more experience in advice-giving[50] or when contextual factors shift, such as when sanctions are introduced.[51] Thus, given that the effects of disclosing COIs on advisers (as on advisees) vary widely, it is important to understand the circumstances in which disclosure could increase or decrease advisers' bias.

Interventions and Results

While studying the effect of disclosing COI on advisers in the lab, I discovered that participants who took the role of medical advisers gave significantly less biased advice with disclosure than without. I conducted many more experiments to investigate why this finding contradicted the prior lab finding of increased bias with disclosure.

First, I randomized participants from the same nonexpert subject pool (US university community members) to give advice in either a real estate context, as in the prior study,[52] or a medical context. In both contexts, advisers were subject to similar real monetary incentives that created real COIs. Advisers gave more biased advice with disclosure in the real estate context but less biased advice with disclosure in the medical context (see Sah, 2019, Study S1 in Supplement).[53]

As the two contexts had different design elements, I next created similarly structured advice-giving scenarios in both the medical and financial contexts. I again subjected advisers to real monetary COIs and randomized participants from a US graduate school to give advice in either a medical or financial context, with or without COI disclosure. Once again, nonexpert advisers gave more biased advice with disclosure in the financial context and less biased advice with disclosure in the medical context.[54] Such dramatic reversals are often a symptom of context effects.[55] What about these contexts changed the nonexpert advisers' behavior?

Further investigation revealed that nonexperts had different norms for how medical and financial advisers should behave.[56] Moral licensing and strategic exaggeration did not explain (or mediate) the relationship between disclosure and bias in advice in either context, but when nonexperts were informed they had to disclose their COI, the disclosure statement increased norm salience. In the medical context, a profession viewed by nonexperts as "patient first," this salience decreased advice bias; in the financial context, a profession viewed by nonexperts as "self-interest first," it increased advice bias.

People tend to draw on multiple sources of information to perceive norms, including other people, mass media, and institutional/legal signals such as sanctions, other penalties, and rewards.[57] Naturally, these perceptions and role expectations differ between expert and nonexpert advisers as well as by context;[58] thus, it is important to understand how real-world expert advisers view the norms of their profession and how those norms might affect their reactions to COI disclosures.

Framed Field Experiments

The field evidence from the medical studies suggests that physicians themselves have a "patient first" norm because bias in their advice decreased with COI disclosure. However, little field evidence was available to determine how financial advisers viewed the norms of their profession and thus how they would react to COI disclosures. To address this gap, I conducted two "framed field experiments," in which the nature of the participant pool and task are relevant to the field context.[59] Framed field experiments offer a controlled environment in which to compare advice quality from real financial and medical advisers with and without disclosure. Table 1.2 shows the differences and similarities between the laboratory studies that inspired this research and the framed field experiments.

Table 1.2. Similarities and differences between field and laboratory studies: Advisers

	Framed Field Experiments (Sah, 2019)	Lab Experiments (Sah, 2019)	Lab Experiment (Cain et al., 2011)
Experimental Design	Two randomized conditions (two experiments – one in a medical content and one in a financial context): • No-disclosure • COI disclosure	Relevant randomized conditions over four experiments (medical, financial, real estate contexts): • No-disclosure • COI disclosure • COI reminder • COI disclosure with fiduciary norm education	Relevant randomized conditions (one experiment in a real estate context): • No-disclosure • COI disclosure
Setting	Online studies in the United States	Online studies in the United States	Online studies in the United States
Participants	Real-world medical and financial advisers	Non-expert university community members and MTurk participants	Non-expert university community members
Sample Size	184 advisers (approx. 46 per condition)	1,101 advisers (ranging from approx. 53 per condition to 122 per condition)	126 advisers (approx. 32 per condition)
Main Outcome Measure	• Quality of advice	• Quality of advice • Strategic exaggeration • Moral licensing • Norm salience	• Quality of advice
Key Results	• For expert advisers, disclosure increased advice quality in both medical and financial contexts.	• For nonexperts, disclosure increased advice quality in a medical context and decreased advice quality in financial and real estate contexts. • Norm salience explained (mediated) the relationship between disclosure and bias in advice; strategic exaggeration and moral licensing did not explain the relationship. • COI reminders worked similarly to COI disclosures. • For nonexpert financial advisers, providing information on financial adviser's fiduciary norm to place clients first increased advice quality.	• For nonexperts, disclosure decreased advice quality in real estate context.

For expert medical advice, I recruited 109 senior clinical medical students from two US medical schools with at least one full year of clinical experience in patient care (response rate = 50 percent). The study was designed to present practicing medical advisers with realistic medical COIs. Medical advisers were presented with information on three different "patients" and had to decide between one of two treatment options to recommend. Due to their COI, one of the options gave the adviser an additional payment but was less beneficial to the patient. In the disclosure (vs. nondisclosure) condition, advisers were informed that their advice would be accompanied by a disclosure statement revealing the additional payment.

For example, one of the scenarios described Patient P, a sixty-four-year-old man who was present for a routine annual examination. His paternal uncle had been diagnosed with colorectal cancer at age sixty-seven. Previously, the patient had two clear colonoscopies, the most recent one four years ago. The medical adviser was reminded of the American Cancer Society's guidelines, which recommend a colonoscopy every ten years for average-risk individuals. Advisers learned they would receive more payment if they conducted the colonoscopy that day (a $5 bonus). They then had to choose whether to offer to conduct a colonoscopy immediately or to recommend waiting (see Figure 1.3). Reassuringly, most medical advisers gave unbiased advice – that is, they recommended waiting. Also, consistent with the outcomes for nonexpert medical advisers and with the evidence on physician prescribing from the medical field, expert medical advisers gave less biased recommendations with disclosure than without it.

To achieve expert financial advice, I recruited seventy-five financial advisers from an alumni database of a US university (approx. response rate = 40 percent) who were working in various financial institutions, such as Goldman Sachs, Edward Jones, and Morgan Stanley. In this comparable framed field experiment, advisers advised three different "clients" on different fund options. Most advisers gave unbiased advice, and disclosure again *decreased* advice bias as compared to nondisclosure. This suggests that expert financial advisers and medical advisers have similar perceptions of professional norms: to place their advisees first. Indeed, like physicians,[60] many of the practicing financial advisers, who were unaware of the hypotheses and different disclosure conditions, did not want to be viewed as biased. In written comments, they revealed they were offended by the notion that a COI would bias their advice and that they might not place their clients' interests first.[61] Thus, it appears that, at least for this sample of financial advisers, their professional norms aligned with their fiduciary duty to place "clients first."

Figure 1.3. Medical adviser instructions for Patient P

In this study, you will provide medical advice. You will see three patients in turn. After reviewing relevant information on each patient, you will make a recommendation between two options and then will move onto the next patient. You will receive $10 (in Amazon gift cards) plus an opportunity to receive an additional $10 for completing this survey.

Please note that your recommendations are real, in that they will be presented to other participants who will play the role of the patients. Patients' payments will be determined by the option they choose after viewing your advice.

Next, you will see Patients P, Q, and R in turn and make a recommendation for each patient.

Please **carefully** review the abbreviated medical history for **Patient P** shown below and then make a recommendation.

Name:	Gender:	Age:	Race:	Occupation:
Patient P	Male	64	White	IT

Relevant family medical history:

Paternal uncle diagnosed with Stage IIA colorectal cancer at age 67

Relevant medical history:

Today	**Scheduled routine examination. Nothing suspicious to report.**
November 2012	**Colonoscopy at age 60, results were clear**
November 2002	**Colonoscopy at age 50, results were clear**

According to the American Cancer Society guidelines for colorectal cancer prevention and early detection, a colonoscopy for average risk individuals is recommended first at 50 years of age, and then following at 10 year intervals.

Patient P's last colonoscopy was 4 years ago. You could recommend a repeat colonoscopy today if you determine that the medical history of Patient P warrants more attention or wait another 6 years as the guidelines recommend. As with all medical procedures and diagnostic examinations, there are risks and benefits for the patient. Risks include complications such as adverse reactions to the sedative used during the exam, bleeding, or a perforation of the colon or rectum wall. Benefits include potential early detection of colon cancer.

As you are paid by a fee-for-service compensation model, if you conduct the colonoscopy today, you will receive more payment (you'll receive a $5 bonus if the patient chooses to accept the colonoscopy now rather than waiting 6 more years).

[Disclosure condition] Due to a mandatory disclosure policy at your work, patients will receive a disclosure statement (as shown below) informing them that you, the physician, receive additional payment for each colonoscopy performed.

COMMUNICATION FROM THE PHYSICIAN (YOU):

TO PATIENT P

[The disclosure statement seen below is only shown in the disclosure condition]
Disclosure: I, your physician, receive additional payment for each colonoscopy I perform.

I, your physician, recommend that you:

☐ **Wait before taking another colonoscopy**   ☐ Take a repeat colonoscopy today

---

Please indicate the strength of your recommendation.

☐ I'm 100% sure that this choice is the best option for you
☐ I'm very sure that this choice is the best option for you
☐ I'm fairly sure that this choice is the best option for you

---

Reprinted from supplementary material from Sah, S. (2019). Conflict of interest disclosure as a reminder of professional norms. Clients First!, *Organizational Behavior and Human Decision Processes, 154*, 62–79, with permission from Elsevier.

Note: The advice was converted to a 1–6 scale representing honest advice that placed the interests of the patients first (score = 1, Treatment A, 100 percent sure) to self-interested biased advice (score = 6, Treatment B, 100 percent sure).

Additional surveys revealed that both medical and financial experts rated the norms of their profession to place clients first high. Nonexperts' assessments of their professional norms were similar to those of experts in the medical context but not in the financial context; nonexpert financial advisers rated norms to place clients first significantly lower than expert financial advisers.

Additional Experiments and Discussion

Two further laboratory experiments provided additional evidence that disclosure changes advisers' behavior by increasing norm salience. In these experiments, simply reminding advisers that they have a COI produced similar effects as COI disclosure. A key difference between disclosure and nondisclosure of COIs is the advisees' knowledge of the COI. With disclosure, advisees' knowledge of the COI may cause advisers to either (i) believe that their advisees will discount their advice, thus leading them to strategically exaggerate their advice, increasing bias; (ii) feel less guilty about providing biased advice, thus increasing bias; or (iii) believe that their advisees will scrutinize their advice more, leading to potential negative legal or reputational consequences for giving biased advice, thus decreasing bias. If the effects of disclosure are contingent on the advisee's knowledge of the COI, then the effects on advice with COI disclosure would not match those with a COI reminder. But if the effects of COI disclosure on advice serve mainly to remind advisers of their professional norms, we would expect, and indeed find, similar results with COI disclosures and COI reminders in both the medical and financial (see Figure 1.4) contexts. Furthermore, as the norms for expert and nonexpert financial advisers diverged, when nonexpert financial advisers are encouraged to focus on a "client first" norm (as expert financial advisers appeared to do in my framed field experiment), we would expect disclosure to decrease bias in nonexperts' financial advice. In one condition in the financial context, I informed nonexpert financial advisers of their fiduciary duty to place clients first. Although this information is not equivalent to time-intensive professional training that could indoctrinate professional responsibilities, it should still effectively inform nonexperts unfamiliar with this responsibility of financial advisers. Indeed, the "client first" condition did significantly reduce bias as compared to the COI disclosure and COI reminder conditions but did not reduce it significantly below the nondisclosure condition (Figure 1.4).

The series of laboratory experiments with nonexperts and framed field experiments with experts revealed that the effects of COI disclosure

Figure 1.4. Advice quality from nonexpert financial advisers

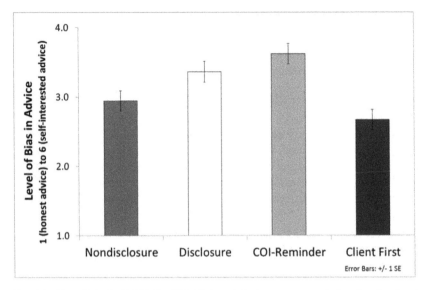

Reprinted from Sah, S. (2019). Conflict of interest disclosure as a reminder of professional norms. Clients First! *Organizational Behavior and Human Decision Processes, 154,* 62–79, with permission from Elsevier.

Note: Disclosure decreased advice quality (increased bias) for nonexpert advisers in a financial context. COI reminders worked similarly to COI disclosures – in this context increasing the bias of nonexpert financial advisers. For nonexperts, providing information on fiduciary norms – that financial advisers need to place "clients first" – increased advice quality.

on advisers depend on the sample population and their norms. Notably, experts, who had spent time training in their profession and who had frequent work interactions with other experts, had different perceptions of the moral rules and norms of their profession than did research participants asked to role-play an adviser in an experiment. Not surprisingly, then, real financial advisers behaved differently than role-playing research participants. The professional advisers (financial and medical alike) all decreased their advice bias with COI disclosure versus without. We cannot assume, however, that this will be true of all professional advisers. The financial advisers in my sample were all alumni from the same university and included both brokers and registered investment advisers at different financial institutions. Different institutions can signal different professional norms, and some employees may perceive their workplace to have "self-interest first" norms.[62]

But when norms emphasize placing advisees' interests first, and advisers are averse to being viewed as biased, my findings suggest that COI disclosure is more beneficial than previously assumed at increasing the salience of norms that place clients first and encouraging advisers to reduce bias in their advice[63] or, if possible, reject COIs.[64]

Beyond Disclosing Conflicts of Interest

In our efforts at translating laboratory research on conflict of interest disclosures to the field, we found some promising results. For recipients, such as patients, providing a single mailed letter with information on their physicians' financial relationships with industry was successful in educating patients on their physicians' conflicts of interest but it did not affect patients' trust in their physicians or the hospital. Such disclosures would be better served if they are provided to patients *before* they choose their physicians so that they can act on any preferences to avoid physicians with large financial conflicts more easily. For advisers, I found conflict of interest disclosures can increase the quality of advice if it reminds advisers of their professional responsibilities to place patients or clients first, but such disclosures may also decrease advice quality if norms to prioritize profit or self-interest are more salient.

The importance of using real-world actors in examining the effects of COI disclosure cannot be overstated, given the very different effects disclosure can have on advisers and advisees in different contexts and circumstances. Due to these and other potential effects of disclosing COIs, pilots for COI disclosure should be tested in the field in each context to determine whether they have only beneficial consequences. Importantly, more stringent efforts to eliminate or reduce COIs are likely to be much more effective at improving advice quality than policies such as disclosure or mandatory second opinions.[65] Policymakers must be cautious to avoid any indirect harm that COI disclosure could cause if it displaces more effective measures taken against COIs.

NOTES

1 See Sah, S., & Fugh-Berman, A. (2013). Physicians under the influence: Social psychology and industry marketing strategies. *The Journal of Law, Medicine & Ethics, 41*(3), 665–72. https://dx.doi.org/10.2139/ssrn.2286433; Wazana, A. (2000). Physicians and the pharmaceutical industry: Is a gift ever just a gift? *The Journal of the American Medical Association, 283*(3), 373–80. https://doi .org/10.1001/jama.283.3.373; and Campbell, E.G., Gruen, R.L., Mountford,

J., Miller, L.G., Cleary, P.D., & Blumenthal, D. (2007). A national survey of physician-industry relationships. *The New England Journal of Medicine, 356*(17), 1742–50. https://doi.org/10.1056/nejmsa064508.

2 Boatright, J.R. (2000). Conflicts of interest in financial services. *Business and Society Review, 105*(2), 201–19. https://doi.org/10.1111/0045-3609.00078.

3 Pham-Kanter, G., Mello, M.M., Lehmann, L.S., Campbell, E.G., & Carpenter, D. (2017). Public awareness of and contact with physicians who receive industry payments: A national survey. *Journal of General Internal Medicine, 32*(7), 767–74. https://doi.org/10.1007/s11606-017-4012-3.

4 See Davis, M., & Stark, A. (2001). *Conflict of interest in the professions.* Oxford University Press; Moore, D.A., Tetlock, P.E., Tanlu, L., & Bazerman, M.H. (2006). Conflicts of interest and the case of auditor independence: Moral seduction and strategic issue cycling. *Academy of Management Review, 31*(1), 10–29. https://doi.org/10.5465/amr.2006.19379621; and Mullainathan, S., Noeth, M., & Schoar, A. (2012). *The market for financial advice: An audit study.* National Bureau of Economic Research; and Sah, S. (2015). Investigations before examinations: This is how we practice medicine here. *JAMA Internal Medicine, 175*(3), 342–3. https://doi.org/10.1001/jamainternmed.2014.7549.

5 Sims, R.R., & Brinkmann, J. (2003). Enron ethics (or: Culture matters more than codes). *Journal of Business Ethics, 45*(3), 243–56. https://doi.org/10.1023/A:1024194519384.

6 Kassirer, J.P. (2005). Physicians' financial ties with the pharmaceutical industry. In D. Moore, D. Cain, G. Loewenstein, & M. Bazerman (Eds.), *Conflicts of Interest: Challenges and Solutions in Business, Law, Medicine, and Public Policy* (pp. 133–41). Cambridge University Press.

7 Sah, S. (2017). Policy solutions to conflicts of interest: The value of professional norms. *Behavioural Public Policy, 1*(2), 177–89. http://dx.doi.org/10.1017/bpp.2016.9.

8 Securities and Exchange Commission. (2010). *17 CFR Parts 275 and 279.* [Release No. IA-3060; File No. S7-10-00]. https://www.sec.gov/rules/final/2010/ia-3060.pdf.

9 Federal Trade Commission. (2013). *.com Disclosures: How to Make Effective Disclosures in Digital Advertising.* https://www.ftc.gov/business-guidance/resources/com-disclosures-how-make-effective-disclosures-digital-advertising.

10 Johns, M.Z. (2007). Informed consent: Requiring doctors to disclose off-label prescriptions and conflicts of interest. *Hastings Law Journal, 58*(5), 967–1024. https://repository.uclawsf.edu/hastings_law_journal/vol58/iss5/2.

11 Thompson, D.F. (1993). Understanding financial conflicts of interest. *New England Journal of Medicine, 329*(8), 573–6. https://doi.org/10.1056/nejm199308193290812.

12 Crawford, V.P., & Sobel, J. (1982). Strategic information transmission. *Econometrica: Journal of the Econometric Society, 50*(6), 1431–51. https://doi .org/10.2307/1913390.

13 Grady, C., Horstmann, E., Sussman, J.S., & Hull, S.C. (2006). The limits of disclosure: What research subjects want to know about investigator financial interests. *The Journal of Law, Medicine & Ethics, 34*(3), 592–9. https://doi.org/10.1111/j.1748-720x.2006.00073.x.

14 Rosenthal, M.B., & Mello, M.M. (2013). Sunlight as disinfectant – New rules on disclosure of industry payments to physicians. *New England Journal of Medicine, 368*(22), 2052–4. https://doi.org/10.1056 /nejmp1305090.

15 Sah, S. (2016, July 8). The paradox of disclosure. *The New York Times.* http://www.nytimes.com/2016/07/10/opinion/sunday/the-paradox -of-disclosure.html?_r=0.

16 Sah, S. (2019a). Conflict of interest disclosure as a reminder of professional norms: Clients first! *Organizational Behavior and Human Decision Processes, 154,* 62–79. https://doi.org/10.1016/j.obhdp.2019.07.005.

17 Hwong, A.R., Sah, S., & Lehmann, L. (2017). The effects of public disclosure of industry payments to physicians on patient trust: A randomized experiment. *Journal of General Internal Medicine, 32*(11), 1186–92. https://doi.org/10.1007/s11606-017-4122-y; Sah, S., & Feiler, D. (2020). Conflict of interest disclosure with high quality advice: The disclosure penalty and the altruistic signal. *Psychology, Public Policy, and Law, 26*(1), 88–104. https://psycnet.apa.org/doi/10.1037/law0000215; and Kesselheim, A.S., Robertson, C., Myers, J.A., Rose, S.L., Gillet, V., Ross, K.M., Glynn, R.J., Joffe, S., & Avorn, J. (2012). A randomized study of how physicians interpret research funding disclosures. *New England Journal of Medicine, 367*(12), 1119–27. https://doi.org/10.1056/nejmsa1202397.

18 Campbell, M.C., & Kirmani, A. (2000). Consumers' use of persuasion knowledge: The effects of accessibility and cognitive capacity on perceptions of an influence agent. *Journal of Consumer Research, 27*(1), 69–83; Friestad, M., & Wright, P. (1994). The persuasion knowledge model: How people cope with persuasion attempts. *Journal of Consumer Research, 21*(1), 1–31. https://doi.org/10.1086/209380; and Van Swol, L.M. (2009). The effects of confidence and advisor motives on advice utilization. *Communication Research, 36*(6), 857–73. https://doi .org/10.1177/0093650209346803.

19 Sah & Feiler (2020).

20 Sah & Feiler (2020).

21 Sah, S., Loewenstein, G., & Cain, D.M. (2013). The burden of disclosure: Increased compliance with distrusted advice. *Journal of Personality and Social Psychology, 104*(2), 289–304. https://psycnet.apa.org/doi/10.1037

/a0030527; and Sah, S., Loewenstein, G., & Cain, D.M. (2019). Insinuation anxiety: Concern that advice rejection will signal distrust after conflict of interest disclosures. *Personality and Social Psychology Bulletin, 45*(7), 1099–12. https://doi.org/10.1177/0146167218805991.

22 Sah et al. (2013).

23 Sah et al. (2019).

24 Sah, S., Fagerlin, A., & Ubel, P.A. (2016). Effect of physician disclosure of specialty bias on patient trust and treatment choice. *Proceedings of the National Academy of Sciences, 113*(27), 7465–9. https://psycnet.apa.org /doi/10.1073/pnas.1604908113; and Sah, S., Malaviya, P., & Thompson, D. (2018). Conflict of interest disclosure as an expertise cue: Differential effects due to automatic versus deliberative processing. *Organizational Behavior and Human Decision Processes, 147,* 127–46. https://psycnet.apa .org/doi/10.1016/j.obhdp.2018.05.008.

25 Sah et al. (2018).

26 Sah et al. (2018).

27 See Sah & Fugh-Berman. (2013); Wazana. (2000); Pham-Kanter et al. (2017); Sah. (2015); and Robertson, Rose, S., & Kesselheim, A.S. (2012). Effect of financial relationships on the behaviors of health care professionals: A review of the evidence. *The Journal of Law, Medicine & Ethics, 40*(3), 452–66. https://doi.org/10.1111/j.1748-720X.2012.00678.x.

28 See Sah. (2017); and Rosenthal & Mello. (2013).

29 Rose, S., Sah, S., Raed, D., Schmidt, C., Mercer, M., Mitchum, A., Kattan, M., Karafa, M., & Robertson, C. (2021). Patient responses to physician disclosures of industry conflicts of interest: A randomized field experiment. *Organizational Behavior and Human Decision Processes, 166,* 27–38 https://doi.org/10.1016/j.obhdp.2019.03.005.

30 Crawford & Sobel (1982).

31 Johns (2007).

32 Sah et al. (2018).

33 Sah et al. (2019).

34 Sah & Feiler (2020).

35 Sah, et al. (2013); and Sah et al. (2019).

36 Sah et al. (2018).

37 See Sah et al. (2019); and Spece, R., Yokum, D., Okoro, A.-G., & Robertson, C. (2014). An empirical method for materiality: Would conflict of interest disclosures change patient decisions. *American Journal of Law and Medicine, 40*(4), 253–74. https://doi.org/10.2139/SSRN.2378524.

38 See Joel, S., Teper, R., & MacDonald, G. (2014). People overestimate their willingness to reject potential romantic partners by overlooking their concern for other people. *Psychological Science, 25*(12), 2233–40. https:// psycnet.apa.org/doi/10.1177/0956797614552828; Nordgren, L.F.,

Harreveld, F., & Pligt, J. (2009). The restraint bias: How the illusion of self-restraint promotes impulsive behavior. *Psychological Science, 20*(12), 1523–8. https://psycnet.apa.org/doi/10.1111/j.1467-9280.2009.02468.x; and Patrick, V.M., & MacInnis, D.J. (2006). Why feelings stray: Sources of affective misforecasting in consumer behavior. *Advances in Consumer Research, 33*(1), 49–56. https://ssrn.com/abstract=3604570.

39 Evans, M. (2014, October 5). *How patients will use physician payment data.* Morning Consult. https://morningconsult.com/2014/10/05/health -sunday-10-5/.

40 Sah, S., & Loewenstein, G. (2015). Conflicted advice and second opinions: Benefits, but unintended consequences. *Organizational Behavior and Human Decision Processes, 130*, 89–107. https://psycnet.apa.org/doi/10.1016 /j.obhdp.2015.06.005.

41 Kunda, Z. (1990). The case for motivated reasoning. *Psychological Bulletin, 108*(3), 480–98. https://psycnet.apa.org/doi/10.1037/0033-2909.108.3.480.

42 See Kunda. (1990); and Gibbons, R.V., Landry, F.J., Blouch, D.L., Jones, D.L., Williams, F.K., Lucey, C.R., & Kroenke, K. (1998). A comparison of physicians' and patients' attitudes toward pharmaceutical industry gifts. *Journal of General Internal Medicine, 13*(3), 151–4. https://doi.org/10.1046 /j.1525-1497.1998.00048.x.

43 Kassirer, J.P. (1995). Managed care and the morality of the marketplace. *New England Journal of Medicine, 333*(1), 50–2. https://doi.org/10.1056 /NEJM199507063330110.

44 Sah, S., & Loewenstein, G. (2014). Nothing to declare: Mandatory and voluntary disclosure leads advisors to avoid conflicts of interest. *Psychological Science, 25*(2), 575–84. https://doi.org/10.1177 /0956797613511824.

45 Omer, T.C., Bedard, J.C., & Falsetta, D. (2006). Auditor-provided tax services: The effects of a changing regulatory environment. *The Accounting Review, 81*(5), 1095–117. https://doi.org/10.2308/ACCR.2006.81.5.1095.

46 Cain, D.M., Loewenstein, G., & Moore, D.A. (2011). When sunlight fails to disinfect: Understanding the perverse effects of disclosing conflicts of interest. *Journal of Consumer Research, 37*(5), 836–57. https://psycnet.apa .org/doi/10.1086/656252.

47 See Sah & Fugh-Berman. (2013); Chren, M.M., & Landefeld, C.S. (1994). Physicians' behavior and their interactions with drug companies. *The Journal of the American Medical Association, 271*(9), 684–9. https:// doi.org/10.1097/00006254-199408000-00019; and Goldfinger, S.E. (1987). A matter of influence. *New England Journal of Medicine, 316*(22), 1408–9. https://doi.org/10.1056/nejm198705283162211.

48 See Chao, M., & Larkin, I. (2017). *Regulating conflicts of interest through public disclosure: Evidence from a physician payments sunshine law.* https://

www.researchgate.net/publication/320684814_Regulating_Conflicts
_of_Interest_through_Public_Disclosure_Evidence_from_a_Physician
_Payments_Sunshine_Law; and Guo, T., Sriram, S., & Manchanda, P.
(2020). "Let the Sunshine in": The Impact of Industry Payment Disclosure
on Physician Prescription Behavior. *Marketing Science, 39*(3), 516–39.
https://doi.org/10.1287/mksc.2019.1181.

49 Guo et al. (2020).

50 Koch, C., & Schmidt, C. (2010). Disclosing conflicts of interest–Do
experience and reputation matter? *Accounting, Organizations and Society,*
35(1), 95–107. https://doi.org/10.1016/j.aos.2009.05.001.

51 Church, B.K., & Kuang, X. (2009). Conflicts of interest, disclosure, and
(costly) sanctions: Experimental evidence. *The Journal of Legal Studies, 38*(2),
505–32. https://doi.org/10.1086/596117.

52 For full results for this direct replication of Cain et al. (2011), see Sah, S.
(2019b). Understanding the (perverse) effects of disclosing conflicts of
interest: A direct replication Ssudy. *Journal of Economic Psychology; Special*
Issue on Replications in Economic Psychology and Behavioral Economics, 75(A).
https://doi.org/10.1016/j.joep.2018.10.010.

53 Sah (2019a).

54 Sah (2019a).

55 Johns, G. (2006). The essential impact of context on organizational
behavior. *Academy of Management Review, 31*(2), 386–408. https://
doi.org/10.5465/amr.2006.20208687; and Merton, R.K. (1957). The role-set:
Problems in sociological theory. *The British Journal of Sociology, 8*(2), 106–20.
https://doi.org/10.2307/587363.

56 Sah (2019a).

57 Tankard, M.E., & Paluck, E.L. (2016). Norm perception as a vehicle for
social change. *Social Issues and Policy Review, 10*(1), 181–211. https://doi
.org/10.1111/sipr.12022.

58 March, J.G., & Olsen, J.P. (2004). *The logic of appropriateness.* Arena Centre
for European Studies Working Papers. http://www.sv.uio.no/arena
/english/research/publications/arena-publications/workingpapers
/working-papers2004/wp04_9.pdf.

59 Harrison, G.W., & List, J.A. (2004). Field experiments. *Journal of Economic*
Literature, 42(4), 1009–55. https://doi.org/10.1257/0022051043004577.

60 See Gibbons et al. (1998); and Sah, S. (2012). Conflicts of interest and your
physician: Psychological processes that cause unexpected changes in
behavior. *The Journal of Law, Medicine & Ethics, 40*(3), 482–7. https://doi
.org/10.1111/j.1748-720x.2012.00680.x.

61 Sah (2019a).

62 See Sah, S. (2018). *FSRC Research Paper: Conflicts of Interest and Disclosure.*
Report to the Royal Commission into Misconduct in the Banking,

Superannuation and Financial Services Industry. https://financialservices
.royalcommission.gov.au/publications/Documents
/research-paper-conflicts-interest-disclosure.pdf; Also see https://www
.effectivegovernance.com.au/page/knowledge-centre/news-articles
/conflicts-of-interest-and-disclosure and https://treasury.gov.au/sites
/default/files/2019-03/fsrc-volume1.pdf; and Smith, G. (2012, March 14).
Why I am leaving Goldman Sachs. *The New York Times*. http://www
.nytimes.com/2012/03/14/opinion/why-i-am-leaving
-goldman-sachs.html.

63 Sah (2019a).

64 Sah & Loewenstein (2014).

65 Sah (2018).

CHAPTER TWO

Translating and Scaling Laboratory Research on Time-Saving Services to Increase Well-Being of Working Mothers

Ashley Whillans

AT A GLANCE

- **Our Goal:** To increase the well-being of working mothers living in Kenya by providing one of two time-saving services: meals or laundry.
- **The Intervention:** Working mothers were randomly assigned to a control condition, or to receive equivalently valued time-saving services or unconditional cash transfers.
- **The Results:** We predicted that working mothers who received the time-saving services would report greater well-being at the end of the study compared to the control and cash transfer conditions. In contrast to this prediction, all three conditions significantly improved well-being.
- **Lesson Learned:** When implementing studies with at-risk populations, even a "neutral" control condition that involves a small incentive fee for completing surveys could benefit well-being.

Motivation and Objective

Poverty entails more than a scarcity of money – it also involves a shortage of *time*.[1] Time-use data shows that people living in poverty spend more time on unpaid labor as compared to those who are wealthier. In this project, we conducted a lab-in-the-field experiment to test whether reducing the burden of unpaid labor causally improved the well-being of working mothers living in an informal settlement in East Africa who were struggling to make ends meet.

Poverty involves both material limitations and time constraints. In this project, we explored whether alleviating the time poverty that is often associated with financial ill-being could promote well-being and improve economic mobility.

Time poverty most severely affects poor women living in developing countries.[2] For example, women in East Africa spend 4.2 hours per day on unpaid work, and women in India spend upward of 6 hours per day.[3] Poorer women tend to lack basic amenities in their households, requiring them to spend far more time on household production tasks such as cooking and cleaning as compared to their richer counterparts. In turn, these burdens reduce the amount of time available to participate in paid labor and invest in the development of children.

Despite potentially far-reaching consequences, little is known about the effects of time poverty on the well-being of women living in poverty. Economic measurements of poverty often neglect the time deficits that poor households face in developing countries.[4] This incomplete understanding of time poverty may undermine public and private sector initiatives that are designed toward reaching UN Sustainable Development Goals related to poverty, employment, economic growth, and inequality. In contrast, having a better understanding of time poverty could improve the effectiveness of NGOs engaged in economic development efforts. Economic aid programs tend to focus on material constraints; spending billions of dollars to provide monetary and non-monetary aid to people living in poverty such as by providing food, livestock, fertilizer, and services such as agricultural training. This experiment provides the first rigorous causal test of whether reducing unpaid labor through the provision of time-saving services such as meals and laundry can promote well-being and productivity for working women living in poverty. In doing so, this experiment examines whether the effectiveness of economic aid programs could be increased by directly intervening on recipients' time demands.[5]

Inspiration

This experiment is part of a larger initiative to apply rigorous behavioral science methodologies to poverty alleviation efforts. Over the past twenty years, there has been a growing debate on the effectiveness of international aid for economic development efforts and a subsequent movement toward a more rigorous evaluation of aid programs.[6] This evaluation approach includes the use of randomized control trials (RCTs) to identify the causal impact of aid on key outcomes like mental and physical health, health behavior, and economic mobility.[7]

The current experiment applied these rigorous methods to the evaluation of time-saving services. The time costs linked to material poverty are especially severe for working women living in developing countries where there is minimal provision of basic services and infrastructure like childcare, school, and health services.[8] By using a rigorous RCT design, we were directly able to evaluate the effectiveness of an aid program designed to address time poverty against a traditional program designed to alleviate recipients' financial constraints.

RCTs are increasingly being used in economic development research and policymaking to compare the cost-effectiveness of aid programs. One type of aid that has been identified as especially cost-effective is unconditional cash transfers (UCTs) – sending money directly to low-income recipients via an SMS-based mobile money platform. Unconditional cash transfers have been shown to improve psychological and economic well-being. In one highly cited study of the unconditional cash transfer program "Give Directly," researchers found that providing cash transfers resulted in large and persistent effects on well-being over a nine-month period.[9] Sending money directly to recipients limits administrative costs and empowers recipients to use the money in creative ways to solve their own idiosyncratic economic challenges. Given the well-documented benefits of cash, we compared time-saving services against unconditional cash transfers, given that UCTs are considered the gold standard of economic development efforts.

This experiment built on existing research showed that time-saving services causally improve happiness and reduce stress.[10] In a small experiment of sixty working adults living in Vancouver, Canada that demonstrated this initial effect, participants received two $40 CAD windfalls over two consecutive weekends. On the first weekend, participants were instructed to spend this money on a material purchase for themselves. On the second weekend, participants were instructed to spend this money on a time-saving service. The order was counterbalanced and did not influence outcomes. After making each purchase, at the end of the day, participants reported how happy and time-stressed they felt. Participants were happier and less stressed after making a time-saving purchase than after making a material purchase for themselves.[11]

In the current work, we translated this initial experiment by conducting an experiment with larger and more financially valuable time-saving services (i.e., meals and laundry) and by recruiting participants who could stand to benefit most from these services: working mothers living in East Africa who were struggling financially. We conducted the study over six weeks and explored whether the benefits of time-saving services extended to measures of financial well-being. See Table 2.1 for a table that reports the similarities and differences of these studies.

Interventions and Method

We recruited 1,070 working mothers who were living in Kibera, Kenya, and had at least one school-aged child living at home.[12] See Figure 2.1 for a procedural diagram. Adapting the paradigm from Whillans et al. (2017), participants were randomly assigned to one of three conditions in a between-subject design:

1. **Time-saving services:** Participants received three weekly vouchers for a time-saving service that totaled ~1500 KSH or US$15; the mean daily wage for this sample was ~600 KSH per day. Participants received a ~500 KSH voucher once per week for three consecutive weeks. We selected the time-saving services through extensive piloting. Vouchers were provided for one of two time-saving services: laundry or prepared meals. Participants received one type of voucher throughout the duration of the study. Our pilot data indicated that both services reduced a disliked chore and saved a significant amount of time. On average, these services saved 3–7 hours per week according to our pilot data.
2. **Unconditional cash transfer condition:** Participants received a cash transfer via MPesa (a ubiquitous mobile money platform used by Kibera residents) that was matched to the value of the time-saving services at 500 KSH per week for a total of 1500 KSH. Participants received a payment once per week for three consecutive weeks. On average, participants assigned to this condition experienced a 33 percent average increase in their total income during the intervention period during Weeks 3–5 of the study.
3. **Control Condition:** Participants received no windfalls. This condition provided a benchmark to evaluate the effectiveness of the treatment conditions.

Figure 2.1. Study flow diagram from Whillans & West (2022)

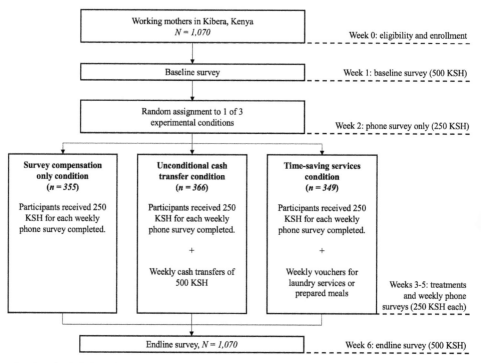

Overview of study design and timeline.

All participants completed baseline measures of positive and negative mood, stress, and relationship conflict. These measures served as our primary outcome measures of interest. After completing these and other baseline measures, participants were randomly assigned to the time-saving, UCT, or control conditions. Each week, participants completed a short well-being and spending survey over the phone. In Week 6, participants completed the identical measures of positive and negative mood, stress, and relationship conflict from the baseline measures.

At baseline, we also collected comprehensive demographic measures. These measures allowed us to explore whether the benefits of time-saving services were stronger when participants worked more hours, were married, or owned their own small businesses.

Table 2.1. Similarities and differences between Whillans & West (2022) and Whillans et al. (2017)

Feature	Whillans & West (2022)	Whillans et al. (2017); Study 8
Experimental Design	- Between-subject design - Preregistered	- Within-subject design - Preregistered
Setting	- Kibera, Kenya - Informal settlement	- Vancouver, Canada - Wealthy suburb
Participants	- Working mothers - Full-time employed - Average income: 700 USD per year (82K KSH)	- Working adults - Full-time employed - Average income: 50K USD per year (65K CAD)
Sample Size	- N=1,070 - 98% statistical power to detect a small effect of condition on well-being	- N=60 - 95% statistical power to detect a small effect of condition on well-being
Measures	- Positive and Negative Affect over Past Month - Perceived Stress Scale over Past Month - Relationship Conflict over Past Month	- Positive and Negative Affect over Past Day - Time Stress over Past Day
Procedures	- Six-week study - Received 500 KSH (4 USD) in cash or equivalently valued laundry or meal vouchers in Weeks 3, 4, and 5 - Baseline and Endline Measures in Week 1 & 6 - Phone surveys asked in Weeks 3–5	- Two-week study - Received 30 USD (40 CAD) for two weekends - Instructed to spend the money on a material purchase (Wk 1) or time-saving purchase (Wk 2); order counterbalanced - End of day measures after making each purchase
Implementation	- Cash was given via MPesa (mobile money) - Time-saving services involved walking ~30 minutes to a community center to receive the meals or drop off and pick up laundry	- Cash was given via electronic bank transfers - Time-saving services did not incur time costs because participants could make purchases of any time-saving services they desired

Results

We predicted that women who were assigned to the time-saving service condition would report greater positive mood, lower stress, and lower relationship conflict as compared to women assigned to the

Figure 2.2. Condition assignment on subjective well-being, stress, and conflict across time

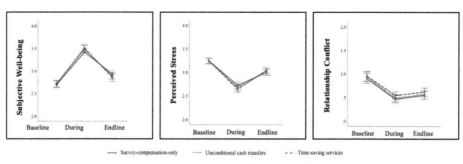

Effect of condition and time point on subjective well-being, perceived stress, and relationship conflict. This figure reports estimate marginal means and 95% confidence intervals by each condition and time point: at baseline (Week 1), during the intervention (weighted average of Weeks 3–5), and at endline (Week 6). As indicated by the confidence intervals that do not overlap, all outcome measures differed significantly from the baseline to endline measurements, suggesting that the positive impact of the condition assignments persisted even after the intervention ended. Outcome measures during the intervention were calculated as a weighted average of participants' responses in Weeks 3, 4, and 5. For subjective well-being, the measure during the intervention was a weighted average of positive affect and negative affect in Weeks 3–5. The Satisfaction with Life scale was not included because it required a visual aid and was not administered in the phone survey during intervention weeks.

unconditional cash transfer and control conditions. In contrast to this prediction, all three conditions produced lasting benefits for participants' well-being, stress, and relationship conflict. Collapsing across conditions, study participation significantly increased well-being ($d=0.21$), reduced stress ($d=0.29$), and reduced relationship conflict ($d=0.36$) as depicted in Figure 2.2.

Time-saving services and cash transfers had similar well-being benefits regardless of participants' educational background or occupation. At endline, participants who were assigned to the time-saving (vs. cash) condition and owned their own businesses reported earning 68 percent higher profits. Why? Instead of allocating money to their business, female business owners in the cash transfer condition spent the majority of their transfers on household expenses and bills. In contrast, women who received the time-saving services reported saving money (e.g., saving money on soap or food expenses) *and* time, which they directly allocated to their business.

Reconciliation

Before the start of the study, participants earned a median income of 1250 KSH per week and had a median total savings of 0 KSH. All three conditions provided sizable survey compensation. Even participants assigned to the control condition experienced a 14 percent increase in their total income as a result of completing our study-related surveys. Under dire financial circumstances, it is possible that any small cash aid could have a positive psychological impact.

It was surprising that the survey compensation-only control condition did not differ from the cash or time-saving conditions. It is possible that women in the control condition derived psychological benefits from working for the money that they earned during the study. In contrast, women in the cash and time-saving conditions could have experienced lower well-being as a result of receiving "aid," thereby explaining the similar well-being benefits observed across conditions. This proposition is supported by an experiment conducted in Kenya showing that working for pay improved well-being relative to waiting for an equivalently valued windfall.[13] This proposition is also supported by research showing that receiving cash or assistance from a higher-status actor can increase feelings of guilt and shame and undermine well-being.[14] These findings highlight the importance of understanding "neutral" control conditions. It is possible for control participants to derive direct and indirect benefits such as social interactions with research assistants or small survey payments that should be quantified and understood.

According to our surveys, 20 percent of our sample was at high risk for depression. During weekly phone calls, participants reported serious events like illness, hospitalization, theft, death, and arson. Through weekly phone surveys, it is possible that our study provided participants across all three conditions with the chance to share their feelings and reflect. Indeed, this weekly phone call may have provided "social support" and "economic support via survey compensation" that – coupled together – produced powerful psychological benefits.[15] Future research should systematically quantify the benefits of interactions between participants and field officers, especially when studying well-being in vulnerable populations.

We made several methodological decisions that likely strengthened the benefits of the time-saving condition. We chose time-saving services that were desirable but unaffordable. In Kibera, small businesses offered laundry services, and women reported that these services were desirable, but they often could not afford them. A single load of laundry cost 500 KSH per average, which was over three times the average daily wage for participants in our study. As a result, in our pilot data, 77 percent of working women reported "never" paying for laundry services, and 83 percent reported "never" paying for prepared meals. The fact that these services were desirable but not frequently purchased likely increased their positive impact. We were also careful to avoid using time-saving services that removed a positive experience such as socializing. For example, women in our pilot studies disliked taking their waste to the dump but reported that this activity was a significant source of social interaction, thus we did not outsource this chore in our study. When designing time-saving interventions, researchers should avoid eliminating chores that provide positive experiences like the chance to socialize with friends or family members.

Discussion and Prescriptive Advice

From an implementation perspective, this study was a success as we observed low rates of attrition (7.2 percent). Despite the successful implementation of this research, there are several different decisions that we would have made in retrospect when conducting this research.

First, we would have included a pure time-saving condition. In the current design, the time-saving services saved both time *and* money. In our initial design, we included a condition where some women received staple food ingredients such as rice and vegetables and had to cook the food themselves. This condition controlled for the objective value of the goods, while directly manipulating the time saved. We submitted our study proposal as a preregistered report and had to make a series of changes to the study design during peer review, including omitting this condition. Understanding why an intervention works is critical when translating studies to policy.[16] Future research should more directly manipulate time-savings such as by varying whether aid involves waiting in line or not to understand the unique benefits of saving time.

Second, we would have included additional measures of the quantity and quality of field officer interactions, felt belonging, and subjective feelings of wealth. With these items, we would have been better positioned to understand why all three conditions had significant benefits.

Third, we would have further tailored the time-saving services to the local context. Meal and laundry services were desirable and saved time. These services were also easy to implement because of our partnership with a non-profit. However, our pilot data pointed to other time-saving services that might have had more impact. Female business owners spent a lot of time traveling to the market to restock their goods.[17] Providing women business owners with drivers to restock their goods could have produced even larger profit benefits. This point underscores the importance of *learning from the field* in addition to replicating lab research in the field.[18]

Finally, it is important to consider when to measure critical outcomes. In this study, we *wanted* to measure well-being through text messages immediately after participants had received cash transfers or time-saving services, yet the text message data we collected was unusable due to low response rates. Thus, we had to rely on end-of-week and end-of-study measures. When conducting behavioral interventions that measure well-being, it is important to include immediate *and* long-term measures that capture sustained changes. By omitting immediate mood, it is possible that we failed to observe the differential benefits of the cash vs. time conditions.

Conclusion

It is a worthwhile exercise to try to translate small lab studies into large field studies. As a researcher, I gained new skills by conducting extensive pilot studies, working with field officers, and cooperating with non-profit organizations to establish complex lab infrastructure in a developing market. I also gained first-hand knowledge of pre-registered reports. The protocol and analysis plan for this study was accepted as a preregistered report, which ensured a guaranteed publication. For junior scholars who are considering conducting a field experiment in a new or untested context, submitting the study design as a preregistered report can be a helpful step. If the results do not turn out as expected (such as the results reported here), preregistered reports guarantee at least one publication, regardless of the study outcomes. A preregistered format requires an openness to changing your study design, but the guarantee of a publication is – in my opinion – worth the flexibility, especially given the inherent risk, time cost, and challenge of running large-scale translational studies in the field like the one reported here.

By piloting and submitting a detailed protocol for peer review before study launch, my research team and I overcame challenges that often arise when conducting field research.[19] We knew that our measures were reliable, that our interventions were scalable, and that our participants and field officers understood the study protocol. When we received our data, we knew exactly what analyses to run. Thus, writing detailed protocol and analysis plan documents and sharing them for feedback before launching your experiment are highly recommended – even if you do not submit a preregistered report. Only through rigorous implementation of behavioral ideas in the field can we truly begin to understand what works, when, and why, and clarify the foundation of our field.

NOTES

1 Giurge, L.M., Whillans, A.V., & West, C. (2020). Why time poverty matters for individuals, organisations and nations. *Nature Human Behaviour*, 4(10), 993–1003. https://doi.org/10.1038/s41562-020-0920-z.

2 Antonopoulos, R., & Hirway, I. (2010). Unpaid work and the economy. In R. Antonopoulos & I. Hirway (Eds.), *Unpaid work and the economy: Gender, time-use, and poverty in developing countries* (pp. 1–21). Palgrave Macmillan.

3 OECD (2014). *Gender, institutions, and development database*. OECD.Stat. https://stats.oecd.org/Index.aspx?DataSetCode=GIDDB2014.

4 Hirway, I. (2017). *Mainstreaming unpaid work: Time-use data in developing policies*. Oxford University Press.

5 For a review, see West, C., & Whillans, A. (2023). Don't waste recipients' time: How to save and give time in cash transfer programs. In J. Zhao, S. Datta & D. Soman (Eds.), *Cash Transfers for inclusive societies: A behavioural lens* (pp. 130–62). University of Toronto Press.

6 See Burnside, C., & Dollar, D. (2000). Aid, policies, and growth. *American Economic Review*, 90(4), 847–68. https://doi.org/10.1257/aer.90.4.847; Bourguignon, F., & Sundberg, M. (2007). Aid effectiveness: Opening the black box. *American Economic Review*, 97(2), 316–21. https://doi .org/10.1257/aer.97.2.316; and Rajan, R.G., & Subramanian, A. (2008). Aid and growth: What does the cross-country evidence really show? *The Review of Economics and Statistics*, 90(4), 643–65. https://doi.org/10.3386 /w11513.

7 Banerjee, A.V., & Duflo, E. (2009). The experimental approach to development economics. *Annual Review of Economics*, 1(1), 151–78. https:// doi.org/10.3386/w14467.

8 Hirway (2017).

9 Haushofer, J., & Shapiro, J. (2016). The short-term impact of unconditional cash transfers to the poor: Experimental evidence from Kenya. *The Quarterly Journal of Economics*, 131(4), 1973–2042. https://doi.org/10.1093 /qje/qjw025.

10 Whillans, A.V., Dunn, E.W., Smeets, P., Bekkers, R., & Norton, M.I. (2017). Buying time promotes happiness. *Proceedings of the National Academy of Sciences*, 114(32), 8523–7. https://doi.org/10.1073/pnas.1706541114.

11 Dunn, E.W., Whillans, A.V., Norton, M.I., & Aknin, L.B. (2020). Prosocial spending and buying time: Money as a tool for increasing subjective well-being. In B. Gawronksi (Ed.), *Advances in experimental social psychology* (pp. 67–126). Elsevier Academic Press.

12 For eligibility and recruitment information see Whillans & West (2023).

13 Bhanot, S.P., Han, J., & Jang, C. (2018). Workfare, wellbeing and consumption: Evidence from a field experiment with Kenya's urban poor.

Journal of Economic Behavior & Organization, 149, 372–88. https://doi
.org/10.1016/J.JEBO.2018.01.007.

14 See Lee-Yoon, A., Donnelly, G.E., & Whillans, A.V. (2020). Overcoming
resource scarcity: Consumers' response to gifts intending to save time
and money. *Journal of the Association for Consumer Research, 5*(4), 391–403.
https://doi.org/10.1086/709887; and Sandstrom, G.M., Schmader, T.,
Croft, A., & Kwok, N. (2019). A social identity threat perspective on being
the target of generosity from a higher status other. *Journal of Experimental
Social Psychology, 82,* 98–114. https://doi.org/10.1016/j.jesp.2018.12.004.

15 Haushofer, J., Mudida, R., & Shapiro, J.P. (2020). *The comparative impact of
cash transfers and a psychotherapy program on psychological and economic well-
being* (No. w28106). National Bureau of Economic Research. https://doi
.org/10.3386/w28106.

16 Bryan, C.J., Tipton, E., & Yeager, D.S. (2021). Behavioural science is
unlikely to change the world without a heterogeneity revolution. *Nature
human behaviour, 5*(8), 980–9. https://doi.org/10.1038/s41562-021-01143-3.

17 Delecourt, S., & Fitzpatrick, A. (2021). Childcare matters: Female business
owners and the baby-profit gap. *Management Science, 67*(7), 4455–74.
https://doi.org/10.1287/mnsc.2021.3976.

18 Jachimowicz, J.M. (2022). Embracing field studies as a tool for learning.
Nature Reviews Psychology, 1, 249–50.

19 For a detailed description of the methods and results of this experiment
please see: Whillans, A., & West, C. (2022). Alleviating time poverty among
the working poor: A pre-registered longitudinal field experiment. *Scientific
Reports, 12,* 719. https://www.nature.com/articles/s41598-021-04352-y.

CHAPTER THREE

Behaviorally Informed Reminders: Translating Mindset Research to Improve Task Persistence

Joonkyung Kim and Dilip Soman

AT A GLANCE

- **Our Goal:** To help people accomplish tasks and goals by invoking implementation intentions through making choices.
- **The Intervention:** A behaviorally informed (BI) smartphone app that delivered reminders for tasks along with a series of binary choice questions.
- **The Results:** We predicted that users of the BI-app would a) complete more tasks and b) do them sooner relative to those getting regular reminders. Unfortunately, we did not find this consistently or reliably.
- **Lesson Learned:** Success in user experience (UX) testing and repeated lab testing does not ensure efficacy. Interventions that need attention and engagement might be particularly hard to scale in real-world conditions.

Motivation and Objective

People routinely set personal goals that require them to undertake a series of tasks that extend over time, whether training to climb a mountain, doing a fitness or weight-loss program, or learning a new language. Indeed, there is an active segment of human enterprise – personal coaches, mobile applications, and self-help books – dedicated to help people to set personal and professional goals, make plans, and execute on those plans to get things done.

Put simply, success at any goal requires the individual to get started (as Aristotle and Mary Poppins have proclaimed), and then to persist. Yet, folklore and consumer narratives are replete with the idea that performance and the motivation to accomplish tasks typically flags in the middle of the task. Motivation is typically high at the start of a task and toward the end when the target is in sight.[1] As the author Martha Wells so eloquently wrote,

> Writing the beginning of a book is exciting, everything is new, you're creating the world, meeting the characters for the first time. The end is also exciting, because all the plot threads are tying up and you should be done soon. … The middle is the hard part, where you have to make the magic happen and start pulling things together.[2]

This narrative about a "middle slump" has academic support in research as well: the engagement in goal-consistent behavior was lowest in the middle relative to the start and the finish.[3] As a result, individuals are likely to (a) perform poorly, (b) procrastinate and delay, and perhaps (c) drop out altogether in the middle.

We were interested in developing a solution that would mitigate the effects of the middle slump and help people accomplish goals that require the completion of multiple tasks. For instance, success in a weight-loss program might entail a certain number of visits to the gym and dietician appointments; learning a new language might involve a specific number of classroom sessions and conversation workshops. The goals we study are neither extreme (i.e., we will not study a mountain climbing expedition to Mt. Everest) nor mundane (i.e., waiting in queue for service).

There are several explanations for why the middle slump occurs. One set of explanations suggests that the outcome loses value in the middle relative to when the individual initiated goal pursuit. The second set relates to the inability to convert plans into actions, either due to a decline in motivation or due to the lack of a proper mindset. In particular, the appropriate mindset that tunes a person's cognitions to implementing the chosen goals is known as an implementation mindset.[4] Our interest is in helping individuals stay the course by using a behavioral intervention that helps them convert plans into action by promoting an implementation intention. Based on published work, we hypothesized that promoting an implementation intention by encouraging individuals to make a series of choices would improve persistence and help people accomplish a series of tasks in a timely matter.

Inspiration

Ordinary household appliances like ovens or washing machines can be set to different modes (e.g., baking, broiling, or roasting). While the apparatus remains the same, each mode activates some parts of the apparatus and dampens other parts. The human brain is no different – it can adopt different modes of operating. These modes are called mindsets.

The term mindset is used to refer to "a state of mind that influences how people think about and then enact their goal-directed activities in ways that may systematically promote or interfere with optimal functioning."[5] The research makes a distinction between the two types of mindsets activated during the two stages of goal pursuit: the first stage (motivation), which involves goal setting, and the second stage (volition), which involves implementation.[6] At the beginning of goal pursuit, people adopt a *deliberative* mindset, a mode characterized by planning and evaluation. As individuals move to the stage of volition, they adopt an *implemental* mindset, which is characterized by action orientation, goal commitment, and willingness to make choices.[7] Features of an implemental mindset include the formulation, monitoring, and progress made on action plans that have activities and timelines associated with them and the willingness to make choices that allow for a sequence of actions to unfold.[8]

The effect of mindset on task completion has been demonstrated in many contexts, including exercise, cancer screening, eating fruit, getting flu shots, and making better financial decisions.[9] A field study conducted by the Behavioral Insights Team (BIT) in the UK used the idea of implementation mindsets and action planning to help job seekers.[10] In this study, the implementation mindset was activated by making an action plan for when, where, and how they would apply for jobs. Prospective job seekers in the implementation mindset intervention were more likely to apply for and find employment.

An oven or washing machine comes with a knob that can be turned to change modes. What knobs can be turned to change mindsets? One knob was illustrated in the example of the BIT study – the formation of action plans has been shown to create an implemental mindset. A second knob has to do with getting people to practice or rehearse specific cognitive operations that are central to the mindset.[11] A central feature of the implementation mindset is making tradeoffs and choices.

Consistent with this, the act of making choices has been shown to make individuals action oriented by invoking a comparative mindset.[12] In particular, Xu and Wyer demonstrated the action-boosting effect of making binary choices.[13] In Experiment 2 of their paper, participants viewed two computers A and B and indicated whether they would choose A, choose B, or contemplate further and not make an immediate choice. In two treatment conditions, participants made a series of binary choices between animals (e.g., hippos or elephants) prior to the computer task to indicate either (a) which computer they preferred or (b) which one dominated on a particular attribute (e.g., weight). Participants in both these treatment conditions were significantly more likely to make a choice between computers, whereas those in the control condition (who were not given any animal choice task) were more likely to wait and deliberate further.

We were intrigued by the demonstration that making binary choices in a completely unrelated domain (attributes of animals) to the focal task (of choosing computers) boosted decisiveness, and we felt that idea could be translated into a realistic field setting to help people get things done.

Interventions and Method

With funding from the New Paths to Purpose Project and in partnership with an app developer, we created a smartphone application (app) that acted as a behaviorally informed reminder system. Simple reminders have been shown to have an effect on task completion.[14] However, our goal was to go beyond mere reminders and to test interventions that were based on the Xu and Wyer study.

Prior to the app development process, we conducted laboratory studies to pretest the efficacy of the intervention. We realized that the original studies had demonstrated the effects of making choices on making an unrelated choice, and not on getting things done per se. In that sense, we were not just translating the finding but also extending it and wanted to collect some evidence to support the extension. In one online study, for example, participants were randomly assigned to one of two conditions – a treatment condition in which they first answered three (binary choice) trivia questions or a control condition in which they did not. Participants then read a gift-buying scenario and had to respond on a scale as to whether they were ready to make a decision or to wait and deliberate. We also measured their implemental vs. deliberative mindsets on standard scales.[15] Results showed that participants who answered three trivia questions first were subsequently more likely to

Figure 3.1. General structure of reminders in the smartphone app

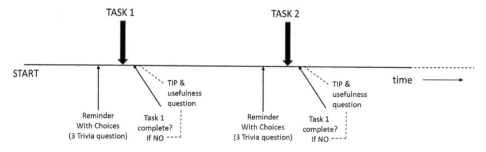

Note: The most general version of the app could be customized to change a) number of choice questions asked or b) whether the questions are related or unrelated (e.g., trivia) to the task.

make a choice, and that it was the change in mindset that drove these results. Reassured by the results of our laboratory studies, we pressed on with app development.

The key functions of the mobile app were to record upcoming tasks, to set and deploy reminders for scheduled tasks, and to track task completion (see Figure 3.1 for a schematic). Users first entered the series of tasks they needed to pursue as part of their goal and indicated a name, start time, and end time for each task. At the time for a reminder, a notification (hereafter "reminder notification") was displayed on the phone (see web appendix for screenshots). At the planned task ending time, another type of notification (hereafter "completion notification") popped up, asking people whether they had completed the task or not.

We developed a control version of the app that simply provided reminders, and a treatment version, which also displayed trivia questions that asked users to make trivia choices. After each reminder notification, the treatment version of the app displayed three trivia questions with binary response options (see Table 3.1 for sample questions) sequentially. These trivia questions were randomly drawn from a bank of 298 questions. When these questions were answered, the feedback for the answers was immediately displayed, and the notification was dismissed. As an added intervention in the treatment version of the app, if the previous task was reported as incomplete, the app delivered a "tip" – a helpful hint at how others have succeeded in persisting with the task. That is, the reminder notification displayed a tip, asked the user whether the tip was helpful or not, and again offered a binary

Table 3.1. Sample trivia questions and tips

Sample Trivia Questions (Library of 298), Correct Response Is Indicated by a*	Binary Choices Presented	
1 In what place was Christmas once illegal?	Russia	England*
2 In California, it is illegal to eat oranges while doing what?	Gardening	Bathing*
3 Coulrophobia means fear of what?	Clowns*	Clouds
4 How many teeth does a human have?	32*	36
5 An anaconda is a South American what?	Snake*	Spider
6 What continent covers about 20 percent of the earth?	Africa*	Asia
7 What relative of the alligator is native to Central and South America?	The caiman*	The crocodile
8 Which US capital city lies at the highest altitude above sea level?	Santa Fe*	Juneau
9 Half the world population lives near what body of water?	Pacific Ocean*	Atlantic Ocean
10 What instrument in an orchestra has the highest pitch?	Piccolo*	Flute
Sample Tips (Library of 97)	**Binary Choices Presented**	
1 Keep calm and drink another glass of water.	Useful	Not Useful
2 Eat breakfast. It will energize you for the day and keep your diet in check.	Useful	Not Useful
3 Use the three-bite rule with dessert. Have three small bites and put your fork down.	Useful	Not Useful

choice ("useful" and "not useful"). When users answered the questions, the reminders were cleared from the notification screen. However, it was not essential for users to respond to the questions – they could manually dismiss the notification if they wanted to. We worked with a professional mobile application development company to conduct workshops, complete user research (UX testing), iterate on concepts, finalize the architecture, and develop the app.

One hundred and twenty-five students (male = 24 percent, mean age = 20.8) from the University of Toronto participated in the eight-week panel study for monetary compensation (maximum compensation of $125, see Figure 3.2 and Table 3.2 for details). The sample size was determined by posting a recruitment advertisement for a predetermined duration of time and recruiting everyone who applied to participate. The recruitment flyer said the research project is about tracking goals

Figure 3.2. CONSORT flow diagram

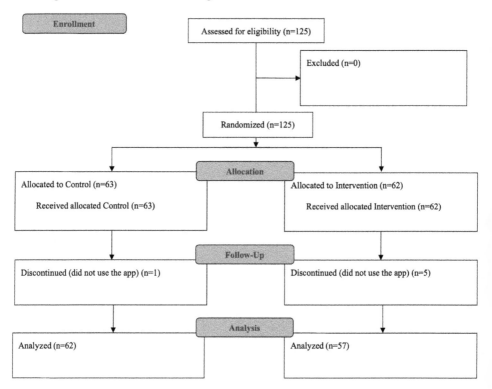

and that students who used an iPhone were eligible to participate. The flyer was posted on bulletin boards in the Rotman School of Management and the university library. Participants randomly received one of the two (control and treatment) versions of the app and were asked to use it for their own task management for an eight-week period. Each participant chose their own goals and specified their own tasks. Given that we had a broad range of goals, the treatment version of the app only used trivia questions.

The app tracked the following usage data: basic task information (title, task start time, task end time, the reminder time), task completion status, the time when the user interacted with the reminder notification and the first and the last time when the user reported task completion. Additionally in the treatment condition, we knew whether the user interacted with the questions in the reminder notification (i.e., whether they made trivia question choices or simply dismissed the

Table 3.2. Panel study timeline

Week	Session	Activity	Compensation
-3		Recruitment flyers posted	
0	Session 1	Introduction and app download (lab)	$25 (immediate)
1			
2	Session 2	Interim survey (online)	$15
3			
4	Session 3	Interim survey (online)	$15
		Office hour for compensation (lab)	
5			
6	Session 4	Interim survey (online)	$15
7			
8	Session 5	Final survey (lab)	$15
		Compensation for ongoing app engagement	$5 / week (max $40)

notification). Using this data, we focused on the task completion status (i.e., whether they completed the task) and if completed, the time delay to complete (i.e., the time between when they were supposed to complete the task and when they actually completed it) to examine the effectiveness of the intervention. For example, if the scheduled task completion time is 3 p.m. on May 20 and the user first reported task completion at 3 p.m. on May 21, the delay is recorded as one day. Likewise, if the reported completion happens at 9 p.m. on May 20, the delay is 0.25 days.

Differences and Similarities with the Original Study

The trivia question intervention in the current study is adapted from Experiment 2 in Xu and Wyer (2008) but with a few changes (see Table 3.3).[16] In the Xu and Wyer study, the participants who first made a series of choices were more likely to purchase a product in an unrelated subsequent product choice task compared to participants who did not make previous choices. The intervention in the current study is similar to the prior work in that the trivia questions nudge participants to make a choice among given options. On the other hand, the current study is different from the previous work in terms of the context. The current study focuses on the consequences of making choices in the context of implementing planned tasks, rather than choosing one of given products.

Table 3.3. Differences and similarities between Xu and Wyer (2008) and the current study

	Xu & Wyer (2008), Experiment 2	Current Study
Study Type	Laboratory	Panel
Experimental Design	Choice (which animal preferred) vs. Choice (Which animal dominates on a given attribute) vs. control	Choice task (trivia question) vs. control
Setting	Product choice	Task completion
Participants	86 University students	125 University students
Measures	Willingness to purchase one of the two products	Completion of reminded tasks, the delay between the actual and planned task completion
Nature of Outcome Variable	Hypothetical and perhaps irrelevant / uninteresting to participants	Real tasks that were presumably meaningful to the participants
Interface	Paper	Smartphone app
Procedures	Participants in the two judgment task conditions completed questions related to animals and evaluated two computers. The control participants did the computer evaluation only.	Participants created tasks and set the time they wanted to complete them and be reminded. Participants in the treatment condition were then prompted to make a choice when the reminder triggered. The control participants did not receive the choice task when the reminder triggered.
Additional Intervention	None	Tips were provided in addition to trivia questions

Results

Over the eight weeks, 119 students created at least one task using the app, resulting in 3492 separate task entries in total. However, our main analysis is based on 3218 entries; 274 entries had to be eliminated because some task entries used a date format that was difficult to interpret (for example, it was unclear whether 02/03/2015 referred to March 2 or February 3) thus it was unclear when the task was created and completed. This was not something we had planned for – we had expected all users to follow a standard dd/mm/yyyy that is common in Canada and elsewhere, but we realized that we had a few users who followed the American mm/dd/yyyy convention. We caution other

Table 3.4. Means and standard deviations of completion rate and delay

	Completion Rate		Delay (Days)	
	Control Mean (SD)	Treatment Mean (SD)	Control Mean (SD)	Treatment Mean (SD)
Week 1	0.663 (0.473)	0.709 (0.455)	1.36 (3.575)	0.75*(2.952)
Week 2	0.585 (0.494)	0.701*(0.460)	2.68 (4.224)	1.14*(2.474)
Week 3	0.715*(0.452)	0.630 (0.484)	2.11 (3.933)	1.49*(3.222)
Week 4	0.596 (0.492)	0.714*(0.453)	2.09 (3.119)	1.96 (3.159)
Week 5	0.631 (0.484)	0.709 (0.455)	1.93 (3.596)	1.84 (3.021)
Week 6	0.637 (0.483)	0.596 (0.493)	1.97 (2.630)	1.64 (2.470)
Week 7	0.641 (0.481)	0.580 (0.495)	1.11 (1.987)	1.69 (3.126)
Week 8	0.681 (0.468)	0.659 (0.476)	1.63 (2.133)	1.46 (2.182)

Note: A * indicated that the completion rate [delay] value was statistically greater [lower] than the other condition in a given week.

applied scientists to critically examine their data collection plans and anticipate all the ways in which users might respond differently from expectations.

We examined the effectiveness of the current intervention by comparing different groups. First, we compared the differences between the treatment app users and the control app users in their task completion and delay measured in days. To confirm whether making choices before a task increases the implementation, we further sliced the data from the treatment group into a) users that interacted with the questions (trivia or tip) in the reminder notification, and b) users that did not interact with the questions, and we then compared the two groups.

We conducted a 2 (app version) × 8 (week) two-way analysis of variance (ANOVA) each for completion and delay measured in days to investigate how the app version and time influenced task performance. The overall task completion rate was around 65 percent, and there was no difference between the control and treatment groups nor significant change over time ($ps > .2$). However, there was an interaction effect between the two factors, $F(1, 3202) = 2.78, p = .007, \eta_p^2 = .006$). The average completion rate and delay for each of the eight weeks is shown in Table 3.4.

Contrast tests showed that the completion rate for treatment users was significantly higher than control users in the second ($F(1, 3202) = 4.73, p = .03, \eta_p^2 = .001$) and the fourth week ($F(1, 3202) = 6.68, p = .01, \eta_p^2 = .002$). Although not significant at the 95 percent confidence level, treatment users had a higher completion rate in the fifth week as well ($F(1, 3202) = 2.72$, $p = .09$, $\eta_p^2 = .001$). Interestingly, control users had a higher completion rate in the third week ($F(1, 3202) = 3.58$, $p = .05$, $\eta_p^2 = .001$). The two groups did not differ in other periods ($ps > .22$). To examine whether the effect of using treatment on event completion differs by interaction with the reminder, we additionally conducted a 2 (interaction: yes vs. no) × 8 (week) ANOVA with event completion. However, we did not find any significant effect in the analysis ($ps > .5$). In sum, the effects of the treatment were inconsistent and varied over time.

Next, we conducted the same set of analyses with delay as the dependent variable. First, the 2 (app version) × 8 (week) ANOVA revealed a main effect of the app type. The delay in the treatment group ($M = 1.48$, $SD = 2.91$) was significantly lower than for the control group ($M = 1.81$, $SD = 3.37$, $F(1, 3119) = 9.45$, $p = .002$, $\eta_p^2 = .003$). Also, consistent with the middle slump, the delay was slightly longer in the middle than the beginning and end of the period ($F(1, 3119) = 5.08$, $p < .001$, $\eta_p^2 = .01$). There was an interaction between the app type and time ($F(1, 3119) = 3.10$, $p = .003$, $\eta_p^2 = .007$). Contrasts showed that the delay among the treatment group was shorter than that among the control group in the first to third weeks, but not in subsequent weeks. As an example, the treatment group scored a shorter delay compared to the control group in the first week ($t(3119) = 5.60$, $p = .01$ $\eta_p^2 = .002$). In the fourth week, the difference became indistinguishable ($p > .6$).

Why did the effect weaken over time? One possibility is that the treatment users kept interacting with choice questions but adapted to the intervention, thereby weakening its effectiveness. Second, the weakened effect could be due to a decrease in the level of interaction with the choice questions. In Figure 3.3, we plot the data for treatment app users who interacted with the choice questions separately from those who did not interact. If adaptation is responsible for the weakening over time, there should be a similar pattern between the interacted treatment group and no-interaction treatment group toward the later weeks. A visual glance at the figure suggests that this is not the case. A 2 (interaction with app: yes vs. no) × 8 (week) on the delay (day) variable in the treatment group ($n = 1351$) showed only a main effect of interaction with the app only ($M_{interacted} = .43$, $SD_{interacted} = 1.17$, vs. $M_{not\_interacted} = 1.59$, $SD_{not\_interacted} = 3.24$, $F(1, 1335) = 15.39$, $p < .001$, $\eta_p^2 = .01$, ps for other effects $> .6$). There is also a significant drop in the level of interactions with the choice questions in the middle phase ($M_{week1} = 16\%$, $SD_{week1} = .37$, $M_{week4} = 10\%$, $SD_{week4} = .31$, $t(1387) = 1.96$, $p = .05$). Therefore, this suggests that the weakening of the effect is due to people simply interacting less with the trivia questions and notifications over time.

Figure 3.3. Delay (days) as a function of treatment and week

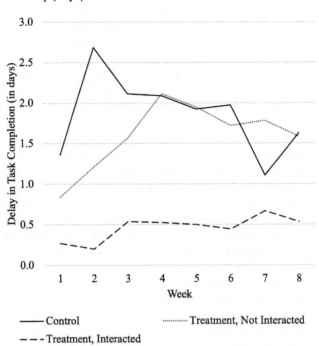

Reconciliation

We had expected that users who received the treatment version of the app would have a higher rate of task completion and shorter delays than users who received the control version of the app. Unfortunately, our results found no consistent support for either prediction. While there was an effect of the treatment version on reducing delays early in the eight-week period, the effect dissipated after three weeks. At this time, people reduced their level of engagement with the trivia questions, resulting in the weakening. While we don't know why this reduced engagement occurred, we suspect that the novelty and fun associated with the trivia questions wore off over time. The effect of the treatment on task completion was noisy – there was no overall effect, the treatment outperformed the control in three weeks, but there was no trend.

In Week 2 (and only in Week 2), we could claim to recreate the results of the study that inspired us – people in the treatment condition that answered a series of three trivia questions both completed more tasks and did so with significantly lower delays. In Week 4, as we got to "the middle," the treatment had an effect on the completion rate but not on delays. And there was no effect anywhere else in the middle. The reassurance that we had experienced after completing our laboratory studies had faded after our panel study.

In thinking through why we ended up with noisy and messy results, we generated a number of "what if" scenarios. We found that the level of engagement with the trivia questions dropped after three weeks (presumably when the novelty wore off), precisely when we expected the middle slump to hit. What if we had simply delivered regular reminders for the first three weeks and then started with the trivia questions later? Alternatively, what if we had gamified the trivia questions by introducing scores, badges, or competitions to keep the level of engagement high? While these sounded like easy things to do in a laboratory setting, our app developers highlighted the development complexities they would raise. What if we did not allow users to dismiss notifications without answering the trivia questions? Our app developer cautioned us against doing this because the resulting annoyance might reduce app usage overall. What if we had four or five trivia questions?

A number of our "what if" questions were empirical questions, and if experimentation were relatively costless, they could have been tested in trials with large samples. However, even if we did find a combination of app features where we consistently found the treatment app to outperform the control app, we would still be left with the conclusion that the effect is fragile and that small changes in the situation could significantly change outcomes.[17]

Discussion and Prescriptive Advice

We started this project with a practical problem of how to help people stay the course and maintain progress toward their goals. In diagnosing why people don't get things done, we quickly narrowed down to three sets of explanations – (a) that the final outcome loses value as people start working toward their goal, (b) that there is a loss of motivation, and (c) that people need to be put in an implemental mindset in order to improve volition and their ability to get things done. In thinking through possible solutions, we realized that the first explanation meant that the goal was truly not worth achieving, and the second had solutions that were relatively more complex. For the third explanation relating to mindsets, we were struck by the elegance and simplicity of prior laboratory research on the competitive mindset, which showed that the act of making unrelated choices could push people toward being more implemental. That is how we came to use the trivia question interventions in the design of our app. As an aside, the most general version of the enterprise version of the app (designed for the iOS operating system) is open source and available to researchers, practitioners, and organizations interested in customizing it for their needs.

There is a growing chorus of voices in the applied behavioral science community that has raised the point that many of our findings, especially those demonstrated in the lab, are not readily portable or scalable, and are dependent on the population and the specific situation in which the intervention is delivered.[18] For instance, a previous result might not hold true if participants belong to a different age or socioeconomic group, speak a different language, or live in a different country. Likewise, results might not replicate if there are changes in the situation – for instance, an intervention delivered with paper and pencil might work differently from one delivered electronically, an intervention done in the morning might work differently than one delivered in the evening, or an intervention might work differently as a function of whether the target audience received it individually or in a social setting surrounded by other people. These warnings about the lack of portability increase the need for applied behavioral scientists to test ideas before they are scaled up. In our case, the panel study reported here was an example of such a test. Unfortunately, our panel results (unlike our own lab experiments) did not give us enough confidence to proceed with a fully scaled version of the app given the cost and effort involved. Of course, had the cost of experimenting been lower (in this case, the cost of (a) generating multiple versions of the app, (b) recruiting large sample sizes in a multi-arm trial over longer periods of time, and (c) collecting and analyzing large volumes of data), we could have tested further.

We note that our app did very well on standard "UX testing"[19] – the app was deemed highly usable, easy to navigate, engaging, and was well liked in testing. Unfortunately, it just did not succeed in doing what we had hoped it would do. UX testing is important, but we caution others from solely relying on it for two reasons. First, while it may help assess the usability in a static sense (i.e., at one point in time), UX testing might not be able to capture adaptation or the reduction in novelty and engagement over time. Second, usability does not imply efficacy and effectiveness. We had a well-liked app that simply did not reliably help people get things done.

In this process, we were reminded that translating laboratory studies to the field is inherently difficult. For one, interventions are easier to deliver in the lab as compared to the field. The lab allows the researcher to customize interventions, to make sure that the participant pays attention to the intervention, and to change the nature of the intervention over time. An intervention delivered in the field needs to compete with a large number of other things for attention. Thus, it is incumbent on the designer of field interventions to build in mechanisms to ensure that the intervention receives the attention that is needed to make it effective. Unfortunately, this adds to the complexity of the real-world setting, in this case, the complexity of designing an app.

In reflecting on the portability of findings from the lab to the field, we recognize that there are certain interventions that might be more portable than others. For instance, interventions that are perceptual in nature (visual depictions, framing interventions) might be more portable than interventions that are procedural in nature and need more attention (interventions that activate certain mindsets or prime certain cognitive operations). In hindsight, we were perhaps expecting too much from an app that recreated a laboratory intervention in the field, given the nature of this particular intervention. Further research could start cataloging and documenting interventions to suggest which types of interventions are more likely to successfully translate and scale.

Because we were interested in developing a solution that was easily scalable, we were attracted to the possibility of developing a smartphone app, given how easy it is to download, install, and use these apps. Our conceptual development in this project was then dictated by what was possible and what was not in the context of an app. We ended up choosing the interventions we did because it was relatively easy to duplicate in the context of an app. However, in hindsight, we should have probably spent more time thinking through what might have been the best solution to the problem of the middle slump and then determine whether an app was the best vehicle to deliver that solution.

Note that we do not mean to suggest that there will always be problems of attention when scaling interventions to an app. A recent paper reported a field trial to test the effects of performance monitoring, performance feedback, target setting, and prosocial incentives on commercial airline pilots' productivity on the targeted fuel-saving dimensions.[20] Some of these ideas were used to develop an app that reportedly has saved airlines significant amounts of fuel.[21] In this particular situation, pilots were motivated to save fuel because it was presumably central to their performance evaluations. This was also a population that routinely used data and technology to make decisions, so the app likely did not suffer from an attention problem as ours did.

Finally, it is trite to say that the real world is much more complex than the lab. The beauty of the lab is that the researcher can rule out anything else that might have an effect on the outcome. Looking at the erratic nature of results over the eight weeks, we could not help but wonder if there was something else going on in the lives of our target populations in some of the weeks in this time window that we were unable to observe. Perhaps our students were taking an exam or were on vacation and had more time to devote to goal achievement in some weeks. As Goswami and Urminski recently point out, outcomes seen in the field are often an aggregate of multiple effects arising from the intervention.[22] In the lab, we are able to isolate all but one of these, but in the field, we need to be more sensitive to the fact that other effects could change the outcome. This essentially means that we need to focus on interventions that are not only quick, simple, and scalable but have been shown to have large effect sizes. Interventions with small and subtle effects might likely get washed out by other psychological processes that happen in the wilderness of the real world.

NOTES

1 See Bonezzi, A., Brendl, M.C., & De Angelis, M. (2011). Stuck in the middle: The psychophysics of goal pursuit. *Psychological Science, 22*(5), 607–12. https://doi.org/10.1177/0956797611404899; Cheema, A., & Bagchi, R. (2011). The effect of goal visualization on goal pursuit: Implications for consumers and managers. *Journal of Marketing, 75*(2), 109–23. https://doi.org/10.1509/jm.75.2.109; and Heath, C., Larrick, R.P., & Wu, G. (1999). Goals as reference points. *Cognitive Psychology, 38*(1), 79–109. https://doi.org/10.1006/cogp.1998.0708.

2 Wells, M. (2022). Getting unstuck. *Apex Magazine.* https://apex-magazine.com/nonfiction/getting-unstuck/.

3 Bonezzi, A., Brendl, M.C., & De Angelis, M. (2011). Stuck in the middle: The psychophysics of goal pursuit. *Psychological Science, 22*(5), 607–12. https://doi.org/10.1177/0956797611404899.

4 See Gollwitzer, P.M., & Bayer, U. (1999). Deliberative versus implemental mindsets in the control of action. In S. Chaiken & T. Yaacov (Eds.), *Dual-process theories in social psychology* (pp. 403–22). Guilford Press; Gollwitzer, P.M. (2012). Mindset theory of action phases. In P.A.M. van Lange (Ed.), *Handbook of theories of social psychology* (pp. 526–45), SAGE Publications; and Xu, A.J., & Wyer, R.S. (2007). The effect of mind-sets on consumer decision strategies. *Journal of Consumer Research, 34*(4), 556–66. https://doi.org/10.1086/519293.

5 See Gollwitzer (2012); and American Psychological Association. (2022). *Mindset.* APA Dictionary of Psychology. https://dictionary.apa.org/mind-set.

6 Heckhausen, H., & Gollwitzer, P.M. (1987). Thought contents and cognitive functioning in motivational versus volitional states of mind. *Motivation and Emotion, 11*(2), 101–20. https://doi.org/10.1007/BF00992338.

7 See Gollwitzer (2012); and Xu, A.J., & Wyer, R.S. (2008). The comparative mind-set from animal comparisons to increased purchase intentions. *Psychological Science, 19*(9), 859–64. https://doi.org/10.1111/j.1467-9280.2008.02169.x.

8 See Lippke, S., Ziegelmann, J.P., & Schwarzer, R. (2004). Behavioral intentions and action plans promote physical exercise: A longitudinal study with orthopedic rehabilitation patients. *Journal of Sport and Exercise Psychology, 26*(3), 470–83. https://doi.org/10.1123/jsep.26.3.470; Sniehotta, F.F., Scholz, U., & Schwarzer, R. (2006). Action plans and coping plans for physical exercise: A longitudinal intervention study in cardiac rehabilitation. *British Journal of Health Psychology, 11*(1), 23–37. https://doi.org/10.1348/135910705X43804; and Milne, S., Orbell, S., & Sheeran, P. (2002). Combining motivational and volitional interventions to promote exercise participation: Protection motivation theory and implementation intentions. *British Journal of Health Psychology, 7*(2), 163–84. https://doi.org/10.1348/135910702169420.

9 See Milne et al. (2002); Milkman, K.L., Beshears, J., Choi, J.J., Laibson, D., & Madrian, B.C. (2011). Using implementation intentions prompts to enhance influenza vaccination rates. *Proceedings of the National Academy of Sciences, 108*(26), 10415–20. https://doi.org/10.1073/pnas.1103170108; Ameriks, J., Caplin, A., & Leahy, J. (2003). Wealth accumulation and the propensity to plan. *The Quarterly Journal of Economics, 118*(3), 1007–47. https://doi.org/10.1162/00335530360698487; Milkman, K.L., Beshears, J., Choi, J.J., Laibson, D., & Madrian, B.C. (2013). Planning prompts as a means of increasing preventive screening rates. *Preventive Medicine, 56*(1), 92–3. https://doi.org/10.1016/j.ypmed.2012.10.021; and Armitage, C.J. (2007). Effects of an implementation intention-based intervention on fruit consumption. *Psychology and Health, 22*(8), 917–28. https://doi.org/10.1080/14768320601070662.

10 OECD. (2017). *Behavioural insights and public policy: Lessons from around the world*. OECD Publishing. https://doi.org/10.1787/9789264270480-en.

11 Xu, A.J., & Wyer, R.S. (2008). The comparative mind-set from animal comparisons to increased purchase intentions. *Psychological Science, 19*(9), 859–64. https://doi.org/10.1111/j.1467-9280.2008.02169.x.

12 See Xu & Wyer (2008); and Dhar, R., Huber, J., & Khan, U. (2007). The shopping momentum effect. *Journal of Marketing Research, 44*(3), 370–8. https://doi.org/10.1509/jmkr.44.3.370.

13 Xu & Wyer (2008).

14 Karlan, D., McConnell, M., Mullainathan, S., & Zinman, J. (2016). Getting to the top of mind: How reminders increase saving. *Management Science, 62*(12), 3393–411. https://doi.org/10.1287/mnsc.2015.2296.

15 Dhar, R., Huber, J., & Khan, U. (2007). The shopping momentum effect. *Journal of Marketing Research, 44*(3), 370–8. https://doi.org/10.1509/jmkr .44.3.370.

16 Xu & Wyer (2008).

17 Schmidt, R., & Stenger, K. (2021). Behavioral brittleness: The case for strategic behavioral public policy. *Behavioural Public Policy*, 1–26. https:// doi.org/10.1017/bpp.2021.16.

18 See Mažar, N., & Soman, D. (Eds.). (2022). *Behavioral science in the wild*. Rotman-UTP Publishing; and List, J.A. (2022). *The Voltage effect: How to make good ideas great and great ideas scale*. Currency.

19 See Barnum, C.M. (2020). *Usability testing essentials: Ready, set…. Test*. Morgan Kaufmann.

20 Gosnell, G.K., List, J.A., & Metcalfe, R.D. (2020). The Impact of management practices on employee productivity: A field experiment with airline captains. *Journal of Political Economy, 128*(4), 1195–233. https:// doi.org/10.1086/705375.

21 Polek, G. (2022). *UK software startup helping pilots fly more efficiently*. Aviation International News. https://www.ainonline.com/aviation-news/air-transport /2022-08-18/uk-software-startup-helping-pilots-fly-more-efficiently.

22 Goswami, I., & Urminsky, O. (2022). Why many behavioral interventions have unpredictable effects in the wild: The conflicting consequences problem. In Mažar, N., & Soman, D. (Eds.), *Behavioral science in the wild* (pp. 65–81). Rotman-UTP Publishing.

CHAPTER FOUR

A Conceptual Replication of the Effects of Gamification on UK Adults' Ability to Reach a Saving Goal

Nethal Hashim, Irene Scopelliti, and Janina Steinmetz

AT A GLANCE

- **Our Goal:** To understand whether gamification can motivate behaviors that are typically not enjoyable to pursue, such as saving money.
- **The Intervention:** A gamified web app to track savings which would motivate participants' pursuit of a saving goal over a four-week period using progress bars, badges, and a leaderboard.
- **The Results:** We expected participants in the gamified condition to save more toward their goal and find the process of reaching their saving goal more enjoyable than participants in the control condition, but we only found tentative support for the first prediction and no support for the second prediction.
- **Lesson Learned:** Gamification-based interventions that were effective in lab studies may be less immersive and engaging in field settings due to distractions and the inherent "noisiness" of the field.

Motivation and Objective

Gamification refers to the use of game elements in otherwise "serious" settings with the intent to motivate a target behavior (e.g., using a fitness app or studying a language).[1] For example, the app Zombies, Run! motivates users to be physically active by immersing them in a virtual world in which they go on running missions to help their town survive a zombie apocalypse; the app Duolingo motivates users to study a new language by displaying their progress on a leaderboard and awarding badges for doing well in lessons. The virtual environments, leaderboards, and badges used by these apps are typical game elements.

A gamified behavior becomes more enjoyable[2] than its non-gamified counterpart because gamification introduces some immediate psychological rewards:[3] for example, those experienced when climbing a leaderboard or winning a badge.[4] Several lab studies show that gamification can be effective at, for example, motivating people to engage with brands[5] or to complete a task,[6] but lab studies also show that gamification is not always effective at increasing motivating to pursue a behavior.[7] Similarly, research on the effectiveness of gamification-based interventions in field settings shows mixed results. For example, people were motivated to reduce household energy consumption,[8] increase their daily step count,[9] and eat more fruits and vegetables[10] through gamification, but students also performed worse on a gamified university course than a non-gamified one,[11] and some people reported that gamification did not motivate them to exercise more.[12] Against this backdrop, we conducted an experiment that conceptually replicates two previous field studies that use gamified interventions to motivate target behaviors that share similar characteristics.

Inspiration

The two field studies that inspired our experiment examined the effects of gamification on reducing household energy consumption[13] and improving students' performance in a university course.[14] The target behaviors examined by these studies have something in common: they involve short-term costs and sacrifices (changing habits to reduce energy consumption and foregoing other activities to study) in favor of benefits that will be experienced in the long term (saving money on bills and better academic performance). Since gamification is intended to make the pursuit of a behavior more enjoyable,[15] we expected gamification to be effective at motivating behaviors that are not immediately rewarding by making the pursuit of these behaviors more enjoyable in the short term.

In the first study, Mulcahy and colleagues assigned 326 participants to use a gamified application to reduce household energy consumption over a four-month period or to use no application (control group).[16] The gamified application allowed participants to choose an avatar to earn points playing minigames related to reducing household energy consumption. The study predicted greater enjoyment in reducing household energy consumption in the gamified condition, which would lead to lower energy bills. The results showed that households in the gamified condition did indeed lower their energy consumption more than households in the control condition. In the gamified condition, savings amounted to approximately $55 over the four months study period, compared to only $5 in the control condition. However, the reduction in energy consumption was not driven by energy saving becoming more enjoyable.[17]

Hanus and Fox assigned seventy-one students to a gamified course in which they could win badges and compete on a leaderboard for engaging with class materials.[18] The students' course performance was compared to a control group of students in a non-gamified version of the same course. Students in the gamified course condition had lower exam scores at the end of the course than students in the non-gamified course condition. Additionally, students in the gamified course condition had significantly lower enjoyment of the course than students in the non-gamified course condition.[19]

The two studies described show that there is no conclusive evidence for the effectiveness of avatars, minigames, badges, and leaderboards to motivate the pursuit of a target behavior in field settings. Although using avatars to earn points playing minigames motivated a reduction in household energy consumption, students who could win badges in class and competed on a leaderboard with fellow students performed worse in the exam compared to students in the non-gamified course. Additionally, in contrast to the commonly held belief that gamification makes pursuing a behavior more enjoyable, none of the game elements used in the two studies made the target behaviors more enjoyable compared to the non-gamified alternatives. One of the big challenges in examining the effects of gamification is that the concept of gamification itself is a collection of potentially different behavioral phenomena (e.g., competing on a leaderboard, winning badges, or being immersed in a virtual environment). Because the specific implementation of gamification varies across studies it may be more appropriate to draw conclusions on the effectiveness of individual game elements featured by each study, rather than drawing conclusions for the concept of gamification as a whole.

Given the mixed results of the previous studies, we decided to specifically test the effectiveness of three game elements that are commonly used in implementing gamification (a leaderboard, a progress bar, and badges) in a conceptually similar behavioral domain, that is, reaching a saving goal (i.e., saving as a behavior that lacks immediate rewards but offers long-term benefits). We predicted that gamification would motivate people to reach a saving goal. The long-term benefits of saving are substantial, protecting people from financial shocks and poverty. However, saving for the future is typically not an enjoyable task since one forgoes purchases in the present.[20] It is also a behavior for which interventions are needed. For example, four in ten Americans are unable to come up with $400 in case of a financial emergency.[21]

Interventions and Method

To investigate the effectiveness of gamification as an intervention to help people reach a saving goal, we ran a four-week study for which we recruited 331 UK-based online participants. At the beginning of November, we invited participants to set themselves a saving goal for the coming four weeks (e.g., save £50) in preparation for the holidays, and to use a custom designed web app (justsavemore.net) to track their progress toward that goal. The web app displayed the goal participants had set and how much they had already saved. Participants were able to use an "add-savings" button and a "decrease-savings" button to adjust and monitor the amount of money they had saved. The web app also showed participants an indicator of how many days were left to achieve their goal. Additionally, the web app included a guide with saving tips and instructions on how to set up a virtual piggy bank.

Participants were randomly assigned to either a gamified version of the web app (n = 169) or a control condition (n = 162) in which the web app was not gamified. The gamified version included a leaderboard on which participants competed with other participants based on their progress toward their saving goal (participants competed against nine other randomly selected participants in the same condition), a progress bar, and badges that could be achieved for reaching saving milestones (e.g., reaching 50 percent of their goal). In the control condition, the web app did not feature any game elements. To maintain comparable levels of visual appeal with the gamified condition, we replaced the leaderboard and progress bar with equally sized, colored objects and the badges with saving-related icons. Figure 4.1 includes screenshots of both versions of the web app (gamified and control).

The study was conducted between November 9 and December 6, 2020. We timed the study to end at the beginning of the winter holiday season because people are likely to want to save during this period to prepare for the holidays. The design of the study, the main predictions, and the analysis plan were preregistered.[22]

When recruiting participants for the study, we initially administered to 509 UK-based participants a screening survey consisting of

Figure 4.1. Non-gamified (control) version of the web app (left) and gamified version of the web app (right)

demographic questions (age, gender, education) and questions about their behavior in relation to saving and habit tracking. These included how satisfied they were with their ability to save money, how likely they were to set saving goals, whether they used any apps to track their behavior, their net personal monthly income, and what percentage of that income they typically spent each month.

After completing the first part of the screening survey and receiving compensation, all participants were offered the opportunity to take part in a four-week study on saving behavior for additional compensation. Out of 509 participants, 457 participants chose to find out more about the field study. These participants were given detailed information about the study and compensation. Out of these 457 participants, 332 decided to enroll in the study and set a saving goal for the subsequent four-week period. One of these 332 participants failed to set a saving goal (i.e., set a saving goal of £0) and was not assigned to a condition. Therefore, we had 331 participants in our final sample. In terms of sample size, our preregistered goal was to recruit 250 participants, but our final sample size was larger. This is because we underestimated how many participants who took the screening survey would decide to participate in the four-week study (i.e., we forecasted that 50 percent of the participants who took the initial survey would enroll, whereas 65 percent did).

The 331 participants who enrolled in the study completed the second part of the screening survey, which measured individual differences in the pain of paying (tightwad vs. spendthrift scale),[23] debt aversion,[24] propensity to plan for money in the short- and in the long-run,[25]

Figure 4.2. CONSORT flow diagram

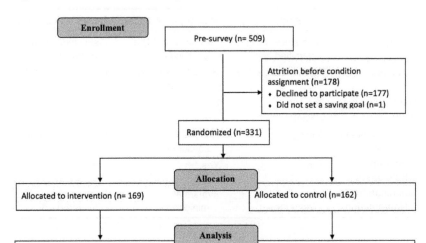

self-control,[26] financial literacy,[27] and future orientation.[28] We also measured participants' playfulness[29] in the final week of the study. Figure 4.2 is a flow diagram of the study.

The main dependent variable was the percentage of the saving goal participants achieved each week. This percentage was calculated by dividing the total amount saved in that week by the goal set by the participant at the beginning of the study. The amount saved was directly retrieved from the logs of the web app. We also observed the frequency with which participants accessed the web application and the overall percentage of the saving goal achieved at the end of the study. Each week, we reminded participants to log their savings on the web app and to complete a weekly survey, which measured their satisfaction with the amount of money they saved, and how enjoyable and useful they found using the web app. In the final weekly survey, administered at the end of the fourth week, we also measured participants' likelihood to recommend the web app and likelihood to continue using the web app after the end of the study.

All participants received £0.20 for completing the first part of the initial recruitment survey. If they decided to enroll in the four-week study, they received an additional £1.30 for completing the second part of the

Table 4.1. Summary of main similarities and differences between studies

	Our Study	Mulcahy et al. (2020)	Hanus & Fox (2015)
Setting	Field study using a gamified app	Field study using a gamified app	Field study during a university course
Participants	Prolific users in the UK	Households recruited via Facebook	University students
Sample Size	331	326	71
Duration	4 weeks	4 months	16 weeks
Main Dependent Variable	Saving	Household energy consumption	Course performance
Measured Enjoyment	Yes	Yes	Yes
Gamification Manipulation	Badges and leaderboard	Avatars and minigames	Badges and leaderboard

screening survey. Each week, participants further received £1.00 for logging their savings on the web app and completing the weekly survey. Participants were incentivized to complete all the weekly surveys with a bonus of £2.00 to be received in week four and entry in a lottery to win one of two £50 Amazon vouchers. Over the entirety of the study, participants could therefore earn £7.50 in compensation in addition to the lottery entry.

Differences (and Similarities)

We summarize the main differences and similarities between our study and the two other field studies discussed in this chapter in Table 4.1. All three studies test interventions in the field, but with samples drawn from different populations, i.e., prolific users, students, and regular households. Hence, the three studies test the effectiveness of gamification to motivate the pursuit of target behavior across a wide range of people. Sample sizes and duration of the studies differ as well, with studies recruiting between 71 to 331 participants and study duration ranging from four weeks to four months. Each of the three studies focuses on a different yet conceptually similar behavior that tends to be costly or not rewarding in the short term. We suggest that people are likely to benefit from gamification to pursue these behaviors because gamification will make the pursuit of these behaviors more enjoyable. All three studies measured enjoyment as an additional variable.

Results

In our study, participants achieved larger shares of their saving goals in the gamified condition than the control condition. Participants in the gamified condition saved on average 27.28 percent ($SE = 1.52$) of their goal each week, whereas participants in the control condition saved on average 22.90 percent ($SE = 1.52$) of their goal each week $F(1, 328) = 4.14$, $p = .043$). However, this difference emerged only once we excluded an extreme observation in the control group (whose percentage of saving goal achievement was 11.88 SDs above the condition mean). Including the extreme observation, there was no difference in saving goal achievement between the two conditions. Participants in the gamified condition saved on average 27.28 percent ($SE = 2.76$) of their goal each week, whereas participants in the control condition saved on average 26.19 percent ($SE = 2.76$) of their goal each week $F(1, 329) = 0.07, p = .788$). The exclusion was not preregistered.

Additionally, we observed no differences between conditions on additional measures that were included in the study (participants' satisfaction with their savings, the web app's perceived enjoyability, its perceived usefulness, likelihood to recommend, and likelihood to continue using it). This was regardless of whether we excluded the extreme observation or not. Since the gamification literature suggests that gamification makes the pursuit of a behavior more enjoyable,[30] it was somewhat surprising that we did not find a difference in perceived enjoyment between the conditions. Participants in the gamified condition perceived the app as equally enjoyable (M = 4.71, $SE = 0.12$) as participants in the control condition (M = 4.61, $SE = 0.12$; $F(1, 281) = 0.36$, $p = .552$, enjoyment measured on a 7-point scale). Not all participants answered each weekly survey in which perceived enjoyment was measured, which is why the degrees of freedom are lower in this analysis compared to the main analysis on the percentage of saving goal achieved.

The individual difference measures we collected for exploratory purposes highlighted some interesting patterns. Participants with a lower (vs. higher) debt aversion and higher (vs. lower) financial literacy were more likely to reach their saving goal. Additionally, participants who were more (vs. less) likely to plan for money in the long run were more likely to reach their saving goal. Finally, more (vs. less) playful participants were more likely to achieve their saving goal in the gamified condition than the control condition, hence it could be that more playful participants found the gamification condition especially motivating. Although this evidence is preliminary, this result could highlight a possible boundary condition for the effects of leaderboards, progress bars, and badges, in that they may be an effective intervention only for people who are inherently more playful.

Some individual differences showed no relationship with saving goal achievement, for example, short-term money planning. Furthermore, tightwads and spendthrifts were equally likely to achieve their saving goals. Likewise, although saving is typically considered a future oriented behavior that requires self-control, participants' future orientation and self-control had no impact on saving goal achievement.

We also asked participants in both conditions whether they logged their savings accurately each week. We wanted to ensure that participants in the gamified condition were not lying when logging their savings because they, for example, wanted to reach the top of the leaderboard. We found no significant differences in self-reported accuracy across the two conditions.

Reconciliation

Broadly speaking, our results are in line with the effects of the two fields studies that we built on. Hanus and Fox showed that gamification interventions in field studies may be ineffective at motivating a target behavior.[31] Similarly, our results only provided tentative support for the effectiveness of gamification on the achievement of saving goals because the significance of the focal effect is contingent on the exclusion – albeit arguably justifiable – of a very extreme observation. Furthermore, as with the previous two studies, we did not observe that gamification makes pursuing a behavior more enjoyable. Participants did not perceive tracking their savings to be more enjoyable in the gamified condition compared to the control condition in our study.

We find limited support for the effect of a leaderboard, a progress bar, and badges on motivating participants to achieve their saving goal in the gamified condition compared to the control condition and no support for the effect of these game elements on increasing participants' perceived enjoyment of the web app. We can only speculate about possible reasons why the intervention might not have been as effective at motivating people to achieve their saving goals as we expected. The first reason has to do with the setup of the experiment. We likely made the study a more conservative test of the effectiveness of gamification at motivating participants to achieve a saving goal by asking participants to set themselves realistic saving goals, which might have led participants to set goals that were too easy to achieve. This could have resulted in a high likelihood of achieving those goals irrespective of the experimental condition (even in the control condition participants saved more than 90 percent of their goal on average) and a lower likelihood of measuring the true effect of gamification on motivating the behavior.

Second, the intervention might not have been as effective as expected at motivating participants to reach their saving goals because of how gamification was operationalized. Perhaps the game elements employed in the study might not have been immersive or engaging enough. This could explain why we did not find significant differences in enjoyment between the conditions and why participants were equally likely to plan to continue using the web app and to recommend it regardless of the experimental condition.

Discussion and Prescriptive Advice

Our results provide three key takeaways for researchers and practitioners who wish to use gamification in field settings. Given that gamification is a collection of different game elements, the application of the findings in this chapter may be limited to certain forms of gamification. However, the game elements discussed in this chapter – leaderboards, badges, and progress bars – are among the most widely used, so the findings can inform a large number of gamified designs and applications.

First, we highlight that the effectiveness of gamification to motivate behaviors in lab studies does not necessarily translate to field settings. Although gamification has been shown to motivate people to perform tasks more effectively in lab studies, our experience highlights the potential difficulties that may occur when applying the same type of intervention in field studies, where its salience may not be as prominent as in a controlled lab environment. In noisier field settings, the same game elements might not make enough of a difference to be experienced as a motivating factor. Therefore, interventions may need to be more immersive and engaging, possibly by utilizing a wider range of game elements. These game elements could, for example, include virtual environments and narratives.

Second, we hypothesize that, in principle, gamification should be more effective at motivating people who lack the experience of immediate rewards when pursuing a behavior versus those who may already perceive a behavior as immediately rewarding. We hypothesize that gamification will be effective at motivating behaviors that people do not find immediately rewarding but have long-term benefits. Saving money and reducing household energy consumption are behaviors that we think typically fall within this purview and gamification should (if designed as immersive and engaging enough) be effective at motivating the pursuit of such behaviors. However, some behaviors, such as studying, might also be intrinsically motivating for some people (i.e., some people have an inherent motivation to pursue these behaviors because they like to study).[32] These people might already experience the behavior as immediately rewarding, which might render additional rewards through gamification superfluous.

Finally, we suggest that gamification may be more effective for people that are inherently more playful, rather than in general. People who are more playful tend to be those with more experience in playing games and those that hold more positive attitudes toward play.[33] Domains that attract more playful consumers (e.g., online shopping[34]) may be more likely to benefit from the implementation of gamification. Conversely, product categories that inhibit fun may be the least likely to benefit from gamification. For example, using gamification to motivate physical activity for patients that have degenerative diseases can have a negative impact on their well-being because it reminds them of their condition.[35]

In conclusion, we suggest that gamification could be more effective at motivating the pursuit of a target behavior in field settings when designed to be highly immersive and engaging thanks to the simultaneous use of multiple game elements. These effects may be more pronounced for people that do not find pursuing the target behavior inherently rewarding and for people who tend to be naturally more playful. We hope these suggestions can spark new interest in testing gamification-based interventions in the field.

NOTES

1 Huotari, K., & Hamari, J. (2017). A definition for gamification: Anchoring gamification in the service marketing literature. *Electronic Markets, 27*(1), 21–31. https://doi.org/10.1007/s12525-015-0212-z.

2 See Koivisto, J., & Hamari, J. (2019). The rise of motivational information systems: A review of gamification research. *International Journal of Information Management, 45*, 191–210. https://doi.org/10.1016/j.ijinfomgt.2018.10.013; and Müller-Stewens, J., Schlager, T., Häubl, G., & Herrmann, A. (2017). Gamified information presentation and consumer adoption of product innovations. *Journal of Marketing, 81*(2), 8–24. https://doi.org/10.1509/jm.15.0396.

3 Woolley, K., & Fishbach, A. (2017). Immediate rewards predict adherence to long-term goals. *Personality and Social Psychology Bulletin, 43*(2), 151–62. https://doi.org/10.1177/0146167216676480.

4 See Friedrich, J., Becker, M., Kramer, F., Wirth, M., & Schneider, M. (2020). Incentive design and gamification for knowledge management. *Journal of Business Research, 106,* 341–52. https://doi.org/10.1016 /j.jbusres.2019.02.009; and Huotari & Hamari (2017).

5 Berger, A., Schlager, T., Sprott, D.E., & Herrmann, A. (2018). Gamified interactions: Whether, when, and how games facilitate self–brand connections. *Journal of the Academy of Marketing Science, 46*(4), 652–73. https://doi.org/10.1007/s11747-017-0530-0.

6 See Landers, R.N., & Armstrong, M.B. (2017). Enhancing instructional outcomes with gamification: An empirical test of the Technology-Enhanced Training Effectiveness Model. *Computers in Human Behavior, 71,* 499–507. https://doi.org/10.1016/j.chb.2015.07.031; and Mekler, E.D., Brühlmann, F., Tuch, A.N., & Opwis, K. (2015). Towards understanding the effects of individual gamification elements on intrinsic motivation and performance. *Computers in Human Behavior, 71,* 525–34. https://doi.org/10.1016 /j.chb.2015.08.048.

7 Sailer, M., Hense, J.U., Mayr, S.K., & Mandl, H. (2017). How gamification motivates: An experimental study of the effects of specific game design elements on psychological need satisfaction. *Computers in Human Behavior, 69,* 371–80. https://doi.org/10.1016/j.chb.2016.12.033.

8 Mulcahy, R., Russell-Bennett, R., & Iacobucci, D. (2020). Designing gamified apps for sustainable consumption: A field study. *Journal of Business Research, 106,* 377–87. https://doi.org/10.1016/j.jbusres.2018.10.026.

9 Patel, M.S., Benjamin, E.J., Volpp, K.G., Fox, C.S., Small, D.S., Massaro, J.M., …Murabito, J.M. (2017). Effect of a game-based intervention designed to enhance social incentives to increase physical activity among families: The BE FIT Randomized Clinical Trial. *JAMA Internal Medicine, 177*(11), 1586–93. https://doi.org/10.1001/jamainternmed.2017.3458.

10 Jones, B. A., Madden, G. J., & Wengreen, H.J. (2014). The FIT Game: Preliminary 60 evaluation of a gamification approach to increasing fruit and vegetable consumption in school. *Preventive Medicine, 68,* 76–9. https://doi.org/10.1016/j.ypmed.2014.04.015.

11 Hanus, M.D., & Fox, J. (2015). Assessing the effects of gamification in the classroom: A longitudinal study on intrinsic motivation, social comparison, satisfaction, effort, and academic performance. *Computers and Education, 80,* 152–61. https://doi.org/10.1016/j.compedu.2014.08.019.

12 Reynolds, L., Sosik, V.S., & Cosley, D. (2013). When Wii doesn't fit: How non-beginners react to Wii Fit's gamification. *ACM International Conference Proceeding Series,* 111–14. https://doi.org/10.1145/2583008.2583027.

13 Mulcahy et al. (2020).

14 Hanus & Fox (2015).

15 See Koivisto & Hamari (2019); and Müller-Stewens et al. (2017).

16 Mulcahy et al. (2020).
17 Mulcahy et al. (2020).
18 Hanus & Fox (2015).
19 Hanus & Fox (2015).
20 See Ainslie, G., & Haslam, N. (1992). Hyperbolic discounting. In G. Loewenstein & J. Elster (Eds.), *Choice over time* (pp. 57–92). Russell Sage; Thaler, R.H. (1994). Psychology and savings policies. *The American Economic Review, 84*(2), 186–92. https://www.jstor.org/stable/2117826; and Thaler, R.H., & Shefrin, H.M. (1981). An economic theory of self-control. *Journal of Political Economy, 89*(2), 392–406. https://doi.org/10.3386/w0208.
21 Benartzi, S. (2020). People don't save enough for emergencies, but there are ways to fix that. *The Wall Street Journal.* https://www.wsj.com/articles/people-dont-save-enough-for-emergencies-but-there-are-ways-to-fix-that-11581951601.
22 See https://aspredicted.org/jb3v5.pdf.
23 Rick, S.I., Cryder, C.E., & Loewenstein, G. (2008). Tightwads and spendthrifts. *Journal of Consumer Research, 34*(6), 767–82. https://doi.org/10.1086/523285.
24 Callender, C., & Jackson, J. (2005). Does the fear of debt deter students from higher education? *Journal of Social Policy, 34*(4), 509–40. https://doi.org/10.1017/S004727940500913X.
25 Lynch, J.G., Netemeyer, R.G., Spiller, S.A., & Zammit, A. (2010). A generalizable scale of propensity to plan: The long and the short of planning for time and for money. *Journal of Consumer Research, 37*(1), 108–28. https://psycnet.apa.org/doi/10.1086/649907.
26 Tangney, J.P., Baumeister, R.F., & Boone, A.L. (2004). High self-control predicts good adjustment, less pathology, better grades, and interpersonal success. *Journal of Personality, 72*(2), 271–324. https://doi.org/10.1111/j.0022-3506.2004.00263.x.
27 Lusardi, A., & Mitchell, O.S. (2017). The economic importance of financial literacy: Theory and evidence. *Journal of Economic Literature, 52*(1), 5–44. https://doi.org/10.3386/w18952.
28 Bartels, D.M., & Rips, L.J. (2010). Psychological connectedness and intertemporal choice. *Journal of Experimental Psychology: General, 139*(1), 49–69. https://psycnet.apa.org/doi/10.1037/a0018062.
29 Proyer, R.T. (2012). Development and initial assessment of a short measure for adult playfulness: The SMAP. *Personality and Individual Differences, 53*(8), 989–94. https://doi.org/10.1016/j.paid.2012.07.018.
30 See Koivisto & Hamari (2019); and Müller-Stewens et al. (2017).
31 Hanus & Fox (2015).
32 Ryan, R., & Deci, E.L. (2000). Intrinsic and extrinsic motivations: Classic definitions and new directions. *Contemporary Educational Psychology, 25*(1), 54–67. https://doi.org/10.1006/ceps.1999.1020.

33 See Bittner, J.V., & Shipper, J. (2014). Motivational effects and age differences of gamification in product advertising. *Journal of Consumer Marketing, 31*(5), 391–400. https://doi.org/10.1108/JCM-04-2014-0945; Huotari & Hamari (2017); and Landers & Armstrong (2017).

34 Perea Y Monsuwé, T., Dellaert, B.G.C., & De Ruyter, K. (2004). What drives consumers to shop online? A literature review. *International Journal of Service Industry Management, 15*(1), 102–21. https://doi.org/10.1108/09564230410523358.

35 Hammedi, W., Leclercq, T., & Van Riel, A. (2017). The use of gamification mechanics to increase employee and user engagement in participative healthcare services: A study of two cases. *Journal of Service Management, 28*(4), 640–61. https://doi.org/10.1108/JOSM-04-2016-0116.

CHAPTER FIVE

Translating Interventions to Improve Competence, Motivation, and Support of Heating Professionals to Increase Energy Efficiency in Swiss Buildings

Ulf J.J. Hahnel, Christian Mumenthaler,
Tessa Dent Ferrel, and Tobias Brosch

AT A GLANCE

- **Our Goal:** To develop a multimodular intervention aiming to improve competence, motivation, and supervisor support of heating technicians to promote more energy-efficient heating system adjustments and thus reduce the energy demand of energy-intensive buildings.
- **The Intervention:** Heating professionals were provided with a checklist in the boiler rooms to structure their work tasks, allow individual goal setting, and – depending on the experimental condition – get feedback from their responsible supervisors.
- **The Results:** We predicted reduced actual energy consumption in the buildings where responsible heating technicians were assigned to one of the experimental conditions compared to controls. We did not find this consistently across experimental conditions.
- **Lesson Learned:** Implementing behavioral interventions to increase energy efficiency of professionals should encompass various levels, including interventions at the level of the supervisor – which seems to be the most promising approach to foster behavior change in the given context.

Motivation and Objective

Energy demand in residential buildings is a key contributing factor to worldwide CO_2 emissions. In Switzerland, for instance, energy demand in residential buildings accounts for 16.4 percent of overall CO_2 emissions.[1] The use of fossil fuels for heating and hot water use are the main sources of emission generation in buildings. The behavior of residents plays a key role in this context as efficient heating practices and investment in building insulation may substantially reduce CO_2 emissions in the building sector. Despite the relevance of residents' individual behavior, heating energy consumption also depends on the adjustment of the central heating systems. Optimally adjusted heating systems ensure a certain level of comfort by concomitantly avoiding unnecessarily high baseline temperatures in the building and thus inefficient behavioral counteractions by residents (e.g., opening the window to reduce room temperature). Adjustments of the heating systems in large multifamily buildings are often effectuated by specialized heating technicians that visit the central boiler rooms at certain intervals. Thus, the adjustment practices of the technicians have a significant influence on energy efficiency of the buildings. However, optimization practices such as reducing the baseline temperature may backfire when residents complain due to perceived discomfort. Energy efficiency optimization thus may be sanctioned, increasing the likelihood that heating technicians lean toward higher baseline temperatures and thus lower energy efficiency to avoid complaints by inhabitants.

In the present research, we developed a multimodular behavioral intervention targeting energy efficiency practices of professional heating technicians in Geneva, Switzerland. This study thus aimed to contribute to the scarce research on behavioral interventions aiming to promote energy efficient behaviors in the work context. Whereas most theoretical and empirical research on environmental psychology and behavioral economics in the field focuses on private energy behavior,[2] research on professional behavior in the work context is limited – despite its high relevance for CO_2 emissions. Our main goal was to develop a multimodular intervention that supports heating technicians in making more energy-efficient heating system adjustments and thus reducing the energy demand of energy-intensive buildings. Semi-structured interviews with relevant stakeholders (e.g., heating technicians, technical supervisors, and energy efficiency experts) pointed to potential behavioral and communicative barriers that prevent an effective optimization process. The identified barriers could be clustered into three areas of change: *competence, motivation,* and *support*.

The developed behavioral interventions aimed to address these three areas on two main levels: The level of heating technicians and the level of the technicians' supervisors. At the heating technician level, the intervention targeted either technicians' competence only or both their competence and their motivation. At the technical supervisor level, the intervention targeted the support heating technicians receive from their technical supervisor. We tested this intervention in a field experiment in Geneva, Switzerland. Based on an experimental design, we were able to test whether the specific components of our intervention (competence, competence + motivation, support) were associated with a decrease in total actual heating energy consumption in the sample buildings.

Inspiration

Our qualitative analysis including relevant stakeholders revealed the three areas of intervention targets: change competence, motivation, and support. After identification of these promising intervention targets to increase energy efficiency, we aimed to identify suitable behavioral interventions to address these areas. This identification process was inspired by the EAST framework,[3] which incorporates the principles to make behavior change *Easy*, *Attractive*, *Social*, and *Timely*. See Table 5.1 for a summary of the main studies that served as inspiration for the development of our behavioral interventions in the present research.

A lack of *competence* due to insufficient training and experience can impact how energy efficiency measures are applied by heating technicians during the boiler room visits. In order to effectively adjust the heating systems, trial and error practices are necessary, but perceived lack of competence may hinder heating technicians in trying out certain optimization actions. We aimed to address this barrier by providing a checklist at the moment when heating technicians were optimizing the heating systems. In line with the EAST framework,[4] the checklist was expected to make the need for energy optimization salient at the moment of action (*Timely*) and to provide a simple tool highlighting the most pertinent optimization tasks (*Easy*). Checklists have been shown to be effective tools, especially in the medical domain.[5] The implementation of a surgical safety checklist, for instance, resulted in a decrease of complications per 100 patients from 27.3 to 16.7.[6] We thus applied horizontal scaling of an intervention strategy by testing the impact of a checklist in a new domain (i.e., energy) using a new target behavior (i.e., energy optimization tasks).

In addition to missing competence, a lack of *motivation* to optimize the heating systems can hinder energy efficient optimization practices.

Table 5.1. Main studies that inspired the behavioral interventions tested in the present study. The interventions were structured along the dimensions of competence, motivation, and support

Dimension	Original study	Findings
Competence	de Vries et al. (2010)	Providing a checklist (here surgical safety checklist) resulted in better work practices (here reduction of complications per 100 patients)
Motivation	Abrahamse et al. (2007)	Setting energy saving goals resulted in a reduction of household energy consumption
Support	Abrahamse et al. (2007)	Providing tailored energy feedback resulted in a reduction of household energy consumption

For instance, some heating technicians may be reluctant to change their practices due to established working habits that do not include optimization actions. In these cases, the introduction of energy optimization actions may be perceived as coercion, thus resulting in resistance. We aimed to address this barrier by providing heating technicians with the opportunity to set individual goals for energy optimization in order to increase motivation and attractiveness of the optimization task (*Attractive*). In previous research, goal setting, combined with information and feedback provision, led to a reduction in energy consumption by 5.1 percent.[7] We thus applied vertical scaling of an intervention strategy by testing an intervention on a new sample (i.e., shifting from laypersons to professional technicians) within the same domain (i.e., energy).

Finally, missing *support* may be a cause of inefficient work practices.[8] Our qualitative analysis revealed that the level of competence that supervisors ascribed to their heating technicians varied greatly from one supervisor to another. Therefore, even though the majority of heating technicians were responsible for the optimization of the heating systems, only in some cases did they receive the necessary training to acquire the relevant skills. This moreover implies that they did not receive feedback on their energy optimization performance from their supervisors. We aimed to address this barrier to energy efficiency with an intervention aiming to improve the feedback heating technicians receive on their optimization actions and performance from their technical supervisor. In their study, Abrahamse and colleagues provided tailored feedback on energy reduction potential to laypersons, effectively reducing their energy consumption compared to a control group.[9] Our feedback intervention component thus can also be considered as vertical scaling within the energy domain. In order to increase support, our intervention further incorporated joint goal setting of energy optimization goals with the heating technicians and their supervisors (*Social*). We expected this measure to create a social norm, which has been shown to be an effective tool to motivate energy-efficient behavior.[10] In line with the messenger effect,[11] we further expected feedback and this social norm to be especially potent as they were both conveyed by the supervisor.

Interventions and Method

We tested a behavioral intervention aiming to increase energy efficiency practices of heating technicians taking part in an energy efficiency program initiated by the energy provider in Geneva, Switzerland. Our intervention targeted various barriers hindering effective energy efficiency practices that were identified at the *level of heating technicians* and the *level of technical supervisors*. Both levels were addressed by means of a multimodular behavioral intervention. Specifically, two booklets were developed to increase competence and motivation at the level of the heating technicians as well as to increase the support heating technicians received at the level of the supervisors.

Intervention: The Level of Heating Technicians

In line with the notion that interventions should take place at the exact moment the respective behavior change is desired (*Timely*), we developed an intervention that nudges the desired behavior at the moment when the heating technicians have the opportunity to adjust the heating systems. To this end, we developed a booklet to be placed in the boiler room. The goal was for heating technicians to consult the booklet every time they visit the boiler room during the project's intervention period. The booklet incorporated the selected psychological principles and was adapted as a function of the experimental condition, which allowed us to assess whether targeting a single behavioral barrier (i.e., competence) is more or less effective than targeting a combination (i.e., competence + motivation).

Competence Condition

In the competence condition, the booklet consisted of a checklist of the most pertinent energy efficiency optimization tasks (cf. Figure 5.1). In contrast to the study by de Vries and colleagues, we tested whether a checklist could increase energy efficient practices of heating technicians rather than work practices in the medical domain. While long and complicated descriptions of possible optimization actions may be perceived as a barrier to behavior change, we aimed to concisely depict

Figure 5.1. Example of the booklet checklist page for the competence condition

Optimization checklist

| Visit 1 | Visit 2 | Visit 3 | Visit 4 |

Of the many possible optimization tasks, please focus on those listed below. Please check each box to confirm that the task has been completed.

Optimization tasks

- Optimization of day and night non-heating temperatures ☐
- Optimization of day and night setpoint temperatures ☐
- Optimization of the heating curves for radiators or under-floor heating ☐
- Increase of the nocturnal temperature reduction ☐
- Verification of the boiler in/out temperature differentials ☐
- Verification of the number of boiler starts during the visit
- Verification of the orientation of the building facades ☐
- Verification that the outdoor sensor is not in direct sunlight ☐
- Lowering of the DHW primary temperature boost ☐
- Lowering of the primary temperature boost for radiator heating ☐
- Optimization of the domestic hot water (DHW) storage temperature ☐
- Verification of the thermostat's on/off temperature differential
- DHW temperature boost setpoint ☐
- DHW production schedule ☐
- DHW production, the low set point for the thermostat, the high set point and a safety set point ☐
- Shutdown of the DHW pump during non-operating and high operating periods ☐
- Reduction of the air renewal in living spaces
- Check the schedules of the low or high speed verification ☐
- Optimization of the operating speed of the circulating fans ☐

the relevant optimization tasks to maximally reduce behavioral barriers (*Easy*). We moreover aimed to use the checklist to make the need for optimization salient.[12] The checklist, which was located in direct proximity of the heating system, was supposed to serve as a cue, reminding heating technicians of the need for optimization in general and of certain optimization tasks in particular. The checklist further allowed heating technicians to keep track of the adjustment processes they conducted in a simple manner, reducing the likelihood the task will be perceived as an effortful behavioral burden.[13]

Competence and Motivation Condition

While competence was identified as a core area of opportunity for behavior change, the initial analysis of contextual conditions also revealed that a lack of motivation is a relevant issue that may impede optimal adjustment practices. We thus designed an additional intervention condition in which both competence and motivation barriers were addressed simultaneously.

This intervention condition was more dynamic in nature as it was based on three phases (with a duration of approximately two months each) in which optimization tasks were progressively introduced (see Figure 5.2 left panel, for an example from Phase 1). That is, instead of presenting all optimization actions at once, clusters of tasks were emphasized in each phase. In line with the foot-in-the-door technique,[14] the workload slightly increased during the intervention period, allowing heating technicians to focus on more feasible portions of the optimization task. We expected this strategy to provide continuous rewards to the heating technicians as it allowed them to set and attain feasible objectives by avoiding excessive demands. Heating technicians were instructed to focus on the optimization tasks of the current phase in particular, but they were free to conduct additional optimization tasks from the other phases. That is, heating technicians were not restricted in their working processes. Instead, attention was drawn to specific optimization actions. In subsequent phases, reminders of the optimization tasks from the previous phase(s) were included to ensure that already established optimization actions were continued (see Figure 5.2, right panel, for an example from Phase 2).

The booklets in this condition moreover included a space where heating technicians could set individual optimization goals for their next visit to the boiler room (i.e., the number of optimization tasks they wanted to perform in the next visit). This goal setting was expected to increase heating technicians' motivation to optimize heating efficiency

Figure 5.2. Example of the booklet checklist page for the competence and motivation condition in Phase 1 (left). Example of the booklet checklist page for the competence and motivation condition in Phase 2, where optimization tasks of Phase 1 are presented in addition to newly introduced tasks (right)

Optimization checklist

Phase 1

| Visit 1 | Visit 2 | Visit 3 | Visit 4 |

Of the many possible optimization tasks, please focus today on those listed below.
Please check each box to confirm that the task has been completed.

Optimization tasks

- Optimization of day and night non-heating temperatures ☐
- Optimization of day and night setpoint temperatures ☐
- Optimization of heating curves for radiators or under-floor heating ☐
- Increase nocturnal temperature reduction ☐
- Verification of the boiler in/out temperature differentials ☐
- Verification of the number of boiler starts ☐
- Verification of the orientation of the building facades ☐
- Verification that the outdoor sensor is not in direct sunlight ☐

Please update:
How many optimization tasks do you want to perform during the next visit? **New goal** ☐

Optimization checklist

Phase 2

| Visit 5 | Visit 6 | Visit 7 | Visit 8 |

Of the many possible optimization tasks, please focus today on those listed below.
Please check each box to confirm that the task has been completed.

Optimization tasks

- Lowering of the DHW primary temperature boost ☐
- Lowering of the primary temperature boost for radiator heating heating ☐
- Optimization of the DHW storage temperature ☐
- Verification of the thermostat's on/off temperature differential ☐
- DHW temperature boost setpoint ☐
- DHW production schedule ☐
- DHW production, the low set point for the thermostat, the high set point and a safety set point ☐

Are you maintaining the tasks from the previous phase?
Cross out the tasks you did not pursue.
- Optimization of day and night non-heating temperatures
- Optimization of day and night setpoint temperatures
- Optimization of heating curves for radiators or under-floor heating
- Increase of nocturnal temperature reduction
- Verification of the boiler in/out temperature differentials
- Verification of the number of boiler starts
- Verification of the orientation of the building facades
- Verification that the outdoor sensor is not in direct sunlight

Please update:
How many optimization tasks do you want to perform during the next visit? **New goal** ☐

as they could set specific goals for each building and monitor whether they succeeded in reaching them. The goals set at the previous visit were visible during the next boiler room visit, thus providing feedback on individual goal attainment. In accordance with implementation intentions, stimulating behavior is most effective when the goal is linked to a specific situation.[15] In contrast to the study by Abrahamse and colleagues, who used goal setting to reduce direct energy consumption of inhabitants, our interventions aimed to provide dynamic goal setting and feedback to the professional heating technicians who adjust the heating systems but do not directly consume the energy.

Intervention: The Level of Technical Supervisors

In addition to competence and motivation, the third area of opportunity identified in the analysis of decision context was support. In particular, our analysis suggested that increasing the communication between heating technicians and their technical supervisor might be a promising lever to make energy optimization action more likely. In line with our modular intervention approach, interventions at the supervisor level were modularly integrated and combined with the interventions at the heating technician level (see section "Experimental design and dependent variable").

Support Condition

This intervention part was aimed at increasing the support heating technicians receive from their technical supervisors. The core of this intervention component was to establish regular meetings between the technical supervisors and the heating technicians (i.e., four feedback sessions during the heating period). During the meetings, the supervisors were asked to provide feedback on the heating technicians' energy optimization performance. The fact that the feedback was provided by the supervisor was expected to increase the value of the feedback as well as the perceived motivational relevance of the related tasks. This notion is supported by research on the messenger effect showing that the source of a message significantly determines whether the message will be implemented by the recipient.[16]

The intervention was structured by means of a booklet that was provided to the technical supervisors. One booklet was provided for each heating technician. Before the kick-off meeting at the beginning of the heating season, the supervisor was asked to sign a statement in which they committed to providing regular feedback to the respective heating technician (see Figure 5.3). Commitment contracts have

Figure 5.3. Supervisor booklet with the commitment contract page (left) and the feedback page for the kick-off meeting (right). The feedback page refers to the optimization phases in accordance with the competence + motivation condition at the heating technician level.

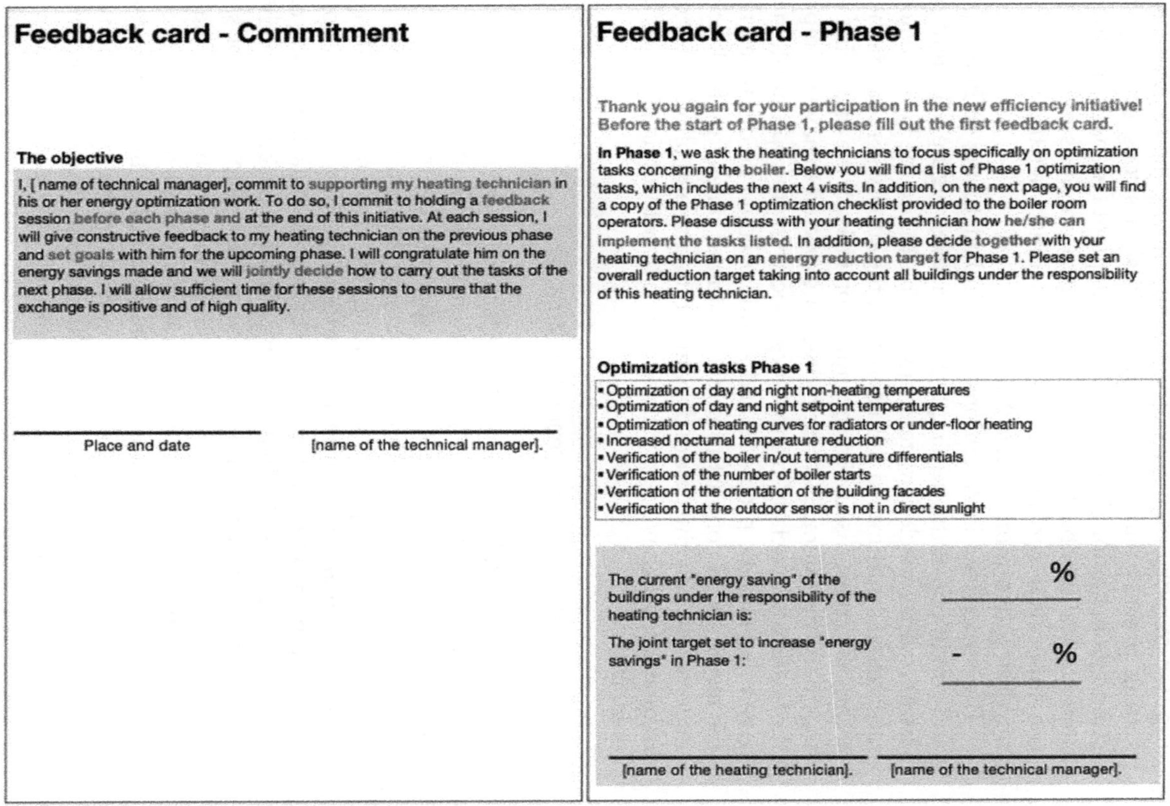

Feedback card - Commitment

The objective

I, [name of technical manager], commit to supporting my heating technician in his or her energy optimization work. To do so, I commit to holding a feedback session before each phase and at the end of this initiative. At each session, I will give constructive feedback to my heating technician on the previous phase and set goals with him for the upcoming phase. I will congratulate him on the energy savings made and we will jointly decide how to carry out the tasks of the next phase. I will allow sufficient time for these sessions to ensure that the exchange is positive and of high quality.

_____   [name of the technical manager].

Place and date

Feedback card - Phase 1

Thank you again for your participation in the new efficiency initiative! Before the start of Phase 1, please fill out the first feedback card.

In Phase 1, we ask the heating technicians to focus specifically on optimization tasks concerning the boiler. Below you will find a list of Phase 1 optimization tasks, which includes the next 4 visits. In addition, on the next page, you will find a copy of the Phase 1 optimization checklist provided to the boiler room operators. Please discuss with your heating technician how he/she can implement the tasks listed. In addition, please decide together with your heating technician on an energy reduction target for Phase 1. Please set an overall reduction target taking into account all buildings under the responsibility of this heating technician.

Optimization tasks Phase 1

- Optimization of day and night non-heating temperatures
- Optimization of day and night setpoint temperatures
- Optimization of heating curves for radiators or under-floor heating
- Increased nocturnal temperature reduction
- Verification of the boiler in/out temperature differentials
- Verification of the number of boiler starts
- Verification of the orientation of the building facades
- Verification that the outdoor sensor is not in direct sunlight

The current "energy saving" of the buildings under the responsibility of the heating technician is: _____ %

The joint target set to increase "energy savings" in Phase 1:   - _____ %

[name of the heating technician].   [name of the technical manager].

been shown to increase the likelihood that an intended behavior will actually be executed.[17] In the kick-off meeting, the supervisor provided the heating technician with feedback on their performance during the previous year. In addition, they set a joint goal for the heating technician's energy reduction performance for the upcoming two months. Inclusion of the technical supervisor into the goal setting process was expected to establish a strong social norm to stimulate behavior change. In the subsequent feedback sessions, the supervisors' feedback referred to the two previous months. Again, the supervisor and heating technician jointly set the goals for the upcoming two-month periods.

The supervisor interventions were linked to the different phases and conditions at the heating technician level. Figure 5.3 (right panel) displays a feedback card referring to Phase 1 of the competence and motivation condition. In this condition, the supervisor and the heating technician could discuss the optimization tasks of the upcoming phase together. This interaction was moreover expected to have an impact on the heating technicians' competence concerning the optimization tasks, given that specific problems and solutions could be discussed during the meetings. In contrast to previous studies on energy feedback, our intervention was thus more dynamic in nature and allowed for direct, frequent, and behavior-specific advice on how to attain energy efficient outcomes.

Experimental Design and Dependent Variable

Our experimental design with the factors *intervention at the heating technician level* (competence / competence + motivation / control) and *intervention at the supervisor level* (support / control) resulted in six different conditions (see Table 5.2). Due to the implementation of the intervention in an applied field setting, we faced major challenges in creating a balanced experimental design. Specifically, it was not possible to implement the intervention at the level of each building and to randomly assign individual buildings to the experimental conditions. The reason was that heating technicians were responsible for several buildings simultaneously, which would have produced potential confounding effects if the same person was assigned to different experimental conditions depending on which building they were working in on a specific day. We therefore implemented the intervention at the level of the heating companies, meaning that the same experimental condition was allocated to all the buildings operated by a given heating company and all the heating technicians working for this company.

Table 5.2. Complete experimental study design with the six experimental conditions based on interventions at the heating technician and technical supervisor levels

		Technical Supervisor	
		Support	Control
Heating Technicians	**Competence**	Competence & Support	Competence
	Competence + Motivation	Competence/Motivation & Support	Competence/ Motivation
	Control	Support	Control Only

Our behavioral intervention was embedded within a general energy efficiency strategy of the local energy provider, which included various "classic" technical interventions and non-technical interventions (e.g., workshops and consultancy on optimization procedures). Here we test whether a behavioral intervention can contribute to energy efficiency on top of classic interventions.

As illustrated in the CONSORT flow diagram (see Figure 5.4), 167 buildings serviced by twenty-two heating companies were included in the intervention. As previously mentioned, the intervention was implemented at the level of the heating companies. Therefore, we assigned each heating company to an experimental condition with the aim of balancing the number of buildings as well as variables specific to each building, such as previous energy performance and participation duration in the energy efficiency program of the local energy provider. The aim of this approach was to obtain experimental conditions comparable with regards to important energy efficiency indicators at baseline prior to our intervention. Our dependent variable was the percentage of energy economy achieved for each building compared to the previous heating period. The local energy provider calculated these performance values by accounting for multiple variables such as the orientation of each building, external temperature, sunshine rate, and season. Given that the empirical evaluation of the intervention took place during the heating season of autumn/winter 2017–18, we considered buildings that have been part of the general energy efficiency program since before 2016 as "senior," and buildings that have joined the program after that date as "recent."

Balancing the cells of the experimental design based on a consideration of building performance and participation length in the program was essential, given that preliminary analyses of the data from

Figure 5.4. CONSORT flow diagram illustrating the experimental design of the field study

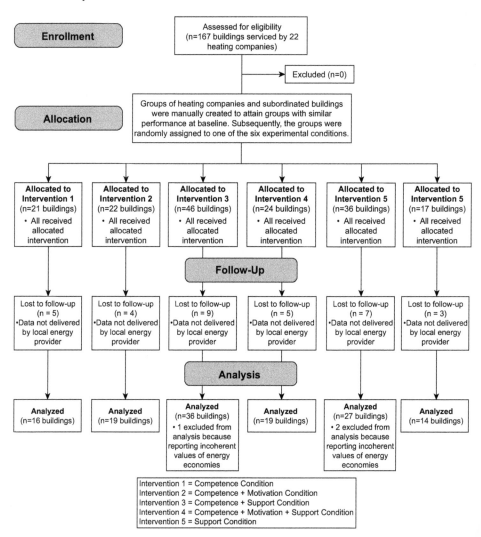

Intervention 1 = Competence Condition
Intervention 2 = Competence + Motivation Condition
Intervention 3 = Competence + Support Condition
Intervention 4 = Competence + Motivation + Support Condition
Intervention 5 = Support Condition

previous heating periods revealed that in some cases, the best performances (i.e., the largest gains in energy efficiency) were achieved during the first months after joining the program, but that continually improving performances is more challenging. However, even though we considered these variables in assigning buildings to the different

Table 5.3. The total number of buildings allocated to each experimental condition based on their performance and participation length in the energy efficiency program

Experimental Condition	Total Heating Companies	Total Buildings	SDP	RDP	SIP	RIP
Competence	3	21	2	4	9	6
Competence and Motivation	3	23	3	7	7	6
Competence and Support	3	46	9	10	17	10
Competence, Motivation, and Support	3	24	3	5	9	7
Support	4	36	4	5	21	6
Control	6	17	3	4	4	6

SDP = Senior in the program and showing a decrease in performance (i.e., energy consumption increase); RDP = Recent in the program and showing a decrease in performance; SIP = Senior in the program and showing an increase in performance (i.e., energy consumption decrease); RIP = Recent in the program and showing an increase in performance.

experimental conditions, we were not able to achieve a perfectly balanced experimental design with the restrictions imposed by the field conditions. This resulted, for instance, in differences in group sizes and performance indicators between the different experimental conditions, which should be taken into account in the interpretation of our results. Table 5.3 illustrates the total number of heating companies and buildings that were allocated to the six experimental conditions, including the previous energy efficiency performance of the buildings and the duration of participation in the general energy efficiency program.

Differences (and Similarities)

The original studies presented above served as inspiration for the present research but given the novel and specific research context of the present research, which encompasses professional technicians responsible for energy efficiency practices and their supervisors, our research design substantially differed from previous work, including differences in research setting, participants, experimental design, measurement of the dependent variable, and procedures (see Table 5.4. for an exhaustive list of differences).

Table 5.4. Significant differences between previous research and the present study

Dimension	Original Study	Differences
Competence	de Vries et al. (2010)	Participants: Hospital professionals (original study) versus heating technicians (present study) Dependent variable: Number of complications per 100 patients (original study) versus actual reduction in building energy consumption (present study) Intervention: Surgical safety checklist (original study) versus energy efficiency checklist (present study)
Motivation	Abrahamse et al. (2007)	Participants: Laypersons (original study) versus heating technicians (present study) Dependent variable: Reduction of energy consumption on the household level (original study) versus reduction of energy consumption on the (multi-family) building level (present study) Intervention: Fixed goal setting of 5% energy consumption reduction (original study) versus personalized goal setting of the number of energy efficiency measures (heating technician level; present study) and personalized energy reduction targets (supervisor level; original study)
Support	Abrahamse et al. (2007)	Participants: Laypersons (original study) versus heating technicians (present study) Dependent variable: Reduction of energy consumption on the household level (original study) versus reduction of energy consumption on the (multi-family) building level (present study) Intervention: Tailored information on energy saving measures and feedback provided through a website (original study) versus tailored information and feedback on energy optimization measures and performance provided by the supervisor (present study)

Results

The intervention took place during the heating period from October 1, 2017, to April 1, 2018. At the end of this period, we obtained performance data for 134 of the 167 buildings initially available for the study. Thirty-three buildings were not included in the study because of incomplete or nonconsolidated data, or because some buildings had switched between heating companies during the intervention period. A drop-out rate of 20 percent is not uncommon in interventions applied in a real-world setting.

A preliminary analysis of the performance data for the intervention period led to the exclusion of three buildings reporting invalid percentage values of energy economies (e.g., 8000 percent). Moreover, the distribution of the daily values of energy economies reported for the remaining buildings in the data set included many outliers. Therefore, we computed a trimmed mean by removing 20 percent of the highest and lowest daily scores for each building in order to obtain a robust statistic representing the mean percentage of energy economies achieved during the heating period from October 1, 2017, to April 1, 2018. Although different approaches to deal with extreme values in distributions exist, there is good evidence that a 20 percent trim will usually stabilize the mean and its confidence intervals and produce robust sample statistics.[18]

As we were not able to obtain a completely balanced experimental design but faced groups with different sample sizes (see Table 5.3), we performed Levene's test to assess the homogeneity of variances between groups, an assumption that is required, especially with groups of different sizes, to perform comparisons of means between experimental conditions using a conventional parametric test like ANOVA or Student's t-test. Results indicated that for the mean percentage of energy economies during the heating period of interest, variances differed significantly between the six groups, $F(5, 125) = 3.397, p = .007$. We therefore tested the effectiveness of each intervention individually by comparing the mean percentage of energy economies in the respective experimental condition to the control condition, relying on a series of independent two-tailed Welch's t-tests, which can correct for violations of the assumption of homogeneity of variances. In addition, effect sizes were calculated using Cohen's d instead of Pearson's r as the latter is likely to be biased more strongly by differing group sizes compared to Cohen's d.[19]

Mean values revealed reduced energy consumption in all conditions compared to the previous periods. This reduction can be attributed to the fact that the intervention presented here was embedded within a larger energy efficiency program, which resulted in an overall reduction of energy consumption across conditions. Results moreover revealed that buildings allocated to the support condition achieved on average a greater percentage of energy savings ($M = 14.1$, $SE = 2.55$) than those allocated to the control condition ($M = 6.82$, $SE = 1.92$). This difference was statistically significant $t(38.86) = 2.266, p = 0.029$, representing a medium-sized effect $d = .62$. The mean percentages of energy savings achieved by buildings allocated to all other experimental conditions did not statistically differ from those allocated to the control condition (see Table 5.5).

Table 5.5. Results of five two-tailed Welch's t-tests comparing the mean percent of energy savings in each experimental condition to the control condition

Experimental Condition	Total Buildings	Mean Percent of Energy Savings	Comparison to Control Condition	
			Welch's t-tests (two-tailed)	Effect Size (Cohen's d)
Competence	16	7.79 (3.34)	t(23.59) = .252, p = .803	d = .09; CI [−.66, .84]
Competence and Motivation	19	7.69 (2.22)	t(30.99) = .295, p = .77	d = .1; CI [−.62, .82]
Competence and Support	36	8.58 (1.27)	t(24.96) = .766, p = .451	d = .24; CI [−.4, .87]
Competence, Motivation, and Support	19	6.76 (1.23)	t(23.08) = -.024, p = .981	d = -.01; CI [-.73, .71]
Support	27	**14.1 (2.55)**	**t(38.86) = 2.266,** **p = .029**	**d = .62;** **CI [−.06, 1.3]**
Control	14	6.82 (1.92)	–	–

Standard errors of the mean are reported in parentheses, next to the mean values. 95 percent confidence intervals of Cohen's d are reported in brackets.

It is important to note that with a Bonferroni-adjusted alpha of 0.01 ($\alpha_{original}$ = .05 / number of tests = 5), the difference between the support and control condition is no longer significant ($p > .01$), despite the medium-sized effect of $d = .62$. This is driven by the fact that buildings rather than individuals served as our unit of observation, thus reducing our statistical power. In a similar vein, we observed a small effect ($d = .24$) in the "competence plus support" condition, but this difference was not statistically significant $t(24.96) = .766, p = .451$.

Reconciliation

We did observe some differences between our results and the original studies we based our interventions upon. Especially, providing check-lists and individual goal setting at the level of heating technicians in the competence and competence + motivation conditions did not result in higher energy efficiency compared to the control condition. This may be because our study was applied in a complex field setting or because we transferred the interventions to other target groups and/or other domains. One additional shortcoming of our field design was that the heating companies varied in the extent to which they implemented the

Figure 5.5. Evolution of the entry rate of data into the booklets for heating technicians across the twelve visits in the competence and competence + motivation conditions (N = 114)

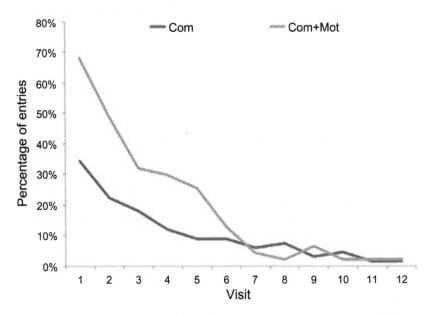

behavioral intervention, despite a number of measures taken by the project team aiming to increase companies' involvement in the project (e.g., presentations, reminders). As a result, it is possible that some of the potential effects of the interventions were attenuated due to loose implementation practices by some participating heating companies. Consistent with this assumption, qualitative analyses revealed that only 27 percent of the companies in the support condition completed all four feedback sessions as indicated by the number of filled-in feedback cards (9 percent of the companies filled in three cards, 9 percent two cards, 18 percent one card and 37 percent no card).

A similar pattern was observed with regards to the interventions at the level of heating technicians. Figure 5.5 illustrates the percentage of entries into the booklets in the boiler rooms in the "competence" and the "competence + motivation" conditions. While at the beginning of the intervention period, heating technicians did indeed fill in the booklets to optimize energy efficiency, these numbers drop considerably over time, reaching values close to zero in the last visit. It is thus possible that the repeated confrontation with the checklist increased fatigue or reactance. In line with our assumption that a more dynamic version of the booklet increases motivation, more optimization actions were indeed initially reported by heating technicians in the "competence + motivation" condition. However, this difference disappeared over time and did not result in measurable efficiency gains.

Discussion and Prescriptive Advice

Our efforts at translating prior research into behavioral interventions that aimed to increase the energy efficiency practices of heating technicians in Geneva yielded mixed results. The development of the behavioral intervention was grounded in an analysis of the existing literature from psychological science and behavioral economics as well as in a qualitative analysis of the context in which the intervention was applied. The findings shed light on various factors fostering and hindering effective energy efficiency practices that were identified at two levels: the level of heating technicians and the level of technical supervisors. Both levels were addressed by means of a multimodular behavioral intervention. The context of our intervention targeting professional work behavior including the employee and leadership level is highly novel and may point to new, promising research avenues in environmental psychology, which usually focuses on individual layperson behavior, but largely neglects professional behavior.

We were moreover able to apply an experimental design in the field, which allowed us to test the intervention modules separately in order to examine which intervention component was most effective in triggering behavioral change (Table 5.2 and Figure 5.4). Specifically, several booklets were developed that aimed to increase competence and motivation at the heating technician level and to increase the support heating technicians receive at the supervisor level. We used actual energy consumption data of multifamily Geneva buildings to test the effectiveness of the developed intervention components.

The behavioral intervention presented here was embedded within a larger energy efficiency program of the energy provider in Geneva, including a variety of technical and non-technical interventions to reduce energy consumption in the target buildings. The energy saving effects presented here can thus be considered as savings over and above already established technical and non-technical interventions, indicating that "soft" and relatively simple behavioral interventions can result in additional effects on top of energy efficiency measures such as workshops and consultancy on optimization procedures.

Our findings suggest a potential effectiveness of behavioral interventions aiming to increase the support heating technicians receive from their supervisors. In the *support* condition, supervisors gave their commitment to providing feedback to heating technicians and setting energy saving goals jointly with them. Importantly, this condition did not include any of the intervention modules targeting the heating technician level. As this condition was most successful in reducing energy consumption, without additional measures at the heating technician level, the results illustrate that "less can be more."

These findings, however, have to be interpreted with caution. The field conditions in which our experimental intervention modules were embedded need to be considered, including imperfect allocation of buildings to experimental conditions, variance due to already established energy efficiency measures and heating companies, and the relatively small sample size since buildings rather than individuals were the unit of observation. The ensuing reduction in statistical power resulted in the fact that the observed difference was not statistically significant when applying Bonferroni correction, despite a substantial observed reduction in energy consumption of 14.1 percent compared to a reduction of 6.8 percent in the control condition.

The present project illustrates that a successful implementation of behavioral interventions needs to be accompanied by a thorough analysis of the context in which the intervention will be applied. A contextual analysis can be based on observations and qualitative interviews with key stakeholders at different organizational levels as conducted in the present project. Here, the interviews revealed that many heating technicians faced a lack of support from their hierarchy, which we addressed with a behavioral intervention to increase social support at the technical supervisor level. After the initiation of the project, we realized that it would be wise to continuously monitor the implementation of the intervention in the field. As described in the Reconciliation section, we observed significant variations in the extent to which our intervention was implemented by the responsible actors in the field and the extent to which we were able to contact the concerned heating companies during the intervention. Concrete measures that can be applied when a successful implementation of the intervention cannot be ensured should be defined prior to implementation.

Finally, the present project illustrates the value of considering the different levels of the organizational context instead of focusing on the "end actor" only. We jointly considered the behavior of heating technicians *and* their technical supervisors. Our findings indicate that interventions on the supervisor level may be the most promising to increase energy efficiency in this context. At the level of intervention mechanisms, the support condition was constructed by combining a commitment contract, feedback sessions, and joint goal setting. Future research could examine the different intervention components at the technical supervisor level in more detail by separating experimental groups according to the aforementioned intervention components. The findings would provide more detailed insights into the effectiveness of the different aspects of organizational support and would thus facilitate the development of more specific interventions at this level. We hope that our intervention is a starting point for a more systematic analysis of behavioral interventions in the work context, including employees with significant direct impacts on energy consumption as well as relevant actors at the organizational level.

NOTES

1 Swiss Federal Office for the Environment. (2022, April 11). *Greenhouse gas emissions from buildings*. https://www.bafu.admin.ch/bafu/en/home/topics/climate/state/data/greenhouse-gas-inventory/buildings.html.

2 See Hahnel, U.J.J., Chatelain, G., Conte, B., Piana, V., & Brosch, T. (2020). Mental accounting mechanisms in energy decision-making and behaviour. *Nature Energy, 5*, 952–8. https://doi.org/10.1038/s41560-020-00704-6; and Mertens, S., Hahnel, U.J.J., & Brosch, T. (2020). This way, please: Uncovering the directional effects of attribute translations on decision making. *Judgment and Decision Making, 15*(1), 25–46. https://doi.org/10.1017/s1930297500006896.

3 Service, O., Hallsworth, M., Halpern, D., Algate, F., Gallagher, R., Nguyen, S., Ruda, S., Sanders, M., Pelenur, M., Gyani, A., Harper, H., Reinhard, J., & Kirkman, E. (2014). *EAST – Four simple ways to apply behavioural insights*. https://www.bi.team/wp-content/uploads/2015/07/BIT-Publication-EAST_FA_WEB.pdf.

4 Service et al. (2014).

5 Borchard, A., Schwappach, D.L.B., Barbir, A., & Bezzola, P. (2012). A systematic review of the effectiveness, compliance, and critical factors for implementation of safety checklists in surgery. *Annals of Surgery, 256*(6), 925–33. https://doi.org/10.1097/SLA.0b013e3182682f27.

6 de Vries, E.N., Prins, H.A., Crolla, R.M.P.H., den Outer, A.J., van Andel, G., van Helden, S.H., Schlack, W.S., van Putten, M.A., Gouma, D.J., Dijkgraaf, M.G.W., Smorenburg, S.M., & Boermeester, M.A. (2010). Effect of a comprehensive surgical safety system on patient outcomes. *New England Journal of Medicine, 363*(20), 1928–37. https://doi.org/10.1056/nejmsa0911535.

7 Abrahamse, W., Steg, L., Vlek, C., & Rothengatter, T. (2007). The effect of tailored information, goal setting, and tailored feedback on household energy use, energy-related behaviors, and behavioral antecedents. *Journal of Environmental Psychology*, 27(4), 265–76. https://doi.org/10.1016/j.jenvp.2007.08.002.

8 Euwema, M.C., Wendt, H., & van Emmerik, H. (2007). Leadership styles and group organizational citizenship behavior across cultures. *Journal of Organizational Behavior*, 28(8), 1035–57. https://doi.org/10.1002/job.496.

9 Abrahamse et al. (2007).

10 Schultz, P.W., Nolan, J.M., Cialdini, R.B., Goldstein, N.J., & Griskevicius, V. (2007). The constructive, destructive, and reconstructive power of social norms: Research article. *Psychological Science*, 18(5), 429–34. https://doi.org/10.1111/j.1467-9280.2007.01917.x

11 Dolan, P., Hallsworth, M., Halpern, D., King, D., Metcalfe, R., & Vlaev, I. (2012). Influencing behaviour: The mindspace way. *Journal of Economic Psychology*, 33(1), 264–77. https://doi.org/10.1016/j.joep.2011.10.009.

12 Dolan et al. (2012).

13 See for example Borchard et al. (2012).

14 Freedman, J.L., & Fraser, S.C. (1966). Compliance without pressure: The foot-in-the-door technique. *Journal of Personality and Social Psychology*, 4(2), 195–202. https://doi.org/10.1037/h0023552.

15 Gollwitzer, P.M., & Sheeran, P. (2006). Implementation intentions and goal achievement: A meta-analysis of effects and processes. In *Advances in Experimental Social Psychology*, 38, 69–119. https://doi.org/10.1016/S0065-2601(06)38002-1.

16 See for example Dolan et al. (2012).

17 Giné, X., Karlan, D., & Zinman, J. (2010). Put your money where your butt is: A commitment contract for smoking cessation. *American Economic Journal: Applied Economics*, 2(4), 213–35. https://doi.org/10.1257/app.2.4.213.

18 Wilcox, R.R. (2001). Fundamentals of modern statistical methods. In *Fundamentals of Modern Statistical Methods*. Springer New York. https://doi.org/10.1007/978-1-4757-3522-2.

19 McGrath, R.E., & Meyer, G.J. (2006). When effect sizes disagree: The case of r and d. *Psychological Methods*, 11(4), 386–401. https://doi.org/10.1037/1082-989X.11.4.386.

CHAPTER SIX

Taking Context Seriously: Iteratively Translating Behavioral Interventions to Create Anemia Preventing Habits in Rural India

Anisha Singh and Steve Wendel

AT A GLANCE

- **Our Goal:** To help women in rural India take iron and folic acid supplements during pregnancy and lactation to avoid anemia and its deadly consequences through the use of value perception and recall interventions.
- **The Intervention:** A behaviorally informed counseling card that normalized the side effects and a behaviorally informed peel-off calendar.
- **The Results:** The interventions were effective at two specific decision-making points – the calendar was effective in reminding women when their dosage was complete and they could stop the supplements, and the counseling card was effective in reducing drop-offs from side effects.
- **Lesson Learned:** Successful translation of research findings from prior work can come from the thoughtful combination of qualitative and quantitative methods, and the interweaving of iterative prototyping, lab testing, and field testing.

Motivation and Objective

Anemia is a pervasive public health problem in India, where 53 percent of women aged fifteen to forty-nine years are anemic.[1] Approximately 20 percent of maternal deaths are anemia related, and the condition can cause low birth weight and cognitive challenges for children. Thankfully, there are highly effective means to boost iron levels such as iron-folic acid (IFA) pills, which are especially valuable for pregnant women and new mothers.

IFA pills are widely, though not universally, available to women in India through free government programs.[2] IFA pills should be taken during pregnancy and for six months afterward, but according to Indian government data,[3] only 28 percent of those who received IFA pills took the pills for one hundred days or more.[4] Women thus face a significant intention-action gap: a mother's desire to protect her life and the health of her child can be assumed, but when pills that do so are available, only a minority take them as needed.

In this study, we encouraged pregnant and lactating women to take iron-folic acid supplements to improve their health and that of their babies. We focus on areas in which the supply of iron-folic supplements is consistent. There is a rich literature on medication adherence and on techniques to overcome the intention-action gap; new intervention development was not required. Instead, the study sought to winnow down the set of possible interventions to those that were likely to be effective and then assess their impact in practice, in the local context and to the specific problem statement.

Inspiration

The growing body of literature on medication adherence includes a host of individual interventions and systematic reviews of the evidence,[5] as does the more general literature on the intention-action gap. We started out ambitious with a list of roughly fifty interventions that we derived from a combination of the existing literature and internal brainstorming. For example, inspirations from the existing literature included:

- A tailored immunization calendar for parents of one-year-old children, studied in St. Louis, Missouri (USA), which boosted rates of complete immunization from 47 percent to 66 percent in a randomized control trial.[6]
- The use of reminder or recall systems to support vaccination; a systematic review of twenty-nine studies from 1997 to 2012 by the US

Department of Health and Human Services Community Preventive Services Task Force found a median increase in vaccination rates with this technique alone of 6 percent, and 11 percent in combination with other techniques.[7]

- UNICEF's counseling cards to support infant feeding; for example, an implementation of the cards in Ghana found qualitative support among parents of children under three years old.[8]

Interventions and Method

Our approach did not treat prior studies as templates to be simply replicated or re-implemented in the context of our population. Instead, we treated all empirically supported approaches as inspiration for locally grounded analyses, selection, and tailoring, before the interventions were finalized and subjected to field testing. Specifically, we employed a process of selecting from and translating our list of evidence-informed ideas to the local context.

First, we employed qualitative interviews and workshops to identify five viable candidates. Then we employed rapid prototyping to iterate on these five candidates. We conducted a hybrid field/lab test of these remaining concepts and selected the two most promising interventions for further iteration and scaling. We then conducted a randomized control trial to assess their impact.

Selecting Viable Candidates for the Local Context

As a first step to translating prior research to the specific setting of this project, we conducted initial qualitative research and mapped out the barriers that women in rural India might face. These included behavioral, informational, and logistic barriers. Although women in rural areas were aware of IFA supplements, our exploratory analysis found persistent gaps in information retention, value perceptions, and adherence that needed to be addressed to ensure they took the pill.

Our qualitative phase employed a series of design workshops with our partner organization and allowed us to validate barriers to IFA use (and medication adherence more broadly) from the literature for our population. It also provided the foundation for adapting these interventions to the specific barriers at work in this context. Table 6.1 shows one of the outputs of that process, in which we combine lessons in the field with potential intervention ideas.[9]

We narrowed down the concepts to five interventions, each designed to promote follow through in the use of IFA pills: (1) counseling cards,

Table 6.1. Analysis of the situation and intervention design

	Determinants		
	Motivation	**Ability**	**Opportunity**
Barriers	Not linked to goals Beliefs – IFA not effective because it is free, government programs usually not effective, might be slow acting	Low procedural knowledge – when to take, how to take Side effects of counseling	Inertia; Procrastination
Intervention Design Principles	Vividness Social comparison Source credibility	Cognitive ease	Reminders Rewards Goal progress
Interventions	Food equivalency Testimonial	Counseling card (visual aid)	Calendar (goal progress, reward) Interactive Voice Response (IVR, reminder)

(2) food equivalency images, (3) IVR reminders, (4) testimonial video, and a (5) daily tracking device – calendar.

Iteration and Initial Testing

We developed prototypes of these five concepts and subjected them to rapid A/B testing to understand which contextual cues mattered the most (e.g., how big should the baby's face be in the calendar, should the doctor on the counseling card be female or male). For example, in our food equivalency intervention we tried out different food items from milk to pomegranate before settling on spinach. Figure 6.1 provides these prototype variations.

The rapid prototyping phase resulted in the final list of five specific interventions for field testing, as shown in Figure 6.2.

Next, we sought to test these five prototypes with women in a semi-controlled environment. Before investing in a massive field trial to test the five interventions, we wanted to narrow these interventions down to the ones we thought would be most effective. We did this through a series of lab experiments that created hypothetical environments to test habit formation. But cultural norms in rural Haryana meant that women couldn't travel to a centralized location for the lab. We had to

Figure 6.1. Four versions of the food equivalency card, from the rapid prototyping stage. Translation in notes[10]

Figure 6.2. Five prototyped interventions, ready for field testing. Translation in notes[11]

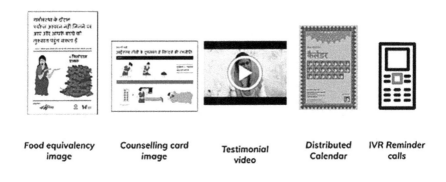

Food equivalency image	Counselling card image	Testimonial video	Distributed Calendar	IVR Reminder calls

take the lab to them. We fitted out a public bus and drove through villages to reach a sample of 1,150 women.

The counseling card and goal tracking device showed the strongest effects and became our final two concepts. Through focus group discussions with frontline health workers after the lab testing, we also validated the two main barriers they addressed (perception of side effects, and lack of habit formation) and gathered additional feedback on the interventions.

Experimental Testing

Given our two refined and polished interventions, we tested them through a field randomized control trial with 1,200 women across two districts in Madhya Pradesh. We randomized the interventions at the

Figure 6.3. Experimental design used to test the final two polished interventions

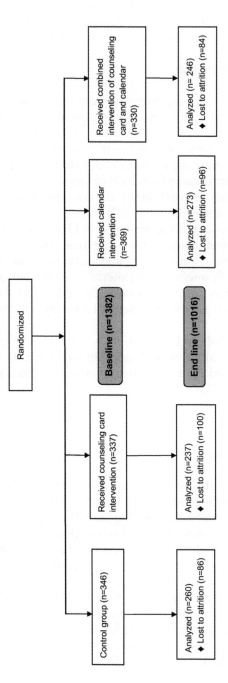

Differences between the end line sample and regression outputs are due to missing data for various outcome and control variables as women might have chosen to refuse to answer.

village level, and we included an observational component at the point of intervention to capture mechanisms and nuances that we might miss out on due to the experimental nature of the study.

Differences and Similarities

As noted above, we treat interventions from the existing literature as a starting point for localized intervention design and validation, and not a template to be blindly followed. As such, our study had quite a few differences from the original academic literature. Similarly, the existing literature simply does not provide the level of detail required to make a complete intervention – this must come from local innovation and development.

For example, prior research offers the concept of food equivalency but does not offer a specific food with a specific design featuring the female decision maker with specific text in Hindi to help guide them. These extensions and adaptations to the local context occurred especially during the rapid prototyping and iteration phase. Similarly, we pretested our specific intervention materials with women on the ground to inform our designs during this phase. This included various versions of the doctor's image for the endorsement message and the baby image for the calendar.

We further adapted our interventions based on the lab study and the quantitative and qualitative feedback gathered from it. The feedback further differentiated the materials to produce the final interventions tested during the RCT.

Results

Phase 1: Lab Findings

In our lab test, we tested the following five interventions: food equivalency image, counseling card image, testimonial video, distributed calendar, and IVR reminder calls (see Figure 6.2).

We found that the presentation of counseling cards demonstrated a positive effect of visual information on recall of side effects and coping strategies (~21 percent treatment vs. ~13 percent control; Figure 6.5, left hand side). However, including a doctor-endorsed graphic to the counseling card had no significant effect on trust. Using images with food equivalency information, we found that the images significantly increased the value perception of IFA pills (~34 percent treatment vs. ~26 percent control). The images also increased the recall rate of information pertaining to dosage of the pills.

Table 6.2. Differences and similarities between existing work and our work

Dimension/ Aspect of Project	Existing Work	Our Work
Translations from Previous Work to Our Work		
Intervention Type	Personalized immunization calendar tested in US to boost immunization: in this intervention, monthly calendars included information matched to the child's current age in months; ongoing tracking of the baby's height and weight; a digital picture of the baby; professional graphics matched to the ethnicity of the baby; a reminder of the baby's next immunization appointment; the name, address, and telephone number of the health center; and monthly birthday greetings for the baby and yearly greetings for parents and siblings.	Borrowing from the idea of having a visual reminder, we implemented a behaviorally informed calendar by incorporating peel-off stickers that revealed a happy baby's face to act as positive reinforcement for each time the mother took the IFA supplement. These were different from the original calendar in that each calendar was not personalized to each baby as we predicted this would be costly in India and we might not be able to get mothers' consent as easily. Instead, we borrowed the idea of a visual reminder and a way to track pill-taking.
	Reminder systems to increase vaccination rates in the US: these interventions focus on sending clients reminders through mail or phone that are less costly to implement. Post our trial, the pandemic spurred a number of vaccination reminders through SMS.	Building off previous research, we had to adapt the platform to our context and tried an IVR based messaging system. We chose this due to the literacy levels and context of our population. Mail is not a common channel of communication in rural India, and personalized phone calls were expensive.
	Counseling cards for infant feeding in Ghana with Ghanaian children. Counseling cards focused on dimensions of responsive feeding and were assessed through focus group discussions to ensure cultural appropriateness and accompanying messages.	We borrowed the idea of visual tools to reinforce key messages by health workers and created locally relevant images to normalize side effects of taking IFA pills. Similar to original work, our counseling cards went through a prototyping process with both health workers and mothers to ensure contextualization and relevance.

(*Continued*)

Table 6.2. (Continued)

Dimension/ Aspect of Project	Existing Work	Our Work
Translations from Lab to Field		
Sample	Our own lab study, which focused on women of childbearing age.	In our field trial, we further tested the interventions with the specific target audience: women who were pregnant or lactating.
Geography	Our original lab study, which was conducted in Haryana.	The new location was in districts in Madhya Pradesh wherein the supply of IFA tablets was not a barrier. This translation helped validate our measures within a geographically different context within India.
Intervention Design	Our lab study design with a "cute baby" photo. Feedback from that lab study highlighted that women associated the "cute baby" with more painful delivery as the baby had a bigger head and bigger cheeks. The woman in our counseling card looked too old to be giving birth and the black stool needed to be placed in context.	We tweaked our lab-based interventions to meet this feedback from the community. Our final counseling card intervention included a younger looking woman and a latrine next to the stool. Our final calendar intervention included a dated calendar that could replace their current calendar, a peel-off sticker and baby faces of different sizes.

Figure 6.4. Further refinements on the interventions based on our lab study

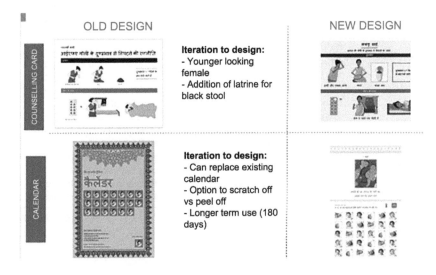

Figure 6.5. Lab results from calendar and counseling card interventions

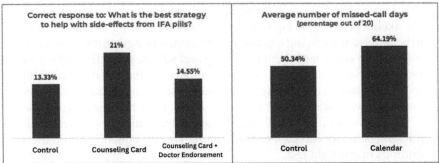

In addition, we found that participants who received a calendar with peel-off stickers were more likely to adhere to a proxy behavior (giving a "missed call" to a number daily)[12] than those who did not receive the calendar (64 percent treatment vs 50 percent control; Figure 6.5, right hand side), thus women could benefit from having an interactive tracking mechanism alongside the pills. Last, we did not find any significant effect of showing a testimonial video from a pregnant woman.

Results from the counseling card and goal tracking device seemed promising. We validated the two main barriers as perception of side effects and lack of habit formation as well as our interventions to target them through focus group discussions with frontline health workers such as ASHA (Accredited Social Health Activist) workers after the lab testing.

Our two headline learnings were that visual information is more memorable (hardly a surprise!) and that daily tracking behavior can increase adherence.

Visual Information Is More Memorable

Even though most women had heard of IFA pills before, participants were more likely to recall the new information about side effects and coping strategies if the information was accompanied by the counseling card. We posited that adding this counseling information along with the card to current health information shared by frontline health workers may be effective at disseminating information on coping strategies and therefore increasing overall adherence to the IFA pill. In relation to this, we also captured that counseling information should be kept brief to reduce the risk of information overload.

Daily Tracking Behavior Can Increase Adherence

Based on our findings, being able to track a particular behavior increased the likelihood of adhering to it. Pregnant and lactating women seemed to benefit from receiving a goal tracking device alongside their dosage of pills to help encourage them to take up and adhere to the IFA pill for the recommended time period. It is also important that the daily tracking tool be interactive (for example a peel-off or scratch calendar) with some positive reward such as an image of a healthy baby to incentivize its use.

We concluded that visual information is more memorable and daily tracking behavior can increase adherence. We subsequently tested these findings in our field test.

Phase 2: Field RCT Findings

To better understand the effect of these interventions in the final leg, the Centre for Social and Behavior Change (CSBC), Busara, and Clinton Access for Health Initiative (CHAI) came together to pilot the counseling card and goal tracking interventions in a randomized controlled experiment field setting with pregnant women across two districts in Madhya Pradesh. Frontline health workers, in this case "Anganwadi workers," were the main channel of delivery for these interventions. We tested:

- Control: Received regular interactions and communication
- Treatment 1: Counseling card only
- Treatment 2: Goal tracking device (calendar) only
- Treatment 3: Counseling card and goal tracking device

We looked at outcomes such as self-reported adherence, biomedical markers of anemia levels, and observation of the pill packets (how empty were they?) and the calendar (how many stickers had been peeled off?). We also looked at trust and value perceptions of the pills, changes in knowledge of side effects, and recall of pill-related benefits and information.

Both the Counseling Card and the Calendar Improved
Self-Reported Adherence

In terms of adherence, participants who received either or both treatments provided self-report data indicating that they kept to the shared guidelines as compared to the control group. Self-report

Figure 6.6. Combined graph showcasing (i) self-report measure of whether women were taking IFA supplements at the time of the survey, (ii) proportion of women who reported the correct response for when they should stop taking IFA supplements and (iii) proportion of women who report not taking IFA supplements due to side effects

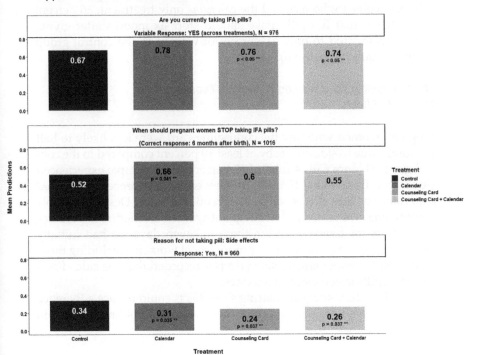

responses are highly susceptible to social desirability bias (telling the interviewer what they think they want to hear), but the same issue would be expected to occur with the control group. In our case, self-report responses were easier to collect. We also used a list randomization method to collect data on adherence, hoping that would be more "accurate." Findings from our list randomization measure did not show any significant effect of the treatments on adherence. We found that both enumerator hiccups in understanding the measure and women's lack of clarity on how to answer made this a noisy measure. We were also likely not well-powered to detect effects on the list measure.

The Calendar Was Most Effective at Reminding Women
When Their Dosage Was Complete

On an intervention level, the goal tracking device (the calendar) was the most effective at helping women remember when to stop taking IFA pills. Of women who received the calendar only treatment, 66 percent remembered that IFA pill intake should stop six months after giving birth as compared to only 51 percent of women in the control group doing the same (Figure 6.6).

The Counseling Card Worked to Reduce Drop-Offs
from Side Effects

Pregnant women who saw the counseling card were less likely to halt pill intake due to side effects by at least 10 percent compared to the control group (Figure 6.6). A total of 37 percent of the sample experienced side effects from taking IFA pills; there were no differences in reported experience of side effects across intervention groups. Despite multiple prototyping, we realized that pregnant women seemed to experience side effects for longer than the three to seven days we had initially thought. Across all intervention groups, most women – including those who reported experiencing side effects – recorded that the side effects from IFA pills lasted eight to ten days.

Some literature suggests sharing side effects could reduce adherence due to perceived negative effects. However, we did not find this within our sample.

Maybe We Had Overloaded the Combined
Treatment Group with Information

Consistently, the group that received the counseling card and calendar did not outperform the group that received either only the counseling card or only the calendar.

Our Interventions Didn't Address Everything,
Can Any Intervention?

We still found gaps in knowledge and perceptions around anemia, which ultimately affect uptake of, and adherence to, IFA pills. Despite the high prevalence of anemia among pregnant women, most women are not aware of its symptoms. Although 56.4 percent of the total sample had previously been diagnosed with anemia, most of the women incorrectly cited the symptoms of anemia, suggesting a lack of knowledge on its negative effects. Further, the pregnant women perceived anemia to be more dangerous to their unborn baby than to themselves, suggesting an urgent need for awareness campaigns on the condition.

Our Interventions Still Need Further Tweaking
before Scaling Up

As we write this chapter, our partner CSBC is in talks with the Behavioral Insights Unit of India at NITI Aayog (the National Institution for Transforming India) to scale up the successful interventions across the Government's Aspirational District program. Quantitatively, we learned that the duration of side effects on our counseling card might be inaccurate. Observational research at the point of intervention delivery, and further qualitative research with the frontline health workers after the endline, gave us rich data to further improve our interventions.

Observational data suggested that the frontline health worker didn't show the counseling card to the pregnant woman about a quarter of the time but instead used it for themselves to explain the side effects. Even though we had provided a detailed intervention script (available in the notes), in almost half the cases, the health workers delivered the message around how to use the calendar or about side effects in their own words. This seemed more natural and engaging than the ones who narrated our script verbatim. For example, health workers elaborated on taking vitamin C in the form of citrus fruits as a coping strategy to overcome the side effects of IFA. Although these are some factors researchers would like to maintain strict control over, it's not always possible in the real world, and iterations and adaptations need to be made. A certain level of messiness should be expected in field work, even after efforts to eliminate it.

Reconciliation

In our study, we found that both final interventions – a planning calendar and a counseling card – show an impact. At a high level, these results are consistent with prior research that has offered these techniques. However, when one analyzes the details of the interventions and the supposedly irrelevant factors (SIFs) that differ between them, we fear that a point-by-point comparison would provide little value, or, worse, may actually be misleading.

In our study, there could be a range of different SIFs. We conducted our field trial over summer, and summers in Madhya Pradesh are brutal.

We don't have data to ascertain whether the heat in the health centers hindered women's attention to the counseling card. Similarly, women might not travel to the health centers by themselves. As a result, their relatives accompanying them could also overhear the counseling intervention. It's impossible for us to know whether there is a peer effect. We assume pregnant women are a category and don't measure all the intersections of religion, beliefs, and so on. Thus, we would not know enough on how these beliefs might affect their interactions with health-care workers. One can make a guess as to which of these "supposedly irrelevant" factors, and countless more, are actually "irrelevant." However, it would be just that: a guess. Given limited budget, resources, and participant attention spans, it's not feasible to measure and assess all possible SIFs.

The primary challenge that one faces in selecting among potential published interventions is that all of them "could" work: otherwise, they would not have been published.[13] Field studies always have numerous differences from prior published work – especially those done in a laboratory or controlled environment. Some of these differences are ones that a thoughtful researcher could guess will change the outcome of the study (usually when the underlying mechanism should not be relevant in the new context). More often, however, the practitioner is faced with myriad small differences and no guide to determine which are SIFs that increase impact, which are SIFs that decrease impact, and which are truly irrelevant factors. Alternatively, there simply is not enough information about the detailed design of prior studies to identify and assess these myriad differences if only because the authors of those papers would struggle to identify which SIFs are in fact irrelevant, and which are vital to mention.

These limitations certainly apply to our studies – we started with roughly fifty concepts directly from the literature and from literature-informed brainstorming. We extended these ideas by instantiating them in specific prototypes, adding countless SIFs on top of the original hypothesized mechanism, and then injected numerous additional changes to prototypes through feedback from the people we sought to help. The most honest assessment of the specific SIFs that drove differences in our outcomes versus existing literature is that we simply do not know – and that it is probably impossible to know.

From our experience in this study and more generally, we believe it is wise to be cautious about focusing too strongly on a specific set of SIFs in a particular field application. Instead, it is reasonable to assume that the impact of any given intervention, in the face of numerous and only partially understood SIFs, has a range of possible outcomes (a distribution). Each field application is a potentially random draw from that range, and in one application variation A may appear stronger, and in another variation B; those results could reflect nothing more than random chance in drawing from their underlying range of potential impacts. The literature – both of academic studies and field studies – provides a set of empirically tested tools that can "work" (sampling from their impact distributions often results in measurable and positive outcomes) but does not provide the level of clarity and insight that we would wish as researchers into the structure and causes of that impact distribution.

Discussion and Prescriptive Advice

In this study, our attempt at translating previous research on medication adherence to boost IFA update in India was successful. Specifically, we found:

- Both our treatments (calendar and counseling card) increased self-reported measures of adherence.
- The calendar was most effective at reminding women when to stop taking IFA pills.
- Pregnant women who saw the counseling card were less likely to halt pill intake due to side effects.

Second, while we caution against seeking undue generalizations from the findings – given the numerous and difficult to assess SIFs at play – we believe strongly in the applicability and value of the process. In this study, we demonstrated an effective way to translate academic lab work into the field through a structured process. That process consists of five components:

1. Gather the existing academic or lab work on known interventions and behavioral obstacles.
2. Use iterative, qualitative field work to target those materials to the audience – to place it in their language, their context.
3. Use a hybrid of lab and field testing to winnow down and adapt the set of interventions to those that appear to be most effective.
4. Scale up the remaining set of interventions for the full project.
5. As the full project is rolled out, continue to measure and test.

Overall, this approach is one of continued learning in the face of context-dependence. Even when conducting the full project, one employs both a rigorous impact assessment and integrates qualitative ethnographic work. Randomized control trials for impact assessment are now a standard, though not universal, practice. Open-ended, embedded observation of both the "final study" and the steps leading up to it are not. The combination of rapid quantitative testing and qualitative work helps the team both tune impact for future rounds and understand the broader implications of its work (positive and negative) beyond the targeted behavior.

In order to move from the realm of possible interventions to successful ones, we suggest that other researchers invest in their iterative feedback gathering process. Specifically, the process has three departures from a standard field study. First, we advocate for creating lower-cost ways to winnow down and target those suggestions to identify which are most valuable for a specific context and population. Second, add observational or interactive, qualitative approaches throughout the testing so you can answer the "why" along with establishing what does and doesn't work. And finally, look for the implications of your intervention above and beyond the target behavior. Field work involves changing the lives of real people, and there will be effects beyond what are expected – for good and for ill.

NOTES

1 See, for example: Bahri, C. (2017, November 21). *50% Indian women are anaemic: Why it persists after 70 yrs of freedom.* Business Standard. https://www.business-standard.com/article/current-affairs/50-indian-women-are-anaemic-why-it-persists-after-70-yrs-of-freedom-117112100219_1.html.

2 See: Anemia Mukt Bharat. (n.d.). *View Your Data (Cum. Monthly).* https://anemiamuktbharat.info/view-your-data-monthly/ (Page no longer available); Halli, S.S., & Biradar, R.A. (2020). Is distribution a problem in iron-folic acid consumption in India? An exploration of district level household survey. *The Open Family Studies Journal, 12*(1). 34–9. https://www.semanticscholar.org/paper/Is-Distribution-a-Problem-in-Iron-Folic-Acid-in-An-Halli-Biradar/ef86f9a6341d82d2dbdacbf31648c06c689cd99b; and Varghese, J.S., Swaminathan, S., Kurpad, A.V., & Thomas, T. (2019). Demand and supply factors of iron-folic acid supplementation and its association with anaemia in North Indian pregnant women. *PLoS ONE, 14*(1), e0210634. https://doi.org/10.1371/journal.pone.0210634.

3 Indian Institute for Population Sciences (IIPS) & MoHFW. (2017). *National family health survey* (NFHS-4). https://rchiips.org/nfhs/NFHS-4Report.shtml.

4 Even one hundred days is itself an insufficient threshold (since they should be taken both during pregnancy and for six months afterwards).

5 See Marcum, Z.A., Hanlon, J.T., & Murray, M.D. (2017). Improving medication adherence and health outcomes in older adults: An evidence-based review of randomized controlled trials. *Drugs & Aging, 34*(3), 191–201. https://doi.org/10.1007/s40266-016-0433-7; Nieuwlaat, R., Wilczynski, N., Navarro, T., Hobson, N., Jeffery, R., Keepanasseril, A., Agoritsas, T., Mistry, N., Iorio, A., Jack, S., Sivaramalingam, B., Iserman, E., Mustafa, R.A., Jedraszewski, D., Cotoi, C., & Haynes, R.B. (2014). Interventions for enhancing medication adherence. *Cochrane Database of Systematic Reviews, 11.* https://doi.org/10.1002/14651858.CD000011.pub4; Ogedegbe, G., & Schoenthaler, A. (2006). A systematic review of the effects of home blood pressure monitoring on medication adherence. *The Journal of Clinical Hypertension, 8*(3), 174–80. https://doi.org/10.1111/j.1524 -6175.2006.04872.x; and Yap, A.F., Thirumoorthy, T., & Kwan, Y.H. (2016). Systematic review of the barriers affecting medication adherence in older adults. *Geriatrics & Gerontology International, 16*(10), 1093–101. https:// doi.org/10.1111/ggi.12616.

6 Kreuter, M.W., Caburnay, C.A., Chen, J.J., & Donlin, M.J. (2004). Effectiveness of individually tailored calendars in promoting childhood immunization in urban public health centers. *American Journal of Public Health, 94*(1), 122–7. https://doi.org/10.2105/ajph.94.1.122.

7 Community Preventive Services Task Force. (2015, July 15). *Vaccination programs: Client reminder and recall systems.* The Guide to Community Preventive Services (The Community Guide). https://www .thecommunityguide.org/findings/vaccination-programs-client -reminder-and-recall-systems.

8 See https://www.unicef.org/media/108406/file/Counselling%20 Cards.pdf for examples of the cards; for an example of a study using them in the field, see: Hromi-Fiedler, A.J., Carroll, G.J., Tice, M.R., Sandow, A., Aryeetey, R., & Pérez-Escamilla, R. (2020). Development and testing of responsive feeding counseling cards to strengthen the UNICEF infant and young child feeding counseling package. *Current Developments in Nutrition, 4*(9), nzaa117. https://doi.org/10.1093 /cdn/nzaa117.

9 The figure builds on the COM-B model, among others. For more information see Michie, S., Stralen, M.M. van, & West, R. (2011). The behaviour change wheel: A new method for characterising and designing behaviour change interventions. *Implementation Science, 6,* 42. https:// doi.org/10.1186/1748-5908-6-42.

10 **Image 1: Headline: You and your baby may be harmed if you do not get enough iron during pregnancy.**

- Byline: How much food do you have to consume to get the same iron content as in one iron and folic acid supplement?
- Above the image: 4 Kilograms of Spinach
- Image 2: Headline: You and your baby may be harmed if you do not get enough iron during pregnancy.
- Byline: How much food do you have to consume to get the same iron content as in one iron and folic acid supplement?
- Above the image: 100 liters milk.
- Image 3: Headline: You and your baby may be harmed if you do not get enough iron during pregnancy.
- Byline: How much food do you have to consume to get the same iron content as in one iron and folic acid supplement?
- Above the image: 3 Kilograms of chickpeas.
- Image 4: Headline: You and your baby may be harmed if you do not get enough iron during pregnancy.
- Byline: How much food do you have to consume to get the same iron content as in one iron and folic acid supplement?
- Above the image: 33 Kilograms pomegranate

11 **Image 2: Strategy to deal with the side effects of IFA (Iron and Folic Acid) tablets.**

- Side Effects (written in black bold highlighted line)
- Upper left hand: Retching (feeling of having vomiting) and dizziness
- Upper middle: Constipation
- Upper middle: Black defecation/black human fecal matter
- Upper right: Side effects usually go away after 3–7 days
- Red bold highlighted line: Doctor's suggestion
- Take one tablet before going to bed

Intervention Scripts:

Script for Counseling Card Intervention

All respondents who participated in this intervention listened to the same script:

"From the fourth month of pregnancy till a child is 6 months old, women must take the iron pill everyday day after having a healthy nutritious dinner. Even if they are not anemic, they should take the iron pill once a day during pregnancy and 6 months after birth together along with Vitamin C rich foods which increases the absorption of iron. If they do this, it will benefit both mother and child. The woman will grow stronger and solid and the child will be healthy. It will also help a pregnant woman have a smooth delivery."

"At the beginning of a course of IFA tablets, a woman might experience some side effects for a few days. You might feel nauseous and dizzy, or constipated, or start to see a black stool when you go to the toilet. Do not worry too much about these effects, as they can be reduced and usually go away after a short time. The best way to reduce these effects is simply to take the IFA tablet soon before you go to sleep at night. This way, you allow your body to rest and you won't feel the side effects as much. You should stop feeling the side effects after 3–7 days."

Script for Calendar Intervention

All respondents who participated in this intervention listened to the same script:

"From the fourth month of pregnancy till a child is 6 months old, women must take the iron pill everyday day after having a healthy nutritious dinner. Even if they are not anemic, they should take the iron pill once a day during pregnancy and 6 months after birth together along with Vitamin C rich foods which increases the absorption of iron. If they do this, it will benefit both mother and child. The woman will grow stronger and solid and the child will be healthy. It will also help a pregnant woman have a smooth delivery."

"We would like you to share with you a daily pill tracking tool. The goal of sharing this will be to keep track of your day-to-day pill usage starting from today. This will act as a reminder to remind you to take your pills every day for the next 6 months. You should place this calendar on your wall or somewhere you can see and access every day. You should hang this tracking pill at a place that will remind you to take one pill at night before you sleep. This should also be in a place where children cannot reach it to avoid them from tearing or playing with it. This calendar is to help remind you to take your pill. Every time you take a pill you should scratch of one box from the top left side, and as the days progress, move towards the right corner. Once the row ends, start again from the left side as you move to the right side."

"[Scratch the demo scratch box placed at the top of the calendar on the first page – help them do so on their own.]"

12 A missed call is a telephone call that is intentionally disconnected before it is answered. However, the recipient often sees the number that was attempting to call them. This practice is common in the Global South as a means of communicating a pre-agreed message without incurring any costs (which only kick in if the call is completed).

13 While null findings are increasingly seeing the light of day, these null findings are often on existing techniques that prior published work showed to be effective – and not on the broad range of completely novel ideas that had no prior evidence of support.

CHAPTER SEVEN

Translating Research on Goal Setting to Enhance the Wellness of UK Social Workers

Shibeal O' Flaherty, Michael T. Sanders, and Ashley Whillans

AT A GLANCE

- **Our Goal:** To improve well-being and reduce sickness absence and turnover among child protection social workers in the UK.
- **The Intervention:** A goal-setting task to support time-poor social workers over several weeks, following an approach that had been effective with civil servants previously.
- **The Results:** The intervention did not have an effect on well-being, and compliance with the intervention was very low.
- **Lesson Learned:** Social workers are in a "time poverty trap," having insufficient time to take actions that would save them time later.

Motivation and Objective

When What Works for Children's Social Care was established in 2019, its purpose was to support policymaking and practice by identifying gaps in the existing evidence base and filling them by conducting original empirical research. The children's social care workforce in England has consistently high rates of turnover and sickness absence rates – with a turnover rate of 16 percent (5,150 leavers) in the year ending September 30, 2018.[1] This rate of leavers in the workforce was over 50 percent higher than in other public-sector workforces such as teaching as of

2018, where the turnover rate was 10.3 percent.[2] Sickness absence rates for staff employed in human health and social work was one of five industries that was statistically significantly higher than the rate for all industries in the UK.[3] Beyond descriptive research detailing the extent of the problem, fairly little research had been done that addressed this area. It was because of this confluence of practice needs and a shortfall in research that workforce well-being was one of the center's first priorities.

We launched the Happier, Healthier Professionals research program[4] in January 2019 to design interventions to promote social worker well-being, motivation, and retention, and to test them using randomized trial methodology. The program was ambitious for a number of reasons. First, the use of behavioral science to increase public-sector employee well-being has been underexamined in the literature, and there is a lack of research demonstrating the causal impact of workplace well-being interventions.[5] Second, we set out to rigorously test and evaluate our interventions in collaboration with UK Local Authorities (LAs), many of whom had not previously engaged in this type of research. Third, to build early success for the center and to show that our work was having an impact – particularly in its early days – we needed to do everything within our power to promote the success of each of our interventions, with a small team of researchers, little funding, and only a year to prove ourselves to our funders and the wider sector. Thus, it was important that we were able to show that our interventions could meaningfully impact social workers' well-being: we needed to show that they could be cost-effective and had the potential to improve organizational outcomes – including turnover and sickness absence rates.

The research unfolded in several phases (see Figure 7.1). During the Consultation and Co-Design phase, we conducted site visits, focus groups, and interviews with social workers and managers to build relationships with future research sites and to understand the issues affecting them. We also held internal brainstorming meetings to create a long list of potential interventions, carefully considering which ones might be most feasible and applicable based on the key issues identified. Finally, we had a short list of intervention ideas which were decided upon with the policy priorities of LAs in mind (e.g., addressing social workers' feelings of time pressure and a lack of feeling recognized or valued), and we launched an official countrywide call for LAs to partner with us on the interventions.[6] We then

Figure 7.1. Our approach

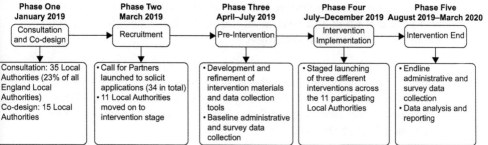

built a "pitch deck" which we used to consult LA senior leaders on our ideas, outlining why and how we thought they might work – for example, decreasing burnout by alleviating administrative burden. It was also vitally important to explain the process of randomization, and what this might look like in practice. This was to create buy-in with each of our potential partners for our methodology as well as our interventions – in a context where this kind of research was novel. As we gathered more feedback through consultation, we developed a short list of ideas, and detailed two-page project pitches for each, which could be disseminated regularly to potential field partners (i.e., LA senior leaders). This provided us with content for our outreach to potential field partners – something to guide our discussions and let them know what would be involved if they took part in the research.

Findings from Co-Design

During the consultation phase we spoke to social workers on the ground, as well as their managers and senior leaders at thirty-five LAs. Despite the many different contextual factors across these LAs, such as their size (with some employing less than one hundred social workers, and others over a thousand) and location (some in large cities in London, and others in remote and rural areas), the same themes emerged throughout our discussions with them. These themes are summarized below:

Time Pressure, Overtime Worked, and Low Work-Life Balance

Social workers reported having higher than average caseloads; working outside of work hours (9 a.m. to 5:30 p.m.) thus disrupting their leisure and personal time; and having an unpredictable schedule (e.g., emergency visits or court proceedings).

> [I am] in and out of the office, other days might be spent in office – it's varied. [There is a sense of] not knowing how your day is going to go. When there is an emergency to go and see a family – you don't know what time you're going to be finished.
> – Focus group member, Lambeth Council

Consistent with other research on the burdens that social workers face, we found that social workers often experienced a great deal of time pressure and challenges with work-life balance.[7]

Administrative Burden

In line with prior research,[8] social workers also reported a high level of administrative burden, dealing with a high volume of paperwork and reporting requirements that was seen as repetitive, cumbersome, and time-consuming.[9] This also meant less time for direct work for the people they serve – children, young people, and their families.

In the past, social workers were supported by administrative staff who would support administrative tasks – including reports which are due forty-eight hours after each visit with a child.[10] However, rising demand for services coinciding with substantial reductions in spending due to austerity measures introduced in the UK starting in 2010 had led to reduced administrative support for social workers.[11] This meant that the burden was now with social workers for the majority of their administrative tasks, on top of their already busy workload of direct, in-person contact with children and families. Additionally, new regulations,[12] passed by the UK government in 2014, meant that social workers had only twenty-six weeks (as opposed to forty-nine weeks) to ensure successful completion of their cases in care proceedings, resulting in them having to accomplish a lot more within a shorter duration.

Lack of Recognition and Feeling Valued

Our consultations revealed that social workers reported rarely receiving positive feedback for their work (either from their beneficiaries or from management). When we asked senior leaders about any existing positive feedback mechanisms in their departments, this varied across the LAs – some made an effort to provide positive feedback (e.g., through large staff meetings). While other senior leaders said that there was an option on their website to provide feedback, it was more usual for service users to use this to issue a complaint rather than a compliment. This lack of positive feedback for social workers seemed to also be compounded by social workers often being portrayed negatively in the media,[13] with the perception that they would be to blame when anything happened with one of their cases.[14]

Building on these focus groups and prior research, our long list of interventions included ideas focused on solving the three concerns that were frequently mentioned: time stress, difficulties tackling administrative burdens, and feeling a lack of appreciation for their work.

To ensure that each of our intervention ideas could be taken forward by LAs if they were found to be effective, we developed a list of criteria that aided our decision-making process of which interventions should make the final shortlist – namely that each intervention should be:

1) **Low-cost,** so that LA leaders could implement the intervention with little funding or staff time,
2) **Light-touch,** requiring little resource or time on the part of LAs to implement, and
3) **Scalable,** so that if our intervention was found to be effective, it could be implemented across different organizational contexts with varying contextual factors. This meant interventions needed to be cheap to deploy (less than £50 per staff member), not require new or specialized equipment, and not require people to all be in the same place (which would work in urban local authorities, for example in London, but not in a rural area like Cornwall).

The Interventions

In the sections that follow, we will describe the two primary experiments that we implemented: goal setting and letters of appreciation.

Addressing Time Scarcity: An Adaptation of a Goal-Setting Intervention

Our first intervention was focused on helping social workers manage their time and target social workers' feelings of time scarcity, "a feeling of having too much to do and not enough time to do it."[15]

The intervention we focused on to increase efficiency and reduce time stress was goal setting. Why did we choose goal setting? There is an established literature of overcoming intention-action gaps – that is, when a person's intention to do something is not followed up with action – through the use of various forms of planning and goal setting.[16] The act of explicit planning – also known as implementation intentions – involves encouraging people to write how and when they will accomplish their goals, and it can increase follow-through across a range of behaviors, including voting,[17] and in personal planning and goal-pursuit.[18] One of the key issues voiced by social workers was fitting in all of their important tasks – visits to children and families and preparing legal documents – alongside the urgent issue of the day. As such, we thought that goal setting – which in previous studies had been found to aid task completion – would be an ideal intervention to test with social workers.

Our intervention choice was also inspired by a prior successful goal-setting experiment conducted with UK civil service workers.[19] This intervention took the form of a randomized controlled trial, allocating half of 307 UK civil servants to an intervention group, and the other half to a control group. The intervention involved six online modules that were completed over a five-week period, with each module encouraging individuals to engage in various goal-setting strategies, e.g., asking participants to set personal goals, imagining what it would be like to achieve them, and creating a written plan of how to do so. Treated participants reported significantly higher positive affect and flourishing compared to those in the control group at three- and six-month follow-up points after the intervention ended.

The authors shared their intervention materials, and we adapted them for the social work context, using tailored language (i.e., demonstrating them to social workers on our team), and creating an online platform for social workers to access the materials more easily.[20] Another adaptation we incorporated was to allocate the intervention randomly at the team-level, since social workers work closely within their team, and spillover effects to individuals within teams would be likely. Thus, we delivered the intervention to teams (which on average had six members) via team managers.

Table 7.1. Comparison of goal-setting intervention and original study

Study Element	Current Study	Original Study (Oliver & MacLeod, 2018)
Experimental design	• Team-level RCT • Intention-to-treat design	• Individual-level RCT (waitlist control design) • Intention-to-treat design
Setting	Delivered online	Delivered online
Participants	UK children's social workers	UK civil service workers
Sample size	$N = 871$	$N = 307$
Measures	• Sickness absence • Turnover • Subjective well-being • Time pressure • Workplace self-efficacy	• Positive and negative affect scale • Life satisfaction scale • Flourishing scale • Adherence and skills survey
Procedures	• Staff recruited via email • Baseline (T1) and endline (T2/2-weeks after intervention end) survey data collection, with raffle incentives • Baseline and endline administrative data collection	• Staff recruited via email • Baseline (T1), interim (T2/ directly after intervention end) and endline (three-month follow-up) survey data collection, with raffle incentives
Implementation details	• Six modules (thirty mins each) over six-week period; small tweaks applied to original study materials from Oliver and MacLeod (2018) to be suitable for the social work context • Treated participants asked to organize weekly time block agreed with manager where they would complete the modules	• Six modules (thirty mins each) over five-week period • Treated participants received email reminder sent two weeks after launch to encourage completion of modules; offered twenty-min call with researcher to discuss progress

The Findings: A Failure to Replicate

Across the five LAs who participated, 130 teams (containing 934 social workers) were randomized, 66 to control and 64 to treatment. We stratified randomization on median team sickness absence rates. Balance checks suggested no difference between the treatment and control groups on participants' seniority ($p = 0.30$), or gender ($p = 0.21$) at the outset of the trial.

Figure 7.2. Goal-setting intervention: Study procedure

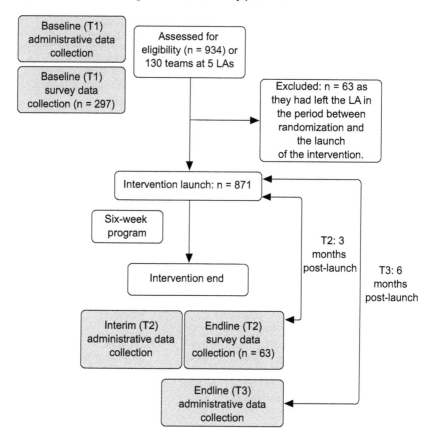

Data on participants' turnover and attendance was collected through LA administrative records. Administrative data was returned by all five LAs and included 871 participants in the trial out of 934 (93.3 percent). A small number of participants (6.7 percent) were not included due to leaving the LA between randomization and the beginning of the trial. Our primary outcomes of participants' attendance were calculated by subtracting their number of absences (including if they left their job) from the total number of days they could have been present.

Per our preregistered protocol,[21] analyses were conducted using linear regression, controlling for participants' gender, job role, tenure in post, and LA, with standard errors clustered at the level of randomization (the team). This regression analysis yielded a null result for impacts on participant attendance, with a negative coefficient of 0.29 days ($p = 0.64$), which was not sensitive to specification. The lack of significance, and small effect sizes, are present in all LAs.

Data on employees' well-being, time pressure, and self-efficacy were collected through surveys administered to social workers at baseline (one month prior to intervention launch) and at endline (six months following intervention launch). 297 participants responded to the baseline survey, while only 63 participants responded to the endline survey, in large part due to disruption to the trial as a result of the COVID-19 pandemic. Of these, only 24 had also completed the baseline survey. For the remaining 39, null imputation was used to preserve their data and the predictive power of the baseline data, as the assumptions for multiple imputations were unlikely to be valid in a sample this small. This substantively impacts the statistical power available for this analysis. Specifically, we had 80 percent power to detect a Cohen's d of approximately 0.35 after controlling for baseline covariates.

We found no statistically significant impact of the intervention on any of these survey outcomes, and the directionality of effects is mixed, relative both to each other and to their hypothesized relationships, consistent with these effects being driven largely by noise.

What Did We Learn?

We attempted to replicate the use of an intervention that was previously successful in the UK civil service in a frontline public service setting.[22] Although our experiment was drawn short as a consequence of the COVID-19 outbreak, we are still able to report results from some surveys (approximately 27.8 percent) and administrative data for the whole sample. While our experiment was a prima facie failure to replicate, we argue that this does not constitute a real failure, or a challenge to the theoretical underpinnings of the original study. Instead, we assert that it is important to share results of a study, even when they are inconclusive, in order to avoid the "file drawer problem."[23] This study demonstrates an important cautionary tale about implementing interventions in a frontline setting, especially one in which workers are responding to tasks that are difficult to forecast.

While workplace interventions can improve subjective well-being,[24] implementation failure of such interventions is common, for example due to contextual factors such as workload and time constraints.[25] Perhaps the most notable finding from this study was the level of uptake, which was far lower than we had anticipated: only 20 percent of individuals who were assigned to the intervention logged in at least once, and just ten participants out of a possible 712 assigned to the treatment group (1.4 percent) completed the full program. The manipulation check in our endline survey indicated an implementation failure, with approximately two-thirds of participants who were allocated to the treatment group reporting that they either had not received the intervention invitation or could not recall receiving it. Thus, there may have been issues with delivery on the LAs' ends – for example, managers in the treatment group may not have sent the email to their team members program despite being instructed to do so, or social workers simply may not have read or noticed the email. Additionally, four participants in the control group reported receiving the intervention invitation, suggesting some accidental spillover – for instance, managers and social workers allocated to the treatment group may have inadvertently forwarded the email invitation to their colleagues in the control group, despite being instructed not to do so.

It is important to highlight the specific context of social work – a profession that is laden with time pressure, tight reporting deadlines, and a chaotic schedule – could have adversely affected the uptake of the intervention. Social workers were already severely time-constrained and susceptible to being in a "time poverty trap," in which they did not have sufficient resources to engage in interventions that would ultimately save them time.[26] Perceptions of time pressure can negatively impact goal-oriented behaviors and reduce the motivation to engage in goal-setting behaviors.[27]

Making Social Workers Feel Recognized: The Value of Nonmonetary, Symbolic Awards

Symbolic awards – or nonpecuniary workplace incentives such as certificates, awards, or notes of gratitude – can motivate employees and enhance their well-being. For this study we drew inspiration mainly from a series of studies conducted by economist Jana Gallus: for example, one field experiment was conducted with new contributors on the online encyclopedia Wikipedia, whose contributions were critical to maintaining the accuracy of articles.[28] Contributors who were randomized to receive a note of gratitude on the platform showed higher rates of productivity and were retained at a higher rate compared to those who did not receive one, despite the award having no financial value. We also drew on insights from research conducted by Adam Grant showing how symbolic awards – messages and stories indicating how the employees' work has had a positive impact on others – could increase employees' perceived social impact (i.e., feeling that their work has an impact) and perceived social worth (i.e., sense of feeling valued and recognized), as well as their intrinsic motivation.[29]

We designed "Symbolic Awards: Letters of Gratitude" as an intervention specifically for the children's social workers context.[30] The first adaptation we made was that our "messenger" in this case was a senior leader in the LA,[31] based on our findings that social workers did not feel valued or recognized for their work. Second, we had physical letters sent to social workers' home addresses, based on feedback from LA senior leaders who thought that a tangible letter would be better received by social workers. By sending personalized letters to home addresses (rather than other alternatives we considered such as emails or notes placed on social workers' desks), we predicted that this would reduce the likelihood of spillover – social workers in the control group inadvertently seeing the letters and being negatively impacted as a result.

One ethical concern we considered during the design of the intervention was that social workers who may not have been performing adequately in their work would receive the letter, and thus would receive an inaccurate signal of their performance, preventing improvement. To address this, we asked participating LA sites to exclude any participants already involved in performance management. Another concern was that social workers in the control group would learn about the intervention from others (i.e., spillover effects as mentioned above), and this would have a negative impact on their well-being, having not received a letter themselves. To tackle this risk, we employed a waitlist control design with a short amount of time (approximately one month) between delivery of the letters to participants in the treatment and control groups to ensure that all social workers received the potential positive benefits of the intervention and to reduce the likelihood that they would discuss the letters with one another in the office. This was a trade-off in design that allowed us to address the ethical concern while limiting our ability to measure outcomes longer-term.

The Findings: A Small Win

Our primary outcome measure in this study was social workers' subjective well-being, based on the rationale that subjective well-being is the outcome variable where we expected to see the largest increase from baseline scores as a result of our intervention. We also tested a number of secondary outcomes, including attendance, motivation, belonging, and perceived social worth. We collected survey and administrative data twice; once at pre-intervention, approximately one month prior to the launch of the intervention, and again one week after the intervention was implemented (i.e., after the letters were expected to have arrived at social workers' home addresses).

For one of our secondary outcomes, perceived social worth, there was a statistically significant increase in perceived social worth for participants in the intervention group compared to the control group: a 1.7 percent increase in perceived social worth for participants who received the treatment. We also found directionally positive, though nonstatistically significant results for our other preregistered outcomes.

What Did We Learn?

As we relied on manager feedback to complete the design of the letters for each social worker, we experienced significant delays in the study implementation for each of the sites. This reliance on our LA points of contact – to gather individual feedback from all managers, and then to collate this in a spreadsheet, meant that not all participants at the LA who were assigned to the intervention group were provided with feedback and thus did not receive the intervention. These individuals were included in the analysis as this was an intention-to-treat design which may have attenuated the treatment effect, but we wanted to replicate conditions as they would occur if LAs were to implement the intervention themselves, outside of the evaluation.

We observed significant attrition from baseline to endline, and despite an original sample of 345 participants, only 66 responded to the endline survey. This substantially impacted the robustness of our findings. Several of our outcome measures showed directional changes, though these fell below the conventional thresholds for statistical significance, possibly as a result of collecting less outcome data than we had planned due to the survey response rates, as well as the impact of the COVID-19 pandemic forcing two participating LAs to withdraw prior to launching.

Discussion and Prescriptive Advice

Our efforts at horizontally scaling a previously successful intervention that involved delivering a goal-setting program to public-sector workers to reduce time pressure and increase self-efficacy ended in failure, and we found no effect of our intervention on any of our outcomes. Yet there was much to learn.

Most of the LAs we worked with had not engaged in experimental research prior to being involved in the program. Some learnings we have taken forward in our work to develop a smooth relationship with research partners included:

Senior-level buy-in: Having a senior-level individual who is responsible for decision-making in the organization, is excited about the research, and allocates the necessary resources to ensure smooth delivery of the intervention is vital.

Importance of creating buy-in with field partners: Future research could do more work to build a higher rate of buy-in early on with organizational partners – for example, through in-person presentations on the research design with senior leaders as well as those responsible for coordinating with researchers on the project. While our team involved organizational partners and key stakeholders early on in the process of research design, it may be that some organizational partners have less capacity as well as knowledge in terms of being involved in behavioral interventions – and indeed, from the team's collective experience, it is often an organization's first time engaging in such research. This may have been a factor in many of the challenges we faced throughout the trials such as LA dropout prior to starting trials, and low response rates observed to our surveys. The issue of having field partners who were new to this kind of research was also compounded by the impacts of the COVID-19 pandemic, which resulted in a lack of endline data collection as well as halting of the trials completely at several sites.

Future research could aim to provide some initial training on the basics of conducting research to field partners early on in the process in order to address their needs and to promote more smooth progress from beginning to end. To support this, there is an argument for working with fewer research partners more intensively to produce better results.

Day-to-day contact: Allocating someone at the field site who is responsible for "on-the-ground" work necessary for the delivery of the intervention and its evaluation, for example, collecting administrative data, sending surveys, and preparing intervention materials would be helpful. It is important that this role is not just "assigned" to an individual by senior leaders, but rather it is someone who has an active interest in the research and a ground understanding of what you are trying to achieve with a particular intervention. The point of contact's role was key to ensuring that we were able to collect outcome data and that we were sufficiently powered to detect an effect if one existed. If they were not sufficiently motivated, or there were other issues (e.g., our point of contact was unexpectedly off work for a period of time), we would experience issues such as delays in getting access to data or being unable to launch the intervention and surveys. Another option could be to provide funding to sites to hire a staff member or buy out an existing employee's time to deliver the intervention.

Careful design and prework: Doing ample prework and holding meetings with relevant stakeholders are necessary to ensure that the intervention is designed with the specific workplace context in mind. One key learning which we have taken forward in a follow-up phase of this research, conducted during 2020–1,[32] is that since social workers are operating in a time-pressured, often chaotic work environment, it is difficult (and perhaps not appropriate) to place extra demands on their time, such as engaging in a goal-setting program or completing surveys. While we had picked up on social workers' time pressures during our prework, we did not sufficiently consider the impact of this on their ability to participate in the intervention. It is important to carefully consider whether and how to collect new data in this type of context, or whether it is sufficient to rely on existing administrative data to measure outcomes. We imagine that this would apply to other public-sector settings, too.

Appropriate facilitator/messenger for the interventions: During the design phase of a trial, it is important to get a sense of who the right messenger might be across different elements of the research – including the delivery of the intervention materials and distribution of surveys. For the Symbolic Award letters, we asked each of the LAs who they thought was the right senior leader at the organization to sign off on each of the letters, and this appeared to have been in our favor. On the other hand, for the goal-setting intervention, while our LA partners thought that team managers would be the best delivery mechanism for the intervention, managers may not have understood the task correctly, were too busy, or forgot to send the goal-setting link to their team members, or simply did not think that the intervention was worth their team's time.

Interventions with larger, more structural changes: Social workers are time poor, operating under conditions that involve high caseloads, significant overtime work and thus, low work-life balance. It may therefore be that larger, more structural changes are needed to their working environment in order to result in any meaningful change – for example, employing more social workers to reduce caseloads or increasing administrative support. Once healthy work conditions are in place and social workers' basic needs are met, it may be that light-touch interventions could be more beneficial. In our case, we were unable to consider more heavy-handed interventions due to funding and time constraints, and so we focused on individual-level changes to promote well-being. However, we want to recognize the importance (and perhaps need, in the social work context) of changing the context and addressing the system in which individuals operate.[33]

NOTES

1 Department for Education. (2018a). Children's social work workforce 2018. https://www.gov.uk/government/statistics/childrens-social-work -workforce-2018.

2 Department for Education. (2018b). School workforce in England: November 2018. https://www.gov.uk/government/statistics/school-workforce-in -england-november-2018.

3 Health Safety Executive. (2018). Health and safety at work: Summary statistics for Great Britain 2018. https://www.hse.gov.uk/statistics /overall/hssh1718.pdf.

4 The report detailing the findings from the HHP Phase One interventions (detailed in this chapter) can be found here: https://whatworks-csc .org.uk/research-report/happier-healthier-professionals-small-scale -interventions-to-improve-social-worker-well-being/.

5 See Linos, E., Ruffini, K., & Wilcoxen, S. (2021). Reducing burnout and resignations of front line workers. *Academy of Management Proceedings, 2021*(1). https://journals.aom.org/doi/abs/10.5465/AMBPP.2021.14886abstract; and Jones, D., Molitor, D., & Reif, J. (2019). What do workplace wellness programs do? Evidence from the Illinois workplace wellness study. *The Quarterly Journal of Economics, 134*(4), 1747–91. https://doi.org/10.1093/qje/qjz023.

6 See web appendix 7A for a long list. https://www.biorgpartnership.com /what-works

7 Holmes, L., & McDermid, S., 2013. How social workers spend their time in frontline children's social care in England. *Journal of Children's Services, 8*(2), 123–33. https://doi.org/10.1108/JCS-03-2013-0005; and Holmes, L., McDermid, S., Jones, A., & Ward, H. (2009). *How social workers spend their time: An analysis of the key issues that impact upon practice pre and post implementation of the integrated children's system.* Centre for Child and Family Research Loughborough University. https://www.researchgate .net/publication/237598971_How_Social_Workers_Spend_Their_Time _An_Analysis_of_the_Key_Issues_that_Impact_on_Practice_pre-_and _post_Implementation_of_the_Integrated_Children's_System.

8 Holmes & McDermid (2013).

9 See Baginsky, M., Moriarty, J., Manthorpe, J., Stevens, M., MacInnes, T., & Nagendran, T. (2010). *Social workers' workload survey: Messages from the frontline. Findings from the 2009 survey and interviews with senior managers.* Social Work Task Force. https://dera.ioe.ac.uk/1945/1/SWTF%20

Workload%20Survey%20(final).pdf; and White, S., Wastell, D., Broadhurst, K., & Hall, C. (2010). When policy o'erleaps itself: The "tragic tale" of the Integrated Children's System. *Critical Social Policy*, *30(3)*, 405–29. https://doi.org/10.1177/0261018310367675.

10 Forrester, D., Westlake, D., McCann, M., Thurnham, A., Shefer, G., Glynn, G., & Killian, M. (2013). *Reclaiming social work? An evaluation of systemic units as an approach to delivering children's services*. University of Bedfordshire. https://core.ac.uk/download/pdf/30322069.pdf.

11 Webb, C.J., & Bywaters, P. (2018). Austerity, rationing and inequity: Trends in children's and young peoples' services expenditure in England between 2010 and 2015. *Local Government Studies*, *44(3)*, 391–415. https://doi.org/10.1080/03003930.2018.1430028.

12 Department for Education (2015). *The impact of family justice reforms on front-line practice*. https://assets.publishing.service.gov.uk/government/uploads/system/uploads/attachment_data/file/450254/RR478A_-_Family_justice_review_the_effect_on_local_authorities.pdf.pdf.

13 Lawson, D. (2021). *Social workers don't question broken families' dangers*. Daily Mail Online. https://www.dailymail.co.uk/debate/article-10327475/DOMINIC-LAWSON-Social-workers-dont-question-devastating-danger-modern-broken-families.html.

14 Leedham, M. (2022). "Social workers failed to heed warnings: A text-based study of how a profession is portrayed in UK newspapers. *The British Journal of Social Work*, *52(2)*, 1110–28. https://doi.org/10.1093/bjsw/bcab096.

15 Perlow, L.A. (1999). The time famine: Toward a sociology of work time. *Administrative Science Quarterly*, *44(1)*, 57–81. https://doi.org/10.2307/2667031.

16 See Gollwitzer, P.M. (1999). Implementation intentions: Strong effects of simple plans. *American Psychologist*, *54(7)*, 493–503. https://psycnet.apa.org/doi/10.1037/0003-066X.54.7.493; and Locke, E.A., & Latham, G.P. (1990). *A theory of goal setting & task performance*. Prentice-Hall, Inc.

17 Nickerson, D.W., & Rogers, T. (2010). Do you have a voting plan? Implementation intentions, voter turnout, and organic plan making. *Psychological Science*, *21(2)*, 194–9. https://doi.org/10.1177/0956797609359326.

18 Rogers, T., Milkman, K.L., John, L.K., & Norton, M.I. (2015). Beyond good intentions: Prompting people to make plans improves follow-through on important tasks. *Behavioral Science & Policy*, *1(2)*, 33–41. https://doi.org/10.1353/bsp.2015.0011.

19 Oliver, J.J., & MacLeod, A.K. (2018). Working adults' well-being: An online self help goal based intervention. *Journal of Occupational and Organizational Psychology*, *91(3)*, 665–80. https://doi.org/10.1111/joop.12212.

20 See web appendix 7B. https://www.biorgpartnership.com/what-works

21 What Works for Children's Social Care (2019). *Trial evaluation protocol happier healthier professionals: Goal-setting and wellbeing programme.* https://whatworks-csc.org.uk/wp-content/uploads/WWCSC_HHP_-goal_setting_trial_protocol_Nov2019.pdf.

22 Oliver & MacLeod (2018).

23 See DellaVigna, S., & Linos, E. (2022). RCTs to scale: Comprehensive evidence from two nudge units. *Econometrica, 90*(1), 81–116. https://doi.org/10.3982/ECTA18709; and Franco, A., Malhotra, N., & Simonovits, G. (2014). Publication bias in the social sciences: Unlocking the file drawer. *Science, 345*(6203), 1502–5. https://doi.org/10.1126/science.1255484.

24 Koydemir, S., Sökmez, A.B., & Schütz, A. (2021). A meta-analysis of the effectiveness of randomized controlled positive psychological interventions on subjective and psychological well-being. *Applied Research in Quality of Life, 16*(3), 1145–85. https://doi.org/10.1007/s11482-019-09788-z.

25 Daniels, K., Watson, D., Nayani, R., Tregaskis, O., Hogg, M., Etuknwa, A., & Semkina, A. (2021). Implementing practices focused on workplace health and psychological wellbeing: A systematic review. *Social Science & Medicine, 277*(113888). https://doi.org/10.1016/j.socscimed.2021.113888.

26 Giurge, L.M., Whillans, A.V., & West, C. (2020). Why time poverty matters for individuals, organisations and nations. *Nature Human Behaviour, 4*(10), 993–1003. https://doi.org/10.1038/s41562-020-0920-z.

27 Beck, J.W., & Schmidt, A.M. (2013). State-level goal orientations as mediators of the relationship between time pressure and performance: A longitudinal study. *Journal of Applied Psychology, 98*(2), 354–63. https://doi.org/10.1037/a0031145.

28 Gallus, J. (2017). Fostering public good contributions with symbolic awards: A large-scale natural field experiment at Wikipedia. *Management Science, 63*(12), 3999–4015. https://doi.org/10.1287/mnsc.2016.2540.

29 Grant, A.M. (2008a). Does intrinsic motivation fuel the prosocial fire? Motivational synergy in predicting persistence, performance, and productivity. *Journal of Applied Psychology, 93*(1), 48–58. https://psycnet.apa.org/doi/10.1037/0021-9010.93.1.48; and Grant, A.M. (2008b). The significance of task significance: Job performance effects, relational mechanisms, and boundary conditions. *Journal of Applied Psychology, 93*(1), 108–24. https://doi.org/10.1037/0021-9010.93.1.108.

30 See web appendix 7C for a sample letter. https://www.biorgpartnership.com/what-works.

31 Dolan, P., Hallsworth, M., Halpern, D., King, D., Metcalfe, R., & Vlaev, I. (2012). Influencing behaviour: The mindspace way. *Journal of Economic Psychology, 33*(1), 264–77. https://psycnet.apa.org/doi/10.1016/j.joep.2011.10.009.

32 We conducted a second phase of this research between 2020–1, the details of which can be found on the WWCSC website here: https://whatworks -csc.org.uk/research-report/happier-healthier-professionals-phase-two/.

33 Chater, N., & Loewenstein, G. (2022). The i-frame and the s-frame: How focusing on the individual-level solutions has led behavioral public policy astray. *Behavioral and Brain Sciences, 46,* E147. https://doi.org/10.1017 /s0140525x22002023.

CHAPTER EIGHT

Horizontal Scaling of Accuracy Prompts to Reduce Digital Misinformation Sharing in Canada

Lauryn Conway, Nicholas B. Diamond, and Chiara Varazzani

AT A GLANCE

- **Our Goal:** To increase the overall reliability of COVID-related news information circulating on social media, without affecting individuals' autonomy or the content itself.
- **The Intervention:** A randomized controlled trial testing two brief and scalable prompts adapted from the academic literature: an attention-to-accuracy cue and a set of digital media literacy tips, presented to individuals before they viewed verifiably true and false COVID-related news headlines.
- **The Results:** An attention-to-accuracy cue had a subtle but significant effect on news-sharing intentions, but digital media literacy tips elicited a very strong effect driven by a selective reduction in sharing intentions for false news headlines.
- **Lesson Learned:** Briefly boosting individuals' digital media literacy may be one way to improve the overall reliability of news information circulating on social media. More broadly, cross-national collaboration and replication is a fruitful way to test solutions to global problems.

Motivation and Objective

Advancements in digital technologies and information ecosystems have fundamentally reshaped the way we consume and share information. Modern communication technologies – social media, in particular – link individuals in a large-scale interconnected network on which people increasingly rely for important news. The diffusion of information on these networks transcends geographical proximity, is shaped by proprietary algorithms optimizing for engagement, and lacks traditional filters on the reliability of news information (e.g., quality control and fact-checking mechanisms of news institutions). On one hand, this interconnected network has facilitated greater civic participation in political, economic, and social life, while also enhancing governments' capacity to communicate with and respond to the evolving needs of the public they serve. On the other hand, continuous exposure to conflicting and rapidly changing information – often algorithmically personalized to each user – further complicates an already overwhelming landscape of information and knowledge exchange. These conditions provide a fertile breeding ground for harmful false or misleading information, which individuals and organizations may spread unintentionally (i.e., "misinformation") or intentionally for political, financial, or otherwise self-serving ends (i.e., "disinformation").[1]

Exposure to false or misleading yet persuasive statements can cast doubt on authoritative and reliable information (e.g., information emerging from the scientific process and expert peer review), eroding the integrity and credibility of democratic institutions.[2] The effects of misinformation on the dynamics between government and the public became especially apparent during the COVID-19 pandemic,[3] when access to accurate, timely, and actionable information could be the difference between life and death. The World Health Organization (WHO) thus declared an "infodemic" in the early days of the pandemic, highlighting that, like the COVID-19 virus itself, false news and misinformation were spreading virally and causing harm.

The borderless nature of the misinformation problem – a common characteristic of today's most pressing policy challenges (e.g., COVID-19 response and climate change) – demands transnational understanding and countermeasures. Recognizing the need for solidarity among and across governments and sectors, the OECD convened a first-of-its-kind partnership between the Government of Canada's Impact and Innovation Unit (IIU), the Direction Interministérielle de la Transformation Publique (DIPT) in the French government, and academic experts. At its core, this partnership aims to develop and share behaviorally informed best practices that can inform government response in this space. As part of this collaborative effort, the IIU led a randomized controlled trial aimed at understanding and improving the quality of information shared on social media, replicating and extending recent high-impact academic work. A complimentary description of the results and implications of this work is available in a recent OECD Public Governance Policy Paper.[4]

Why Focus on the Sharing of (Mis)Information Online?

Information can rapidly spread beyond three to four degrees of separation from the initiator,[5] with verifiably false information potentially spreading further and faster than true information.[6] Consequently, *sharing* of misinformation is a behavioral intervention target that could have substantial impact on the overall reliability of news information circulating online.[7] The latter point is of particular importance, as mere exposure to misinformation can increase subsequent accuracy perceptions.[8]

This study was designed as a first step toward understanding how Canadians engage with COVID-related misinformation online and how they make choices about what types of information to amplify within their social networks. Our objectives were threefold: (1) establish a baseline understanding of Canadians' accuracy perceptions of reliable and unreliable COVID-19 new headlines on social media and their willingness to share those headlines within their social network, (2) better understand the individual- and environmental-level factors contributing to news-sharing decisions, and (3) evaluate the effectiveness of two scalable, behaviorally informed interventions aimed at curbing the spread of misinformation without limiting individuals' autonomy.

Inspiration

In the past five years, we've seen growing scientific interest in the psychology of misinformation, with a burgeoning academic literature circling three key lines of investigation:

i.   *Are some individuals more resistant to misinformation than others?*
ii. *What factors – related to individuals, to information itself, and to information environments – lead to greater resistance to believing and sharing misinformation?*
iii. *What kinds of solutions can reduce the spread and/or the harmful effects of misinformation?*

Several recent reviews have started to tackle these important questions.[9] Broadly, this research suggests that some individuals are more resistant to misinformation than others, with a host of cognitive factors (e.g., analytical thinking), socio-affective factors (e.g., world-view, trust in information sources), and demographic factors (e.g., age) found to be commonly associated with degree of resistance to misinformation.

Building on this work, two overarching (and often competing) accounts have emerged in the recent literature to explain why people share misinformation: the *motivated reasoning* account and the *inattention-to-accuracy* account.[10] The former suggests that we tend to process information in a way that is nonthreatening to and protective of our pre-existing beliefs and identities,[11] beginning our reasoning process with predetermined goals (whether conscious or not) and interpreting new information in alignment with those goals. According to this account, the types of content that people share in online environments are driven by and further reinforce deeply held political, religious, or social beliefs and identities.[12] By contrast, the inattention-to-accuracy account suggests that most people *do* tend to care about sharing accurate information and can discern true from false content; however, they fail to attend to accuracy when making decisions in digital social media contexts.[13] By this account, other features of the social media user experience and incentives compete with our analytical thinking processes and pull attention away from signals of accuracy or reliability when making decisions about what to share in our social networks.[14]

In the last few years, Pennycook, Rand, and their colleagues have published a series of influential studies supporting the inattention hypothesis and proposed a corresponding solution (or set of solutions). The authors designed a series of survey-based and field experiments demonstrating the promise of shifting attention to content accuracy – through subtle, scalable *primes*, or prompts – as means of tilting individuals' news-sharing decisions toward true information or away from false information.[15] Here we highlight one particular study from Pennycook, Epstein et al., published in *Nature* in 2021,[16] which inspired our efforts to replicate and extend evidence for attention-to-accuracy interventions on misinformation sharing in a Canadian context.

Cueing Attention to Accuracy to Reduce the Spread of Misinformation

To test and address the inattention account of digital misinformation sharing, Pennycook, Epstein et al. (2021) conducted a series of experiments online using Amazon Mechanical Turk and Lucid (online experiment and survey hosting platforms) for a large sample of American participants. In each study, participants viewed a series of real, politically charged news headlines presented as they would be seen on Facebook. Half of the headlines were true, and half were false – that is, debunked by independent fact-checking websites. First, Pennycook, Epstein et al. demonstrated a *disconnect between people's beliefs and sharing intentions*. When asked to simply rate the accuracy of the headlines, participants could reliably discern between true and false headlines – yet when asked if they would share these same headlines on social media, participants were much less discerning. People, therefore, may share information that they do not perceive as accurate. Accordingly, the authors then tested *a subtle intervention to cue people's attention to accuracy prior to making decisions about what to share online*. They asked participants to judge the accuracy of a single random, neutral headline, priming the concept of accuracy in participants' minds prior to engaging with social media content. Remarkably, compared to various control conditions, this simple *accuracy evaluation prompt* improved the quality of news that participants intended to share, nudging sharing intentions away from false information and toward true information. The authors also provided preliminary evidence for the effectiveness of this intervention "in the wild," deploying it to real sharers of unreliable (i.e., objectively disreputable) news content on Twitter.

Overall, this series of studies by Pennycook et al. make a compelling case that inattention to accuracy – a clear and addressable cognitive factor – may be one key driver of misinformation sharing on social media for some, including with COVID-related misinformation in particular.[17] Accuracy prompts offer quick, subtle, and potentially scalable interventions for shifting people's information-sharing decisions, which could have significant effects if deployed in real-world contexts, given the network effects of information circulation on digital social networks. The fact that these types of interventions preserve the autonomy of social media users and do not require a centralized definition of truth versus falsehood make them a particularly attractive tool in the broader arsenal.

Building on this original research, researchers have begun to assess the utility of other prompts for influencing accuracy perceptions and sharing decisions for news encountered on social media. For example, in another online survey experiment using COVID-related news headlines, Epstein et al. (2021) assessed the impact of a menu of different attention-to-accuracy prompts in a sample of approximately nine thousand American social media users.[18] The authors replicated prior findings and identified an additional approach – a minimal "digital literacy tips" intervention taken from a campaign developed by Facebook and the nonprofit First Draft and used in other academic research,[19] which they found to be similarly effective in decreasing participants' intentions to share false news headlines about COVID-19. Digital media literacy may, therefore, offer another potentially fruitful avenue to reduce the spread of viral misinformation, and an especially important one given the increasing complexity of our online information ecosystems. Importantly, though, the effects of these interventions have tended to be relatively subtle, and more work is needed to understand which approaches are most effective, for whom, and in what contexts – particularly in samples beyond those recruited for typical online psychology experiments.

Of particular interest, a recent preprint details results from a large international experiment testing the impact of various interventions (i.e., accuracy prompts and digital literacy tips) aimed at reducing the spread of COVID-related misinformation across sixteen countries.[20] The findings point to considerable variation in baseline beliefs and sharing intentions across countries, as well as variability in the effectiveness of interventions across contexts. Canada, though, was not one of the countries investigated. Despite a growing global evidence base, we continue to see a dearth of policy-relevant evidence about misinformation belief and spread, even though Canada is experiencing negative consequences of fragmented online information ecosystems like other countries.[21] Consequently, as behavioral scientists and public servants with a mandate to provide evidence-based advice to policymakers at home and abroad, we set out to address this gap. We replicated and extended prior experimental interventions and took a deeper dive on understanding individual differences in information belief and sharing.

Interventions and Method

Participants

This experiment used a four-condition experimental design embedded in the context of a larger longitudinal study measuring Canadians' beliefs, attitudes, and behaviors related to the COVID-19 pandemic (the COVID-19 Snapshot Monitoring Study [COSMO Canada]).[22] The first phase of COSMO Canada included sixteen waves of data collection, fielding every two months from April 2020 to November 2021 (a second, independent phase of COSMO Canada followed and was recently completed). COSMO sampled two thousand adult Canadian residents over time. Participants were recruited through an online panel managed by Leger Consulting, the largest Canadian polling firm. Using a nonprobability sampling design, Census-matched sampling quotas were applied for gender, age, and region. New participants were recruited to replace those that did not return or otherwise failed to complete each new wave.

The present experiment was a one-time, between-subjects design embedded within the fifteenth wave of COSMO, collected from August

14 to 16 (inclusive), 2021. There were 1872 participants in this experiment. The mean age was 52.19 years (*SD* = 17.09), and there were 959 women (906 men, and 7 in other gender categories).

Design

We tested the impact of two interventions on intentions to share true and false news headlines about COVID-19, informed by the cognitive science literature: an attention-to-accuracy prompt[23] and a set of digital media literacy tips.[24]

All participants completed a news headline-rating task. Participants viewed fourteen real COVID-19-related news headlines presented in a randomized order. The headlines appeared as they would as links on Facebook, with an accompanying source and image. They were drawn from openly shared stimulus repositories,[25] from which we selected headlines that were politically neutral and that translated to the Canadian context (they were originally used in American studies). Half of the headlines were true, and half were false, as determined by third-party fact-checking websites. Prior to viewing the headlines, participants were randomly assigned to one of four conditions (see Figure 8.1 for visualization of the conditions):

Accuracy Judgment Control: This group served as a baseline measure of how true or false these headlines were in the eyes of the Canadian public. For each headline, participants (*n* = 282) were asked, "To the best of your knowledge, is this claim in the above headline accurate?" They then responded using a four-item Likert scale: "not at all accurate," "not very accurate," "somewhat accurate," "very accurate."[26]

Sharing Control: This group served as a passive control condition for comparison with the two treatment conditions. For each headline, participants (*n* = 525) were asked, "If you were to see the above article online (for example, through Facebook or Twitter), how likely would you be to share it?" They responded using a six-item scale: "extremely unlikely," "moderately unlikely," "slightly unlikely," "slightly likely," "moderately likely," "extremely likely." In our analyses of sharing, we excluded participants who provided the minimum possible sharing intention for every headline.

Accuracy Evaluation Intervention (Treatment 1): Participants (*n* = 532) were shown a single neutral headline – "Scientists discover 'the most massive neutron star ever detected,'" – and asked, "To the best of your knowledge, is the claim in the above headline accurate?"[27] The idea here is to make the concept of accuracy salient to participants prior

Figure 8.1. Schematic depiction of the four experimental conditions

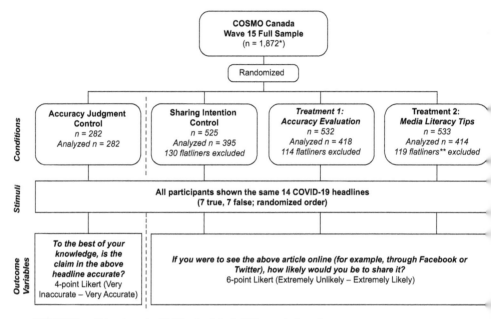

*COSMO Wave 15 target sample of 2,000 not met due to 2021 snap election call.
**Flatliners reported the minimum sharing intention for every headline.

to engaging with social media content. They then rated their sharing intentions for each headline, like the Sharing Control group.

Digital Media Literacy Intervention (Treatment 2): Participants ($n = 533$) were shown the following digital media literacy tips, a subset of those developed by Facebook in collaboration with First Draft and used in prior academic research[28]: "Investigate the source. Ensure that the story is written by a source that you trust with a reputation for accuracy. If the story comes from an unfamiliar organization, check their 'About' section to learn more." "Check the evidence…"; "Look at other reports…"; "Be skeptical of headlines…"; "Watch for unusual formatting…" (full text only shown here for the first tip). Participants then performed a multiple-choice attention check question to confirm they read the tips. They then rated their sharing intentions for each headline, like the Sharing Control and Accuracy Evaluation conditions.

Differences (and Similarities)

Our study is principally inspired by, and comparable to, studies by Pennycook et al. in 2020 and 2021.[29] We first set out to replicate the effects

Table 8.1. Comparing the present study to prior publications

	Pennycook, Epstein et al. (2021), Study 3 & 4	Epstein et al. (2021)	Present Study
Experimental Design	Two experimental conditions: Control (no instructions) or Treatment (Accuracy Evaluation Prompt)	Ten experimental conditions (including an array of misinformation interventions), three of relevance: Control, Accuracy Evaluation Prompt, Digital Media Literacy Tips	Four experimental conditions (see Figure 8.1), three of relevance here: Sharing Intention Control, Accuracy Evaluation Prompt,[32] or Digital Media Literacy Tips[33]
Setting	Online (MTurk)	Online (Lucid)	Online (Leger panel)
Participants	**American** participants recruited on Amazon Mechanical Turk (MTurk)	**American** participants on Lucid	**Canadian** participants recruited by Leger
Sample Size	Study 3: **727** participants; Study 4: **779** participants (both divided into two conditions)	**9,070** participants (divided into ten conditions)	**1,872** participants (divided into four conditions)
Measures	Sharing intentions measured on a **six-point scale** ranging from "Extremely unlikely" to "Extremely likely"	Sharing intentions measured with **binary** yes/no response	Sharing intentions measured on a **six-point scale** ranging from "Extremely unlikely" to "Extremely likely"
Procedures	Participants were randomly assigned to conditions. In the treatment condition, participants first rate the accuracy of a single random headline (Accuracy Evaluation Prompt), then rate sharing intentions for twenty-four headlines, half false (as determined by third-party fact-checking website) and half true.	Participants were randomly assigned to conditions. The Accuracy Evaluation Prompt is replicated from Pennycook, Epstein et al. (2021). The Digital Media Literacy Tips intervention involved exposing participants to four tips (Guess et al., 2020) prior to engaging with the headlines. They then rate sharing intentions for twenty headlines, half false and half true.	Participants were randomly assigned to conditions (Control, Accuracy Evaluation Prompt, or Digital Media Literacy Tips). Our tips condition included five tips.[34] All participants went on to rate sharing intentions for fourteen headlines, half false and half true.
Implementation Details	The headlines were **political**; half were pro-Democrat and half pro-Republican.	The headlines were **COVID-19 related.**	The headlines were **COVID-19 related,** nonpartisan, and applicable to the Canadian context. They were drawn from public repositories shared by Pennycook, Epstein et al. (2021).

of their Accuracy Evaluation prompt on news-sharing intentions in a Canadian context, using a subset of their stimulus materials, and following their analysis flow and logic. We also drew on Epstein et al. (2021) for their media literacy tips manipulation[30] (derived from Guess et al., 2020[31]), which we compared to the Accuracy Evaluation prompt. Both our study and these original publications contain multiple subsamples and/or substudies addressing different questions. Here, for the sake of parsimony, we focus only on features of our main experiment on shifting sharing intentions and the corresponding elements and substudies of these prior publications.

Results

We present three main results from our experiment. The first two are replications and extensions of prior published work discussed above; the third is a novel multivariate analysis of individual differences in misinformation belief and sharing, aimed at advancing our understanding of *why* people come to have such different reactions to true and false news content in the first place. We present this novel approach to demonstrate the utility of using rigorous replication as a scaffold upon which to advance new research questions.

A Disconnect between Beliefs and Sharing Intentions

Following Pennycook, Epstein et al. (2021),[35] we first measured the degree to which the accuracy perceptions and sharing intentions of Canadians vary across true vs. false news headlines. As can be seen in Figure 8.2 (A), participants can reliably discern between true and false COVID-19-related news: they rate true headlines as significantly more accurate than false headlines. Headline veracity, however, had a much smaller effect on participants' sharing intentions (Figure 8.2 (B)). In fact, the effect of headline veracity on accuracy ratings was four times larger than the effect on sharing intentions (based on effect sizes [Cohen's d] accounting for differences in the measurement scale). People, therefore, may share false news that they don't believe, as demonstrated by prior work.

Priming Accuracy Improves Sharing Intentions, but Providing Digital Media Literacy Tips Improves Sharing Intentions More

As discussed above, Pennycook, Rand and their colleagues have repeatedly demonstrated that subtly cueing participants' attention to accuracy – by having them consider the accuracy of a single, random

Figure 8.2. Accuracy ratings (A) and sharing intentions (B) for true vs. false headlines

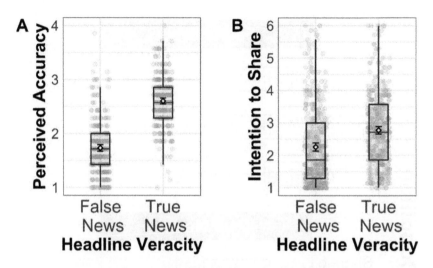

Note: Along with boxplots, diamonds with white fill depict group means, error bars depict 95 percent confidence intervals, and small gray dots depict individual participants. We note that there is a potential floor effect in false-news sharing intentions; it is not clear if this is the case in prior published work, which did not visualize individual participant data.

headline – improves the quality of their sharing decisions when subsequently engaging with social media content. As shown in Figure 8.3, we replicated this effect: when analyzing the Sharing Control and Accuracy Evaluation conditions, there was a significant interaction between headline veracity and condition. That is, the Accuracy Evaluation prompt elicited a subtle but statistically significant improvement in *sharing discernment:* the preference for sharing true over false news headlines (driven in this case by a subtle reduction in sharing intentions for false news). The size of this effect is comparable to prior publications.

The Digital Media Literacy Tips intervention had an even larger effect on sharing intentions (Figure 8.3 – strikingly large, by comparison to the established literature).[36] This effect was driven by a 21 percent decrease (Cohen's d = .41) in sharing intentions (relative to the control group) for false news headlines. Thus, even a one-time exposure to a brief set of digital media literacy tips has, in this case, an outsized effect on reducing intentions to spread false news online.

Figure 8.3. Sharing intentions for false vs. true headlines across the three experimental sharing conditions

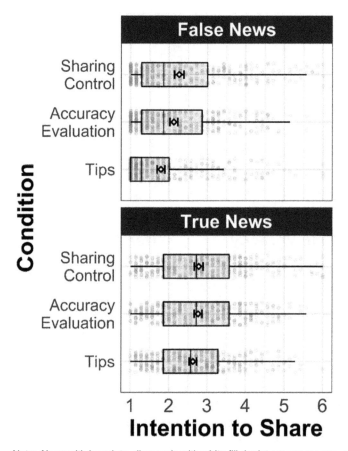

Note: Along with boxplots, diamonds with white fill depict groups means, error bars depict 95 percent confidence intervals, and small gray dots depict individual participants.

Individual Differences in Trust and Information Consumption as a Predictor of Misinformation Belief and Spreading

Both practitioners and academics often evaluate the outcomes of interventions in terms of average effects on the sample or population of interest, inferring that these averages meaningfully generalize to a whole country's (or world's) worth of people. While useful, this approach can render us inattentive to meaningful *variability* in behavior across people.

In our case, having replicated and extended two interventions on misinformation sharing interventions in a Canadian context, several key questions remained: *who believes and spreads misinformation in the first place, and why? And do our interventions work similarly for different subgroups of respondents?* To answer these questions, we leveraged the richness of the COSMO Canada survey, which included a variety of validated measurements of respondents' COVID-related attitudes, beliefs, and related cognitive factors. We hypothesized that differences in the sources respondents trust for COVID-related information, and the way they seek out and react to that information, would be associated with differences in misinformation belief and sharing.

We used a multivariate machine learning approach (k-means clustering) to identify underlying subgroups of participants based on their *trust and information consumption profiles*, reflecting: self-rated trust in a variety of sources for COVID-related information, conspiratorial thinking tendency,[37] psychological reactance (oppositional response to change when one perceives threats to one's freedom),[38] and openness to evidence.[39] This analysis identified three distinct clusters of respondents, visualized in Figure 8.4:

1. **Non-Trusting:** low self-reported trust in all sources, high conspiratorial thinking and psychological reactance, and low openness to evidence.
2. **High/Social Trusting:** high trust in all sources (especially social media, relative to the other clusters), high psychological reactance, and low openness to evidence.
3. **Institution Trusting:** high trust in institutional/authoritative sources and low trust in social sources, low conspiratorial thinking and psychological reactance, and high openness to evidence.

We next investigated whether these subgroups exhibited different belief in and sharing intentions for the true and false headlines. Indeed, as shown in Figure 8.5, subgroups differed significantly in their belief in (A) and sharing intentions for (B) false news headlines about COVID-19. Specifically, respondents in the *Non-Trusting* and *High/Social Trusting* clusters reported significantly higher accuracy ratings and sharing intentions for false COVID-19 news headlines than *Institution-Trusting* respondents. These results empirically show how the information people trust, and the way they react to it, are associated with their accuracy perceptions and the information they choose to amplify in their social networks.

Finally, we asked whether the effects of the two interventions – Accuracy Evaluation and Digital Media Literacy Tips – differed significantly

Figure 8.4. Three subgroups of participants based on their trust and information consumption profiles, from a k-means clustering analysis

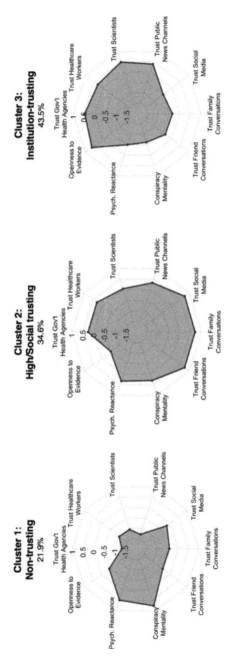

Note: Each variable was mean-centered and standardized prior to the clustering analysis. Absolute levels of trust should therefore not be compared across sources.

Figure 8.5. Accuracy ratings (A) and sharing intentions (B) split by trust and information consumption clusters

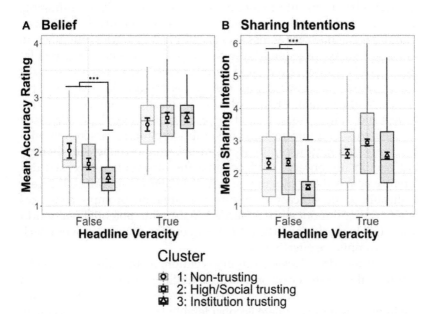

Cluster

- ⦿ 1: Non-trusting
- ⊡ 2: High/Social trusting
- ⊞ 3: Institution trusting

across the clusters. We did not find evidence for this (non-significant interaction between cluster, condition, and headline veracity). We note that this null finding should be interpreted with caution, but tentatively, it suggests that these scalable behavioral interventions are similarly effective in reducing false-news sharing for subpopulations with very different patterns of trust and belief.

Reconciliation

The results of our experiment broadly replicate established findings concerning the effects of accuracy prompts and digital media literacy tips on sharing intentions for true and false news online. Both interventions significantly improved sharing intentions – reducing intentions to share false news in particular. From a policy perspective, it is important to consider the *magnitude* of these effects – both in prior work and in our own data.

First, we found that the *Accuracy Evaluation* prompt had a subtle but significant effect on sharing intentions, replicating a large and growing body of work on the effectiveness of such "attention-to-accuracy" prompts.[40] Our finding of a 6 percent reduction in false-news sharing intentions appears roughly similar to prior studies investigating COVID-related misinformation.[41] This replication is encouraging, given that prior work was conducted predominantly in American samples, or in one case across sixteen different countries, but never in Canada.[42] Here, we extend these findings to a nationally representative Canadian sample recruited through the largest national survey panel provider. We also replicate earlier work suggesting that the *Accuracy Evaluation* prompt is robust to individual differences in various beliefs and traits.[43] We identified three subgroups of individuals based on their trust and information consumption patterns, associated with markedly different susceptibility to misinformation belief and sharing, but we did not observe evidence that the interventions worked differently across these subgroups. While evidence supporting the generalizability and efficacy of accuracy evaluation prompts continues to emerge, still more work is needed to estimate potential real-world impacts.[44] In particular, little is known about the timescales over which these prompts are effective.

The *Digital Media Literacy Tips* intervention, on the other hand, had a substantially greater effect on sharing intentions in our study compared to prior work. Specifically, the 21 percent reduction in false-news sharing intentions observed here is considerably larger (both in percentage difference and in standardized effect size) than we have seen in previous publications using similar sets of tips.[45] For example, in an American study, Epstein et al. (2021) reported a roughly 3–4 percent (though statistically significant) reduction in false-news sharing intentions in their media literacy tips condition (compared to a sharing control condition similar to ours),[46] and Arechar et al. (2022) report reductions of roughly 0–6 percent across sixteen different countries.[47]

Observing large effects is encouraging when considering potential real-world impact in Canada, but raises an obvious question: *why* was the *Digital Media Literacy Tips* intervention so effective in our case? Engaging in some brief post hoc speculation:

- **Conscientious Respondents:** Our experiment was embedded in the fifteenth wave of a longitudinal research program (COSMO Canada) about COVID-related attitudes and behaviors. Our participants may, therefore, have responded in a more effortful and conscientious manner than the typical one-off online experiment participant. This survey context may render participants more responsive to the *Tips* intervention, which is by design more cognitively demanding than the intentionally quick and implicit accuracy evaluation prime.

– **Diverse Respondents:** Our sample may span a broader and perhaps more generalizable distribution of baseline digital media literacy than prior publications. Digital literacy tends to be lower among older adults,[48] who were more represented in our nationally representative study (mean age = fifty-two years here, compared to forty-five[49] or thirty-nine[50]). Additionally, experiment-hosting platforms like Amazon Mechanical Turk (used in prior studies) may overestimate digital literacy levels in a population.[51] Accordingly, in subsequent waves of our COSMO survey, we found poor social media literacy (i.e., awareness of social media algorithms and their influence on what each user sees). This may be one reason that boosting digital media literacy – albeit briefly – was comparatively so effective in reducing false-news sharing intentions.

Discussion and Prescriptive Advice

What did we learn and what would we have done differently? First, systematic replication is the cornerstone of scientific progress and yet, we're reminded through this research effort how challenging it can be, even when building on publications that shared stimulus materials and data. We encourage other practitioners to reach out directly to original study authors for assistance, as we did, and to proactively facilitate future replication efforts when publishing your own results (including null results!).

Second, as is common when applying behavioral science to inform real-world decision-making, we often face trade-offs between basic (i.e., optimizing for more a "pure" isolation of potential mechanisms) versus applied (i.e., optimizing for real-world solutions and impact) research decisions. Through this lens, there are a handful of considerations we will carry forward in future work applying behavioral science to understand and address complex, real-world problems like the misinformation challenge.

Testing Combinations of Interventions: As illustrated throughout this chapter, interventions that empower individuals to consume and share information more discerningly have shown significant promise in online experimental settings. It remains unclear, however, what kind of impact they will have at scale and how they might work synergistically – in combination with other types of solutions – to effectively curb the spread of misinformation. Pitting specific, experimental iterations of interventions against each other is useful for adjudicating between theories, but meaningful real-world impact will likely be best achieved through multiple, additive approaches that tackle the problem at different scales, ideally including both individual- and system-level interventions.[52]

Integrating Qualitative Measures: In replicating, translating, or scaling an intervention, we often rely heavily on experimental designs and quantitative outcome data. While these methods are critical, we also see great value in integrating qualitative research into experimental designs – for example, by including open-ended questions in survey experiments or incorporating semi-structured interviews into field experiment protocols. In our case, these approaches could help us understand *why* and *how* individuals make decisions about what information to share (i.e., linking process to outcome), gauge Canadians experiences with the interventions themselves (e.g., *Were the instructions clear? Did certain tips resonate more than others?*), and predict hidden factors that might create resistance in real-world uptake. O'Cathain et al. (2013) provide a systematic mapping review outlining key benefits of incorporating qualitative research into RCTs.[53]

Better Accounting for Outcome Complexity: Even in basic science, there is usually a trade-off between embracing complexity and ecological validity, on the one hand, and experimental control and measurement precision, on the other. This tension is particularly apparent in the growing scientific literature on misinformation – a topic of clear importance around the world today, but one which varies across multiple scales simultaneously (e.g., person-to-person, region-to-region, topic-to-topic, platform-to-platform), and accordingly, resists clear definitions and measurement strategies. In our case, we took inspiration from some recent high-impact academic work, operationalizing COVID-related misinformation belief and sharing by surveying people's responses to a specific set of real news headlines. This approach has proven fruitful, but (like most scientific operationalizations) paints a simplified picture of a much more complex real-world problem. Krause et al. (2022) highlight a number of confounds in defining the accuracy of scientific truth claims this way, for example: accessibility of evidence to the public, fluidity of evidence, variable harm associated with different falsehoods, and traction on different social media algorithms.[54] Identifying interventions, programs, and policies that produce meaningful and durable change in this space will require more work, measuring misinformation (and its consequences) from a variety of perspectives.

Where Do We Go from Here?

Experimental and mixed-methods research can be instrumental in advancing our understanding of how and why people share misinformation on digital platforms. Behaviorally informed interventions like the one presented here point to potential bottom-up policies that preserve the autonomy of social media users. These results also suggest that there are no one-size-fits-all solutions. Building on existing work, we used analytical tools to identify different population segments based on their trusted news sources and information consumption, finding that these segments had markedly different patterns of misinformation belief and sharing. Future research in this space must move beyond a focus on group averages in order to understand and respond to critical inter-individual (as well as cross-national) differences.

Global challenges such as the spread of mis- and disinformation require a global policy response, informed by intentional efforts to replicate findings across different socio-cultural contexts and among diverse populations. The international collaboration presented here highlights the promise of building applied research programs – grounded in behavioral science – across governments, nongovernmental agencies, and academic partners. Moving forward, we would like to urge academic and policy communities to prioritize opportunities for cross-national research – employing user-centered approaches that are informed by empirical evidence from the behavioral sciences, in concert with a deeper understanding of collective behavior and systems-level forces[55] – to meaningfully move the needle on large-scale behavioral challenges like the spread of pandemic-related misinformation.

NOTES

1 See OECD. (2021). *OECD report on public communication: The global context and the way forward*. OECD. https://doi.org/10.1787/22f8031c-en; and Carrasco-Farré, C. (2022). The fingerprints of misinformation: How deceptive content differs from reliable sources in terms of cognitive effort and appeal to emotions. *Humanities and Social Sciences Communications*, 9(1), 1–18. https://doi.org/10.1057/s41599-022-01174-9.

2 See Greifeneder, R., Jaffe, M., Newman, E., & Schwarz, N. (Eds.). (2021). *The psychology of fake news: Accepting, sharing, and correcting misinformation*. Routledge; Colomina, C., Sánchez Margalef, H., & Youngs, R. (2021). *The impact of disinformation on democratic processes and human rights in the world*. Policy Department for External Relations. European Union; Marshall, H., & Drieschova, A. (2018). Post-truth politics in the UK's Brexit referendum. *New Perspectives*, 26(3), 89–105. https://doi.org/10.1177/233682 5X1802600305; and Bovet, A., & Makse, H.A. (2019). Influence of fake news

in Twitter during the 2016 US presidential election. *Nature Communications*, *10*(1), 7. https://doi.org/10.1038/s41467-018-07761-2.

3 Posetti, J., & Bontchva, K. (2020). *Disinfodemic: Deciphering COVID-19 disinformation* (Policy brief No., 1). UNESCO. https://unesdoc.unesco.org /ark:/48223/pf0000374416/PDF/374416eng.pdf.multi.

4 OECD. (2022). *Misinformation and disinformation: An international effort using behavioural science to tackle the spread of misinformation.* OECD Public Governance Policy Papers, No. 21, OECD Publishing, Paris. https:// doi.org/10.1787/b7709d4f-en.

5 Bak-Coleman, J. B., Alfano, M., Barfuss, W., Bergstrom, C.T., Centeno, M.A., Couzin, I.D., Donges, J.F., Galesic, M., Gersick, A.S., Jacquet, J., Kao, A.B., Moran, R.E., Romanczuk, P., Rubenstein, D.I., Tombak, K.J., Van Bavel, J.J., & Weber, E.U. (2021). Stewardship of global collective behavior. *Proceedings of the National Academy of Sciences*, *118*(27), 1–10. https:// doi.org/10.1073/pnas.2025764118.

6 Vosoughi, S., Roy, D., & Aral, S. (2018). The spread of true and false news online. *Science*, *359*(6380), 1146–51. https://doi.org/10.1126/science. aap9559.

7 Pennycook, G., & Rand, D.G. (2022). Accuracy prompts are a replicable and generalizable approach for reducing the spread of misinformation. *Nature Communications*, *13*(1), 2333. https://doi.org/10.1038/s41467-022 -30073-5.

8 Pennycook, G., Cannon, T.D., & Rand, D.G. (2018). Prior exposure increases perceived accuracy of fake news. *Journal of Experimental Psychology: General*, *147*(12), 1865–80. https://doi.org/10.1037/xge0000465.supp.

9 See van der Linden, S. (2022). Misinformation: Susceptibility, spread, and interventions to immunize the public. *Nature Medicine*, *28*(3), 460–7. https://doi.org/10.1038/s41591-022-01713-6; Ecker, U.K.H., Lewandowsky, S., Cook, J., Schmid, P., Fazio, L.K., Brashier, N., Kendeou, P., Vraga, E.K., & Amazeen, M.A. (2022). The psychological drivers of misinformation belief and its resistance to correction. *Nature Reviews Psychology*, *1*(1), 13–29. https://doi.org/10.1038/s44159-021-00006-y; and Pennycook, G., & Rand, D.G. (2021). The psychology of fake news. *Trends in Cognitive Sciences*, *25*(5), 388–402. https://doi.org/10.1016/j.tics.2021.02.007.

10 van der Linden (2022).

11 Kunda, Z. (1990). The case for motivated reasoning. *Psychological Bulletin*, *108*(3), 480–98. https://psycnet.apa.org/doi/10.1037/0033-2909.108.3.480.

12 Van Bavel, J.J., Harris, E.A., Pärnamets, P., Rathje, S., Doell, K.C., & Tucker, J.A. (2021). Political psychology in the digital (mis) information age: A model of news belief and sharing. *Social Issues and Policy Review*, *15*(1), 84–113. https://doi.org/10.1111/sipr.12077.

13 See Pennycook, G., & Rand, D.G. (2022). Nudging social media toward accuracy. *The ANNALS of the American Academy of Political and Social Science, 700*(1), 152–64. https://doi.org/10.1177/00027162221092342; Pennycook & Rand (2021).

14 See Pennycook & Rand (2022); Pennycook, G., McPhetres, J., Zhang, Y., Lu, J.G., & Rand, D.G. (2020). Fighting COVID-19 misinformation on social media: Experimental evidence for a scalable accuracy-nudge intervention. *Psychological science, 31*(7), 770–80. https://doi.org/10.1177/0956797620939054; and Pennycook, G., Epstein, Z., Mosleh, M., Arechar, A. A., Eckles, D., & Rand, D. G. (2021). Shifting attention to accuracy can reduce misinformation online. *Nature, 592*(7855), 590–5. https://doi.org/10.1038/s41586-021-03344-2.

15 See Pennycook & Rand (2022); Pennycook, McPhetres et al. (2020); and Pennycook et al. (2021).

16 Pennycook, Epstein et al. (2021).

17 Pennycook, McPhetres et al. (2020).

18 Epstein, Z., Berinsky, A.J., Cole, R., Gully, A., Pennycook, G., & Rand, D.G. (2021). Developing an accuracy-prompt toolkit to reduce Covid-19 misinformation online. *Harvard Kennedy School (HKS) Misinformation Review.* https://misinforeview.hks.harvard.edu/article/developing-an-accuracy-prompt-toolkit-to-reduce-covid-19-misinformation-online/.

19 Guess, A.M., Lerner, M., Lyons, B., Montgomery, J.M., Nyhan, B., Reifler, J., & Sircar, N. (2020). A digital media literacy intervention increases discernment between mainstream and false news in the United States and India. *Proceedings of the National Academy of Sciences, 117*(27), 15536–45. https://doi.org/10.1073/pnas.1920498117.

20 Arechar, A.A., Allen, J.N.L., berinsky, a., Cole, R., Epstein, Z., Garimella, K., Gully, A., Lu, J.G., Ross, R.M., Stagnaro, M., Zhang, J., Pennycook, G., & Rand, D.G. (2022, February 11). *Understanding and reducing online misinformation across 16 countries on six continents.* PsyArXiv. https://doi.org/10.31234/osf.io/a9frz.

21 Mosleh, O. (2022, June 14). "Kind of terrifying": Numbers show racist Great Replacement conspiracy theory has found audience in Canada. *The Toronto Star.* https://www.thestar.com/news/canada/2022/06/14/kind-of-terrifying-numbers-show-racist-great-replacement-conspiracy-theory-has-found-audience-in-canada.html.

22 Impact Canada. (2022). *COVID-19 Snapshot Monitoring (Cosmo Canada).* https://impact.canada.ca/en/cosmo-canada.

23 Replicated from Pennycook, McPhetres et al. (2020); and Pennycook, Epstein et al. (2021).

24 Replicated from Epstein et al. (2021). See also Guess et al. (2020).

25 See Pennycook, McPhetres et al. (2020); and Pennycook, G., Binnendyk, J., Newton, C., & Rand, D. G. (2021). A practical guide to doing behavioral research on fake news and misinformation. *Collabra: Psychology*, 7(1), 1–13. https://doi.org/10.1525/collabra.25293.

26 Following Pennycook, Epstein et al. (2021). (Studies 3–5).

27 Epstein et al. (2021).

28 Guess et al. (2020).

29 Replicated from Pennycook, McPhetres et al. (2020); and Pennycook, Epstein et al. (2021).

30 Epstein et al. (2021); and Arechar et al. (2022, February 11).

31 Guess et al. (2020).

32 Replicated from Pennycook, Epstein et al. (2021) and Epstein et al. (2021).

33 Replicated from Epstein et al. (2021).

34 Guess et al. (2020).

35 See Pennycook, Epstein et al. (2021).

36 Epstein et al. (2021); and Arechar et al. (2022, February 11).

37 Bruder, M., Haffke, P., Neave, N., Nouripanah, N., & Imhoff, R. (2013). Measuring individual differences in generic beliefs in conspiracy theories across cultures: Conspiracy mentality questionnaire. *Frontiers in Psychology*, 4(April). https://doi.org/10.3389/fpsyg.2013.00225.

38 Hong, S.-M., & Faedda, S. (1996). Refinement of the Hong Psychological Reactance Scale. *Educational and Psychological Measurement*, 56(1), 173–82. https://psycnet.apa.org/doi/10.1177/0013164496056001014.

39 Pennycook, G., Cheyne, J.A., Koehler, D.J., & Fugelsang, J.A. (2020). On the belief that beliefs should change according to evidence: Implications for conspiratorial, moral, paranormal, political, religious, and science beliefs. *Judgment and Decision Making*, 15(4), 476–98. https://doi.org/10.31234/osf.io/a7k96.

40 Pennycook & Rand (2022).

41 Pennycook, McPhetres et al. (2020); Epstein et al. (2021); and Arechar et al. (2022, February 11).

42 Arechar et al. (2022, February 11).

43 See Pennycook & Rand (2022); and Pennycook & Rand (2021).

44 Locey, M.L. (2020). The evolution of behavior analysis: Toward a replication crisis? *Perspectives on Behavior Science*, 43(4), 655–75. https://doi.org/10.1007/s40614-020-00264-w.

45 See Epstein et al. (2021); Guess et al. (2020); and Arechar et al. (2022, February 11).

46 Epstein et al. (2021).

47 See Figure S12B in Arechar et al. (2022, February 11).

48 Guess, A.M., & Munger, K. (2022). Digital literacy and online political behavior. *Political Science Research and Methods*, 11(1), 1–19. https://doi.org/10.1017/psrm.2022.17.

49 Epstein et al. (2021).

50 Guess et al. (2020).

51 Epstein et al. (2021).

52 See recent work by Bak-Coleman and colleagues in Bak-Coleman, J.B., Kennedy, I., Wack, M., Beers, A., Schafer, J.S., Spiro, E.S., Starbird, K., & West, J.D. (2022). Combining interventions to reduce the spread of viral misinformation. *Nature Human Behaviour*, 6(10), 1372–80. https://doi.org /10.1038/s41562-022-01388-6.

53 O'Cathain, A., Thomas, K.J., Drabble, S.J., Rudolph, A., & Hewison, J. (2013). What can qualitative research do for randomised controlled trials? A systematic mapping review. *BMJ open*, 3(6), e002889. https://doi.org/10.1136 /bmjopen-2013-002889.

54 Krause, N.M., Freiling, I., & Scheufele, D.A. (2022). The "Infodemic" Infodemic: Toward a more nuanced understanding of truth-claims and the need for (not) combatting misinformation. *Annals of the American Academy of Political and Social Science, 700*(1), 112–23. https://doi.org/10.1177 /00027162221086263.

55 Bak-Coleman et al. (2021).

CHAPTER NINE

Customizing Social Norm Nudges by Format and Reference Group to Reduce Water Consumption among Israeli Households

Eyal Pe'er

AT A GLANCE

- **Our Goal:** To identify the most effective manner to customize social norm nudges, by format and reference group, to reduce water consumption among Israeli households.
- **The Intervention:** Social norm nudge comparing bimonthly household water consumption to the median of a selected reference group (entire city vs. similar households) in a specific format (graph, percent, or cost).
- **The Results:** The nudges decreased water consumption among those that had higher-than-median consumption in previous periods, and the nudges were most effective to smaller households and when the nudge was in graphical format using the similar households as the reference group.
- **Lesson Learned:** Social norm nudges can be effective to reduce water consumption but heterogeneity among households significantly impacts effectiveness.

Motivation and Objective

Using social norms has come, in the last decade, to be one of the common tools used by many organizations to nudge consumers toward more efficient and less wasteful consumption. The use of social norms, typically providing consumers with comparison values of their peers, neighbors, or other referent group, has been found to be generally effective and thus advocated for as a nonrestrictive and unobtrusive means to curb consumption. Most of the studies examined the effects of social norms on electricity usage, while several others focused on water consumption or other types of energy conservation (e.g., towel reuse in hotels).

The motivation behind the current study was several years of drought that were experienced in Israel, roughly from 2010 to 2019, which spurred the Water Authority to seek out solutions, including behavioral ones, that could aid their efforts to curb water consumption among Israeli residents. The Water Authority issued a call for proposals to conduct an experiment that would test and evaluate different implementations of a behaviorally informed intervention in consumers' water bills. I responded to that call and proposed, after reviewing findings of previous studies on the topic, to implement and examine nudges that utilize social norms to curb water consumption.

Inspiration

In a famous experiment in California, 290 households received messages encouraging reduced energy use using descriptive norms (average energy consumption by participating households), with or without an injunctive norm icon (smiley ☺ or frowny ☹), stating whether they were below or above average consumption. Results showed that, for both short term (after two weeks) and longer term (three weeks later), both descriptive and injunctive social norms reduced the consumption of consumers who were above average consumption in the preceding period. Moreover, under the injunctive norm message (smiley/frowny), consumers who were above average reduced their consumption while those who were below average did not increase their consumption. This experiment spurred a wave of field studies in the US and elsewhere that showed how social norm messaging can reduce consumption of electricity.[1]

Focusing on water consumption, Ferraro and Price used a similar paradigm to encourage residents of a large county in the US to reduce their household water consumption.[2] They appended to a certain month's water bill one of three messages including either technical advice on how to save water, an appeal to pro-social preferences, or a social norm message comparing the consumer's consumption to average (median) consumption in the past months. They found that, compared to the control group, consumers who received the social norm message showed the highest reduction in water consumption (4.8 percent vs. 2.7 percent in pro-social appeal, and a null effect for the technical advice) in the subsequent period. This effect was, as expected, more pronounced for consumers who had a higher-than-median consumption level pre-treatment, but no boomerang effect was found for consumers who had a lower-than-median consumption level. When measured again about three months after, the size of the effect (on all experimental groups) was reduced by about a third but remained significant. Interestingly, the reduction in effect size over time was largest among higher-than-median users who received the social norm comparison messages.

Bernedo, Ferrero, and Price revisited the same sample several years after the initial intervention to investigate the potential long-term effect of the social norm nudge.[3] They found that the initial effect size reduced by half after four years but remained statistically significant and practically considerable even four years after the initial treatment. By analyzing the effects observed among households that changed owners during that period, the researchers were able to conclude that most of the effect can be attributed to behavioral changes in consumption habits, rather than to physical changes in capital stock of the home, consistent with other research.[4] Additionally, they found that homeowners are more affected by the social norm message compared to renters. Based on the observed effect sizes over seven summers, the authors estimate that the cost-effectiveness of the social norm nudge, had it been applied to the entire population, would have been $0.24 per 1,000 gallons saved.

Interventions and Method

As part of a policy initiative of the Israeli Water Authority, I partnered with a large water cooperation and examined the effect of displaying social norms on consumers' water bills (distributed bimonthly).[5] The intervention varied on the **format** of the social norm nudge and on the **reference** group it used: the versions included comparing consumers' water consumption to their peers either using graphical information only, or with accompanying textual information highlighting the differences in percentages (e.g., 50 percent above/below the median consumption) or in monetary terms (e.g., 100 NIS above/below the median bill). The social norm used for comparison was either based on the entire city's median consumption or the median of similar consumers (i.e., with the same household characteristics).

The Format of the Social Norm Nudge

In almost all the reported studies that used social norm nudges to curb electricity or water consumption, the comparison has been expressed in absolute or relative terms. For example, the Home Energy Report (HER) displays the individual's consumption as above, at, or below the average consumption, and the consumer can infer how much more electricity they used, compared to the average.[6] Some studies used percentages to directly inform consumers how much above or below the average (or median) their consumption is.[7] Brent and his colleagues also compared the absolute to relative formats in one study, and they found no clear difference in their effectiveness.[8] In none of the cases, however, was the value of the social norm nudge expressed in monetary terms (e.g., the relative added cost/savings compared to the average). This is inconsistent with a body of research that has already shown that converting efficiency or consumption metrics into cost metrics leads to better outcomes. For example, people were found more likely to prefer more fuel-efficient vehicles when fuel economy was presented in terms of fuel costs (estimated dollars per year) than in fuel efficiency (miles per gallon).[9] Similarly, people prefer more energy-efficient refrigerators when their energy efficiency is presented as cost per year,[10] and the same was found for washing machines.[11] Hardisty and colleagues also found that framing energy levels as annual costs nudged consumers to buy more electricity-saving light bulbs.[12] In other domains, Read, Frederick & Scholten showed that under-savings (e.g., for pension) can be moderated if annual interest is displayed as money earned and not as a percent interest rate, if the amount to be saved is large.[13]

Aside from being a more intuitive and familiar metric, monetary costs can also help aid decisions because they can be easily compared to other expenses. For example, spending twenty dollars on your water bills can be easily compared to how much you spend on other utilities, whereas consuming fifty gallons of water a month cannot be easily compared to how much electricity (or any other product or service) you consumed in the same month. Thus, our study also included a version of the social norm nudge that used the average (median) cost and how much the target consumer was above or below that norm. By this, we also test the monetary version of social norm nudge in a manner that is more straightforward than was previously tested by Brent, which only displayed costs in terms of relative savings compared to a 10 percent reduction benchmark and did not include a comparison to the median consumer.[14]

Reference Group

A key component of the social norm nudge is that it compares individual-level behavior to a group-level norm. Thus, setting the group-level norm could be critical for its success. When trying to curb water (or other resource) consumption, individual-level consumption could be compared to several different norms, including people living in the same neighborhood, people living in the same town, city, or county, or to people who are otherwise similar, in some sense, to the individual. The common perception is that the more specific and similar a group is to the individual, the more the individual will be affected by the norm. For example, Goldstein, Cialdini, & Griskevicius found that telling hotel guests that the majority of guests in their particular room reuse towels is more effective in persuading them to do the same, and such a "provincial" social norm is more effective than a descriptive social norm or other pro-social appeals.[15]

Probably because of these reasons, previous studies that used social norm nudges acted under the assumption that showing a comparison to consumers' neighbors would be more effective than comparing to a larger referent group (e.g., all city residents). However, from a policy perspective, comparisons to smaller groups could be more difficult to achieve, would require the collection and usage of consumers' personal information, and might not be feasible or sensible in all cases (e.g., in less habituated rural areas). If comparing to one's neighbors is indeed more effective, then it is important to estimate that effect's size, so it can be used to inform policy decisions within a cost-benefit analysis. On the other hand, if it is found that such personalization does not carry with it a marginal benefit, policymakers could do better to suffice with a coarser but less costly and more privacy-preserving comparison to a larger referent group such as the entire city, county, etc.

However, similarity must not be only local. In fact, when it comes to water consumption, it is not necessarily best to compare individuals' behavior to people who only live nearby. For example, a neighborhood could be diverse and include spaces for apartment buildings, which have a smaller size and less water-consuming facilities, next to townhouses, which take up a larger piece of land and use much more water for irrigation and landscaping, as well as for recreational uses such as an outdoor pool or hot tub. Thus, when it comes to nudging water consumption, it might be more effective to compare to a group of consumers who use water similarly. For instance, individuals' water consumption could be compared to the average (or median) consumption of other consumers with similar characteristics (e.g., who live in the same type of residence with a similar number of inhabitants). Thus, in the current study we tested whether making comparisons based on the type of residence and number of inhabitants in the residence could prove to be more effective than comparing to a more general norm available (e.g., the city level).

To summarize, our field study provided us with the ability to test for the effects of the format of the comparison (percent above/below median consumption vs. cost above/below median bill), and the reference group (the entire city vs. only consumers with same residency attributes).

Method

Our sample originally included 23,132 households in a mid-size city in the center of Israel: 76.9 percent of participants lived in apartments and 23.1 percent resided in houses. Family size ranged from zero (unknown but assumed to be one or two)[16] to ten, with a median of three persons. Out of the total sample, 3,067 were excluded because a leak was reported on their household either before, during, or after the treatment period. Also, 199 households were excluded for not showing any water consumption (zero) in any of the experiment periods. The final sample included 18,819 households of which 80 percent resided in apartments and the rest resided in houses.

Design

Participants were randomly allocated to one of seven groups, which included the control (N=3,116, 14.2 percent) that received the same bills as before. All the other six experimental groups received a modified bill that included a new graph that compared their consumption in the last six billing periods (twelve months) to the social norm. For half of these groups, the values used for the social norm were the median consumption levels among all city residents ("general referent group" conditions), and for the other half it was the median consumption of households similar to them in both type of house and family size ("similar referent group"). A third of the experimental groups only saw the graph with a sentence explaining what is shown on the new line ("descriptive norms only" conditions). For another third of the groups, the graph was accompanied by the difference (in percentages) between the consumers' consumption and the referent median consumption in the current billing period.

If the difference was positive (i.e., the consumer used more water than the norm), it was accompanied by a frowny face ☹, and if it was negative it was accompanied by a smiley face ☺ ("injunctive norms"). The last third of the groups had the difference in consumption presented in difference in costs above or below the norm median. Allocation to conditions was made randomly at the consumer level based on the list of consumers who received a water bill in the period right before the first treatment.

Procedure

The experimental messages were added to the bimonthly bills of participants with the help of the water corporation personnel in two bimonthly bills consecutively. Participants were allocated to the same condition in all bills and received the same type of message on all bills. However, the specific values on the graph and the respective text varied according to the specific bill's consumption values.

Results

Table 9.2 shows the average weekly consumption pre-treatment (in thousands of liters) by the condition of treatment (format and reference group) and the percent change in water consumption in the first and second post-treatment, in relative terms compared to last years' difference in consumption in the respective time periods. That is, the difference between the two time periods (pre- vs. post-treatment) is subtracted from the respective difference in consumption that was measured in the same time periods last year (as was done in Ferraro and Price's study).[17] For example, in the control group, water consumption between pre- and post-treatment decreased by 8.23 percent compared to the same difference in the previous year. This means that conditions in which the percent change was larger (in size) than that of the control condition show an effect of the treatment. The last column in Table 9.2 shows the relative effect size by comparing the percent change of each treatment to that found in the control. For example, the treatment that showed a graph comparing to the general city level led to a decrease in water consumption in a degree that was 183 percent (almost triple) the size of the change found in the control group. Overall, the treated households showed a larger percent change in water consumption compared to the control (-13.45 percent vs. -8.23 percent) but this difference was not statistically significant, t (2616.4) = 0.45, p = 0.65.

Comparing between treatments, ANOVA showed that while the format of the nudge (graph, percent, or cost) did not show a significant effect, F (3, 15744) = 0.79, p = 0.49, the reference group did show a

Figure 9.1. CONSORT flow diagram for the intervention

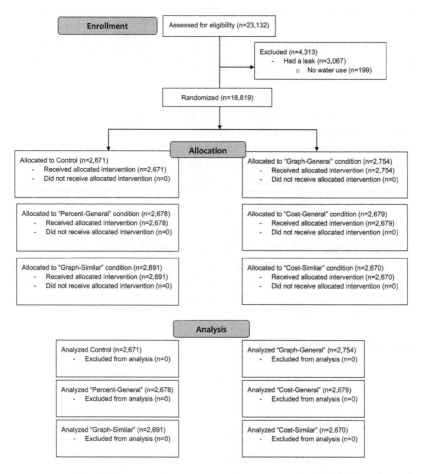

Table 9.1. Similarities and differences between current study and Ferraro & Price's (2013) study

Similarities	Differences
Uses similar intervention (social norm nudge in water bills) as previous studies	Experimental design includes variations of the social norm nudge (by format and reference group)
Uses similar procedure and implementation (nudges added to water bills)	Sample size is smaller (18,300 in the current research vs. 106,669 households in Ferraro & Price [2013])
Uses similar measure (change in actual water consumption between conditions and households)	

Table 9.2. Mean effects of nudges on water consumption

Format	Reference group	N	Average difference in liters (trimmed)	Percent Change relative to last year	Relative effect size
Control		2,671	−254.41	−8.23%	
Graph	General	2,754	−331.87	−23.33%	−183%
Percent	General	2,678	−267.24	−9.07%	−10%
Cost	General	2,679	−320.72	−5.12%	38%
Graph	Similar	2,691	−62.97	−14.98%	−82%
Percent	Similar	2,675	121.59	−19.65%	−139%
Cost	Similar	2,670	−16.45	−8.17%	1%

significant effect, $F(1, 15744) = 4.29$, $p = 0.03$. The interaction between the type of nudge and reference group was also not significant, $F(2, 15744) = 0.6$, $p = 0.55$. Additionally, the type of residence (house vs. apartment) and the size of the household[18] did not show significant effects, $F < 1$, $p > .05$.

Nudging Those Who Matter

More important, however, are the results of the effects of the nudges among consumers who showed an above-than-median consumption in the previous period, and thus were expected to decrease their consumption following the nudge, compared to those that already consumed below the median. As Figure 9.2 shows, the percent change among those who had an above-than-median consumption was much more pronounced than their counterparts, who did not show any significant change from the previous period. ANOVA showed that in addition to the significant effect of the level of previous consumption (above or below median), $F(1, 15737) = 78.79$, $p < .001$, there was a significant effect for the reference group, $F(1, 15737) = 4.31$, $p = .03$. This effect showed that the group that received a nudge with a reference to the general norm (the entire city) reduced their water consumption a little less than those who received a reference to similar other consumers. ANOVA between treatment conditions only (without control) of consumers in the "Above" group showed significant effects for both nudge and reference group, $F(1, 6895) = 4.1, 5.49$, $p = 0.04, 0.02$, but no significant interaction, $F(1, 6895) = 0.01$, $p = 0.92$. These effects showed

Figure 9.2. Percent change of water consumption between consumers who had above vs. below median consumption in previous period, between the different nudges

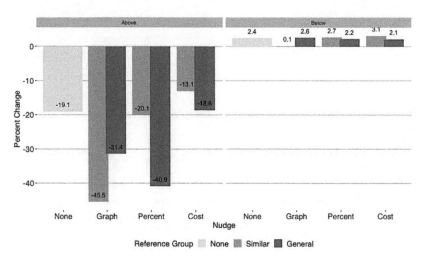

that the change in water consumption was higher when the nudge only included a graph (mean change of –38.48 percent), followed by the percent (–30.43 percent), and the cost (–15.8 percent). As seen in Figure 9.2, the highest percent change was when the nudge included a graph with reference to the similar group of other consumers (–45.5 percent).

Heterogeneity in Effects

Further analyzing the households that were above the median in previous period also showed differences depending on the household characteristics. The difference between houses and apartments was significant, $F (1, 6863) = 13.89, p < .01$, as houses showed a larger percent change compared to apartments (–32.8 percent vs. 27.01 percent on average). There was also a significant interaction between the type of residence and the type of nudge, $F (2, 6863) = 3.01, p = 0.049$, and between the type of residence and the reference group, $F (1, 6863) = 3.82, p = 0.05$. Moreover, there was a significant four-way interaction between the type of nudge, reference group, type of residence, and household size, $F (4, 6863) = 3.63, p < .01$. As Figure 9.3 shows, the effects of the nudges were more pronounced among small houses and small apartments. Surprisingly, there was a counter-effect (increase in consumption) among small houses that received a graph with reference to

Figure 9.3. Percent change in water consumption between types of nudges and households

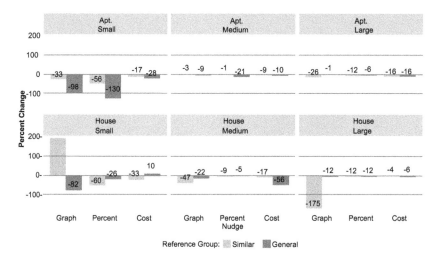

similar consumers. Other than that, though, the effects of the nudges were in the expected direction.

Reconciliation

Our efforts at replication of a previous social norms intervention yielded mixed results. The overall effect of the nudge was not significant when analyzed in aggregate, which is different from previous results. This is because there were significant differences between the types of nudges, which differed both in their format and the reference group used. Additionally, previous research did not measure or consider household characteristics – such as type of residence and household size – which appear to also matter significantly in moderating the effects of the nudges. Another finding that was consistent with previous literature is that consumers who were already below median consumption did not significantly alter their behavior (down or up) following the treatment.

Discussion and Prescriptive Advice

From this research, two major lessons should be learned. First, while social norm nudges can impact households' consumption, the method of implementation is key. Thus, researchers and practitioners should carefully consider how to best tailor and design the social norm nudge to impact water consumption behavior. Second, individual differences matter too. The effects of the nudges were most pronounced among smaller households and also more effective among houses compared to apartments. This finding was made possible in this research due to the existing data in the participating water corporation. If such data is also available in future settings, it should be taken into account when designing the specific implementation of this behavioral policy.

NOTES

1 See for examples Costa, D.L., & Kahn, M.E. (2013a). Energy conservation "nudges" and environmentalist ideology: Evidence from a randomized residential electricity field experiment. *Journal of the European Economic Association, 11*(3), 680–702. https://doi.org/10.3386/w15939; Costa, D.L., & Kahn, M.E. (2013b). Do liberal homeowners consume less electricity? A test of the voluntary restraint hypothesis. *Economics Letters, 119*(2), 210–12. https://doi.org/10.1016/j.econlet.2013.02.020; Allcott, H. (2011). Social norms and energy conservation. *Journal of Public Economics, 95*(9–10), 1082–95. https://doi.org/10.1016/j.jpubeco.2011.03.003; Ayres, I., Raseman, S., & Shih, A. (2013). Evidence from two large field experiments that peer comparison feedback can reduce residential energy usage. *The Journal of Law, Economics, and Organization, 29*(5), 992–1022. https://www.jstor.org /stable/43774381; and Kim, J.H., & Kaemingk, M. (2021). Persisting effects of social norm feedback letters in reducing household electricity usage in Post-Soviet Eastern Europe: A randomized controlled trial. *Journal of Economic Behavior & Organization, 191*, 153–61. https://doi.org/10.1016 /j.jebo.2021.08.032.
2 Ferraro, P.J., & Price, M.K. (2013). Using nonpecuniary strategies to influence behavior: Evidence from a large-scale field experiment. *Review of Economics and Statistics, 95*(1), 64–73. https://doi.org/10.3386/w17189.
3 Bernedo, M., Ferraro, P.J., & Price, M. (2014). The persistent impacts of norm-based messaging and their implications for water conservation. *Journal of Consumer Policy, 37*(3), 437–52. https://doi.org/10.1007/s10603 -014-9266-0.
4 Allcott, H., & Rogers, T. (2014). The short-run and long-run effects of behavioral interventions: Experimental evidence from energy conservation. *American Economic Review, 104*(10), 3003–37. https://doi.org/10.1257 /aer.104.10.3003.
5 I would like to thank the invaluable contributions to the research design, implementation, and analyses by Dr. Itay Sisso.

6 See Costa & Kahn (2013a); and Costa & Kahn (2013b).

7 Ferraro & Price (2013).

8 Brent, D.A., Lott, C., Taylor, M., Cook, J., Rollins, K., & Stoddard, S. (2017). *Are normative appeals moral taxes? Evidence from a field experiment on water conservation*. Department of Economics Working Paper No. 2017–07. http://faculty.bus.lsu.edu/papers/pap17_07.pdf.

9 Camilleri, A.R., & Larrick, R.P. (2014). Metric and scale design as choice architecture tools. *Journal of Public Policy & Marketing, 33*(1), 108–25. https://doi.org/10.1509/jppm.12.151.

10 Anderson, C.D., & Claxton, J.D. (1982). Barriers to consumer choice of energy efficient products. *Journal of Consumer Research, 9*(2), 163–70. https://doi.org/10.1086/208909.

11 Bull, J. (2012). Loads of green washing – can behavioural economics increase willingness-to-pay for efficient washing machines in the UK? *Energy Policy, 50*, 242–52. https://doi.org/10.1016/j.enpol.2012.07.001.

12 Hardisty, D., Shim, Y., Sun, D., & Griffin, D. (2016). Encouraging energy efficiency: Product labels activate temporal tradeoffs. *ACR North American Advances*. https://dx.doi.org/10.2139/ssrn.3576266.

13 Read, D., Frederick, S., & Scholten, M. (2013). DRIFT: An analysis of outcome framing in intertemporal choice. *Journal of Experimental Psychology: Learning, Memory, and Cognition, 39*(2), 573–88. https://doi.org/10.1037/a0029177.

14 Brent et al. (2017).

15 Goldstein, N.J., Cialdini, R.B., & Griskevicius, V. (2008). A room with a viewpoint: Using social norms to motivate environmental conservation in hotels. *Journal of Consumer Research, 35*(3), 472–82. https://doi.org/10.1086/586910.

16 The water corporation assigns a value of zero to households who have not recently reported the number of persons that occupy the household. However, these are assumed to contain one or two persons at the most because (a) the long-term consumption patterns of these groups are highly similar and (b) consumers have an incentive to report the number of persons in the household only if that is above two, in order to get the discounted base fare.

17 Ferraro & Price (2013).

18 Household size was categorized by number of residents as small (up to two residents, 38.6 percent), medium (three to four residents, 31 percent) or large (five or more, 30.4 percent).

CHAPTER TEN

Translating Research on Ease of Payment and Driver Engagement to Reduce Bus Fare Evasion in Santiago

Shannon O'Malley, David A. Pizarro,
Olga E. Rodriguez-Sierra, Juan Camilo Salcedo,
Wardah Malik, and Kelly Peters

AT A GLANCE

- **Our Goal:** To reduce fare evasion rates on the bus system in Santiago by making fare payments easier and by increasing the connection between drivers and riders.
- **The Intervention:** The two interventions tested were (1) adding payment machines near the back door to make payment easier and (2) adding a whiteboard near the driver where they could post friendly messages for riders to increase connection between riders and drivers.
- **The Results:** Adding payment machines near the back door significantly reduced fare evasion relative to the control condition, whereas adding messages from the driver had no added benefit.
- **Lesson Learned:** Simple interventions can often provide the biggest impact, and testing remains a valuable tool to provide clarity on the impact of behavioral interventions, particularly when existing beliefs run counter to those interventions.

Motivation and Objective

As traffic congestion and pollution burden cities with extraordinary costs and consequences, there is an increasing need for expansive, inter-modal public transit networks. Funding of these public transit systems often relies on all users paying a small fare to access the system – a cross-city ride usually costs about the same as a good cup of coffee – but some people are still willing to risk penalty by evading the fare. Fare evasion is estimated at approximately 4 percent globally which translates to hundreds of millions of dollars lost. This leads to added strain on already underfunded systems.[1] Long term, the funds lost due to evasion contribute to poorer service and fewer updates to vehicles and infrastructure.

This problem is seen in cities across the world, where fare evasion takes different forms – from a commuter jumping the turnstiles to enter the subway, to boarding a bus through the back doors to slyly bypass the bus driver – depending on the structure of the system and what is deemed socially acceptable. In some cases, fare evasion is a chronic commuter behavior, while in other cases, it occurs only when opportunity knocks, like when a fare collector is absent from their booth. The nature of fare evasion is also changing as fare control hardware evolves and contactless technology becomes more common.

Transit systems have responded to fare evasion with various oversight and punitive countermeasures, including closed-circuit television monitoring, penalty fares, ticket inspectors, and undercover transit guards. In addition to being resource-intensive to administer, traditional measures such as fines and penalties have been shown to be unreliable at changing behavior and may at times even backfire. Many transit systems operate on a proof of payment system, in which the rider is not monitored during payment, but is expected to provide evidence that they paid if an inspection officer asks. Within these types of systems, fare inspection typically takes place on less than 10 percent of rides.

Given the significant costs, the resource-intensiveness of measures typically deployed, plus the clear connections to human psychology and behavior, fare evasion represents a challenge well-suited to the deployment of behavioral science strategies.

From 2017 to 2018, we (BEworks.com) worked with the Inter-American Development Bank and Transantiago to develop tactics aimed at reducing fare evasion on the transit system in Santiago, Chile.[2] The history of the Transantiago transit system is complicated and includes a number of missteps along the way.[3] This resulted in pervasive negative social sentiment toward the system and higher than average fare evasion for a city of this size. While fare evasion was a challenge across transit systems (buses and metro), the bus system was a key focus, as it was experiencing up to an estimated 28 percent fare evasion on buses within some months.

Our objective was to use techniques from behavioral science that would reduce fare evasion rates without increasing inspection rates. With this objective clear from the start, we needed to identify where in the customer journey we wanted to target and what interventions to use.

As a first step in the process, three of the authors visited Santiago, Chile, to observe rider behavior and interview the people directly involved in the transit system including operators, bus drivers, and local government officials. This provided a clearer picture of the challenges the system faced, including negative sentiment, aggression toward drivers, and fear of confrontation. We also conducted an extensive literature review to identify the types of psychological barriers riders faced in making a payment. We identified three main stages of the journey and key psychological factors that would influence the decision to pay to each stage:

1. **Planning Stage (Intention to Pay):** The only available payment method on the Transantiago system is the BIP! payment card, which requires riders to purchase and preload the card, then tap when boarding to deduct the funds from their account.
   - Key psychological factors relevant to this stage: pain of paying,[4] planning fallacy,[5] procrastination, social norms.[6]
2. **Acting (Making a Payment):** Once people have sufficient funds on their transit card, as they board transit, they make a choice in the moment to tap their payment card or not.
   - Key psychological factors relevant to this stage: ease (or lack thereof) of payment, empathy toward driver,[7] social norms, rationalization, confirmation bias.[8]
3. **Post-ride Evaluation & Updating Intentions:** Once a rider has made a payment (or not), their experience and decision can inform how they behave in the future through reinforcement and learning.
   - Key psychological factors relevant to this stage: post hoc rationalization[9] and habit formation.[10]

In observing rider behavior, we also noticed key differences in the underlying motivation for evading payment. While some people evade because the payment machine is broken or they couldn't reach the validator, others would go so far as to jump over turnstiles and habitually avoid paying. Research in Australia and in Italy supports the idea of three broad categories of fare evaders: accidental, unintentional (or opportunistic), and deliberate (or chronic). Those who evade for accidental reasons intend to pay their fare, but something gets in the way, like a broken validator or lost card.[11] People in the unintentional or opportunistic category do not have a set intention to evade, but may choose to when the opportunity arises, like when they are in a rush or they slip through the backdoors. Deliberate or chronic evaders typically have a strong preference to not pay. Reasons for evading might include only going a couple stops or a strong stance against the system. Regardless of the reason, people in this category actively avoid paying and do so on a routine basis. In our conversations with officials in Santiago, it was also noted that a subset of deliberate fare evaders likely did so because the cost of transit was too high relative to their income. It's important to note that behavioral science techniques are unlikely to influence people who evade for this reason, as barriers to payment are systemic rather than psychological. Therefore, we did not expect to influence evaders of low income.

Following our assessment of the rider payment journey and reasons for evasion, we determined that the best opportunity to maximize impact would be to focus on accidental and opportunistic evaders, during the "Acting: Making a Payment" stage, targeting riders in the moment of boarding the bus. This meant we would focus on behavioral science techniques that could be implemented near the doors of the bus where people were loading.

Inspiration

With our objective in mind, there were two concepts that were repeatedly identified during the research phase: ease of payment and empathy/connection with the driver. These formed the basis of the interventions that we ultimately tested in field. The exact strategies we developed were a mixture of interventions designed for this context, some inspired by several distinct interventions used in other unrelated settings, and others the direct replication of previous work.

The interventions developed to address ease (or lack thereof) of payment were directly inspired by a similar study conducted on a transit system in San Francisco. The second intervention, designed to address empathy/connection with the driver, was developed on the basis of several behavioral science findings. Below, we describe how each relates to this context, as well as the papers that inspired the interventions that were implemented (see Table 10.1 for a summary).

Table 10.1. Summary of the prior research reports that inspired our interventions

Dimension	Original study	Findings
Ease of Payment	Lee & Papas (2015)	Studied the impact of allowing all-door boarding across the San Francisco Municipal Transportation Agency (SFMTA) system. Two years post-implementation, they found a positive impact of all-door boarding – dwell times and trip durations improved and there was a slight increase for system-wide fare compliance.
Empathy toward Driver	Macintosh (2009)	This study examined the antecedents and outcomes of interpersonal rapport in a professional service context. A survey was deployed to 121 dental patients regarding their relationships with dental professionals. The research findings indicated that all four antecedents (familiarity, mutual self-disclosure, extras, and common grounding) were positively related to rapport.
Empathy toward Driver	Lotz-Schmitt, Siem, & Stürmer (2017)	This study examined the conditions under which empathy becomes "dis-inhibited" as a motivator of out-group helping. They found that when intergroup dissimilarity is high, empathy's influence on helping critically depends upon the out-group target's perceived benevolence (sociability and trustworthiness).

Ease of Payment

On the Transantiago bus system, riders were expected to board through the front doors and deboard through the back doors. This ensured that payment systems were near the driver (to have an authority present) and to create a better flow for boarding and deboarding in busy areas. While all-door boarding had become standard on rail/metro systems, where proof of payment methods are common (riders are responsible for acquiring a ticket and must show proof of payment if asked, else face a fine), in 2018, all-door boarding was still relatively uncommon for bus systems around the world.

There was a general view within the industry that putting payment systems near the back doors would encourage more people to board through the back of the door but increase opportunistic evasion, as people would still not pay when not observed by a driver. In our observation however, the lack of payment near the back door created a barrier to payment. At busy stops, the driver needs to open both doors, and riders who are simply trying to "catch their bus" would often board through both the front and the back doors. The lack of a payment system at the back meant that anyone who boarded at the back would need to make their way to the front (against the general flow of passengers) to tap their card. This resulted in most riders who boarded through the rear doors never paying their fare.

The underlying idea of "making it easy" is common in applied behavioral science and is often one of the first set of strategies practitioners will seek to implement in changing behavior (depending on context). In this case there was a prior study, conducted by the San Francisco Municipal Transportation Agency (SFMTA), examining all-door boarding on buses.[12] In 2012, the SFMTA was the first multimodal transit provider in North America to offer system-wide all-door boarding. Prior to this time all-door boarding was only available on light rail, but within the SFMTA system, it was expanded to include all vehicles including buses, historic streetcars, and cable cars. The study conducted three surveys prior to implementation, and one survey two years after implementation to evaluate the impact of all-door boarding on the system. Their key measures included fare evasion, dwell times (how long buses need to stop to load and unload passengers), and trip duration (overall duration of a route). All-door boarding was expected to reduce dwell times and trip duration and provide a neutral or positive impact on fare evasion. Overall, they found a positive impact on all three measures – dwell times and trip durations improved and there was a slight increase for system-wide fare compliance.[13]

Our primary focus was on fare compliance, and this gave us a strong indication and basis to encourage our client to evaluate the impact of adding card validators to the rear of the bus.

Empathy toward Driver

During our in-field interviews we also observed that riders tend to think of the system as being directly representative of the Chilean government. While there was government oversight across the system, and the government sets fare prices, a number of independent operators are responsible for the actual service provided. In the case of buses, independent operators bid on routes to provide service, and for the duration of the contract they operate, maintain, and provide service to that route, and are paid based on the number of riders that tap their cards on their buses. Fare evasion directly affects the bus operators and their ability to maintain and provide service on those lines. Drivers are employed by the bus operators. However, public perception tends to lump the drivers and the bus operators in with the "system" such that when people evade, they feel as though it is the larger system and government that loses out rather than the private bus systems and drivers.

Drivers expressed that they often avoided interacting with riders, in either a positive or negative manner, particularly in areas with high rates of fare evasion, for fear of confrontation. It was our hypothesis that this creates an environment in which drivers and riders see each other as out-groups, and there is little connection of empathy between them. Therefore, we were interested in ways we could increase the engagement of drivers with riders, to increase a sense of connection and empathy, under the hypothesis that that would increase riders willingness to pay, as they would not want to cheat the driver.[14] While there was not a study that directly looked at this hypothesis in the past, we took inspiration from research by Lotz-Schmitt et al. (2017) showing that empathy could serve as a motivator of helping across intergroup boundaries.[15] In this study they manipulated the similarity between individuals of different groups and found that increasing similarity with dyads predicted higher intentions of helping.

Interventions and Method

We tested three conditions: Rear-door validators (validators); rear-door validators plus driver engagement (validators + engagement); no engagement or rear-door validators (control).

Working directly with bus drivers and bus operators, we developed an intervention that would allow drivers to share something about themselves and greet customers in a safe way that the drivers felt comfortable with and could implement in a reliable and consistent manner. This took the form of a daily message on a whiteboard. In the validators + engagement condition, two 50 cm long and 40 cm wide whiteboards were placed in the bus in locations visible to passengers boarding a bus. One was placed at the front, and another at the rear door. Messages were selected in consultation with stakeholder interviews with the bus drivers who would deliver the intervention. The full list of messages can be seen in Table 10.2.

Experimental Design

TIME AND LOCATION
The experiment was conducted in Santiago, Chile, starting on November 13, 2018. Data was collected on weekdays, between 12.30 and 5.30 p.m., which is the period with the highest evasion in the day at Transantiago.[16]

Table 10.2. Drivers helped generate the below list of thirty-six messages and were instructed to select one of these per route. Messages were always written in Spanish; the English translation is provided below for reference.

List of Messages

All messages were preceded by "¡HOLA! Soy [driver's name] tu conductor."
(HELLO! I'm [driver's name], I am your conductor.)

Hoy llegué más temprano y limpié el bus.	Today I arrived earlier and cleaned the bus.
Hoy verifiqué los niveles de aceite del bus.	Today I checked the oil levels of the bus.
Llegar a tiempo es muy importante para mi.	Being on time is very important to me.
Hoy verifiqué el aire de los neumáticos.	Today I checked the air in the tires.
Hace poco completé un curso de primeros auxilios.	I recently completed a first aid course.
Hoy revisé las luces y las direccionales del bus.	Today I checked the lights and turn signals of the bus.
Hoy revisé los frenos del bus.	Today I checked the brakes of the bus.
Trato de mantener el bus en buenas condiciones.	I try to keep the bus in good condition.
Todas las noches barro el bus.	Every night I sweep the bus.
Cada mañana compruebo que el bus funcione correctamente.	Every morning I check that the bus is working properly.
Mi jugador de fútbol favorito es Alexis Sánchez.	My favorite soccer player is Alexis Sánchez.
Mi actividad favorita es jugar fútbol con mis hijos.	My favorite thing to do is play soccer with my children.
Mi comida favorita son las empanadas de pino.	My favorite food is empanadas de pino.
Soy voluntario en la escuela de mi barrio.	I volunteer at my neighborhood school.
Mi sueño es ir un día a la Isla de Chiloé.	My dream is to one day go to Chiloé Island.
Me encanta el Cerro de Santa Lucía.	I love Santa Lucía Hill.
Recuerdo con alegría la Copa América de 2015.	I remember with joy the Copa América in 2015.
Me encanta el ceviche.	I love ceviche.
Me encanta caminar en el Cajón del Maipo.	I love walking in the Cajón del Maipo.
Mi barrio favorito es Parque Bustamante.	My favorite neighborhood is Parque Bustamante.
¡Mi cumpleaños es esta semana!	My birthday is this week!
Me gusta ver películas.	I like to watch movies.

List of Messages

Me gusta bailar con mi esposa.	I like to dance with my wife.
Amo a mis dos hijos Ana y Jaime.	I love my two children Ana and Jaime.
Siempre llevo a mis hijos a la escuela.	I always take my children to school.
Una parte de mi salario viene de las tarifas de los pasajeros.	Part of my salary comes from passenger fares.
El transporte público es de gran beneficio para todos.	Public transportation is of great benefit to everyone.
Creo que la comunidad se construye en la colaboración.	I believe that community is built on collaboration.
Me gusta contribuir a mi comunidad.	I like to contribute to my community.
El transporte público es un privilegio.	Public transportation is a privilege.
El transporte público te ayuda a ir del punto A al B.	Public transportation helps you get from point A to B.
El transporte público conecta a tu ciudad.	Public transportation connects your city.
El transporte público te conecta con tus seres queridos.	Public transportation connects you to your loved ones.
Este autobús también te pertenece.	This bus belongs to you too.
El transporte público es un servicio para todos nosotros.	Public transportation is a service for all of us.
Los otros pasajeros de este bus son sus vecinos.	The other passengers on this bus are your neighbors.

PARTICIPANTS AND SAMPLE SIZE

A participant was defined as a passenger boarding a bus in Santiago de Chile. Given that we did not expect to influence riders who evade due to low income, we estimated that we needed 1,265 non-low-income evaders to detect a standardized effect size at Cohen's $w = 0.1$, assuming that data would be analyzed with a chi-squared test. Parameters were set at: power= 0.9, alpha = 0.05, Cohen's $w = 0.1$, df = 2. Power analysis was conducted using a parametric-based package in R.[17]

To convert from non-low-income evaders to total ridership required using previous data from socioeconomic status and fare evasion since income cannot be directly observed in individual passengers. We hypothesized that an effect would only be observed in non-low-income passengers, corresponding to 43.6 percent of the sample, and that evasion would be 14.1 percent (evasion data from DTPM from second trimester of 2018, for route 712. C.N. Duk, personal communication, 2018). This yielded a total of 20,577 passengers needed.

Figure 10.1. Example of a message as passengers boarded the bus, at the front of the bus (left) and at the rear of the bus (right)

Across our study period, we observed 144 bus trips, with a total sample size of 20,855 bus riders. Following collection of the data, we compared the in-person observations with the data collected by the card validators (BIP! data), to ensure the in-person observations did not deviate dramatically from the validator data. Considering only people who validated their card, (as the BIP! data does not record fare evaders) the magnitude of error between the two observation types was on average 1.5 transactions. If the magnitude of error between these observations exceeded three standard deviations, then that bus trip was categorized as an outlier and removed from analysis, resulting in 4 bus trips (n= 623) being excluded from the analysis, for a final sample size of 140 bus trips (n=20,323). See the CONSORT flow diagram (Figure 10.2) for further details on the allocation of conditions.

UNIT OF ANALYSIS

Despite our target being passengers, we cannot randomly assign single passengers to conditions. For this reason, the lowest level of aggregation possible was individual bus trips. Eight bus trips (four inbound and four outbound) were selected for the experiment (details below on assignment of conditions to bus trips).

Figure 10.2. CONSORT diagram detailing the allocation of buses and riders to conditions

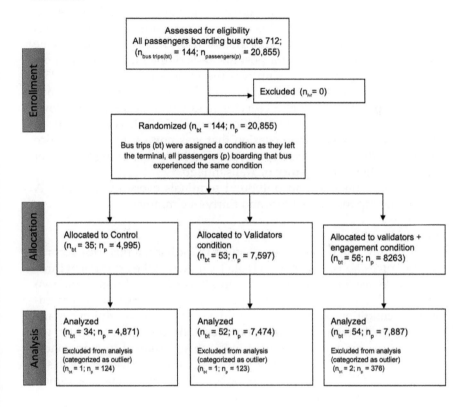

Another alternative would be to test at the level of individual bus routes (the next level of aggregation possible). Aggregation at the level of bus trips, instead of bus routes, was preferred for two reasons: (1) Bus routes are difficult to match in terms of variables that correlate with fare evasion (e.g., socioeconomic status, duration of route, number of bus doors), which would introduce confounds when assigning conditions to bus routes; (2) the first specific hypothesis we are testing – H_1 or immediate localized influence of driver engagement, see section 2 – considers a single boarding of a passenger as the central unit of analysis, assuming boardings are independent of each other.

BUS ROUTE

IDB and DTPM selected route 712 from one of their client bus companies (bus company STP). The following reasons were considered when prioritizing this bus route: (1) Bus company: Route 712 is operated by STP, which has a history of cooperation with the DTPM. Furthermore, other bus companies (Alsacia) were undergoing strikes at the projected time of the experiment. (2) This bus route is a trunk line that connects key hubs and traverses neighborhoods with different socioeconomic statuses, which will allow for post hoc tests of the influence of income on evasion. (3) Daily ridership was the highest (estimated at 21,354) among the list of prioritized routes.[18] (4) In addition, the selected bus company provides the highest service quality (bus cleanliness and lowest delays – personal communication from DTPM). This allowed us to determine an effect of fare evasion that was not a reaction to service quality – which has been hypothesized to have driven high levels of evasion earlier in the history of Transantiago.[19]

Buses left inbound and outbound terminals every ten minutes. A single bus trip took two hours and thirty-one minutes.

RANDOMIZATION

On each day, conditions were assigned to individual bus trips according to a preestablished scheme (Table 10.3). Across the experiment three buses were used for condition VE, three buses for condition V, and two for control (No validators and no treatment). We blocked the assignment of conditions so that there would be one control condition departing from inbound and one from outbound. Beyond this constraint, we used simple random assignment without replacement to map conditions to buses departing the terminals. Once buses arrived at the destination terminal, they would keep the condition they had been assigned to when traveling in the opposite direction.

Differences and Similarities from Past Research

In terms of differences between the Lee & Papas (2015) study conducted in San Francisco, the addition of payment validators near the rear doors was comparable, but there are a number of differences in the design of this study (Table 10.4). In the original study, the implementation of all-door boarding was done system-wide, for an initial six-month period, and was extended indefinitely. Results were evaluated at the two-year mark in a pre-post analysis. In our study, the rear-door validators were only implemented on a small subset of buses within the system (no system-wide promotion of it), for a nine-day period, and results were compared to a control condition (different buses on the same route).

With respect to our driver engagement condition, the design of this intervention was not directly adapted from any one single paper but

Table 10.3. The sequence of conditions assigned to buses as they left the terminal on each day

Day	Inbound	Outbound
1	VE, VE, C, V	C, V, V, VE
2	VE, VE, VE, C	V, V, C, V
3	VE, V, C, VE	V, VE, C, V
4	C, VE, V, V	V, C, VE, VE
5	V, VE, C, V	C, VE, V, VE
6	V, VE, V, C	VE, C, V, VE
7	V, VE, VE, C	V, C, V, VE
8	V, VE, V, C	C, V, VE, VE
9	C, V, VE, VE	C, VE, V, V
10	VE, C, V, V	VE, V, C, VE
11	C, VE, VE, V	C, V, VE, V
12	C, V, V, VE	VE, VE, V, C
13	C, VE, V, VE	V, VE, V, C
14	VE, C, V, VE	V, C, V, VE
15	VE, VE, V, C	V, V, VE, C
16	C, VE, V, VE	C, VE, V, V
17	VE, V, V, C	VE, VE, C, V
18	VE, V, V, C	VE, V, VE, C
19	C, V, VE, VE	V, C, V, VE
20	VE, V, VE, C	V, VE, V, C

Table 10.4. Comparison of the similarities and differences between the Lee & Papas (2015) study and the present study

Parameter	Lee & Papas (2015)	Our study (2018)
City	San Francisco, USA	Santiago, Chile
Location of Validators	Near the rear door	Near the rear door
Experiment Design	Pre-post evaluation, system wide implementation of all-door boarding	Comparison to control condition (within same time frame), inclusion of driver engagement condition, implemented on one bus route (eight buses)
Duration of Data Collection	Unknown (all boarding implemented over two years, survey conducted in 2014 of unknown duration)	9 days

(*Continued*)

Table 10.4 (Continued)

Parameter	Lee & Papas (2015)	Our study (2018)
Participants	Unknown	20,232 passengers
Evaluation of Fare Evasion	In-field survey (observations) conducted across the whole system	Sixteen in-field observers tracked fare evasion during the duration of the study on preselected routes
Measures	Fare evasion, dwell times, trip speed	Fare evasion

rather was developed through at the ideation process at BEworks. During our ideation phase, we review the research conducted so far and consider the psychological factors that are at play. We then develop strategic hypotheses for how to address these barriers. While these strategic hypotheses are grounded in behavioral science techniques, the actual implementation is customized and developed specifically for the context at hand. In this case, that means we do not have a clear reference point for differences and similarities.

Results

We found a significant reduction in fare evasion (2.15 percent) when an additional fare payment machine was placed close to the back door (Figure 10.3) when evaluating people who boarded through either door. When isolating the analysis to people who boarded through the back door, the reduction in fare evasion was 8.39 percent and 9.15 percent (when the payment machine was placed close to the back door and there was driver engagement, respectively) relative to the control condition (Figure 10.3). We saw no impact on evasion when boarding through the front door (Figure 10.3).

In contrast, we did not observe a significant effect in the driver engagement condition over and above the addition of the fare payment machines (whether looking at boarding through the front door, back door, or combined). Based on these findings, we were able to draw several useful conclusions about fare evasion and make concrete suggestions. Our results showed the importance of increasing ease and convenience for paying fares and underscored the powerful potential of relatively small changes to the choice architecture and physical environment.

Figure 10.3. Probability of fare evasion when boarding through (i) both front and back doors, (ii) back door only, and (iii) front door only, for the V and VE conditions relative to the control baseline. Model estimates from Firth logistic regression with covariates. Marginal effect sizes and 95 percent confidence intervals estimated with delta method. Significance tested with Wald test (α = 0.05, Bonferroni corrected)

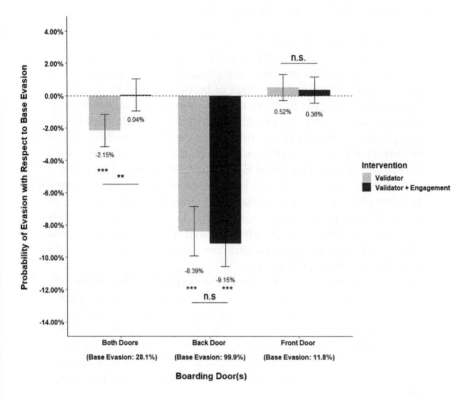

Reconciliation

In the context of our replication of Lee & Papas (2015), we found a similar result in that the addition of validation terminals near the back door reduced fare evasion. While our experiment design was quite different, it is important that we were able to replicate the effect, on a smaller scale, but through a more controlled experiment design. This is also consistent with the positive impact seen through other scenarios where removing barriers or friction to a given action (making it easy) has an overall positive impact on behavior.[20]

In the case of driver engagement, despite our best efforts to create an intervention that would better connect the driver to riders, using messages that were pre-evaluated prior to the in-field experiment, we did not see any additional lift for this condition. There are a number of reasons we think this may have happened:

1. **Interference between conditions:** Because the unit of analysis is a bus trip, it is possible that the same passenger could be exposed to different treatments throughout the duration of the experiment. Assuming the effect of being exposed to driver engagement extends to other rides, this could change the rates of compliance in any condition: for instance, inflate the rate of compliance in the control condition or amplify the effect in the treatment across days. However, given that only a small portion of buses out of the total fleet (three out of sixty) in a day would be treated, which yields a chance to revisit a treatment on any day of 8.6 percent (if experiment runs for ten days) to 26.4 percent (if experiment runs for twenty days), we considered the possibility of interference to be minimal. Unfortunately, because transactions and evasion are not passenger identified, we had no way to measure interference.

2. **Structural barriers may be more relevant to "in-the-moment" decisions:** There was clear indication that there were complex causal factors in fare evasion in Santiago, including social/political dynamics. However, it's possible that for most soft evaders, who tend to evade when the opportunity presents itself (rather than as a matter of principle), simple situational factors are more relevant to their decision to pay or not when they are boarding the bus.

3. **The implemented intervention may not have been correctly attuned to the context or may have needed more time to work.** It's possible that alternative means of implementation, including having the driver speak with riders or share different messages may have been more impactful. This is a challenge often seen in the application of behavioral science when we don't always have the opportunity to run multiple iterations of a study: we cannot distinguish if the hypothesis was wrong or if the implementation was not sufficient to see an effect.

Discussion and Prescriptive Advice

Our efforts at translating and replicating prior research to develop interventions to reduce fare evasion on public transit yielded mixed results – while the replication of implementing all-door boarding[21] (making payment easy) was successful, out attempt to reduce fair evasion by increasing the empathy/connection with drivers was not. Fare evasion is an economically important issue, but it is also a social issue – why do passengers not pay their fair share and what is the best way to motivate citizens to consistently pay? Over the course of this project, we uncovered key psychological barriers to fare payment, including ease (or lack thereof) in making a payment, negative attitudes toward the transit company, and norms in favor of fare evasion.

Some of the most reliable and consistent interventions implemented by practitioners are those that make a given action easier – either by implementing a default, removing friction, or putting the option in the right place at the right time. We see that again in this project: making payment validators more accessible led to a reduction in fare evasion. For many, it will be tempting to view this as an obvious intervention, but it is important to note that within the industry at the time, providing payment machines at the back door was not common, and there was resistance to implementing this change. Adding additional fareboxes likely influenced accidental and unintentional evaders (and not deliberate evaders). There was an underlying perception within the industry that most or all evaders are deliberate, but this simple intervention that provides support that is not the case.

For bus operators, adding additional payment machines costs money, and if they assume that people will not use them because evaders are making a deliberate choice, they are unlikely to invest in them. We calculated that introducing additional fareboxes on buses could help our client collect an additional US$20 million in fare revenue, providing a clear justification for bus operators to invest in the additional payment machines.

This also serves as a good reminder of the value of field experiments[22] – the historic decision to not put payment validators as the back of the bus was rooted in long-standing assumptions about rider behavior. Fare evasion is a complex behavior, with many different underlying reasons, but in-field testing is an effective way to evaluate the ROI of any given intervention prior to large-scale roll out.

An additional lesson that will be familiar to most practitioners is that we often generate many more ideas during the process than what can be tested in field. This requires a process of prioritization that often takes the client needs into consideration. While it was disappointing that the driver engagement condition did not impact fare evasion, this was an important learning for the transit system. The driver empathy hypothesis was compelling, there was ample evidence that negative sentiment impacted fare evasion rates, and the strategy to humanize the drivers was innovative; however, a simple change to the choice architecture (more fareboxes) was sufficient to garner significant benefits. Although there may be other interventions targeting the social/empathy level that might have an effect, it is a good reminder that focusing on simple interventions can yield significant results.

Those seeking to shift transportation modes, increase safety, reduce fare evasion, or tackle any of the other large-scale challenges posed by advances in transportation would be well served to remember the utility of behavioral science in driving positive change.

NOTES

1 Bonfanti, G., & Wagenknecht, T. (2010). Human factors reduce aggression and fare evasion. *International Association of Public Transport (UIPT)*, 59(1), 28–32. https://trid.trb.org/view/915667.

2 In 2019 the system was renamed "Red Metropolitana de Movilidad." Throughout the Chapter we refer to it as Transantiago, as that was the name at the time of study.

3 Muñoz, J.C., & Gschwender, A. (2008). Transantiago: A tale of two cities. *Research in Transportation Economics*, 22(1), 45–53. https://doi.org/10.1016/j.retrec.2008.05.010.

4 Zellermayer, O. (1996). *The pain of paying* [Doctoral dissertation, Carnegie Mellon University]. ProQuest Dissertations Publishing. https://www.researchgate.net/publication/280711796_The_Pain_of_Paying.

5 Buehler, R., Griffin, D., & Peetz, J. (2010). The planning fallacy: Cognitive, motivational, and social origins. *Advances in Experimental Social Psychology*, 43, 1–62. https://doi.org/10.1016/S0065-2601(10)43001-4.

6 Cialdini, R.B., & Trost, M.R. (1998). Social influence: Social norms, conformity and compliance. In D.T. Gilbert, S.T. Fiske, & G. Lindzey (Eds.), *The handbook of social psychology* (pp. 151–92). https://psycnet.apa.org/record/1998-07091-021.

7 Lotz-Schmitt, K., Siem, B., & Stürmer, S. (2017). Empathy as a motivator of dyadic helping across group boundaries: The dis-inhibiting effect of the

recipient's perceived benevolence. *Group Processes & Intergroup Relations,*
20(2), 233–59. https://doi.org/10.1177/1368430215612218.

8 Nickerson, R. S. (1998). Confirmation bias: A ubiquitous phenomenon
in many guises. *Review of General Psychology, 2*(2), 175–220. https://
doi.org/10.1037/1089-2680.2.2.175

9 Blanton, H., Jaccard, J., Christie, C., & Gonzales, P.M. (2007). Plausible
assumptions, questionable assumptions and post hoc rationalizations:
Will the real IAT, please stand up? *Journal of Experimental Social Psychology,*
43(3), 399–409. https://doi.org/10.1016/j.jesp.2006.10.019.

10 Smith, K.S., & Graybiel, A.M. (2016). Habit formation. *Dialogues in Clinical*
Neuroscience, 18(1), 33–43. https://doi.org/10.31887/DCNS.2016.18.1/ksmith.

11 See Delbosc, A., & Currie, G. (2016). Cluster analysis of fare evasion
behaviours in Melbourne, Australia. *Transport Policy, 50,* 29–36. https://doi
.org/10.1016/j.tranpol.2016.05.015; and Salis, S., Barabino, B., & Usell, B. (2017).
Segmenting fare evader groups by factor and cluster analysis. *WIT Transactions*
on The Built Environment, 176, 503–15. https://doi.org/10.2495/UT170431.

12 Lee, J., & Papas, D. (2015). All-door boarding in San Francisco, California.
Transportation Research Record, 2538(1), 65–75. https://doi.org/10.3141/2538-08.

13 Lee & Papas (2015).

14 Macintosh, G. (2009). The role of rapport in professional services:
antecedents and outcomes. *The Journal of Services Marketing, 23*(2), 70–8.
https://doi.org/10.1108/08876040910946332.

15 Lotz-Schmitt et al. (2017).

16 Guarda, P., Galilea, P., Handy, S., Muñoz, J.C., & Ortúzar, J. de D. (2016).
Decreasing fare evasion without fines? A microeconomic analysis. *Research*
in Transportation Economics, 59, 151–8. https://doi.org/10.1016/j.retrec
.2016.06.001.

17 Champely, S., Ekstrom, C., Dalgaard, P., Gill, J., Weibelzahl, S.,
Anandkumar, A., Ford, C., Volcic, R., & De Rosario, M.H. (2018). Package
'pwr'. *R package version, 1*(2). https://nyuscholars.nyu.edu/en/publications
/pwr-basic-functions-for-power-analysis.

18 Guarda et al. (2016).

19 Muñoz, J.C., Batarce, M., & Hidalgo, D. (2014). Transantiago, five years
after its launch. *Research in Transportation Economics, 48,* 184–93. https://
doi.org/10.1016/j.retrec.2014.09.041.

20 Thaler, R.H., & Sunstein, C.R. (2008). *Nudge: Improving decisions about*
health, wealth, and happiness. Yale University Press.

21 Lee & Papas (2015).

22 Barr, N., Hilscher, M.C., Le, A., Thomson, D.R. & Peters, K. (2022). To
effectively apply and scale behavioral insights, practitioners must be
scientific. In N. Mažar & D. Soman (Eds.). *Behavioral science in the wild.*
University of Toronto Press.

CHAPTER ELEVEN

Translating Social and Planning Interventions to Increase Self-Identification among Canadian Public Servants

Haris Khan, Meera Paleja, Renante Rondina,
and Elizabeth Hardy

AT A GLANCE

- **Our Goal:** To encourage Canadian public servants to self-identify as a member of an employment equity group to improve diversity and inclusion in the Government of Canada.
- **The Intervention:** In the two experiments, two social interventions (social norms and messenger variation) and two planning interventions (default appointments and planning prompts) were administered.
- **The Results:** We found that (a) information delivered by a more relevant messenger drove self-ID more successfully than social norms, and (b) contrary to the literature and our predictions, individuals were more likely to self-identify if provided with information-rich, lengthy text about self-ID rather than sparse, direct, and action-oriented text.
- **Lesson Learned:** Without experimentation tailored to our specific context, we would not have been able to determine which (among multiple) interventions would lead to more robust, effective communications to help meet policy objectives.

Motivation and Objective

Ensuring the population of the federal public workforce is representative of the Canadian population is an important building block for fostering diversity and inclusion in the Canadian public service. Self-identification (self-ID) is the process by which an employee identifies as one of the four employment equity groups as defined by the *Employment Equity Act* (women, visible minorities, Indigenous peoples, or persons with disabilities) to their employer for the purposes of understanding representation of these groups in the place of employment.

To understand representation in the public service, the self-ID form must be used by individuals to voluntarily identify themselves as belonging to one of the four designated groups. Data and anecdotal evidence suggest limited participation in the form completion, resulting in an incomplete picture of the composition of the workforce. With limited data, it is uncertain whether we are achieving a representative public service and how far the organization has to go to achieve representation.

The completion of a relatively short and straight-forward form may seem like a simple task, but work from the Research and Experimentation Team (RET) at the Office of the Chief Human Resources Officer (OCHRO) at the Treasury Board Secretariat found in original qualitative research that self-identifying is a complex behavior with a set of contextual factors at play.

To understand whether we can improve self-ID completion rates, we developed two experiments that were inspired by other research. The conditions in the original research were translated and scaled horizontally to the domain of self-identification. This chapter outlines these two translation efforts, detailing their inspirations, interventions, and methods and how they differ from the original studies, before reconciling these differences. At the end of the chapter, we provide some reflections on translating experimental results in industry and nonacademic contexts.

Experiment 1: Using the Messenger Effect and Social Norms to Encourage Self-Identification Among Public Service Executives (EXs)

Inspiration

When considering what kinds of interventions could help increase the proportion of public servants who self-ID, two "tried-and-tested" behavioral insights principles immediately came to mind: the messenger effect and social norms. The messenger effect suggests that people change their behavior based on who is asking them to make that change. Social norms are a bit more nuanced, with the basic idea being that people are more likely to conduct a behavior if they think others are doing so too.

The next step was to consult the literature to determine what has shown to be effective in the past. To our surprise, while the messenger effect is mentioned in almost every behavioral insights framework or popular article we could find, the number of individual experiments that directly manipulate the sender of a behavioral "ask" was very limited. However, using the MINDSPACE framework Dolan et al. (2012) provided,[1] we applied a lens into why messenger effects work and summarized evidence for the different potential pathways for the efficacy of messenger effects. Although this inspired our work and helped us design interventions using a theoretical framework, it did not provide a single concrete study to translate from.

In the end, we found a study by Dean Karlan and John List that approximated the kind of messenger effect we were trying to emulate.[2] In their study, they approach potential donors with a solicitation to donate to an international development charity with the offer of matching funds. The key intervention manipulates whether the matching funds come from an anonymous charity or from the Bill and Melinda Gates Foundation (BMGF). The study found that naming the BMGF increased the average revenue per solicitation by 43 percent and the likelihood of a donation by 26 percent.

When reviewing literature on social norms, we found significantly more experiments. Foremost among them was a meta-analysis which played a similar role to the MINDSPACE framework for the messenger effect by providing overarching principles of what features of social norms are effective in which situations.[3] As with the messenger effect, we searched for a specific experiment for inspiration, and ultimately used an experiment conducted by the Behavioural Insights Team (BIT) and the UK tax authority.[4] In this study, individuals who owed tax debts to the government were sent letters informing them that they were overdue on their payments. Social norms were introduced in the form of a statement informing the recipient that "9 out of 10 people in Britain pay their taxes on time." Some intervention groups also received a more localized social norm specific to their city or town and their postal code. While each social norm increased payment rates, the most local norm was also the most successful, resulting in a 15 percentage point increase in payment rates.

Interventions and Method

RET developed an email campaign to encourage executives to complete the self-ID questionnaire in the Executive Talent Management System (ETMS). ETMS is a common HR software that all executives (high ranking public servants) in the Government of Canada use for the purposes of career management and progression. As part of this experiment, the treatment group executives received an email encouraging them to self-ID, which included a deadline as well as a link to ETMS, while the control group did not receive an email as part of the campaign.

The treatment group emails differed on two dimensions: the messenger and the social norms content of the email. Half of the executives that received an email received it from the Chief Human Resources Officer (CHRO), and the other half received it from their departmental deputy head (the most senior public servant in their department). A fifth group did not receive any email regarding self-ID as part of this campaign.

The emails also differed on their content: half of the emails underlined the fact that self-ID provided a social benefit to the public service, included a social norms statement "7 out of 10 executives self-ID in ETMS," and had a subject line that read: "Join your EX colleagues in Self-IDing in ETMS." The other half of the emails simply provided clear and instructive directions to executives, with the subject line: "To be completed by Nov 5: Self-ID in ETMS." See the online appendix for the full text of the emails.[5]

This experiment was conducted as a clustered randomized trial, in which all the executives of a given department were sent the same email, and the departments themselves were randomly allocated into one of five groups.

While we were inspired by the messenger effect interventions by Karlan and List, we had to redesign the interventions to fit our context, while remaining true to the principle in the original study.[6] In their work, the messenger was in the form of an existing donor who was seeking matching funds from an individual. This donor was either anonymous or the BMGF. Karlan and List provide evidence that attaching the BMGF brand to the ask provides a "quality signal" to potential donors who are likely to recognize the large global charity.[7]

In our study, information regarding the "messenger" was delivered in two ways: the email address that the email came from and the sign-off on the email body itself. This constitutes the major difference in approaches as the CHRO or the DM were not going to "match" the

Table 11.1. Key features for each intervention type

Treatment Group	Sender	Subject Line	Intervention Email Text
Control	–	–	–
CHRO Instructive	CHRO	For Action: Self-Identification in ETMS by November 5	– Request to self-ID in ETMS – Link to ETMS – Deadline – Statement underlining importance of self-ID as a leader
CHRO Social Benefit	CHRO	Join your EX Colleagues in Completing the Self-ID Form	– Request to self-ID in ETMS – Social norm statement (see below) – Link to ETMS – Deadline – Statement underlining importance of self-ID as a leader
DM Instructive	Deputy Head	For Action: Self-Identification in ETMS by November 5	– Request to self-ID in ETMS – Link to ETMS – Deadline – Statement underlining importance of self-ID as a leader
DM Social Benefit	Deputy Head	Join your EX Colleagues in Completing the Self-ID Form	– Request to self-ID in ETMS – Social norm statement (see below) – Link to ETMS – Deadline – Statement underlining importance of self-ID as a leader

behavior of the executive. However, by attaching their names to the request to either donate (or self-ID in our case), the messengers, whether it was the senior government executive or the charity, are implicitly signaling the source of the request and attaching their names to it. While not the same as a quality signal, our hypothesis was that an email from the CHRO would serve a similar purpose as they would be considered an expert on the topic of employment equity. They are also seen as the authority on the matter, vested with a set of powers regarding people management in the public service.

The connection between the social norms intervention in the BIT study and ours was more direct:

Figure 11.1. Study flow diagram

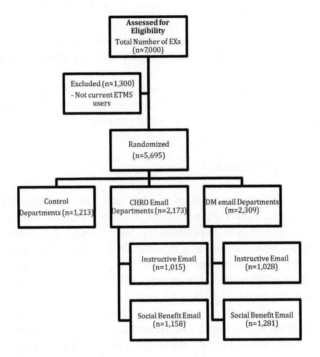

Table 11.2. Comparison with previous study

BIT Social Norms Wording	OCHRO Social Norms Wording
9 out of 10 people in Britain pay their tax on time.	Join the 8 out of 10 GoC executives who have already completed the self-identification questionnaire.

The key differences in the studies were that our wording was slightly more action-oriented, using the verb "join" rather than simply stating the norm. Since self-identifying is usually a one-time action, rather than ongoing, we emphasized the fact that most EXs have already completed the questionnaire, while BIT used an ongoing norm. The BIT study also tested the impact of increasingly local social norms, going down to the recipient's local area, which we were unable to do due to logistic issues.

In order to test these interventions, in the CHRO-sender groups, an email was sent directly from the CHRO's account. For individuals in the DM-sender groups, a template email was shared with the deputy heads' offices, who then sent the emails from the deputy heads' email accounts. The researchers confirmed with executives in each of the DM-sender group's departments that the template email was used, with the only exception being that a select few departments changed the deadline date if it had already passed.

Due to technical constraints, we were unable to track actual self-identification rates among executives. However, unique clickthrough rates attributable to each version of the email provided us with a compelling picture of what works in encouraging executives to self-ID.

Differences (and Similarities)

While we took inspiration from Karlan and List and the BIT Social Norms trial for intervention design, our experiment differed quite significantly in terms of experimental design. First and foremost, we wanted to test both the messenger effect and social norms in our study as well as the interactions between the two principles. For this reason, we landed on a 2x2 matrix design rather than the more traditional one arm RCTs in the two inspiration papers.

The second major difference is in the behavior that we were trying to encourage. Both the BIT and Karlan and List trials were seeking monetary payment, either for tax debts or charity.[8] On our side, we were looking for people to provide information to their employer in support of employment equity initiatives.

Results

The clickthrough rates for each intervention type over time is shown in Figure 11.2, while the overall clickthrough rates by intervention group is shown in Table 11.4.

As previously mentioned, technical issues at the end of the experiment meant that we could not accurately measure actual self-ID rates among executives. We were able to substitute clickthrough rates on the emails as a proxy for self-ID rates but could only measure clickthroughs for experimental groups that got emails. This meant that comparing the four groups that received an email to the control group that did not receive one was not possible. This limitation also meant that more advanced statistical analysis methods (e.g., regressions) were not possible.

Overall, this experiment provided significant statistical results. First, providing clear and authoritative instructions to self-ID was 2.2x as

Table 11.3. Comparison of our study with previous studies

Dimension	BIT Trial	Karlan and List (2020)	ETMS Trial
Experimental Design	Four arm RCT	Two arm RCT	2x2 RCT
Setting	United Kingdom	United States	Canadian Federal Public Service
Participants	Taxpayers with outstanding amounts	Former donors to US charities	Executives in the Government of Canada
Sample Size	140,000	61,466	5,695
Measures	Payment Rate	Donation Rate	Clickthrough Rate
Procedures	Participants were randomly assigned to receive a control letter, a letter with a national-level social norm, or a national-level social norm and a postcode- or town-level social norm.	Participants were randomly assigned to receive a solicitation for a donation including a matching offer from either an anonymous charity or from the Bill and Melinda Gates Foundation.	Participants were clustered into their departments. All participants in the same departments were randomly assigned to receive an email from their Deputy Minister or from the CHRO. Half of these emails emphasized the social benefits of self-ID and the other framed it as a task to be completed.
Implementation details	Participants were notified of their outstanding debts via mail.	Participants were solicited for donations through mail.	Participants were asked to self-ID through email and provided a tracked link to the relevant system.

effective at encouraging self-ID than focusing on social norms and benefits. Second, social norms were significantly more effective coming from the CHRO than from deputy heads. Finally, in general, a message from the CHRO was more effective than from deputy heads. More than twice as many EXs acted before the deadline if they got an email from the CHRO, and 1.4x as many EXs took action after a message from the CHRO overall. The clickthrough rates were analyzed using pairwise z-tests, which showed that all the differences listed above were statistically significant.

Figure 11.2. Clickthrough rate over time

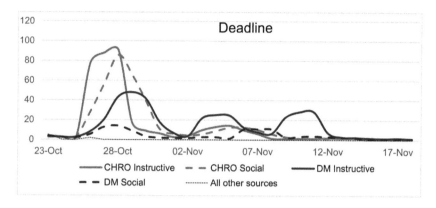

Table 11.4. Overall clickthrough rates

	CHRO Sender	DM Sender	Both Senders
Instructive Content	34.8%	26.8%	30.7%
Social-benefit Content	25.5%	5.0%	14.7%
Both content types	29.8%	14.7%	

Reconciliation

Both Karlan and List and the Behavioural Insights Team found highly positive effects for a recognizable messenger and social norms respectively.

Messenger Effect

Karlan and List find that naming BMGF as the source of matching funds increased the probability of an individual making a donation in the three months following the solicitation by 26 percent (from 0.84 percent to 1.06 percent, p<0.01) and increased the average revenue per solicitation by 42 percent (from $0.31 to $0.44, p<0.01).

Social Norms

BIT found that referring to the social norm of a particular area gave impressive results. There was a 15 percent increase from the old-style control letter that contained no social norm and the localized social norm letter.

In contrast, our experiment showed that the positive effect of the CHRO as the messenger was much greater than for social norms. We suggest that the reason for this is similar to the reason that the inclusion of the BMGF resulted in higher donation rates in Karlan and List. The CHRO is an expert on the topic of employment equity in the public service, and a message sent directly from her on the topic would have underlined the importance of the request and conveyed that the data would be used for government-wide initiatives.

Another nuance of the messenger effect identified in the literature is that we are affected by the feelings we have for the messenger. Assuming nothing about the relationship between executives and their departmental deputy heads, the messenger effect in this case may have been bolstered by the fact that a communication from the CHRO directly to executives is not common practice. Messages from the CHRO are usually relayed to individuals via their departmental deputy heads, along with all the other messages that they may receive from their direct superior. Therefore, we might be able to suggest that the increased activity was due, at least in part, to the fact that individuals have a different, and likely more distant and sporadic, relationship to the CHRO as compared to their deputy heads.

In short, this trial replicates not only the general principle of the messenger effect but also some of its more nuanced findings. The strength of the replication was likely aided by the close connection between the messenger and the behavior that the message was trying to encourage. If the CHRO was trying to encourage a behavior over which they had less responsibility or authority, it is unlikely we would have seen the same amount of responsiveness to her message. The relationship with the deputy head is also likely to have been important. Self-IDing on a central system is quite removed from the deputy head, and so sending a direct message may have underscored the fact that the activity was centrally driven.

BIT's trial finds highly positive results for the inclusion of social norms to encourage tax compliance. On the other hand, our study finds that the inclusion of social norms and the alignment of the email to underline the social benefit of self-ID actually results in lower click-throughs than clear and authoritative instructions.

Knowing the results of the experiment, there are multiple explanations for the weak result for social norms in encouraging executives to self-ID in the federal public service. First, it is possible that the message subject for the social benefit email "Join your EX Colleagues in Completing the Self-ID Form" presented the ask as an optional, nice-to-have activity, especially when compared to the authoritative tone of the alternative: "For Action: Self Identification in ETMS by November 5." This effect is likely particularly pronounced for executives who have staff that prioritize their email traffic for them.

Alternatively, the social norm statement about how many EXs have already self-IDed in the system might suggest to those who have not that it isn't all that necessary. The thinking might be that if 8 out of 10 executives are providing this data, then the marginal gain to the organization for an additional person is minimal.

Experiment 2: Using Default Appointments and Planning Prompts to Encourage Self-ID in a Federal Government Department

Inspiration

This study was inspired by Chapman et al. (2016) in their work with using default appointments to increase rates of influenza vaccination.[9] The participants were a middle-class patient base who were diverse in terms of age and health status, and the appointments themselves were with a suburban New Jersey medical school faculty medical practice.

In this study, participants were placed in one of three conditions: either they received a letter with a default appointment scheduled for their flu shot, a letter with no default appointment scheduled, or no letter. In the default appointment condition, participants had the option to cancel their appointment by phone; in the no-appointment condition, they were provided information to schedule their appointment.

The experiment found that having a default appointment scheduled resulted in a 10 percent increase in flu vaccination. We leveraged some of the key elements of this study to improve self-identification rates in a federal government department.

Planning Prompts

This study was also inspired by Milkman et al. (2011) with their work in planning prompts, which was also to increase the rates of influenza vaccination.[10] The participants were employees at a large Midwestern utility company who were fifty years of age or older and had chronic health conditions that increased the risk of influenza-related complications. On-site clinics were held across sixty-two work locations for one, three, or five days where employees could receive a free seasonal influenza vaccination.

In this study, participants were randomized evenly within work locations into three experimental conditions in which they received one of three versions of a mailer. The control mailer included no additional content. The date mailer included a space on the document where recipients were instructed to write down the date they planned to get their vaccine. And, finally, the time mailer included a space on the document to write down both the date and time. All mailers contained information about how and why to obtain the vaccine.

The experiment found that instructing recipients to write down the date and time of an appointment resulted in a 4.2 percent increase in flu vaccination.

Interventions and Method

RET conducted a trial to uncover what forms of communication are most likely to encourage self-ID. It has been found that low response rates in employees may be due to the *intention-action* gap.[11] On the other hand, default appointments have been associated with an increase in a desired behavior.[12] So we hypothesized that inviting employees to complete the self-ID form at a preselected time may be able to bridge that intention-action gap. Furthermore, it has been found that concrete, actionable steps may also be able to increase the likelihood that a behavior is performed.[13] Therefore, we also hypothesized that, if recipients did not accept the default appointment time, then encouraging them to propose a new time may act as a commitment device to complete the process.[14]

RET partnered with a medium-sized federal government department to increase the proportion of public servants who self-ID and gain evidence-based insights into what works in encouraging self-ID in employees. Participants in the experimental trial included 4,521 public servants. Each participant was randomly assigned to see one version of an email communication: (1) an informative email containing background information on self-ID with no behavioral nudge; (2) an action email with a streamlined, concrete, and actionable message to prompt recipients to complete the self-ID questionnaire; and (3) an action email plus an Outlook calendar invitation with a default appointment that recipients could accept or could use to propose a new time to complete the questionnaire. The outcome measure for the success of different versions of the email communications was the number of participants who agreed to complete the questionnaire.

Differences (and Similarities) from Earlier Studies

These are summarized in Table 11.5 below.

Figure 11.3. Images of emails in each condition

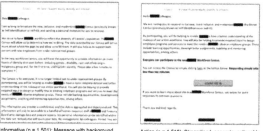

Informative (n = 1,501): Message with background information on the new self-ID form with no behavioral "nudge."

Action (n = 1,518): Streamlined, concrete, actionable message prompting respondents to complete the self-ID form.

Action + Invitation (n=1,502): Same message content as Action, but sent as a meeting invitation blocking time in the employees' calendar.

Figure 11.4. CONSORT diagram for Experiment 2

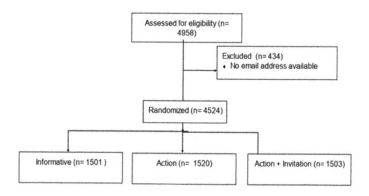

Table 11.5. Experiment 2 – Similarities and differences with previous studies

Dimension	Chapman et al. (2016)	Milkman et al. (2011)	Large Department Trial
Experimental design	Three arm RCT	Three arm RCT	Three arm RCT
Setting	A suburban New Jersey medical school faculty medical practice	A large Midwestern utility company that held on-site clinics across sixty-two work locations	A medium-sized department in the Canadian federal government
Participants	Middle-class patient base diverse in terms of age and health status	Employees who were fifty years of age or older and had chronic health conditions that increase the risk of influenza-related complications	Federal public servants diverse in terms of age, health status, and ethnicity

Dimension	Chapman et al. (2016)	Milkman et al. (2011)	Large Department Trial
Sample size	886	3,272	4,524
Measures	Vaccination rate	Vaccination rate	Survey participation rates
Procedures	Participants were randomly assigned to an opt in, opt out, or a no information condition	Participants were randomly assigned to a control, date, or date and time condition	Participants were randomly assigned to receive an informative (control) email, an action-oriented email, or an action-oriented email with a calendar invitation
Implementation details	Participants were notified of vaccine availability through regular mail and had to make or cancel their appointment by phone	Participants received a mailer with information that free influenza vaccinations were available at the on-site clinics for one, three, or five days	Participants were notified of the self-ID survey through email and had to click on the link to the survey or accept, decline, or reschedule a calendar invitation

Results

Logistic regression analysis found that employees who received the informative email were 5.5 percent more likely to agree to complete a questionnaire than the active email (coefficient = -0.286, S.E. = 0.057, $t = 3.45$, $p < 0.001$), and 7.8 percent more likely than the action plus invitation email (coefficient = -0.417, S.E. = 0.085, $t = 4.956$, $p < 0.001$) (see Figure 11.5).

The findings of this experimental trial show that information-rich communications were better at increasing response rates to the self-ID form than simplified, action-focused messaging.

Reconciliation

Default Appointments and Planning Prompts

The two original studies which our interventions were based on successfully used default appointments and planning prompts to increase influenza vaccination rates in a group of patients and employees.[15] The trial differed from the original studies in their settings and outcome

Figure 11.5. Response rate for letter conditions

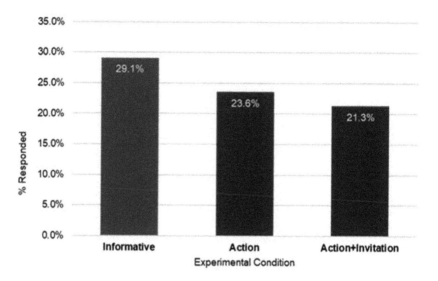

measures. This could potentially explain why default appointments and planning prompts were ineffective in the present study.

Our qualitative research in self-ID identified mistrust and lack of knowledge and understanding about self-ID as key barriers. Therefore, a reasonable explanation for the success of the informative email is that it fulfilled public servants' need for rich information and context that may elicit greater trust. The relatively sparse detail in the simplified, action-oriented emails may have failed to foster the trust that was identified in qualitative work as a key ingredient in willingness to engage in self-ID. It is possible that as a result of mistrust and lack of understanding, employees did not have strong intentions to self-ID, which may have been a prerequisite for activating the intention to eventually perform the behavior. It is possible that since the intention to complete the form was likely not there for self-ID, the nudge used to close the intention-action gap in flu vaccinations was ineffective.

However, these studies also differed in implementation details. Specifically, patients in the original default appointment study had to call the clinic to cancel or reschedule their appointment,[16] whereas participants in the self-ID study could simply decline the email invitation. It is possible that the hassle factors of having to call the clinic were key to the success of default appointments in the original study. In contrast, in our trial, it may have been too easy for employees to cancel the default appointment through Outlook.

There were similar differences in the original planning prompt study.[17] Specifically, work sites were only holding flu shot clinics on one, three, or five days, and patients had to choose a day that worked best for them. In the self-ID trial, participants were allowed to reschedule for any time. It is likely that having fewer options to schedule a flu shot was key to the success of the planning prompts in the original study. In contrast, in our trial, having too many options may have led to a choice overload effect,[18] thereby making it too difficult to choose a day and time to complete the self-ID questionnaire.

Discussion and Prescriptive Advice

Research, even in the absence of expected findings, always offers lessons and learnings. In the ETMS study, we found that self-identification was driven largely by the messenger, with social norms being less effective at producing an increase in self-ID participation. In the default appointment study, contrary to foundational work by Chapman,[19] we found that individuals were less likely to complete the self-ID form if information was more sparse, direct, and action oriented. Despite the failed translation effort for the default appointment experiment, several important learnings resulted.

When developing experimental interventions in practical contexts, the goal is rarely to directly translate findings from academic contexts, nor is it always possible to do so. The primary objective of experimentation in industry and government is to create movement or impact in some key target behavior in a specific context. Academic work is drawn upon to help inform and design solutions that will be tested, but direct translations are rare. Experiments should be designed to be tailored to the context and often that means drawing upon insights from a number of experiments and papers. Therefore, the experiments presented in this chapter are not direct translations but rather were developed to be optimal for the unique context of self-ID in government.

Therefore, if an experiment does not successfully and directly translate, it still has great informative value. Through our ETMS experiment we saw that communication from certain individuals is more optimal than communication from others. In the default appointment experiment we saw that, contrary to our expectations, rich, detailed information is more likely to improve rates of self-ID. Without experimentation that was designed for our specific context, we would not have made this discovery about which of these two approaches results in more robust, effective communications that help to meet policy objectives.

However, there is room for improvement in every study. For the default appointment study, it would have been better designed if the experiment more directly examined the effects of rich versus sparse detail and the effect of appointments. A more informative study design would have been a 2 (Detail: information-rich vs. direct) x 2 (Appointment: calendar invite vs. none). This would allow us to understand whether rich, detailed information in combination with the calendar invite would produce a further heightened effect. For the ETMS study, the inclusion of more localized social norms, down to the department level, for example, would have helped better replicate the BIT trial and may have resulted in larger effect sizes.

To practitioners our advice is threefold. To begin, it is better to focus your efforts in designing an experiment that will lead to practical insights for your organization, even if that means using insights from multiple approaches, authors, and papers to inform your study design. The goals of behavioral science in an organization are usually different from those in academia. In an organizational context, we are not looking to substantiate, support, or refute a theory but rather produce measurable change and drive impact. It is essential to examine evidence-based resources to inform your practical experiments; however, the experiment should be designed with the organization and its context and objectives in mind. Next, null results are still meaningful and valuable. They allow us to understand what doesn't work, which has immense value for an organization, including, for example, reduced costs from no longer using a communication avenue that wasn't producing results. And finally, it is essential to create a body of work to help you understand your challenge and solution from varied angles. Multiple experiments (including some not included here) were executed in the unique context of self-ID in government. This helped to build a body of work that could inform future insights and interventions for this important government priority to improve and modernize self-identification in the public service.

NOTES

1 Dolan, P., Hallsworth, M., Halpern, D., King, D., Metcalfe, R., & Vlaev, I. (2012). Influencing behaviour: The mindspace way. *Journal of Economic Psychology, 33*(1), 264–77. https://doi.org/10.1016/j.joep.2011.10.009.
2 Karlan, D. & List, J.A. (2020). How can Bill and Melinda Gates increase other people's donations to fund public goods? *Journal of Public Economics, 191*(C), 104296. https://doi.org/10.1016/j.jpubeco.2020.104296.

3 Melnyk, V., van Herpen, E., & van Trijp, H.C.M. (2010). The Influence of social norms in consumer decision making: A meta-analysis. *Advances in Consumer Research, 37*, 463–4. https://www.acrwebsite.org/volumes/v37 /acr_v37_15187.pdf.
4 Cabinet Office Behavioural Insights Team. (2012). Applying behavioural insights to reduce fraud, error and debt, 22–24. UK National Archive Reference: 408779/0212. https://assets.publishing.service.gov.uk /government/uploads/system/uploads/attachment_data/file/60539 /BIT_FraudErrorDebt_accessible.pdf.
5 Online appendix available at https://www.biorgpartnership.com/what -works.
6 Karlan & List (2020).
7 Karlan & List (2020).
8 See Karlan & List. (2020); and Cabinet Office Behavioural Insights Team. (2012).
9 Chapman, G.B., Li, M., Leventhal, H., & Leventhal, E.A. (2016). Default clinic appointments promote influenza vaccination uptake without a displacement effect. *Behavioral Science & Policy, 2*(2), 41–50. https:// doi.org/10.1353/bsp.2016.0014.
10 Milkman, K.L., Beshears, J. Choi, J.J., Laibson, D., & Madrian, B.C. (2011). Using implementation intention prompts to enhance influenza vaccination rates. *Proceedings of the National Academy of Sciences, 108*(26), 10415–20. https://doi.org/10.1073/pnas.1103170108.
11 Sheeran, P., & Webb, T.L. (2016). The intention–behavior gap. *Social and Personality Psychology Compass, 10*(9), 503–18. https://doi.org/10.1111 /spc3.12265.
12 Chapman et al. (2016).
13 Benartzi, S., Beshears, J., Milkman, K.L., Sunstein, C.R., Thaler, R.H., Shankar, M., Tucker-Ray, W., Congdon, W.J, & Galing, S. (2017). Should governments invest more in nudging? *Psychological Science, 28*(8), 1041– 155. http://dx.doi.org/10.1177/0956797617702501.
14 Milkman et al. (2011).
15 See Chapman et al. (2016); and Milkman et al. (2011).
16 Chapman et al. (2016).
17 Milkman et al. (2011).
18 See Iyengar, S.S., & Lepper, M.R. (2000). When choice is demotivating: Can one desire too much of a good thing? *Journal of Personality and Social Psychology, 79*(6), 995–1006. https://doi.org/10.1037/0022-3514.79.6.995; and Gourville, J.T., & Soman, D. (2005). Overchoice and assortment type: When and why variety backfires. *Marketing Science, 24*(3), 382–95. http:// www.jstor.org/stable/40056969.
19 Chapman et al. (2016).

CHAPTER TWELVE

Translating and Scaling Social Norms to Reduce Antibiotic Prescription in New Zealand

Alex Gyani

AT A GLANCE

- **Our Goal:** We applied a social norms intervention developed in the UK to reduce the number of antibiotic prescriptions given by high prescribing general practitioners (GPs) in the Aotearoa New Zealand context. Our intervention also aimed to avoid worsening health inequities (by not reducing prescriptions among groups where there was evidence of under-prescription).
- **The Intervention:** The intervention was a letter sent to the highest prescribers of antibiotics in the country.
- **The Results:** The letter led to a 9.2 percent reduction in antibiotic prescriptions and did not reduce antibiotic prescriptions to patient groups where there was evidence of under-prescription.
- **Lesson Learned:** Successful interventions can be scaled from one context to another but doing so requires (a) a clear understanding of the context in which it is being scaled to avoid unintended consequences and (b) an understanding of the theory underpinning the original intervention.

Motivation and Objective

Scaling behavioral interventions is critical to ensuring that they have the greatest impact possible. However, behavioral interventions are often broadly defined, context dependent, and developed using a variety of behavioral theories.[1] Assuming that an intervention does work in one context, it is not clear which of its components are critical to its effectiveness in another. Practitioners may also need to consider whether the original intervention's effectiveness is limited to a very specific context,[2] like an overfit statistical model.

The process of developing behavioral interventions involves the application of behavioral science theory to solve practical (usually policy) problems.[3] So, it can be argued that the process of scaling is the reoperationalization of a behavioral theory into a new context. Viewing the scaling process through the lens of the reapplication of a behavioral theory can aid practitioners in understanding which components of their intervention are likely to be important to scaling.

In the first part of this chapter, I make the case for why the conscientious use of behavioral theory is critical both in the development of an intervention[4] and in the scaling process. This argument draws on discussions on scaling in clinical psychology as there have been numerous innovations in the field of psychotherapy research that will help behavioral insights (BI) practitioners scale their interventions.

In the second part of this chapter, I describe a recent large-scale randomized controlled trial to affect antibiotic prescribing in Aotearoa New Zealand. In my description, I highlight how the theory underpinning the intervention was applied in differing ways to achieve a variety of policy outcomes. I also describe how the Behavioural Insights Team worked with a variety of stakeholders to ensure that the intervention was adapted to meet the needs of the local context.

Part 1: What Does Scaling an Intervention Mean in the Context of Behavioral Insights Practice?

Behavioral insights practice is the translation of behavioral science to public policy. This is acknowledged by the definition offered by Hallsworth and Kirkman: "The behavioral insights approach uses evidence of the conscious and nonconscious drivers of human behavior to address practical issues."[5] It has its roots in the Evidence Based Policy (EBP) movement.[6] The aims of EBP were inspired by arguments for Evidence Based Medicine (EBM).[7] These theoretical roots have unhelpfully left the BI field with the metaphor of the "nudge store" in which practitioners need to decide which invariant nudges they should implement to address a given problem in the same way that a clinician may choose between drugs.[8]

Translating Clearly Defined Interventions Seems Relatively
Straightforward

Moving from clinical treatments to broader policy has made the process of translating evidence into policy more complex. The "nudge store" characterization of EBM asks clinicians to decide whether *intervention* x_1 *would work for problem* y_1 *when offered to population* z_1 *given that intervention* x_1 *has worked problem* y_1 *for population* z_2. This conceptualization relies on interventions being well defined.[9] If interventions are not well defined, it is not possible to understand what it is that is being scaled up. If interventions are not well defined, it is not possible to tell whether intervention x_1 as delivered to population z_1 is the same as intervention x_1 as delivered to population z_2. While interventions can be similar when defined in a certain way, they can differ when defined in a different way (in the same way that two cars may both be red but be different models with different types of transmission from the same manufacturer).[10] For practitioners it is not possible to tell whether any of these differences are meaningful.[11]

Defining a treatment is relatively easy when describing a pharmaceutical intervention but harder when describing an intervention like psychotherapy. In psychotherapy, the implementation of the intervention may vary depending on the person delivering it and the person receiving it. While one patient's treatment may resemble another's in some ways, in many other ways, they will be very different. Treatment developers initially attempted to solve this problem of definition by standardizing and manualizing treatments. This allowed researchers to evaluate these well-defined treatments in the same way that one would evaluate a drug and then advocate for its uptake.[12] The treatments that were shown to work were labeled "empirically supported treatments" (ESTs) and defined as "clearly specified psychological treatments shown to be efficacious in controlled research with a delineated population."[13]

For BI practitioners, this would be the equivalent of categorizing specific interventions (i.e., a reminder text message to get people to attend hospital appointments) and then giving some a stamp of approval to be scaled for specific issues based on whether or not they were shown to be effective in a randomized controlled trial (RCT). It is helpful to know that reminder text messages work in one hospital, but it feels unrealistic to argue that all text messages will work in similar hospitals (i.e., the treatment is defined as any text message).[14] Most of us would also be cautious to argue that the specific text messages that were tested would work in all similar hospitals (i.e., the treatment is defined as the specific text message used).

Defining Interventions as Their Core Components

A criticism that can be levied against ESTs is that they standardize elements that may not be contributing factors to their effectiveness.[15] Subsequent work has focused on distilling the active ingredients of ESTs to identify the core components of a treatment that have to be scaled to a new context in order for the treatment to remain effective and to identify what is termed the "adaptable periphery" in implementation science.[16] These are the elements of a treatment that can be adapted to suit the local context. By understanding what the core components of a treatment are, they can be delivered to a patient, with local adaptations, based on a patient's case formulation.

A case formulation is a hypothesis about the psychological mechanisms that cause and maintain an individual's symptoms and problems. Case formulations are often viewed through a theoretical lens (for example, a behavioral therapist would view a patient's issues by looking at learned responses and a cognitive therapist might view an issue through the lens of cognitive biases). The equivalent process for BI practitioners would involve understanding the theoretically relevant factors that might explain people's behavior in a given system.[17]

Developing case formulations in a clinical setting is an iterative process. Data is initially collected, hypotheses about the mechanisms and precipitating factors in a psychological disorder are generated, and then these ideas are tested with the patient.[18] This process involves moving from a *nomothetic* or general understanding of the issue (i.e., depressive symptoms are caused by schemas activated by stimuli that produce dysfunctional automatic thoughts) to an *idiographic* formulation.[19] An idiographic formulation is one that describes the specific issues in a particular individual.[20] The process of developing an idiographic case formulation allows practitioners to understand an issue through a theoretical lens but also make local adaptations.

Creating Behavioral Case Formulations

The BI approach involves taking interventions and theories from various disciplines (namely behavioral economics, psychology, anthropology, and sociology) and placing them into a variety of different contexts with the aim of changing behavior (in the confines of a policy, program, system, service, or product). When BI practitioners scale one intervention from one context to another, this is similar to a psychotherapist deciding whether an intervention will work for a patient. Rather than matching the active ingredients of a therapy to a case formulation of a patient, they match the behavioral formulation of the policy, program, service, or product with the active ingredients of a theoretically derived intervention.

The nomothetic formulation of the issue will be rooted in behavioral science theory. For example, the theory that people generally will conform to social norms and alter their behavior if they are informed that their current behavior is not aligned with the majority of their peers is a theory derived from social norms theory.[21] From this, an idiographic behavioral formulation can be developed to understand a specific issue. For example, students at a specific university believe that their peers drink more alcohol than they actually drink, so informing them of their peers' actual drinking rates will cause them to drink less.

There are various methods that can be used to develop these idiographic formulations. The Theoretical Domains Framework (TDF) can be used to identify relevant behavioral factors causing a specific issue. Other methods such as the systems thinking methods proposed by Meadows[22] and the use of Directed Acyclic Graphs (DAG) popularized by Pearl and Mackenzie can be used to understand the causal mechanisms in a system without an understanding of behavioral science.[23] Once a DAG or a systems map is created, a (nomothetic) behavioral science theory can be overlaid on these maps to create an idiographic understanding of the issue. The benefit of using a DAG or a systems map is that it allows you to incorporate knowledge from a broad range of stakeholders, who may not be versed in the behavioral science literature.

How Does this Apply to Scaling?

Understanding how a behavioral science theory applies to a specific policy problem is critical in the development of an intervention, but it is also important when scaling an existing intervention to a new context. BI is a translational practice. Both the process for scaling an existing behavioral intervention to a new context and the process of developing a new intervention using an existing behavioral theory require the development of a specific formulation on the basis of a general behavioral theory (or theories).

When scaling, the practitioner should not think of scaling a single invariant intervention but focus on how the original theory underpinning the original intervention applies to the new context. This allows practitioners to focus on the mechanism of action of an intervention and consider what the core components of an intervention are. By describing this as the reapplication of a theory to a new formulation, rather than the scaling of an invariant intervention, it becomes easier to identify the theoretical meaningful components of the intervention.

What Does This Mean for BI Practitioners?

For formulations of a policy problem, the terms *nomothetic* and *idiographic* are perhaps needless jargon for most policymakers. I have only used these terms in order to tie this thinking to the wider literature. However, the idea of mapping out the behavioral and structural processes that regulate behavior and behavior change in the systems that practitioners hope to affect is critical. It is also not completely novel. It is already described by our own TESTS methodology[24] and the TDF.[25]

The novel contribution of this paper is the argument that this process also applies to the scaling of existing behavioral interventions. Rather than thinking about how an intervention is being scaled, practitioners should think about the process as the reapplication of a behavioral theory to a similar but different domain. By doing this, practitioners will be able to identify which components of an existing intervention are theoretically important (i.e., the active ingredients) and which are simply local adaptations in the previous context (i.e., the adaptable periphery).[26]

Part 2: Scaling a Social Norms Intervention to Affect Antibiotic Prescriptions in Aotearoa New Zealand

The second part of this chapter discusses a recent trial to scale an intervention developed in the UK to Aotearoa New Zealand (ANZ).[27] The chapter uses the ideas discussed in part 1 to demonstrate how the same theory was used in both trials. This led to the use of the same core components of the intervention. However, different local adaptations were made on a slightly different idiographic formulation. The results of the trial are not discussed here fully but can be found in the *New Zealand Medical Journal*.[28]

Motivation and Objective

On July 31, 2020, the World Health Organization named antimicrobial resistance (AMR) accelerated by the misuse and overuse of antibiotics as "one of the biggest threats to global health, food security, and development today."[29] They reiterated this point on December 24 by naming it as one of the ten global health threats to track in 2021.[30] Overprescription of antibiotics is especially problematic in ANZ. Work by the OECD found that ANZ had the fourth highest community prescription rate of antibiotics among member countries in 2017, behind Greece, Italy, and Korea.[31]

Most human antibiotic consumption (85–90 percent) in ANZ occurs in the community, with the majority of this being due to prescriptions from GPs.[32] Work by Duffy and his team found that this proportion was higher in ANZ than in comparable countries in Europe.[33] The proposed reasons for inappropriate antibiotic prescribing are manifold. They include GPs not realizing that they are prescribing inappropriately, a belief that other GPs prescribe similarly, a lack of knowledge of which antibiotics they should avoid prescribing, GPs wanting to meet patients' expectations, and GPs habits.[34]

In 2019, the Behavioural Insights Team (BIT) was asked by the Health Quality and Safety Commission (HQSC) and PHARMAC to see whether some of the interventions that the team had developed in the UK along with the UK Department of Health and Public Health England[35] would also work in ANZ. The HQSC and PHARMAC's interest was piqued after reading about the UK trial and its subsequent replication by the Behavioural Economics Research Team in the Australian Department of Health (BERT) and the Behavioural Economics Team of the Australian Government (BETA).[36]

Inspiration

The genesis of the work in the UK was problem led, rather than solution led. The team, led by Michael Hallsworth, looked at the list of public health issues facing the UK and the world and found that AMR was at the top of that list. Unlike much academic research, the team did not start by seeking to test whether or not a specific potential solution would work but whether and how they could address the problem at hand.

The team identified that the top prescribers of antibiotics accounted for a disproportionately large percentage of the overall prescriptions. If they were able to encourage these GPs to reduce their prescribing rates, then the overall number of prescriptions would drop dramatically. Hallsworth and his team developed a behaviorally informed letter that was sent to these over-prescribers and then measured its impact. The letter was evaluated in an RCT in which the top 20 percent of prescribers (n=1,581) were allocated to a group receiving the letter or a group that did not. This RCT found that the intervention reduced the rate at which antibiotic items were dispensed by 3.3 percent over six months. This result was also replicated in Australia by behavioral economics units in the Australian federal government.[37] Follow-up work in Australia found that the results from the interventions were sustained,[38] and in the UK, the results were replicated a year later.[39]

The key "active ingredient" and nomothetic theory behind this intervention had previously already been used by Her Majesty's Customs and Revenue (HMRC) to increase tax compliance in the UK. The project started when an enterprising and curious official at HMRC hypothesized that people in the UK who were not paying their income tax could be spurred to take action if they were given social proof that others paid their tax on time.[40] This hypothesis was sparked after reading Robert Cialdini's work on the power of social proof.[41]

Social proof features in a number of behavioral science theories.[42] These theories have been operationalized into the social norms approach[43] in which descriptive information about the behavior of a group is used to change the behavior of people who do not comply with the group social norms. BIT worked with HMRC to run two experiments to evaluate the impact of social norms messages, with a total sample of over 200,000 individuals in the UK.[44] In both experiments, the social norms messages were found to be effective in encouraging people who had not paid their tax on time to do so.

As discussed in part 1 of this chapter, interventions can be effectively scaled when the theoretically important active ingredients are matched to the problem at hand. In the tax trials and the UK antibiotic project, the formulation of the issue was the same. There was a group of people who were undertaking a behavior that did not align with the group norms.

In the trial to reduce antibiotic prescriptions, Hallsworth and his team added a number of other elements driven by their formulation of the problem at hand. There was evidence that GPs would not respond to a messenger who was not credible.[45] Therefore, the letter was sent from the Chief Medical Officer to draw on the messenger effect.[46] There was also evidence that GPs prescribe antibiotics because they view it as their only option to placate patients who view antibiotics as the only solution. Therefore, the letter included instructions on what actions GPs could take to meet expectations without offering a prescription. The use of multiple theoretical constructs (from different nomothetic theories) in this instance can be accommodated by a single formulation of the issue, which contains a number of specific problems that need to be solved.[47]

Intervention and Method

When it came to thinking about how we can apply this to antibiotic prescribing in ANZ, we investigated whether or not this formulation of the issue also held. We did this by analyzing the national datasets[48] on the number of prescriptions filled[49] and working closely with an expert reference group to identify any differences between the formulation of the issue in the UK and Australia, where the social norms interventions had originally been tested, and ANZ. These discussions identified that the formulation of the issue in the UK was similar to the situation in ANZ.

The group felt that many high-prescribing GPs may not be aware of the fact that they were high-prescribing GPs, and the data showed that high-prescribing GPs accounted for a large proportion of the antibiotics being prescribed. Similarly, the working group also felt that many GPs may be prescribing antibiotics to please patients in short consultations.

These discussions also highlighted critical differences between the UK context and the ANZ context. While overall rates of antibiotic prescriptions are high in ANZ, this does not mean that they are being over-prescribed uniformly to everyone. Work in 2013,[50] and again in 2017,[51] identified that Māori and Pacific people are systematically under-prescribed antibiotics. This under-prescription has been posited to explain the high incidence of rheumatic fever among Māori children.[52]

This deeper understanding of the issue meant that we could not apply the same social norms intervention in this context without potentially exacerbating existing health inequities. By reducing the number of antibiotic prescriptions across the population we were likely to encourage GPs who were under-prescribing to vulnerable groups to use even fewer antibiotics. Therefore, we adapted our formulation of the issue. Rather than solely focus on GPs' overall antibiotic prescription rates, we also used our intervention to bring GPs' attention to whom they were prescribing to. This was presented in a graph, as shown in Figure 12.1 below.[53]

As with the UK and Australian interventions, the letter used in ANZ was signed by a local authority figure who would have been known and respected by the recipients, and it provided the recipients some practical tips on how to reduce their antibiotic prescribing. We did not use the same specific messenger or the same tips used in the UK letter but adapted these to the local context. The authority figure chosen was Dr. Janice Wilson, the chief executive officer of the Health Quality and Safety Commission. This choice was made on the basis that Dr. Wilson is a respected peer to the GPs that would receive the letter.

Similarly, the language used in the letter was adapted to suit the Aotearoa New Zealand vernacular and also incorporated Te Reo Māori phrases. Specific examples include the use of the greeting "Tēnā koe" and "Ngā mihi" as the sign off.

Figure 12.1. Graphs showing how GPs' prescribing rates differed across specific demographic groups

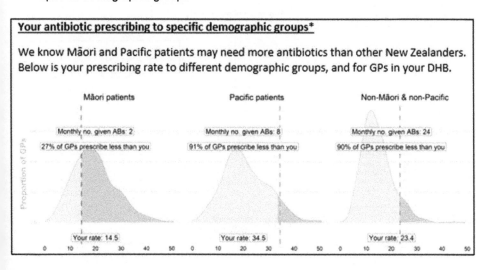

Your antibiotic prescribing to specific demographic groups*

We know Māori and Pacific patients may need more antibiotics than other New Zealanders. Below is your prescribing rate to different demographic groups, and for GPs in your DHB.

Māori patients | Pacific patients | Non-Māori & non-Pacific

Monthly no. given ABs: 2 | Monthly no. given ABs: 8 | Monthly no. given ABs: 24

27% of GPs prescribe less than you | 91% of GPs prescribe less than you | 90% of GPs prescribe less than you

Your rate: 14.5 | Your rate: 34.5 | Your rate: 23.4

Evaluation

The intervention was evaluated using a two-armed RCT, with randomization at the GP level and stratification by District Health Board (DHB).[54] GPs who were in the top 30 percent of antibiotic prescribers in each DHB for the 2018 calendar year were identified using the Ministry of Health's national dispensing data. This data was deidentified and described all dispensing of medicines from community pharmacies in ANZ in 2018. It included the age and ethnicity of patients dispensed to.

We excluded all nurse practitioners, dentists, and all doctors except for GPs. Locums were also excluded on the advice that we would be unable to send them a letter.[55] This gave us a sample of 1,260 high-prescribing GPs, who were then randomized into the control and intervention groups, using R.[56] To account for differences in prescribing and patient characteristics at the DHB level, the sample was stratified by DHB. Balance checks of these two cohorts showed close comparability.

Fifteen intervention GPs could not be linked to a name (which was required to send them a letter), and some were lost in follow-up due to inactivity in the trial period; this gave us a final sample of 602 GPs in the intervention arm and 612 GPs in the control arm (1,214 in total). Figure 12.2 shows how these exclusions affected the sample.

Figure 12.2. CONSORT diagram showing sample composition

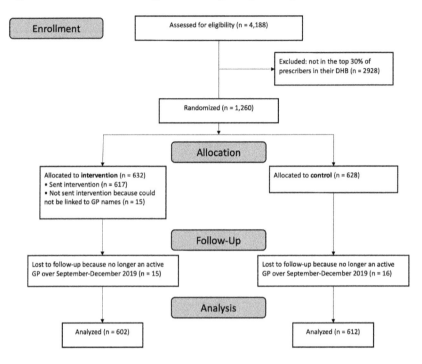

Power calculations showed we would be able to detect an effect size of around 0.75 at p = 0.05 (a 4 percent change in the antibiotic prescribing rate). The rationale for using the top 30 percent rather than the top 20 percent, as was used in the UK trial, was to increase the power of the trial.

Analyses

Our analyses were registered on the American Economic Association's registry for RCTs (AEARCTR-0005526).[57]

Primary Outcomes

Our two primary outcome measures were:

- GPs' antibiotic prescribing rates, averaged across September to December 2019,[58] and
- the number of antibiotic scripts GPs dispensed from prescribing activity between September and December 2019.

These outcome measures differed from the outcome measures used in the UK trial. These differences were largely driven by the way in which the administrative data was reported in both countries rather than our deliberate choice. There were two main differences. Firstly, the data in the UK trial was reported at the practice level. A practice could have a number of GPs working at it. In ANZ, the data was reported at the individual GP level. This has several implications. Having practice-level data means that no individual GP in a practice can be sure that they are responsible for over- or under-prescribing. In fact, it could be the case that a practice looks like it is an average prescriber, when it contains both under- and over-prescribing GPs.[59] Highlighting individual GPs' prescribing is likely to increase the specificity of the intervention (it is more likely to target all high prescribers) and the effectiveness of the intervention (GPs who receive the letter are likely to feel a higher sense of accountability and are therefore more likely to change their behavior).

Second, the outcome measure in the UK was weighted using STAR-PU controls.[60] This is a set methodology used in the UK NHS to control for patient characteristics, namely age and sex. As no such method exists in ANZ, we were not able to weight the outcome measure in the same way. This had the potential to reduce the level of accountability that individual GPs had as they could argue that their patient caseload differs from that of other GPs in their area.

To compensate for any variation in the number of patients that any GP saw, we also used a prescribing rate in ANZ. This rate was defined in consultation with the authors and representatives from the Health Safety and Quality Commission, PHARMAC, the Ministry of Health, the Royal New Zealand College of General Practitioners, the New Zealand Medical Association, and several practicing GPs. The prescribing rate can be described as:

$$\frac{100 * \text{number of patients dispensed an antibiotic}}{\text{number of patients dispensed any medicine}}$$

The antibiotics included in the count were nine commonly prescribed types of antibiotics. The prescribing rate was calculated at a monthly level (i.e., the proportion of patients prescribed any of these nine antibiotics in a given month) and then averaged over the twelve months of 2018 to calculate one antibiotic rate for each GP.

Secondary Outcomes

We also included registered secondary analyses, which examined the effects of the intervention for all high-prescribing GPs in terms of:

- the prescribing rate of antibiotics to Māori, Pacific, and non-Māori and non-Pacific patients, and
- the number of people prescribed paracetamol scripts per 100 prescribed any medicine.

Paracetamol scripts were included as a measure of whether or not there was a general change in prescribing patterns during the trial period.

Exploratory Outcomes

As mentioned above, there is evidence that Māori and Pacific patients are under-prescribed antibiotics. We did not want to exacerbate these inequities, so we investigated whether some GPs were over-prescribing antibiotics to the general population but under-prescribing them to Māori and Pacific patients. We found that a small sample of GPs were in the top 30 percent of overall prescribers but in the bottom 50 percent of prescribers to Māori patients (n=50) or Pacific patients (n=42). Figure 12.3 shows these GPs.[61] While this was a small group, we conducted further analyses to understand whether or not we had increased health inequities.

Statistical Models Used

The effect of the intervention was evaluated using regression analyses conducted in R. The reported regression included the intervention variable, the DHB stratification variable, and the GPs' 2018 value of the prescribing outcome variable to increase precision.[62]

Results

PRELIMINARY ANALYSIS
Before running any inferential analyses, we plotted the average prescribing rate for intervention and control GPs from January 2018 to December 2019. This is shown in Figure 12.4 and was done to sense check any later inferential analyses. Figure 12.4 shows a divergence in antibiotic prescribing rates between the control and intervention groups in the four months after the letters were sent in August 2019.[64]

Figure 12.3. GPs' percentile rank in prescribing to all patients and to Māori patients, January–December 2018

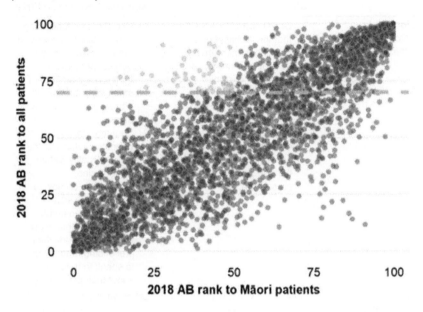

Table 12.1. Overview of differences and similarities

	UK Trial	Aotearoa New Zealand Trial
Case Formulation	Many GPs who over-prescribe antibiotics do so because: 1. They are not aware that they are over-prescribers. 2. They are not aware of the clinical guidelines in place to reduce unnecessary antibiotic prescriptions. 3. They prescribe antibiotics because their patients expect antibiotics.	Many GPs who over-prescribe antibiotics do so because: 1. They are not aware that they are over-prescribers. 2. They are not aware of the clinical guidelines in place to reduce unnecessary antibiotic prescriptions. 3. They prescribe antibiotics because their patients expect antibiotics. However, there is a small group of GPs who might be under-prescribing antibiotics to potentially vulnerable populations.
Nomothetic Components of the Intervention	1. Social norms theory 2. Messenger effect 3. Behavioral instruction	1. Social norms theory 2. Messenger effect 3. Behavioral instruction

(Continued)

Table 12.1. (Continued)

	UK Trial	Aotearoa New Zealand Trial
Idiographic Components of the Intervention	1. Social norm highlighting that the recipients prescribed more than 80% of their peers. 2. Sent from the Chief Medical Officer. 3. Instructions on how to give patients advice on self-care instead, use delayed prescriptions,[63] and advice to speak to their peers about their prescribing.	1. Social norm highlighting that recipients prescribed more antibiotics to the general population than more than 70% of their peers (along with a breakdown of this by ethnicity). 2. Sent from the Chief Executive Officer of the Health Quality Safety Commission. 3. Instructions on how to give patients advice on self-care instead, links to tools that allow them to self-audit their prescribing, and advice to speak to their peers about their prescribing.
Adaptable Periphery in the Intervention	Letter written in British English and in a vernacular and tone that British doctors would be used to.	Letter written in English with Te Reo Māori greetings and in a vernacular and tone that GPs in ANZ would be used to.
Sample Used	1,581 GP practices who were in the top 20% of prescribers in the UK.	1,214 GPs who were in the top 30% of prescribers in ANZ.
Outcome Measures	Practice level prescribing rates, using a national method for weighting prescription rates.	GP level prescribing rates which were not weighted by patient characteristics. We also investigated outcomes broken down by patients' demography to ensure that there was no increased under-prescribing to potentially vulnerable cohorts.
Desired Direction of Change	An overall reduction in antibiotic prescribing across all GP practices.	An overall reduction in antibiotic prescribing across all GPs (with the exception of GPs who were low prescribers to Māori or Pacific patients).

Figure 12.4. GPs' average monthly prescribing by condition (gray dotted line shows when the letters were sent)

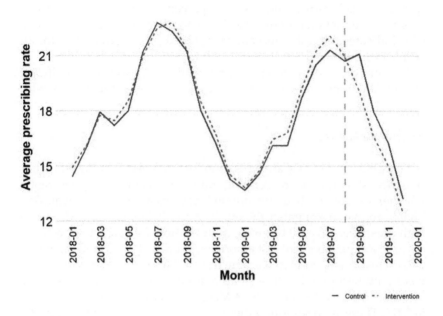

Primary Outcomes

The primary analyses found that there was a difference of 1.65 in the prescribing rate between treatment and control groups. This reflects a 9.2 percent relative difference (p < 0.001). This means that for every 100 patients who are prescribed any medicine by a GP, 1.7 fewer patients will be prescribed an antibiotic.

We also found that there was a significant difference in the total number of antibiotic scripts prescribed by GPs who received the treatment letter. This difference was 13.3 scripts per GP. This represents a 7.1 percent difference between the intervention and control arms (p < 0.01) or eight thousand fewer courses of antibiotics dispensed over the four-month trial period.

Secondary Outcomes

We initially wanted to see if this drop in antibiotic prescribing was seen in GPs prescribing to different ethnic groups. For Māori patients, we saw a significant difference between the treatment and control groups in prescribing rates of 2.22 (p < .001). This corresponds to a

10.2 percent difference compared to the control arm. For Pacific patients, there was a 3.16 reduction in the antibiotic prescription rate (p > .01), which corresponds to a 13.3 percent difference. Finally, there was a 1.69 reduction for non-Māori and non-Pacific patients (p > .001). This indicates that the intervention reduced prescription rates for all ethnic groups.

The analyses on paracetamol prescriptions showed no significant change (although there was a trend suggesting a slight reduction, with p = 0.06).

Exploratory Analyses

Although the secondary analyses found that the letters reduced higher prescribers' antibiotic prescribing rates, we wanted to investigate whether or not we had exacerbated any existing health inequities. Therefore, we investigated the effect of the letters on GPs who were high prescribers overall but were in the bottom 50 percent of prescribers to Māori patients (not just among high-prescribing trial GPs, but all GPs). This corresponds to the blue dots in Figure 12.3. These analyses were only performed with a sample of GPs who had prescribed any medicine to at least ten people of Māori ethnicity in an average month in 2018. These analyses found there was no significant difference in the prescribing rates of GPs who were historically low prescribers of antibiotics to Māori and Pacific patients.

Discussion and Prescriptive Advice

Our efforts at scaling a previous social norms intervention were successful. In particular, the trial described above showed that a theoretically driven intervention developed in the UK to address GPs' over-prescription can work in ANZ. The intervention used the same behavioral theories and applied them to a different context with a series of local adaptations. These adaptations concerned the content of the intervention but also the problem that we were trying to solve (namely the impact of the intervention on existing inequalities).

The work in ANZ had several limitations. Although we argue that the intervention did not exacerbate health inequities, we do not know for certain that the small group of GPs in our sample who were in the bottom 50 percent of prescribers for Māori/Pacific patients were under prescribers. We only know that there were discrepancies in their prescribing. This was also a small group, so we cannot draw strong conclusions from this analysis. Instead, we use this as an example of how the same theory can be applied to an intervention to create intentionally different impacts but still be effective in its policy aims.

Overall, the argument that practitioners should use a theoretically driven approach to scaling interventions and should focus on scaling theories rather than invariant interventions is not based on any effectiveness research. This research would need to use a meta-analytic approach and would need to compare interventions that have been scaled using a theoretical framework to those that do not. So far there is not enough research on the scaling of behavioral interventions to allow for such a meta-analysis. Instead, we advocate for BI practitioners to make sure that they go back to the theoretical underpinnings of their intervention whenever they scale an intervention.

Finally, the application of a behavioral science theory to a context can only be effective if the general theory is true in a wide set of contexts. The replication crisis has identified that many theories in social science may not be "true" effects.[65] It also identified that a number of theories may only hold true in a narrow set of (artificial) contexts and are not generalizable.[66] Throughout the scaling process, BI practitioners will need to constantly check the health of the theory that they are scaling to ensure that it is not suffering its own replication crisis and to avoid suffering the dreaded "voltage drop."[67]

Hopefully the idea of a general or nomothetic theory and a specific or idiographic formulation of a policy problem is a helpful lens through which practitioners can scale their interventions. It can make it easier for practitioners to decide whether an intervention can scale because it helps them understand whether any deviations in the design of an intervention or differences in the context in which they are scaling them to are meaningful. This may also help researchers, as clear definitions of the theoretical elements being scaled in behavioral interventions will help them understand the bounds of a general theory.[68]

NOTES

1 Mažar, N., & Soman, D. (Eds.). (2022). *Behavioral science in the wild.* University of Toronto Press.

2 Cartwright, N., & Hardie, J. (2012). *Evidence-based policy: A practical guide to doing it better.* Oxford University Press.

3 Hallsworth, M., & Kirkman, E. (2020). *Behavioral insights.* MIT Press.

4 See Eccles, M., Grimshaw, J., Johnston, M., Steen, N., Pitts, N., Thomas, R., Glidewell, E., Maclennan, G., Bonetti, D. & Walker, A. (2007). Applying psychological theories to evidence-based clinical practice: Identifying

factors predictive of managing upper respiratory tract infections without antibiotics. *Implementation Science, 2*(26). https://doi.org/10.1186/1748 -5908-2-26; and Michie, S., Johnston, M., Abraham, C., Lawton, R., Parker, D., & Walker, A. (2005). Making psychological theory useful for implementing evidence based practice: A consensus approach. *Quality & Safety in Health Care, 14*(1), 26–33. https://doi.org/10.1136/qshc.2004.011155.

5 See page 21 of Hallsworth & Kirkman (2020).

6 Davies, H.T., & Nutley, S.M. (Eds.). (2000). *What works? Evidence-based policy and practice in public services*. Policy Press.

7 See page 6 of Sackett, D.L., Rosenberg, W.M., Gray, J.M., Haynes, R.B., & Richardson, W.S. (1996). Evidence based medicine: What it is and what it isn't. *Bmj, 312*(7023), 71–2. https://doi.org/10.1136/bmj.312.7023.71.

8 Goodyear, L., Hossain, T., & Soman, D. (2022). Prescriptions for successfully scaling behavioral interventions. In N. Mažar and D. Soman (Eds.), *Behavioral science in the wild* (pp. 28–41). University of Toronto Press.

9 Similarly, the populations, Z, that are receiving the intervention, and the problem at hand, Y, also need to be clearly defined. There are separate issues related to defining a sample too narrowly that I cannot cover here. I would recommend reading Henrich (2020) for a discussion on why having a biased sample reduces the likelihood of effective scaling and Kelly & Moore (2012) for a wider discussion on the problems of external validity in evidence-based medicine.

10 Sanbonmatsu, D.M., Cooley, E.H., & Butner, J.E. (2021). The impact of complexity on methods and findings in psychological science. *Frontiers in Psychology, 11*(580111). https://doi.org/10.3389/fpsyg.2020.580111.

11 Meaningful here being defined as having a moderating impact on its effectiveness.

12 Chambless, D.L., & Ollendick, T.H. (2001). Empirically supported psychological interventions: Controversies and evidence. *Annual Review of Psychology, 52*(1), 685–716. https://psycnet.apa.org/doi/10.1146/annurev .psych.52.1.685.

13 See page 7 in Chambless, D.L., & Hollon, S.D. (1998). Defining empirically supported therapies. *Journal of consulting and clinical psychology, 66*(1), 7–18. https://doi.org/10.1037//0022-006x.66.1.7.

14 Goodyear et al. (2022).

15 Lambert, M.J., & Barley, D.E. (2001). Research summary on the therapeutic relationship and psychotherapy outcome. *Psychotherapy: Theory, research, practice, training, 38*(4), 357–61. https://psycnet.apa.org/doi/10.1037/0033 -3204.38.4.357.

16 See Greenhalgh, T., Robert, G., Macfarlane, F., Bate, P., & Kyriakidou, O. (2004). Diffusion of innovations in service organizations: Systematic review and recommendations. *The Milbank Quarterly, 82*(4), 581–629.

https://doi.org/10.1111/j.0887-378x.2004.00325.x; and Damschroder, L.J., Aron, D.C., Keith, R.E., Kirsh, S.R., Alexander, J.A., & Lowery, J.C. (2009). Fostering implementation of health services research findings into practice: A consolidated framework for advancing implementation science. *Implementation Science*, 4(1), 1–15. https://doi.org/10.1186/1748-5908-4-50.

17 Atkins, L., Francis, J., Islam, R., O'Connor, D., Patey, A., Ivers, N., Foy, R., Duncan, E.M., Colquhoun, H., Grimshaw, J.M., Lawton, R., & Michie, S. (2017). A guide to using the Theoretical Domains Framework of behavior change to investigate implementation problems. *Implementation Science*, 12(1), 1–18. https://doi.org/10.1186/s13012-017-0605-9.

18 "Tested" in this context does not mean testing in the form of a randomized controlled trial, but through a variety of methods ranging from discussions with patients to running behavioral experiments in which patients are asked to predict what the outcome of a behavior will be, undertake it, and see whether or not their predictions are correct. For example, someone with social phobia may be asked what would happen if they tripped in a supermarket. This person may assume that everyone in the supermarket would laugh at them, but when they actually undertake the behavior, they find that no one pays them any attention.

19 In the terminology used by Cartwright and Hardie (2012) this can be referred to as a *vertical search*.

20 Persons, J.B. (2012). *The case formulation approach to cognitive-behavior therapy*. Guilford Press.

21 Berkowitz, A.D. (2005). An overview of the social norms approach. *Changing the culture of college drinking: A socially situated health communication campaign*, 1, 193–214. http://www.alanberkowitz.com /articles/social_norms_short.pdf.

22 Meadows, D.H. (2008). *Thinking in systems: A primer*. Chelsea Green Publishing.

23 Pearl, J., & Mackenzie, D. (2018). *The book of why: The new science of cause and effect*. Basic Books.

24 Behavioural Insights Team. (2022). Target, explore, solution, trial, scale: An introduction to running simple behavioural insights projects. https:// www.bi.team/wp-content/uploads/2022/11/BIT-Handbook-How-to-run -simple-BI-projects.pdf.

25 Atkins et al. (2017).

26 Damschroder et al. (2009).

27 Aotearoa is the Māori name for the country.

28 Chappell, N., Gerard, C., Gyani, A., Hamblin, R., Jansen, R.M., Lawrence, A.J., Mackay, J., Minko, N., Roberts, S., Shuker, C., Te Karu, L., & White, J. (2021). Using a randomised controlled trial to test the effectiveness of social norms feedback to reduce antibiotic prescribing without increasing inequities. *The New Zealand Medical Journal*, 134(1544), 13–34.

29 World Health Organization. (2020, July 31). *Antibiotic resistance.* https://
www.who.int/news-room/fact-sheets/detail/antibiotic-resistance.

30 World Health Organization. (2020, December 24). *10 global health issues to
track in 2021.* https://www.who.int/news-room/spotlight/10-global
-health-issues-to-track-in-2021.

31 OECD Health Statistics. (2019). *Overall volume of antibiotics prescribed,
2017 (or nearest year).* OECD Publishing. https://doi.org/10.1787
/888934015999.

32 Note that GPs are often referred to as family physicians in the US.

33 Duffy, E., Gardiner, S., du Plessis, T., Bondesio, K., & Morar, B. (2015). A
snapshot of antimicrobial use in New Zealand hospitals-a comparison to
Australian and English data. *The New Zealand Medical Journal, 128*(1421),
82–4. https://pubmed.ncbi.nlm.nih.gov/26370766/.

34 King, L.M., Fleming-Dutra, K.E., & Hicks, L.A. (2018). Advances in
optimizing the prescription of antibiotics in outpatient settings. *Bmj, 363.*
https://doi.org/10.1136/bmj.k3047

35 Hallsworth, M., Chadborn, T., Sallis, A., Sanders, M., Berry, D., Greaves,
F., Clements, L., & Davies, S.C. (2016). Provision of social norm feedback
to high prescribers of antibiotics in general practice: A pragmatic national
randomised controlled trial. *Lancet, 387*(10029), 1743–52. https://doi.org
/10.1016/s0140-6736(16)00215-4.

36 Australian Government Department of Health, Department of the Prime
Minister and Cabinet. (2018, June). *Nudge vs superbugs: A behavioural
economics trial to reduce the overprescribing of antibiotics.* https://
behaviouraleconomics.pmc.gov.au/sites/default/files/projects/report
-nudge-vs-superbugs.pdf.

37 Australian Government Department of Health, Department of the Prime
Minister and Cabinet (2018).

38 Australian Government Department of Health, Department of the Prime
Minister and Cabinet. (2020, June). *Nudge vs superbugs: 12 months on.*
https://www.health.gov.au/resources/publications/nudge-vs-superbugs
-12-months-on.

39 Ratajczak M., Gold N., Hailstone S., & Chadborn, T. (2019). The
effectiveness of repeating a social norm feedback intervention to high
prescribers of antibiotics in general practice: A national regression
discontinuity design. *Journal of Antimicrobial Chemotherapy, 74*(12), 3603–10.
https://doi.org/10.1093/jac/dkz392.

40 Halpern, D. (2015). *Inside the nudge unit: How small changes can make a big
difference.* Random House.

41 Cialdini, R.B. (2006). *Influence: The psychology of persuasion* (revised ed.).
William Morrow.

42 Ajzen, I. (1991). The theory of planned behavior. *Organizational behavior and
human decision processes, 50*(2), 179–211. https://doi.org/10.1016/0749
-5978(91)90020-T; and Bandura, A. (2001). Social cognitive theory: An

agentic perspective. *Annual Review of Psychology, 52*(1), 1–26. https://doi
.org/10.1146/annurev.psych.52.1.1.

43 Berkowitz (2005).

44 Hallsworth, M., List, J.A., Metcalfe, R.D., & Vlaev, I. (2017). The behavioralist
as tax collector: Using natural field experiments to enhance tax compliance.
Journal of Public Economics, 148, 14–31. https://doi.org/10.1016/j.jpubeco
.2017.02.003.

45 King et al. (2018).

46 Brinol, P., & Petty, R.E. (2009). Source factors in persuasion: A self-
validation approach. *European Review of Social Psychology, 20*(1), 49–96.
https://doi.org/10.1080/10463280802643640.

47 Note that one of the arguments that Persons (2008) makes for the use of
case formulations is that they allow the clinician to treat multiple issues
in the same person simultaneously, whereas the EST framework would
recommend treating these in series. Persons, J.B. (2008). *The case formulation
approach to cognitive-behavior therapy.* The Guilford Press.

48 Health New Zealand. (2023). *Pharmaceutical collection.* https://www.health
.govt.nz/nz-health-statistics/national-collections-and-surveys/collections
/pharmaceutical-collection.

49 The data in Aotearoa New Zealand does not capture prescriptions that are
not filled.

50 Metcalfe, S., Beyene, K., Urlich, J., Jones, R., Proffitt, C., Harrison, J., &
Ātene, A. (2018). Te Wero tonu – the challenge continues: Māori access
to medicines 2006/07-2012/13 update. *The New Zealand Medical Journal,
131*(1485), 27–47. https://assets-global.website-files.com/5e332a62c703f65
3182faf47/5e332a62c703f6b4832fcc2e_Metcalfe%20FINAL.pdf.

51 Metcalfe, S., Bhawan, S., Vallabh, M., Murray, P., Proffitt, C., & Williams,
G. (2019). Over and under? Ethnic inequities in community antibacterial
prescribing. *The New Zealand Medical Journal, 132*(1488), 65–8. https://
pubmed.ncbi.nlm.nih.gov/31851664/.

52 Hale, M., & Sharpe, N. (2011). Persistent rheumatic fever in New Zealand –
A shameful indicator of child health. *The New Zealand Medical Journal,
124*(1329), 6–8. https://assets-global.website-files.com/5e332a62c703f6531
82faf47/5e332a62c703f68c1f2fd4ce_content.pdf.

53 Chappell et al. (2021).

54 Ethical approval for this work was obtained from the New Zealand Ethics
Committee on 26 July 2019 (ref: NZEC Application 2019_34).

55 Further information on the way in which the data was linked can be found
in Chappell et al. (2021).

56 The R Core Team. (2013). R: A language and environment for statistical
computing. http://www.R-project.org/.

57 Chappell, N., Gyani, A., & Hayward, S. (2020). "Using behavioural insights
to reduce unnecessary antibiotic prescriptions by New Zealand doctors."
AEA RCT Registry. https://www.socialscienceregistry.org/trials/5526.

58 The letters were sent in August 2019.

59 This recalls the joke about a statistician being a person who lays with their head in a oven and their feet in a deep freeze stating, "On the average, I feel comfortable."

60 Lloyd, D.C.E.F., Harris, C.M., & Roberts, D.J. (1995). Specific therapeutic group age-sex related prescribing units (STAR-PUs): Weightings for analysing general practices' prescribing in England. *BMJ*, *311*(7011), 991–4. https://doi.org/10.1136/bmj.311.7011.991.

61 Chappell et al. (2021).

62 Full results can be found in Chappell et al. (2021).

63 Little, P. (2005). Delayed prescribing of antibiotics for upper respiratory tract infection. *BMJ*, *331*(7512), 301–2. https://doi.org/10.1136/bmj .331.7512.301.

64 Chappell et al. (2021).

65 Open Science Collaboration. (2015). Estimating the reproducibility of psychological science. *Science*, *349*(6251). https://doi.org/10.1126/science. aac4716; Camerer, C.F., Dreber, A., Holzmeister, F., Ho, T.H., Huber, J., Johannesson, M., Kirchler, M., Nave, G., Nosek, B.A., Pfeiffer, T., Altmejd, A., Buttrick, N., Chan, T., Chen, Y., Forsell, E, Gampa, A., Heikensten, E., Hummer, L., Imai, T., ... & Wu, H. (2018). Evaluating the replicability of social science experiments in Nature and Science between 2010 and 2015. *Nature Human Behaviour*, *2*(9), 637–44. https://doi.org/10.1038/s41562 -018-0399-z; and Klein, R.A., Vianello, M., Hasselman, F., Adams, B.G., Adams, R.B., Alper, S., Aveyard, M., Axt, J.R., Babalola, M.T, Bahník, Š., Batra, R., Berkics, M., Bernstein, M.J., Berry, D.R., Bialobrzeska, O., Dami Binan, E., Bocian, K., Brandt, M.J., Busching, R., ... & Nosek, B.A. (2018). Many labs 2: Investigating variation in replicability across samples and settings. *Advances in Methods and Practices in Psychological Science*, *1*(4), 443–90. https://doi.org/10.1177/2515245918810225.

66 Van Bavel, J.J., Mende-Siedlecki, P., Brady, W.J., & Reinero, D.A. (2016). Contextual sensitivity in scientific reproducibility. *Proceedings of the National Academy of Sciences*, *113*(23), 6454–9. www.pnas.org/cgi/doi /10.1073/pnas.1521897113; and Gelman, A. (2014). The connection between varying treatment effects and the crisis of unreplicable research: A Bayesian perspective. *Journal of Management*, *41*(2), 632–3. https://doi.org /10.1177/0149206314525208.

67 List, J.A. (2022). *The voltage effect: How to make good ideas great and great ideas scale.* Currency.

68 For an interesting discussion on how scientists can test general or "absolute" theories compared to bounded theories cf. Sanbonmatsu et al. (2021).

CHAPTER THIRTEEN

Horizontally Scaling of Planning Prompt Interventions to Help Tax Compliance in Canada

Nicole Robitaille, Julian House, and Nina Mažar

AT A GLANCE

- **Our Goal:** While planning prompts have been found to successfully encourage numerous individual behaviors, we sought to test their effectiveness with *organizations* in a new behavioral domain (*tax compliance*) and explore the effects over time (*repeat exposure*).
- **The Intervention:** We developed an experimental late notice that reorganized the government's standard late notice into explicit step-by-step instructions of (1) *when* organizations should file their returns as well as (2) *where* and (3) *how* – the three key components of planning prompts.
- **The Results:** Our intervention successfully increased the number of tax returns filed, brought in more outstanding debts, and collected these debts sooner. We also found that being exposed to the letter more than once did not diminish its effectiveness. On the other hand, it is important to note the effects of the intervention did not persist indefinitely.
- **Lesson Learned:** Through careful consideration of the similarities and differences in our audience and context (including design and delivery), we were able to successfully scale a planning prompt nudge in new people, places, and times.

Motivation and Objective

More than a decade of research in behavioral economics has taught us that seemingly small behavioral interventions – such as planning prompts and simplification – can be used to nudge individuals across a variety of areas, including health, finances, and education. Nudges are designed to affect behavior in a predictable way while maintaining individuals' freedom of choice.[1] While often simple and low-cost, across a myriad of studies these interventions have repeatedly been shown to produce impressive results. What is less well understood is how effective a specific intervention will be when it is ultimately applied in practice, especially when the context in which it was initially tested in differs from the context in which it will be implemented. In fact, a recent comprehensive meta-analysis explored a number of nudge studies from both academic and applied research. The authors show that the nudge interventions tested in academia tend to have a significantly larger effect than those tested "at scale" by government nudge units.[2] The authors find that one of the key contributing factors to this gap was differences in the context and features of the interventions that were tested, highlighting that what works well in one context does not always work as well in others.

Research in behavioral science has also taught us that human behavior is highly context dependent. And as such, there is good reason to question whether an intervention such as planning prompts, which worked well in one context, would continue to work as well in others. And there are many aspects of a context to consider. For example, how well would planning prompts which can effectively encourage individuals to get a flu shot work when applied in the context of filing taxes? Does it matter if instead of letting people set their own plans one provides them with a plan to follow? Another question worth considering is whether planning prompts will continue to be effective when encountered several times. Are they only effective the first time? And how long do their effects last? Similarly, does it matter who is seeing the nudge? Despite the breadth of insights on how to improve individuals' behaviors, we know relatively little about how or even whether such behavioral interventions would work to influence organizational behavior.

By horizontally scaling interventions – taking a behavioral intervention that was found to be successful in one field study setting and testing it in a different setting – we can begin to explore some of these questions. And in doing so we can see if and how much the effects of certain behavioral interventions generalize when the specifics change. Moreover, such research can also help establish some of the limits to what can be accomplished with a given tool. In the current chapter, we report on a field experiment[3] that we conducted in collaboration with the Ontario Ministry of Finance that attempted to do just that. Specifically, we sought to test the effectiveness of one of the most well-established behavioral interventions – planning prompts[4] – in new people (organizations), a new place (tax compliance domain), and time (repeated exposure over two separate tax years). In addition to describing what worked and didn't, we will outline the factors that we think most contributed to this successful application, share some of our most important lessons learned, and provide some practical recommendations for others planning to implement behavioral interventions in new contexts.

To begin, let us start by taking a look at the behavioral problem we aimed to address with this research: tax compliance. The public services that we as individuals use and rely on daily – including services such as education, healthcare, fire services, public transportation, infrastructure, waste management, etc. – are all supported through government taxes. Funding these public services relies on both collecting taxes from individuals and organizations as well as minimizing any costs associated with their collection.[5] And while most taxpayers comply with their tax obligations, a substantial number still fail to file and pay their taxes on time.[6] This is problematic because overdue taxes restrict revenue and cost the government time and resources for the subsequently required collection process, and in the end, governments are often unable to recover some of the outstanding debt. In 2001 and 2006, for example, the US Internal Revenue Service estimated that only 83 percent of total taxes were voluntarily collected, and that even with additional enforcement efforts, they were only able to ultimately collect 86 percent of taxes owed.[7] Therefore, finding efficient and cost-effective ways of collecting outstanding taxes is essential.

Governments put in a lot of effort and resources to encourage taxpayers to file on time. The traditional approach, that you see in use almost universally, is to apply hefty penalties and fines when taxpayers do not meet their tax regulations. Yet, even with these significant disincentives, tax compliance continues to be an issue. However, recent behavioral research demonstrates that there is likely more at play for taxpayers than just external, financial motives. First, there is research that argues that noncompliance would even be higher if penalties and fines were the only drivers of our tax behavior as the odds of getting audited are quite low.[8] Moreover, there is a large body of work that has shown that tax morale, or the intrinsic motivation to pay taxes, also predicts compliance behavior.[9] As a result, there has been increased interest among policymakers to supplement the traditional approaches of fines and penalties with techniques from behavioral science to try to motivate taxpayers to file and pay their taxes on time.[10] For example, in two large-scale field experiments, researchers demonstrated that including social norm messages in tax reminder letters (e.g., "nine out of ten people pay their tax on time"), as well as messages highlighting how taxes contribute to the common public good (e.g., "paying tax means we all gain from vital public services like the NHS, roads, and schools"), significantly increased the payment of individuals' overdue tax.[11]

Along these lines, we partnered with the Ontario Ministry of Finance to test whether we could apply behavioral science to improve their tax collection process by specifically improving one of their late notices. Also, we ran our field experiment over two years, allowing us to examine the effects of our interventions on behavior over time. We focused specifically on organizations that failed to file an annual payroll tax return, their Employee Health Tax (EHT), on time. In Ontario, the taxes that organizations pay, which include sales, income, and corporate taxes, make up over 18 percent of the government's total tax revenue. And for this particular payroll tax, 9 percent of organizations fail to file on time each year, and any taxes that are submitted late incur large penalties and compounding interest. The finance ministry sends late notices by mail, informing late-filing organizations that their tax returns have not been received and reminding them to file them immediately to prevent further actions and penalties.

By developing a behaviorally informed (experimental) version of the late notice letter, our goal was to increase the number of these tax returns filed, collect more outstanding debts, and collect these debts sooner, before these accounts entered the traditional collection process. Doing so would also have the added benefit of saving money for those organizations who file sooner as they will avoid unnecessary penalties and fines.

Inspiration

While prior research on tax compliance has focused on increasing either taxpayers' extrinsic motivation to avoid any future penalties and fines or their intrinsic motivation to file by trying to foster and increase tax morale, in this research we examined a behavioral approach that has yet to be applied to tax compliance: encouraging organizations to act on their existing motivation using planning prompts. Planning prompts encourage people to develop simple, concrete plans that include a detailed when, where, and how to perform a given behavior.[12] For example, individuals are more likely to get their annual flu shot when they are asked to write down the date and time that they plan to get their vaccine, as opposed to simply seeing a list of when and where shots are available.[13] Moreover, they have been shown to be effective at encouraging a number of different behaviors, such as increasing cancer screening,[14] voter turnout,[15] writing a report,[16] and perhaps most similarly to our context, improving individuals' credit card debt repayment.[17]

Planning prompts, to our knowledge, had never been shown to improve tax compliance behaviors. However, we had a number of reasons – beyond the fact that they seem to work in several different domains – to believe that planning prompts could also work well here. For one, planning prompts have been shown to be effective because having a specific plan helps people get started on their goals, helps overcome procrastination, and can counteract forgetfulness by reminding people what they need to do at key points in time,[18] all of which we predicted should be very helpful when it comes to filing a tax return. Giving organizations a plan of what they specifically need to do by a given deadline should remind them of their obligations and motivate them to act quickly. Second, planning prompts work especially well when they are tied to goals that are related to people's values,[19] and research on tax morale illustrates the importance of intrinsic values on tax compliance.[20] Therefore, we predicted that encouraging organizations to act on their existing motivation with planning prompts would give them that little nudge in the right direction to improve their tax compliance.

Interventions and Method

We ran a two-wave field experiment in the 2013 and 2014 tax years to test the effects of planning prompts on organizations' tax compliance. Each year, all organizations that were late filing their EHT tax return were randomly assigned to receive one of two letters: a control notice, which was the standard late notice used by the finance ministry, and a behaviorally informed experimental late notice featuring our planning prompt intervention. In both waves, the control and experimental notices were the same, but random assignment of organizations to each notice was carried out independently, with 40 percent of organizations receiving the control letter and 60 percent the experimental letter, as illustrated in Figure 13.1 below. Our goal was threefold: (1) to increase the number of tax returns filed, (2) to collect more outstanding debts, and (3) to collect these returns and debts sooner, before these accounts entered the traditional collection process which is costly for our government partners.

To create our experimental late notice, first, and most importantly, we reorganized information from the control letter into explicit step-by-step instructions of (1) *when* organizations should file their returns as well as (2) *where* and (3) *how* – the three key components of planning prompts. See Figure 13.2 for a side-by-side comparison of the

Figure 13.1. Experimental design in Wave 1 (2013 Tax Year) and Wave 2 (2014 Tax Year)

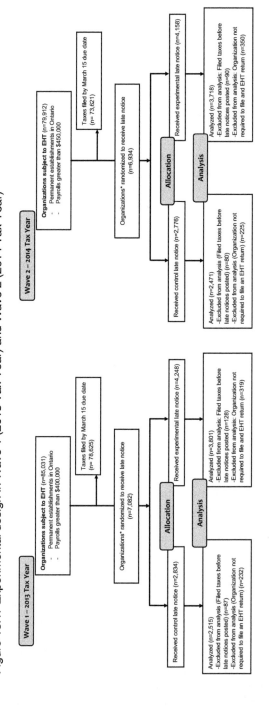

two letters, with the major features of our planning prompt intervention highlighted. It is important to note that our intervention was not designed to give any new information to organizations. All organizations had access to these details of when and how to file a return – they had previously been sent to them in a requirement to file letter, and this information is easily accessible online. Also, over 97 percent of the organizations had previous filing experience. Rather, by organizing this information into a specific plan, our goal was to draw attention to exactly what they needed to do and when they should act by. For example, while both letters highlighted that organizations were late filing their returns and that they must be filed *immediately* to prevent further chargers, in our experimental letter we also added a specific deadline that organizations should file by. This deadline acts as a more concrete goal than asking someone to pay "immediately." Previous research has shown that concrete goals generally produce better performance than abstract goals,[21] and as mentioned, a concrete plan can help people overcome procrastination or forgetfulness. This date also marked the time when additional collections efforts, such as using a call center or hiring a collection's agency, would begin. Therefore, if taxes were collected before this date, the ministry could avoid the costly collections process.

Critically, we also tried to ensure that the plan felt simple and relatively easy to accomplish. For example, there were only two steps, essentially: (1) file and pay, and (2) keep a copy for your records. Feelings of self-efficacy, or the sense that one is going to be able to do the things one needs to do to reach an outcome, can increase goal performance.[22] Last, we supported our intervention with a few small stylistic changes to the letter to improve its clarity and the call to action, including the use of second person pronouns and active voice. Therefore, although imperfectly controlled, we argue that our experiment provides an informative test of the longer-term usefulness of planning prompts as an intervention to accelerate organizations' filing and payment of late taxes.

Similarities and Differences

Planning prompts, to our knowledge, have not been examined within the domain of tax compliance. However, as discussed, given their robust effects shown on numerous domains and given that the mechanisms through which they work (e.g., overcoming procrastination and forgetfulness) should be helpful in this context, we predicted they would be effective here as well. Our study horizontally scaled planning prompts, not only across one dimension (i.e., in a new behavioral domain); we also tested its effectiveness in new people (organizations),

Figure 13.2. Standard Late Notice Letter (left) and Experimental Planning Prompt Late Notice Letter (right)

CONTROL LETTER

Employer Health Tax
Requirement to File

Employer Health Tax: XXXX

If your Employer Health Tax Return has been filed, please disregard this notice.

We have not received your Employer Health Tax Annual Return(s) for the following calendar year(s):

31-Dec-2013

Your return was due on or before 15-Mar-2014. Please complete and file your return with full payment immediately. Interest and penalty charges will apply.

Your return must be filed **immediately** with full payment in order to prevent further interest charges to you or referral to the Collections Branch. *Continued failure to file the required return is a serious offence. If arrangements are not made to correct this situation, the ministry may file an estimated return including applicable penalties and interest for each period that is in default.*

If you have any questions or require additional information, please visit our website or call the Ministry of Finance at the number listed below.

Enquiries	1 866 ONT-TAXS	Fax	1 866 888-3850
	1 866 668-8297		
Teletypewriter (TTY)	1 800 263-7776	Internet	**ontario.ca/finance**

EXPERIMENTAL LETTER

Your Employer Health Tax Annual Return Is Overdue!
You must file immediately.

Employer Health Tax: XXXX

We have not received your Employer Health Tax Annual Return(s) for the following calendar year(s):

31-Dec-2013

Your return was due on or before 15-Mar-2014.

You must file your return(s) immediately with full payment to avoid further interest and penalty charges.

If you fail to deliver your return(s) by 2-May-2014, the Ministry of Finance will refer you to collections. This could have escalating legal consequences as failure to file a return is a serious offence.

Here is what you need to do now and definitely before 2-May-2014:
  1) File and pay your return(s) in full immediately:
     a. By mail to Ministry of Finance, [Street Name, PO Box; City, State, Zip Code]
     b. In person at selected [Government] [centers, see [website address], and click "Visit a Centre"
     c. If you already registered with [website name], log on with your [proprietary key name] at [website address]
  2) Keep a copy for your records.

If you have filed your Employer Health Tax return, please disregard this notice.

If you have any questions or require additional information, please visit our website at [website address] or call the Ministry of Finance at [phone number].

Enquiries	1 866 ONT-TAXS	Fax	1 866 888-3850
	1 866 668-8297		
Teletypewriter (TTY)	1 800 263-7776	Internet	**ontario.ca/finance**

Planning Prompt Intervention
—— How   ····· Where   ▬▬ When

new applications (i.e., providing a detailed plan), and new times (tested effects over two waves).

In chapter 1 of their edited book, *Behavioral Science in the Wild*, Mažar and Soman emphasize that it is often the factors less discussed in an academic paper that impact the ultimate effectiveness of an intervention when applied.[23] To help examine some of these factors, see Table 13.1 below for a comparison of our work versus a select number of planning prompt field studies.[24] Next, we discuss in more detail why each of these contextual differences is important to consider, and how those differences could result in a reduction in effectiveness – a phenomenon coined "voltage drop."[25]

New People

To date, most empirical research on tax compliance has been conducted at the *individual* level, and organizational tax compliance remains a relatively underexplored but growing area of research. Relatedly, even though the field of behavioral economics has amassed more than a decade of research on how to effectively apply behavioral nudges to improve *individuals'* behaviors, we still know relatively little about how such tools influence organizational behavior.[26] On the one hand, organizations are made up of a collection of individuals. Therefore, it is reasonable to think the effects of a given intervention would be similar when applied to firms. On the other hand, there are well-established ways in which organizational decision-making differs from individual decision-making that could dramatically impact an intervention's effectiveness. For one, employees often undergo training and have access to technology and bureaucratic support, which should reduce their reliance on heuristics or biased decisions that nudges often target.[27] Also, experiments have shown that groups tend to act more rationally than an individual.[28] Therefore, we simply do not have a lot of information to draw on when trying to determine how well an intervention tested on individuals will work when applied to organizations.

New Application

Although planning prompt studies have typically asked individuals to form their own goals, we provided the specific *when, where, and how* for their plan. It is entirely possible that providing a plan may not be an effective intervention, as some key features of the intervention are removed. First, when someone creates their own plan, it forces them to consider the details of how they will actually accomplish it, which can

Table 13.1. Comparison of a select number of planning prompt field studies across dimensions of situation and participants

	People		Place	Time		Application	
Field Study	Individual	Organization	Behavior Studied	Intervention Tested 1x	Repeated Testing	Prompt to Form Own Plan	Plan Provided
Armitage (2007)	✓		Eating Fruit	✓		✓	
Gollwitzer & Brandstatter (1997)	✓		Writing a Report	✓		✓	
Holland et al. (2006)		✓*	Recycling		✓*	✓	
Mazar et al. (2018)	✓		Debt Repayment		✓**	✓	
Milkman et al. (2011)	✓		Flu Vaccine	✓		✓	
Milkman et al. (2013)	✓		Cancer Screening	✓		✓	
Nickerson & Rogers (2010)	✓		Voting	✓		✓	
Prestwich et al. (2003)	✓		Exercising	✓		✓	
Current Research (Robitaille et al. 2021)		✓	Tax Compliance		✓		✓

*The study examined the recycling behavior of individual employees in a firm, and while the intervention was applied only once, the effects were measured over several months.

**While the study administered and measured the intervention over several months, it did not explicitly explore the temporal dimension.

help them more accurately estimate how long it will take and any obstacles they may encounter.[29] Second, writing down your own plan acts as a form of commitment, which is known to increase follow through.[30] However, we also know from past research that people are naturally bad at setting concrete plans on their own,[31] so providing the key components in a planning prompt may just be enough to encourage action.

New Timing

Even though many of the behaviors that planning prompts have targeted are behaviors that are repeated over time (e.g., flu shots, voting, debt repayment), prior field studies are mostly unable to talk to the longer-term effects of these prompts as most have administered and measured the effects of the intervention only once. In fact, very few studies have explored the temporal dimensions of behavioral nudges. Yet there are important aspects to consider when a behavior that is being targeted is repeated on a daily, monthly, or annual basis. How long do the effects of a given intervention persist? Would only presenting it once be enough? Based on prior research, the answer likely depends on how much an intervention targets people's beliefs, habits, or the cost of engaging in the behavior, which have all been shown to produce lasting changes.[32] In the case of our planning prompt intervention, which we did not expect would operate in such ways, we would expect the effects to persist once the intervention is removed.

Similarly, what happens if you present the same nudge several times? Does the repetition make it more effective or less? Research on habit formation[33] and the mere exposure effect[34] suggest that the more we see something, the more we may like it, and the more effective it may become. Conversely, research in psychology on habituation suggests that our response to a stimulus decreases over time as the novelty wears off.[35] Therefore, it is unclear to what extent seeing a planning prompt repeatedly would impact its effectiveness. But when designing an intervention to improve tax compliance, something that occurs annually, understanding these temporal effects is critical.

Results

To test the effectiveness of our planning prompt, we compared the tax compliance behavior of organizations that received the standard late notice (our control) to those that received our experimental intervention late notice (featuring the planning prompt). We measured how quickly late-filing organizations filed their taxes, how much money was

Table 13.2. Results: Planning prompts improve organizations' tax filing

	Wave 1 – 2013		Wave 2 – 2014	
	Type of Letter Received by All Late-Filing Organizations			
	Control Letter	Experimental Letter	Control Letter	Experimental Letter
	(n = 2,515)	(n = 3,801)	(n = 2,471)	(n = 3,718)
	Subsequent Tax Behavior of These Organizations			
Average # Days Taken to File *(the lower, the better!)*	51.3	46.9	44.5	39.3
# (%) Returns Filed by the 10-Day Collection Deadline *(the higher, the better!)*	406 (16.1%)	855 (22.5%)	511 (20.7%)	1,072 (28.8%)
Average $ Tax Paid by the 10-Day Collection Deadline *(the higher, the better!)*	$149.88	$241.32	$189.75	$291.70

collected, and we explored the effects over time – looking specifically to see whether our effects replicated, if organizations were affected by our intervention the following tax year, and if our intervention continued to be effective when repeated. Overall, the results of our field experiment were a huge success.

Improved Tax Compliance

We found that, indeed, planning prompts are effective at increasing organizations' timely tax payment (see Table 13.2 above). Organizations that received the planning prompt intervention (the experimental late notice) were significantly faster in filing their taxes, filing an average of four to five days sooner. In addition, across the two tax years studied, the experimental letter brought in approximately $600,000 more before additional collection efforts began, saving the government more than $11,000 in collection costs. Had the experimental letter been sent to all organizations that were late filing their annual return across the two tax years, the government would have

Figure 13.3. No statistically significant evidence for persistence and habituation in the 2nd year

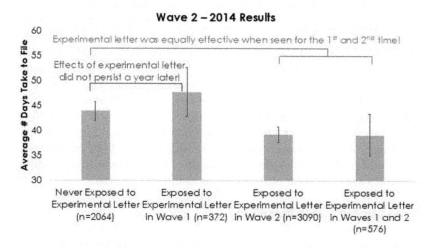

received an additional $1 million and saved approximately $20,000 more in collection costs. Moreover, filing and paying sooner has the added benefit of saving organizations money in terms of accruing any additional penalties and fines.

Effectiveness over Time

Increasing confidence in our findings, we found planning prompts to be equally effective in each of the two years we ran the experiment. And given that tax filing occurs annually, we also found, importantly, that being exposed to the letter more than once did not diminish its effectiveness. Organizations were just as fast to file their taxes after receiving the late notice if it was the first time they saw it or the second. In fact, if anything, the results suggest that the experimental letter may have been more effective for organizations that had already been exposed to it in the first year. That said, we also found that the effects of our intervention did not persist indefinitely. Organizations that received our experimental letter the first year were just as likely to file their taxes late again the following year. As seen in a lot of behavioral research, timing is critical (see Figure 13.3).

By repeating our experiment, we were able to confirm that planning prompts can be effective when seen a second time. However, features of our context may have contributed to the repeated success. In the case of tax returns, there is a year between exposures, which is likely enough time to forget the intervention if they already faced it in the first year. It is possible that if planning prompts were sent more frequently, organizations may habituate and decrease any attention paid to them. Also, organizations are prone to procedural changes and staff turnover that could have caused our nudge to be new to the actual receiver each year. In the end, our research only studied the intervention when it was repeated once, so it's not clear whether the same nudge repeated two, three, or more consecutive years would continue to be as effective. We should continue to explore the effects of nudges over time as these dynamics are critical for ensuring their long-term success.

Discussion and Prescriptive Advice

We were able to successfully scale a behavioral intervention that had previously been used on individuals – planning prompts – to new people, places, and times. So, what led to this success? There are four points that we think are critical for increasing the likelihood an intervention will be successful when applied:

1) Carefully consider which "nudge" should work best in your context.

As research in behavioral science has taught us, not all nudges should be effective in all contexts (across people, places, and time). A lot of care was put into choosing an intervention that we thought should work on organizations' tax compliance behavior and be effective over time. Let us look at one example to illustrate. Recent research on tax compliance showed that social norms can be highly effective at improving an individual's filing behavior. So why didn't we apply social norms in this case? Well, we know that one of the reasons social norms are effective is because they increase the personal moral costs of a particular action.[36] And although individuals are highly concerned with their moral identity, we also know there can be a diffusion of responsibility (it's someone else's fault) when an (in)action occurs in a group.[37] Therefore, we thought a social norms intervention would be more uncertain, and thus risky to run in our context.

What does this mean for practice? It is very important, before simply applying any intervention, that practitioners do careful background research on the domain they are working in to try to identify if there are reasons why their intervention may or may not be effective. First, one may try to consider what might be similar and different in their context, and if any of those differences would impact the likelihood of success. It is also useful to research what is known about why a given intervention works – in other words, the psychological drivers. In our case, we felt social norms likely wouldn't work as well in an organizational context. We felt that planning prompts, which had been shown to help overcome a number of barriers we thought might be at play when it comes to organizational tax compliance, would be a better candidate for a successful intervention.

2) When developing interventions consider message, design, and delivery.

It is one thing to pick the right intervention. However, if the intervention isn't delivered in an effective way, it will not be able to have the desired impact on behavior. Therefore, it is important to consider design and delivery. For example, in our research, to increase the impact of our planning prompt intervention, we also made some stylistic changes to our experimental late notice (e.g., using second person pronouns, active voice, and reorganizing the letter structure). The primary reason we included these changes was to increase the *salience and prominence* of our intervention. In fact, we took care to make sure these edits did not largely change the information in the letter, their meaning, or the reading difficulty. However, if we did not take the time to reorganize the letter and make it easy for firms to attend to the step-by-step plan of what they needed to do, the planning prompt intervention might not have been effective. Therefore, one question to ask is whether one can include other design changes to enhance an intervention's salience and maximize its impact with design.

Second, as we demonstrated in our research, the timing of when to deliver one's intervention is also key. Specifically, we found that if we sent a planning prompt intervention one year, it had no impact on tax filing behavior the following year. As a rule of thumb, research has found it is often optimal to intercept customers at the time of decision-making.[38] However, it would be important to test and confirm this in any given context.

3) To maximize learning, don't throw everything you can think of into one intervention.

Sometimes it is tempting to try to include several different interventions at once. For example, why not add social norms and planning prompts to the late notice? One potential issue with doing so is that it can clutter up the final product. As mentioned above, simplifying as much as possible to increase the salience of key elements is likely the most effective way to implement any intervention. The key message must not be lost. Another issue is that by adding more interventions, one never learns which element was key in driving any behavior change. Knowing which elements caused behavior change is important when applying an intervention in different contexts.

To give one example from this work, planning prompts contain information on *when, where,* and *how* to file taxes. While it is impossible to know how much each of these different features may have ultimately impacted organizational behavior, we suspect that providing a specific deadline may have been critical. For one, most of the information in the experimental letter was not new to organizations. In fact, the only new information was the specific deadline (instead of simply saying file immediately). All organizations who are late filing their returns are told they will ultimately be referred to collections, but we made this point – and more specifically the date – salient.

Second, some of our results support the argument that the deadline may have been key. In both tax years, the experimental late notice significantly increased organizations' likelihood of filing before the ten-day deadline. However, in the two ten-day periods after the deadline, there were no differences in organizations' likelihood of filing between the two late notices. While the differences before and after the deadline may be due, in part, to the fact that additional collections efforts began at that point of time, this pattern of results also suggests that the deadline itself may have provided organizations with a very specific goal to guide their behavior.

In the end, we cannot tell from this experiment alone which aspects or changes in our letter were the most critical for encouraging organizations to file and pay their taxes. It may be the case that just adding the deadline alone may have been enough to encourage change, but without testing it separately, we cannot know.

4) Continue to track data over time, and when possible, repeat experiments.

To date, most field experiments implement their interventions and measure their effects at only one point in time. Therefore, there is still much we do not know about the temporal dimensions of nudges. One of the best ways to learn more about the dynamics of these effects is simply to, as much as possible, continue to track the data over time.

Moreover, repeating an experiment can give lots of meaningful information about the dynamics of these effects: *Does it replicate? Does it work when repeated? Do the effects impact future behavior? How long does it continue to work when removed?* Gathering this data can go a long way in enhancing the understanding of what works, what doesn't (and when).

NOTES

1 Thaler, R.H., & Sunstein, C.R. (2008). *Nudge: Improving decisions about health, wealth, and happiness.* Penguin Books.
2 DellaVigna, S., & Linos, E. (2022). RCTs to scale: Comprehensive evidence from two nudge units. *Econometrica, 90*(1), 81–116. https://doi.org/10.3386/w27594.
3 Robitaille, N., House, J., & Mazar, N. (2021). Effectiveness of planning prompts on organizations' likelihood to file their overdue taxes: A multiwave field experiment. *Management Science, 67*(7), 4327–40. https://doi.org/10.1287/mnsc.2020.3744.
4 Rogers, T., Milkman, K.L., John, L.K., & Norton, M.I. (2016). Beyond good intentions: Prompting people to make plans improves follow-through on important tasks. *Behavioral Science and Policy, 1*(2), 33–41. https://doi.org/10.1177/237946151500100205.
5 Andreoni, J., Erard, B., & Feinstein, J. (1998). Tax compliance. *Journal of Economic Literature, 36*(2), 818–60. https://www.jstor.org/stable/2565123.
6 Matsaganis, M., Leventi, C., & Flevotomou, M. (2012). The crisis and tax evasion in Greece: What are the distributional implications? *CESifo Forum, 13*(2), 26–32. https://www.cesifo.org/en/publications/2012/article-journal/crisis-and-tax-evasion-greece-what-are-distributional.
7 Internal Revenue Service. (2012). *IRS releases new tax gap estimates: Compliance rates remain statistically unchanged from previous study.* https://www.irs.gov/pub/newsroom/overview_tax_gap_2006.pdf.
8 Slemrod, J., & Yitzhaki, S. (2002). Tax avoidance, evasion and administration. In A.J. Auerbach & M. Feldstein (Eds.), *Handbook of public economics* (pp. 1423–70). Elsevier Science.
9 Cummings, R.G., Martinez-Vazquez, J., McKee, M., & Torgler, B. (2009). Tax morale affects tax compliance: Evidence from surveys and an artefactual field experiment. *Journal of Economic Behavior & Organization, 70*(3), 447–57. https://doi.org/10.1016/j.jebo.2008.02.010.
10 Benartzi, S., Beshears, J., Milkman, K.L., Sunstein, C.R., Thaler, R.H., Shankar, M., Tucker-Ray, W., Congdon, W.J., & Galing, S. (2017). Should governments invest more in nudging? *Psychological Science, 28*(8), 1041–55. https://doi.org/10.1177/0956797617702501.

11 Hallsworth, M., List, J.A., Metcalfe, R.D., & Vlaev, I. (2017). The behavioralist as tax collector: Using natural field experiments to enhance tax compliance. *Journal of Public Economics, 148*(C), 14–31. https://doi.org/10.1016/j.jpubeco.2017.02.003.

12 Gollwitzer P.M., & Sheeran, P. (2006). Implementation intentions and goal achievement: A meta-analysis of effects and processes. *Advances in Experimental Social Psychology, 38*(1), 69–119. https://doi.org/10.1016/S0065-2601(06)38002-1.

13 Milkman, K.L., Beshears, J., Choi, J.J., Laibson, D., & Madrian, B.C. (2011). Using implementation intentions prompts to enhance influenza vaccination rates. *Proceedings of the National Academy of Sciences of the United States of America, 108*(26), 10415–20. https://doi.org/10.1073/pnas.1103170108.

14 Milkman, K.L., Beshears, J., Choi, J.J., Laibson, D., & Madrian, B.C. (2013). Planning prompts as a means of increasing preventive screening rates. *Preventive Medicine, 56*(1), 92–3. https://doi.org/10.1016/j.ypmed.2012.10.021.

15 Nickerson, D.W., & Rogers, T. (2010). Do you have a voting plan? Implementation intentions, voter turnout, and organic plan making. *Psychological Science, 21*(2), 194–9. https://doi.org/10.1177/0956797609359326.

16 Gollwitzer, P.M., & Brandstätter, V. (1997). Implementation intentions and effective goal pursuit. *Journal of Personality and Social Psychology, 73*(1), 186–99. https://psycnet.apa.org/doi/10.1037/0022-3514.73.1.186.

17 Mazar, N., Mochon, D., & Ariely, D. (2018). If you are going to pay within the next 24 hours, press 1: Automatic planning prompt reduces credit card delinquency. *Journal of Consumer Psychology, 28*(3), 466–76. https://doi.org/10.1002/jcpy.1031.

18 Rogers, T., & Frey, E. (2015). Changing behavior beyond the here and now. In G. Keren & G. Wu (Eds.), *Blackwell handbook of judgment and decision making* (pp. 725–48). Wiley-Blackwell.

19 Koestner, R., Lekes, N., Powers, T.A., & Chicoine, E. (2002). Attaining personal goals: Self-concordance plus implementation intentions equals success. *Journal of Personality and Social Psychology, 83*(1), 231–44. https://psycnet.apa.org/doi/10.1037/0022-3514.83.1.231.

20 Kirchler, E. (2007). *The economic psychology of tax behaviour.* Cambridge University Press.

21 Locke, E.A., & Latham, G.P. (2002). Building a practically useful theory of goal setting and task motivation: A 35-year odyssey. *American Psychologist, 57*(9), 705–17. https://doi.org/10.1037//0003-066x.57.9.705.

22 Bandura, A. (1977). Self-efficacy: Toward a unifying theory of behavioral change. *Psychological Review, 84*(2), 191–215. https://psycnet.apa.org/doi/10.1037/0033-295X.84.2.191.

23 Mažar, N., & Soman, D. (2022). *Behavioral science in the wild*. University of Toronto Press.

24 See for examples Armitage, C.J. (2007). Effects of an implementation intention-based intervention on fruit consumption. *Psychology and Health*, 22(8), 917–28. https://doi.org/10.1080/14768320601070662; Prestwich, A., Lawton, R., & Conner, M. (2003). The use of implementation intentions and the decision balance sheet in promoting exercise behaviour. *Psychology and Health*, 18(6), 707–21. https://psycnet.apa.org/doi/10.10 80/08870440310001594493; and Holland, R. W., Aarts, H., & Langendam, D. (2006). Breaking and creating habits on the working floor: A field experiment on the power of implementation intentions. *Journal of Experimental Social Psychology*, 42(6), 776–83. https://psycnet.apa.org /doi/10.1016/j.jesp.2005.11.006.

25 List, J.A. (2022). *The voltage effect*. Penguin Books Limited.

26 OECD. (2017). *Applying behavioural insights to organisations: Theoretical underpinnings*. OECD Publishing.

27 Stinchcombe, A.L. (1990). *Information and organizations*. University of California Press.

28 Charness, G., & Sutter, M. (2012). Groups make better self-interested decisions. *Journal of Economic Perspectives*, 26(3), 157–76. https://doi .org/10.1257/jep.26.3.157.

29 Kruger, J., & Evans, M. (2004). If you don't want to be late, enumerate: Unpacking reduces the planning fallacy. *Journal of Experimental Social Psychology*, 40(5), 586–98. https://psycnet.apa.org/doi/10.1016/j .jesp.2003.11.001.

30 Cialdini, R.B. (2009). *Influence: Science and Practice*. Pearson Education.

31 Lynch, J.G., Jr., Netemeyer, R.G., Spiller, S.A., & Zammit, A. (2010). A generalizable scale of propensity to plan: The long and the short of planning for time and for money. *Journal of Consumer Research*, 37(1), 108–28. https://doi.org/10.1086/649907.

32 Rogers et al. (2016).

33 Wood, W. (2019). *Good habits, bad habits: The science of making positive changes that stick*. Farrar, Straus and Giroux.

34 Zajonc, R.B. (1968). Attitudinal effects of mere exposure. *Journal of Personality and Social Psychology*, 9(2), 1–27. https://psycnet.apa.org/doi/10 .1037/h0025848.

35 Thompson, R.F., & Spencer, W.A. (1966). Habituation: A model phenomenon for the study of neuronal substrates of behavior. *Psychological Review*, 73(1), 16–43. https://psycnet.apa.org/doi/10.1037/h0022681.

36 Hallsworth et al. (2017).

37 Bandura, A., Underwood, B., & Fromson, M.E. (1975). Disinhibition of aggression through diffusion of responsibility and dehumanization of

victims. *Journal of Research in Personality, 9*(4), 253–69. https://doi.org/10.1016/0092-6566(75)90001-X.

38 Robitaille, N., Mazar, N., Tsai, C.I., Haviv, A.M., & Hardy, E. (2021). Increasing organ donor registrations with behavioral interventions: A field experiment. *Journal of Marketing, 85*(3), 168–83. https://doi.org/10.1177/0022242921990070.

CHAPTER FOURTEEN

Horizontal Scaling of a Prejudice Reduction Intervention in Australia

Wing Hsieh, Nicholas Faulkner, and Rebecca Wickes

AT A GLANCE

- **Our Goal:** To reduce prejudice against migrants in Australia by increasing people's perception of variability of those within migrant groups.
- **The Intervention:** A video series, "Small Talk," which featured migrants talking about their individual experiences with everyday topics like keeping healthy, work-life balance, and managing stress.
- **The Results:** Although perceived variability-based interventions have worked in France, we found that adapting this approach to a video format and to an Australian audience was not effective at reducing prejudice against migrants.
- **Lesson Learned:** Using a mechanism that has been successful in another context and has good potential for scaling does not ensure successful prejudice reduction – an implementation science for behavioral sciences is needed to better understand how to scale social psychology interventions.

Motivation and Objective

Prejudice against migrants is a pervasive problem in many countries. While immigration brings a range of benefits, such as new and diverse skills, a boost in economic demand and labor force in underpopulated areas, and increased contributions to tax revenues,[1] there often are concerns that increased immigration also leads to competition for scarce resources, such as housing and public infrastructure, and cultural clashes that can harm social cohesion.[2] In response to increased migration, a key concern of many governments is the provision of a suite of services to assist immigrants to settle readily into their new country.[3] In contrast, governments have devoted less attention to programs aimed at enabling receiving communities to more readily tolerate, accept, and include new migrants. This one-sided focus has ignored persistently high levels of prejudice against immigrants occurring in communities throughout the world.[4] Debates in many countries about increased immigration have used language and posturing that alienates migrants, particularly new migrants.[5] Prejudice toward migrants curtails the social, economic, and cultural inclusion of migrants to the detriment of both the receiving community and migrants.[6] A constructive and meaningful approach to managing immigration requires programs that help members of the receiving community manage prejudice relating to immigration as well as programs that help migrants adapt to their new environment.[7]

Despite much research on prejudice reduction, little is known about how to reduce prejudice in real-world settings. Very few interventions are tested in experiments conducted in the real world (field experiments),[8] nor is there much consideration about how to design prejudice reduction interventions in a manner that enables them to be used at scale across large populations.[9] For prejudice reduction interventions to have a widespread impact across the community, an intervention cannot just be effective; it also needs to be scalable. What works in a specific setting may not work in the broader community.[10] Therefore, consideration of the likelihood of successful scaling of an effective intervention is critical for maximizing impact.

In this chapter, we describe our experience with designing a prejudice reduction intervention based on evidence of what works, but also designed with scalability in mind.[11] We tested the horizontal scaling of an intervention – that is, whether an intervention works in other contexts. To do this, we took a theoretical approach to prejudice reduction (perceived variability) that has only been tested in France, adapted it into a digital format to further enhance scalability, and tested its effectiveness in Australia.

Inspiration

Perceived variability has promise as an effective and scalable prejudice reduction approach. It refers to the degree to which individuals view members of an outgroup as being very different from themselves.[12]

According to perceived variability theory, it is harder for a person to dislike a group when they believe that all sorts of people are members of that group. As such, according to the perceived variability approach to prejudice reduction, encouraging individuals to see differences across members of an outgroup may provide a way forward in reducing prejudice, particularly in large-scale interventions.[13] A recent review of prejudice reduction field experiments, which combined the results from all published field experiments, found that interventions based on perceived variability reported the largest average effect size compared to other approaches.[14] Furthermore, perceived variability may be amenable to scaling to the general population according to assessment against a scalability framework designed specifically for prejudice reduction interventions.[15]

Despite these promising findings, research on using perceived variability as a prejudice reduction intervention strategy is in its infancy. Only a small number of studies in laboratory and field settings, mostly conducted by one group of researchers (Abdelatif Er-rafiy and Markus Brauer) have indicated that this approach can reduce prejudice against single-ethnicity groups.[16] Moreover, these studies were all conducted in France, primarily in university environments and laboratory settings with only three studies tested in field conditions (high school, university library, and medical waiting room).[17] A notable feature of these studies is that the authors indicated that the research was conducted in a context where there were recognizable and salient ethnic outgroups. The intervention in these studies featured a prominently displayed poster depicting Arab Muslims of all different appearances and the line "What makes us the same – is that we are all different."[18] This poster was designed to highlight differences within the Arab Muslim outgroup such that the people depicted are of different ages, genders, appearances, and personalities. This approach is yet to be tested outside France and with more diffuse target outgroups such as migrants.

In countries where migration is relatively more widespread and diverse, like Australia, prejudice is often linked to an objection toward immigration and migrants in general rather than toward a particular ethnicity.[19] Out-group definition may also be linked to overall anti-immigrant prejudice,[20] while simultaneously, particular migrant groups may experience more prejudice than others, such as refugees, Africans, and Muslims.[21] Prejudice against immigrants as opposed to specific ethnicities has been observed in many countries across Europe,[22] Canada,[23] and the US.[24] Thus, there remains a need for perceived variability field experiments in other settings, and for more diffuse out-groups like "immigrants" to understand its scalability.[25]

Interventions and Method

In our study, we developed a new intervention – a video series titled "Small Talk." The intervention aimed to reduce prejudice by increasing viewers' perceptions of variability among the featured minority groups.

The intervention was designed with scalability in mind, based on our assessment against a scalability framework covering intervention, delivery, costs, and context factors.[26] A short video format was used as an engaging way to deliver information that is also easy to disseminate.[27] The videos discussed the topics of work-life balance, managing day-to-day stress, and keeping healthy to draw attention away from the actual goals of the study and increase appeal to a broad audience. The presenters discussed their individual viewpoints on the topic of each episode. During the discussion the presenters would make clear that they were born overseas and often contrasted their experiences in Australia with their overseas experiences. The variation in the video for each condition was as follows:

- Treatment 1 – Migrant variability: Three videos featuring three presenters of different migrant backgrounds (New Zealand, Indonesia, and Uganda).
- Treatment 2 – Middle Eastern Muslim variability: Three videos featuring three presenters of the same migrant background (Middle Eastern Muslim).
- Control: Three videos featuring the same single presenter of Indonesian Muslim background.

Each video ended with a single screen depicting images of each presenter from the video series, alongside a summary of their differing views. This was designed to be similar to the poster used in the studies in France.

More than one presenter in the two treatment conditions was included to increase the perception of variability within those groups based on differences in characteristics such as gender, age, personality, and interests (Figure 14.2). The first treatment condition ("migrant treatment") tested whether perceived variability could help to reduce prejudice against broadly defined groups like migrants. It featured migrants from a diverse range of countries, including Western countries, and highlighted that they have a broad range of personalities and beliefs. The second treatment condition ("ethnicity treatment") was designed to reduce prejudice against a specific migrant group of single ethnicity (Middle Eastern Muslims) similar to that tested in the

Figure 14.1. Screenshots of videos

Figure 14.2. Presenters in each condition

Er-rafiy and Brauer studies in France.[28] This condition highlighted the variability within one ethnicity. The idea behind this condition is that if prejudicial stereotypes are based on ethnicity (rather than attributable to migrants as a group), there could be greater perceived homogeneity within one ethnicity than across migrants as a general group. In both treatment conditions we replicated the underlying mechanism of perceived variability but used a video format instead of the poster format used in the Er-rafiy and Brauer studies.[29] These treatment conditions were compared to a control condition featuring only one migrant.

Figure 14.3. CONSORT flow diagram for Study 1

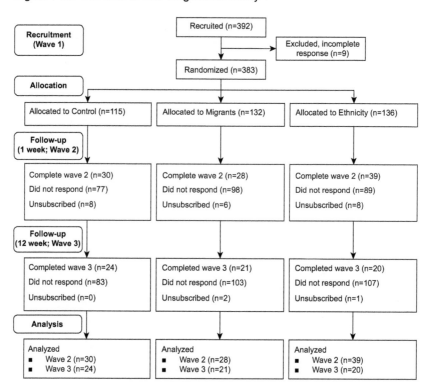

Each of the treatment and control conditions had three episodes (each episode around three minutes). Participants were asked to watch all three videos within the series to which they were randomly allocated (Control, Treatment 1, and Treatment 2).

Specifically, the two preregistered experiments tested the effect of Small Talk on prejudice.[30] In Study 1, we tested the intervention in a field experiment involving the general adult population in Australia. This study gave evidence on the effectiveness of the intervention in a real-world setting, but the unexpectedly low response rate resulted in a small sample, which limited the conclusions that could be made on effectiveness. We then followed with Study 2, which tested the same stimulus materials in a larger, broadly representative Australian sample recruited through a commercial market research company. Both studies were designed to answer the following questions: (1) are perceived variability-based interventions effective in reducing prejudice? and (2) do

Table 14.1. Study procedure

Study 1 – Field Experiment	Study 2 – Panel Experiment
The study was advertised on social media and through postal mailouts. Registration was on a website that invited participants to sign up by completing a pretest that records baseline measures of prejudice and perceived variability. Participants were then randomly assigned one of three conditions, and then for the next three weeks they were sent a weekly email with a link to a new video each week.[31] One week after the final video they were asked to complete a post-test. Three months later they were sent a follow-up email with a request to complete a second post-test. A summary of the procedure is outlined in the CONSORT diagram (Figure 14.3). This study used a pre-post randomized controlled trial design.	Participants signed up through a commercial market research panel provider. After completing some demographic questions, they were then randomly assigned to a condition and asked to watch all three videos in their assigned condition. Following this, participants were asked to complete prejudice and perceived variability questions. This study used a post-test only randomized controlled trial design.

perceived variability-based interventions only reduce prejudice toward a specific ethnic group (that is, "Middle Eastern Muslims"), or can they also work to reduce prejudice against migrants more generally?

The procedure that we followed for each study is outlined above (Table 14.1).

Differences (and Similarities)

Our intervention was designed to stay true to the theoretical underpinnings of the Er-rafiy and Brauer studies, making only the necessary adaptations to ensure suitability in Australian conditions and to adopt a digital video format to enhance scalability. One of the most apparent adaptations that we made was that our intervention videos featured three migrants / Middle Eastern Muslims at a time, whereas the poster designed by Er-rafiy and Brauer featured twelve Arab Muslims. Notwithstanding this, our adaptations were within the theoretical confines of the Er-rafiy and Brauer studies. They ran a number of successful laboratory studies based on other ethnic out-groups in France – one was based on the variability of a smaller group (three) of Chinese students, and the other was based on a travel journal relating to Moroccan people generally as opposed to Moroccan individuals – both presented in written form.[32] Our treatment videos being based on three individual migrants and three individual Middle Eastern Muslims are similar in style and mechanism, and potentially present even greater variability given the deeper engagement with the presenters as individuals in the video format used. Indeed, viewers tend to engage more with video or animated materials than with static materials.[33]

Below we compare other details of our studies to the Er-rafiy and Brauer field experiments that inspired our studies (as discussed above in Inspiration and in Table 14.2).

Results

Study 1 found no evidence indicating that either treatment significantly reduced prejudice against migrants or Middle Eastern Muslims. Most effects across different subgroups were not statistically significant, and the two tests that revealed significant effects slightly favored the control group over treatment groups. As these null results may have been due to recruitment numbers being lower than targeted, we tested the same stimulus materials with a larger sample in Study 2.

Study 2 also did not find a significant effect of the treatments on perceived variability or prejudice. While perceived variability and prejudice were negatively correlated, these correlations were very weak, suggesting that interventions targeting perceived variability may have limited ability to influence prejudice.[38]

Overall, across both experiments, we found that the intervention did not significantly reduce prejudice. In both experiments, correlations between perceived variability and prejudice were in the expected direction – that is, higher perceived variability correlated with lower prejudice. However, the correlations were weak and markedly lower in the higher-powered online laboratory trial. Furthermore, in conducting a mini meta-analysis to summarize the studies, we found that the effect of the intervention was not statistically different from zero on average. Notwithstanding this, equivalence testing suggested that we could not reject the hypothesis that the treatments were equivalent to zero, leaving open the possibility of a small effect of perceived variability on prejudice. These results indicated that perceived variability might have limited application and scaling potential due to apparent low adaptability and effectiveness.[39]

These results contrast with those in the Er-rafiy and Brauer studies, which found that increasing perceived variability was an effective approach to reducing prejudice in France. In the next section we discuss some potential reasons as to why we did not get the same results.

Table 14.2. Comparison of the present study to previous studies

	Er-rafiy and Brauer (2013) and Er-rafiy et al. (2010)	Present Studies
Experimental Design	Poster featuring twelve Arab Muslims with picture, name, age, and adjective for each person RCT with "no treatment" control	Video series of 9–12 min. total viewing time in each condition. Each treatment condition featured three presenters. RCT with control and two treatment conditions
Setting	France, in person, three studies: (1) university library, (2) high school classroom, (3) physical therapist offices. Some studies in laboratory settings were conducted as well.	Australia, online. Study 1 – Field sample through advertising online and with a mailout. Study 2 – paid market research panel sample.
Participants	(1) University library visitors, (2) high school students, (3) medical waiting room patients/attendees	Adults in the community (eighteen years or older)
Sample Size	(1) 50 undergraduate students (average age 19.5 years), (2) 1,012 high school students (average age 16 years), (3) 331 attendees of medical office	Field sample – Data was collected at three points in time: 383 completed the pretest (Time 1), 97 of those participants completed the first post-test at one week (Time 2: i.e., completed both Time 1 and 2), and 65 completed the second post-test at three months (Time 3: i.e., completed both Time 1 and 3). Panel sample – The total sample size was 424 participants (Control, n=143; Migrants, n=139; Ethnicity, n=142).
Measures	Perceived variability measures using (a) range task[34] – assign on a scale the average group member, the group member who possesses the trait least and the group member who possesses the trait most on four traits (selfish, hard-working, aggressive, warm)	Perceived variability was measured using a trait similarity task. Participants were asked to rate specified groups on how similar or dissimilar they are on stereotypic traits.[36] A total of four traits were included in the survey. Two of these were negative traits (threatening and lazy), and two were positive traits

(Continued)

Table 14.2. (Continued)

	Er-rafiy and Brauer (2013) and Er-rafiy et al. (2010)	Present Studies
	and (b) single question asking extent participant thought of the target group on a scale from "not at all different" to "very different."[35] Prejudice measured by Modern Racism Scale.	(family oriented and happy). These traits reflected common stereotypes in Australia that were identified in previous research.[37] Prejudice measured by Modern Racism Scale.
Procedures	Three field experiments – intervention poster put up on (1) university library door, (2) high school classroom, (3) medical waiting room. Post-test only – survey for university and high school / observation of behavior for waiting room.	Field study – advertising on social media and mailout, sign-up online and randomly allocated to a condition. Pre-post surveys. Panel study – signed up through a market research panel and randomly allocated to a condition. Post-test only survey.
Implementation Details	Data collected through observation or in person surveys. Intervention materials were posters in field settings.	Data collected online using Qualtrics. Intervention materials delivered via email with blurb and link to a short video for field study. Videos were built into Qualtrics survey for paid panel study.

Reconciliation

In designing a prejudice reduction intervention based on perceived variability theory, we took care to stay true to the theoretical mechanisms. Our interest in this approach was piqued by the success of previous research and the promise of scalability that this approach had on face value. With this desire to strengthen the evidence base on perceived variability we sought to replicate the findings of the Er-rafiy and Brauer studies in the Australian context.[40] However, we found that the perceived variability approach did not significantly reduce prejudice in Australia. We propose several possible reasons for these findings below.

First, the effectiveness of perceived variability-based prejudice reduction interventions may vary from country to country. Context plays a key role in determining whether a prejudice reduction intervention can successfully be horizontally scaled, or in other words, apply elsewhere.[41] Prejudice reduction programs and interventions are implemented in specific social contexts, which include cultural, linguistic, and religious considerations relevant to a particular community. To illustrate this point, the literature indicating the effectiveness of perceived variability as a prejudice reduction approach has largely been tested in France,[42] where only around 12 percent of the population is born overseas.[43] In contrast, Australia is often recognized as an "immigration nation," with around 30 percent of the population born overseas and over 50 percent of the population having parents born overseas – the second highest among OECD countries.[44] Consequently, there are arguably fewer salient ethnic out-groups in Australia. This significant difference in context could result in differences in perceptions of identity and migrants in the two countries.

Context can influence how someone perceives their own social identity or "social identity complexity." Social identity complexity is a "subjective representation of the interrelationships among his or her multiple group identities."[45] A person has high social identity complexity if they are aware that their memberships in multiple in-groups are not fully overlapping. Typically, that associates with a more complex identity structure and a greater tendency toward inclusion and more limited reliance on stereotypes.[46] So perhaps highlighting multiple categorization (or variability) has a greater effect when participants' perception of their own social identity complexity is low.[47]

Australia's strong migrant history may result in overall higher levels of social identity complexity, which may counter the impact of perceived variability on prejudice. Greater exposure to diverse migrant cultures could result in greater reflection of the complexities associated with social identity and higher social identity complexity. If so, then perceived variability, like multiple categorization approaches, may be less effective. In such contexts, the drivers of prejudice are less predicated on out-group homogeneity bias.

In contexts of greater cultural diversity, threat and conflict of interests may be the more likely causes of prejudice against migrants.[48] These theories postulate that migrants pose economic or political threats to majority groups, which leads to prejudice. Indeed, empirical research has suggested that the greater the perceived competition from an immigrant out-group, the more negatively perceived that group.[49]

This limitation to scaling, based on contextual differences, is what other authors in the social sciences have termed as "representativeness of the situation."[50] The implication of this limitation posed by context is that countries like Australia with a stronger history of migration may require more active strategies for prejudice reduction than perceived variability.

A second possible explanation for the lack of significant effects is that effect sizes in follow-up (replication) studies tend to be lower than those reported in the original study.[51] This may be the case here as we have not been able to conceptually replicate the findings in previous research in both field and market research panel (online laboratory) settings.[52] Without greater transparency of research through preregistration and open science practices, it is difficult to discern the cause of differences beyond the limited information that is published in the academic literature. To tackle prejudice, information about what works is certainly critical, but equally, information about anything and everything that has been trialed (effective or not) is important. The sharing of information on all trials helps to streamline the efforts of all researchers by reducing duplication. Our studies here contribute an understanding of the impact of perceived variability-based interventions over and above general exposure to migrants, helping to better understand the limitations of the perceived variability approach.

A third possible explanation for the null findings is that the adaptations made to the stimulus materials used in our study reduced their effectiveness. As discussed above, we made adaptations to the format of the intervention, from poster to video, while trying to stay true to the theoretical underpinnings. However, it is possible that in allowing the intervention to be suited to an audience in a different country and enhancing its scalability, these adaptations could have affected its effectiveness. Interventions need to be adaptable in order to be scalable.[53] If small modifications render an intervention ineffective, this is a limitation for scale-up. As such, the finding that the adapted materials tested here were ineffective in reducing prejudice indicates that the scaling potential for perceived variability-based prejudice reduction interventions has limits.

Discussion and Prescriptive Advice

Our efforts at horizontally scaling a perceived variability prejudice reduction intervention that had been successful in France uncovered limited applicability in the Australian context, and moreover, the importance of deliberate consideration for scalability.

Perhaps our biggest takeaway is the need for an implementation science for social psychology. Prejudice reduction and the broader field of social psychology face similar challenges to that of the health sciences when it comes to maximizing the impact of interventions evidence in the real world. As far back as the 1940s, health scientists were aware that evidence of what worked did not always translate into broader clinical outcomes.[54] Consequently, the health sciences have devoted significant research effort toward understanding how to systematically improve the take-up of evidence into practice at scale, so much so that such research has become a distinct science – "implementation science."[55]

The concept of scalability has been central to health sciences where taking evidence from academic research and putting it into practice is critical.[56] To this end, several scalability assessments outline strategies for scaling health-related interventions that incorporate the broader suite of real-world factors in the health context.[57] In particular, studies focusing on the effectiveness of health interventions have pointed to the need for adaptation to the local context or cultural accommodation to avoid a reduction in impact in new contexts.[58] Multiple authors have proposed that the key to contextual adjustments is maintaining the causal mechanism of the intervention.[59] Frameworks have been developed in the health sciences to guide in-depth exploration of context when implementing and scaling complex health interventions.[60] This focus on implementation and the development of implementation science has helped individual programs in the health sciences to reach long-term sustainability in complex adaptive environments and to identify the mechanism for effective real-world change.[61]

In contrast, in the prejudice reduction scholarship and across social psychology more broadly, there is limited consideration of how evidence of what works can be implemented and scaled in the real world to have a far-reaching impact. This parallels the state of the health sciences before the development of implementation science. Without deliberate investigation of the methods required to systematically improve the take-up of evidence in real-world settings at scale, grounded in an understanding of scalability, social psychology as a discipline will fail to move the needle on prejudice where it truly matters. An implementation science for prejudice reduction is imperative if we want to effect real change.

As for the question of what works to reduce prejudice, our experience with perceived variability suggests that while there has been some promising evidence of effectiveness and potential for scalability,[62] we could not horizontally scale those results to the Australian context using a video format. The null finding here is an important contribution to knowledge because our attempts to closely replicate an approach that has been found effective by other researchers help to shine a light on the conditions required for effective intervention.[63] These findings and the surrounding learnings are important to share because our overarching aim of reducing prejudice against migrants is achieved not just from understanding what has worked but also where or when an intervention does not work.[64] When we combine the results from our study with other perceived variability field experiments, perceived variability as a prejudice reduction intervention is overall less effective on average.[65] However, we acknowledge that our contribution is only an additional two studies and the first to be conducted outside of France, so we cannot conclusively make claims on the effectiveness of perceived variability as a prejudice reduction approach. As such we encourage other researchers and practitioners to continue to explore and evaluate perceived variability and other approaches with potential for scaling to achieve some success in tackling prejudice in the community.

NOTES

1 See Blanchflower, D.G., Saleheen, J., & Shadforth, C. (2007). *The impact of the recent migration from Eastern Europe on the UK economy.* IZA Discussion Paper Series (No. 2615; Discussion Paper Series, Issue February). https:// dx.doi.org/10.2139/ssrn.969406; and Dumont, J.-C., & Liebig, T. (2014). *Is migration good for the economy?* Migration Policy Debates.https://www .oecd.org/migration/OECD Migration Policy Debates Numero 2.pdf; and Taylor, J.E., Gupta, A., Rojas Valdes, R.I., Filipski, M.J., Alloush, M., & Gonzalez-Estrada, E. (2016). Economic impact of refugees. *Proceedings of the National Academy of Sciences, 113*(27), 7449–53. https://doi.org/10.1073 /pnas.1604566113.

2 Productivity Commission. (2016). *Migrant intake into Australia* (Issue 77). https://www.pc.gov.au/inquiries/completed/migrant-intake/report.

3 See Neudorf, E.G. (2016). Key informant perspectives on the Government of Canada's modernized approach to immigrant settlement. *Canadian Ethnic Studies, 48*(3), 91–107. https://doi.org/10.1353/ces.2016.0027; and Wali, N., Georgeou, N., & Renzaho, A.M.N. (2018). "Life is pulled back by such things": Intersections between language acquisition, qualifications, employment and access to settlement services among migrants in Western Sydney. *Journal of Intercultural Studies, 39*(1), 85–101. https://doi.org/10 .1080/07256868.2017.1410114.

4 See Burnett, L. (1998). *Issues in immigrant settlement in Australia.* National Centre for English Language Teaching and Research; Markus, A. (2021). *Mapping social cohesion: The Scanlon Foundation Surveys.* https:// scanloninstitute.org.au/report2020; Matthes, J., & Schmuck, D. (2017). The effects of anti-immigrant right-wing populist ads on implicit and explicit attitudes: A moderated mediation model. *Communication Research, 44*(4), 556–81. https://doi.org/10.1177/0093650215577859; and Schmuck, D., Heiss, R., & Matthes, J. (2020). Drifting further apart? How exposure to media portrayals of Muslims affects attitude polarization. *Political Psychology, 41*(6), 1055–72. https://doi.org/10.1111/pops.12664.

5 Fox, J.E., Moroşanu, L., & Szilassy, E. (2012). The racialization of the new European migration to the UK. *Sociology, 46*(4), 680–95. https://doi.org /10.1177/0038038511425558.

6 See Chan, C.W.S., Lam, B.O., Teng, Y., & Lee, M. (2015). Making sense of divergent perceptions of racial-ethnic discrimination in Hong Kong. *Multicultural Education Review, 7*(1–2), 41–58. https://doi.org/10.1080 /2005615X.2015.1048608; and Feagin, J.R., & Eckberg, D.L. (1980). Discrimination: Motivation, action, effects, and context. *Annual Review of Sociology, 6*, 1–20. https://doi.org/https://doi.org/10.1146/annurev .so.06.080180.000245.

7 See Burnett (1998); Collins, J. (2013). Rethinking Australian immigration and immigrant settlement policy. *Journal of Intercultural Studies, 34*(2), 160– 77. https://doi.org/10.1080/07256868.2013.781981; and Udah, H., & Singh, P. (2018). "It still matters": The role of skin colour in everyday life and realities of black African migrants and refugees in Australia. *Australasian Review of African Studies, 39*(2), 19–47. https://doi.org/10.22160/22035184 /ARAS-2018-39-2/19-47.

8 See Hsieh, W., Faulkner, N., & Wickes, R. (2022). What reduces prejudice in the real world? A meta-analysis of prejudice reduction field experiments. *British Journal of Social Psychology, 61*(3), 689–710. https://doi.org/10.1111 /bjso.12509; Paluck, E.L., & Green, D.P. (2009). Prejudice reduction: What works? A review and assessment of research and practice. *Annual Review of Psychology, 60*(1), 339–67. https://doi.org/10.1146/annurev .psych.60.110707.163607; and Paluck, E.L., Porat, R., Clark, C. S., & Green, D.P. (2021). Prejudice reduction: Progress and challenges. *Annual Review of Psychology, 72*, 533–60. https://doi.org/10.1146/annurev-psych-071620 -030619.

9 See Hsieh, Faulkner et al. (2022a); and Hsieh, W., Wickes, R. & Faulkner, N. (2022). What matters for the scalability of prejudice reduction programs and interventions? A Delphi study. *BMC Psychology, 10*, 107. https://doi .org/10.1186/s40359-022-00814-8.

10 Caldwell, L. (2018). Public and private sector nudgers can learn from each other. *Behavioural Public Policy, 2*(2), 235–45. https://doi.org/10.1017/bpp .2018.15.

11 This chapter is derived in part from an article published in *Basic and Applied Social Psychology* – Hsieh, W., Faulkner, N., & Wickes, R. (2022b). Perceived variability as a video-media prejudice reduction intervention. *Basic and Applied Social Psychology, 44*(2), 66–83. https://www.tandfonline .com/doi/full/10.1080/01973533.2022.2069025. This research was completed as part of a PhD undertaken at Monash University, supported by the Australian Government Research Training Program and Australia Post. We thank Gilda Good for the filming and editing of the intervention videos.

12 See Brauer, M., & Er-rafiy, A. (2011). Increasing perceived variability reduces prejudice and discrimination. *Journal of Experimental Social Psychology*, *47*(5), 871–81. https://doi.org/10.1016/j.jesp.2011.03.003; Brauer, M., Er-rafiy, A., Kawakami, K., & Phills, C. E. (2012). Describing a group in positive terms reduces prejudice less effectively than describing it in positive and negative terms. *Journal of Experimental Social Psychology*, *48*(3), 757–61. https://doi.org/10.1016/j.jesp.2011.11.002; Er-rafiy, A., & Brauer, M. (2012). Increasing perceived variability reduces prejudice and discrimination: Theory and application. *Social and Personality Psychology Compass*, *6*(12), 920–35. https://doi.org/10.1111/spc3.12000; Er-rafiy, A., & Brauer, M. (2013). Modifying perceived variability: Four laboratory and field experiments show the effectiveness of a ready-to-be-used prejudice intervention. *Journal of Applied Social Psychology*, *43*(4), 840–53. https://doi.org/10.1111/jasp.12010; and Er-rafiy, A., Brauer, M., & Musca, S.C. (2010). Effective reduction of prejudice and discrimination: Methodological considerations and three field experiments. *Revue Internationale de Psychologie Sociale*, *23*(2–3), 57–95. https://www.cairn.info/revue-internationale-de -psychologie-sociale-2010-2-page-57.htm.
13 Brauer & Er-rafiy (2011).
14 Hsieh, Faulkner et al. (2022a).
15 Hsieh, Faulkner et al. (2022a).
16 See Brauer & Er-rafiy (2011); Brauer et al. (2012); Er-rafiy & Brauer (2012); Er-rafiy & Brauer (2013); and Er-rafiy et al. (2010).
17 See Brauer & Er-rafiy (2011); Er-rafiy & Brauer (2012); and Er-rafiy & Brauer (2013).
18 Er-rafiy & Brauer (2013).
19 Berg, J.A. (2015). Explaining attitudes toward immigrants and immigration policy: A review of the theoretical literature. *Sociology Compass*, *9*(1), 23–34. https://doi.org/10.1111/soc4.12235.
20 Cuddy, A.J.C., Fiske, S.T., Kwan, V.S.Y., Glick, P., Demoulin, S., Leyens, J.P., Bond, M.H., Croizet, J.C., Ellemers, N., Sleebos, E., Htun, T.T., Kim, H.J., Maio, G., Perry, J., Petkova, K., Todorov, V., Rodríguez-Bailón, R., Morales, E., Moya, M., ... Ziegler, R. (2009). Stereotype content model across cultures: Towards universal similarities and some differences. *British Journal of Social Psychology*, *48*(1), 1–33. https://doi.org/10.1348 /014466608X314935.
21 See Benier, K., Blaustein, J., Johns, D., & Maher, S. (2018). *"Don't drag me into this": Growing up South Sudanese in Victoria after the 2016 Moomba "riot."* https://www.cmy.net.au/resource/dont-drag-me-into-this-growing -up-south-sudanese-in-victoria-after-the-2016-moomba-riot/; Mansouri, F., & Vergani, M. (2018). Intercultural contact, knowledge of Islam, and prejudice against Muslims in Australia. *International Journal of Intercultural*

Relations, 66, 85–94. https://doi.org/10.1016/j.ijintrel.2018.07.001; Pedersen, A., & Hartley, L.K. (2012). Prejudice against Muslim Australians: The role of values, gender and consensus. *Journal of Community & Applied Social Psychology*, 22(3), 239–55. https://doi.org/10.1002/casp.1110; and Schweitzer, R., Perkoulidis, S., Krome, S., Ludlow, C., & Ryan, M. (2005). Attitudes towards refugees: The dark side of prejudice in Australia. *Australian Journal of Psychology*, 57(3), 170–9. https://doi.org/10.1080/00049530500125199.

22 See Matthes & Schmuck. (2017); and McLaren, L.M. (2003). Anti-immigrant prejudice in Europe: Contact, threat perception, and preferences for the exclusion of migrants. *Social Forces*, 81(3), 909–36. https://doi.org/10.1353/sof.2003.0038.

23 Gordon, J., Jeram, S., & van der Linden, C. (2020). The two solitudes of Canadian nativism: Explaining the absence of a competitive anti-immigration party in Canada. *Nations and Nationalism*, 26(4), 902–22. https://doi.org/10.1111/nana.12570.

24 See Fetzer, J.S. (2000). Economic self-interest or cultural marginality? Anti-immigration sentiment and nativist political movements in France, Germany and the USA. *Journal of Ethnic and Migration Studies*, 26(1), 5–23. https://doi.org/10.1080/136918300115615; and Shattell, M.M., & Villalba, J. (2008). Anti-immigration rhetoric in the United States: Veiled racism? *Issues in Mental Health Nursing*, 29(5), 541–3. https://doi.org/10.1080/01612840801981538.

25 Er-rafiy & Brauer (2012).

26 Hsieh, Wickes et al. (2022).

27 Long, T., Logan, J. & Waugh, M. (2016). Students' perceptions of the value of using videos as a pre-class learning experience in the flipped classroom. *TechTrends*, 60, 245–52. https://doi.org/10.1007/s11528-016-0045-4.

28 Er-rafiy & Brauer (2012).

29 Er-rafiy & Brauer (2012).

30 Preregistration of the studies means that we transparently set out what we are testing before we conducted the tests to make it clear which insights relate to our initial hypotheses and which insights come from subsequent exploratory analysis. Full details can be found in preregistration documents available on Open Science Framework (osf.io/dxf9z [Study 1] and osf.io/zme3t [Study 2]).

31 See examples of emails in the online appendix: https://www.biorgpartnership.com/what-works

32 Brauer & Er-rafiy (2011).

33 See Arguel, A., & Jamet, E. (2009). Using video and static pictures to improve learning of procedural contents. *Computers in Human Behavior*, 25(2), 354–9. https://doi.org/10.1016/j.chb.2008.12.014; Dukic, T.,

Ahlstrom, C., Patten, C., Kettwich, C., & Kircher, K. (2013). Effects of electronic billboards on driver distraction. *Traffic Injury Prevention, 14*(5), 469–76. https://doi.org/10.1080/15389588.2012.731546; and Höffler, T.N., & Leutner, D. (2007). Instructional animation versus static pictures: A meta-analysis. *Learning and Instruction, 17*(6), 722–38. https://doi.org/10.1016/j.learninstruc.2007.09.013.

34 Park, B., & Judd, C.M. (1990). Measures and models of perceived group variability. *Journal of Personality and Social Psychology, 59*(2), 173–91. https://doi.org/10.1037/%2F0022-3514.59.2.173.

35 Er-rafiy & Brauer (2013).

36 See Boldry, J.G. (2007). Measuring the measures: A meta-analytic investigation of the measures of outgroup homogeneity. *Group Processes and Intergroup Relations, 10*(2), 157–78. https://doi.org/10.1177/1368430207075153; Boldry, J.G., & Gaertner, L. (2006). Separating status from power as an antecedent of intergroup perception. *Group Processes and Intergroup Relations, 9*(3), 377–400. https://doi.org/10.1177/1368430206064640; Park & Judd. (1990); and Park, B., & Rothbart, M. (1982). Perception of out-group homogeneity and levels of social categorization: Memory for the subordinate attributes of in-group and out-group members. *Journal of Personality and Social Psychology, 42*(6), 1051–68. https://doi.org/10.1037/0022-3514.42.6.1051.

37 See Callan, V.J., & Gallois, C. (1983). Ethnic stereotypes: Australian and Southern European youth. *Journal of Social Psychology, 119*(2), 287–8; Kabir, N. (2007). Muslims in Australia: The double edge of terrorism. *Journal of Ethnic and Migration Studies, 33*(8), 1277–97. https://doi.org/10.1080/13691830701614072; and McKay, S., & Pittam, J. (1993). Determinants of Anglo-Australian stereotypes of the Vietnamese in Australia. *Australian Journal of Psychology, 45*(1), 17–23. https://doi.org/10.1080/00049539308259114.

38 Underwood, B.J. (1975). Individual differences as a crucible in theory construction. *American Psychologist, 30*(2), 128–34. https://doi.org/10.1037/h0076759.

39 Full results are available in Hsieh, Faulkner et al. (2022b).

40 For a discussion of the importance of replication for building an evidence base see: List, J.A., Suskind, D., & Al-Ubaydli, O. (2019). The science of using science: Towards an understanding of the threats to scaling experiments (Working Paper No. 2019-73). Becker Friedman Institute for Economics. https://doi.org/10.2139/ssrn.3391481.

41 Hsieh, Wickes et al. (2022).

42 See Brauer & Er-rafiy (2011); and Er-rafiy & Brauer (2013).

43 OECD. (2021). *Foreign-born population (indicator).* https://doi.org/10.1787/5a368e1b-en.

44 OECD (2021).

45 Roccas, S., & Brewer, M.B. (2002). Social identity complexity. *Personality and Social Psychology Review, 6*(2), 88–106. https://doi.org/10.1207/S15327957PSPR0602_01.

46 Prati, F., Crisp, R.J., & Rubini, M. (2020). 40 years of multiple social categorization: A tool for social inclusivity. *European Review of Social Psychology, 32*(1), 47–87. https://doi.org/10.1080/10463283.2020.1830612.

47 Prati, F., Crisp, R.J., Pratto, F., & Rubini, M. (2016). Encouraging majority support for immigrant access to health services: Multiple categorization and social identity complexity as antecedents of health equality. *Group Processes and Intergroup Relations, 19*(4), 426–38. https://doi.org/10.1177/1368430216629814.

48 See Campbell, D.T. (1965). Ethnocentric and other altruistic motives. *Nebraska Symposium on Motivation,* 283–311; Duckitt, J., & Fisher, K. (2003). The impact of social threat on worldview and ideological attitudes. *Political Psychology, 24*(1), 199–222. https://doi.org/10.1111/0162-895X.00322; Quillian, L. (1995). Prejudice as a response to perceived group threat: Population composition and anti-immigrant and racial prejudice in Europe. *American Sociological Review, 60*(4), 586–611. https://doi.org/10.2307/2096296; and Stephan, W.G., & Stephan, C.W. (2000). An integrated threat theory of prejudice. In S. Oskamp (Ed.), *Reducing prejudice and discrimination.* Taylor & Francis Group.

49 Lee, T.L., & Fiske, S.T. (2006). Not an outgroup, not yet an ingroup: Immigrants in the Stereotype Content Model. *International Journal of Intercultural Relations, 30*(6), 751–68. https://doi.org/10.1016/j.ijintrel.2006.06.005.

50 See Al-Ubaydli, O., Lee, M.S., List, J.A., Mackevicius, C., & Suskind, D. (2019). How can experiments play a greater role in public policy? Twelve proposals from an economic model of scaling. *Behavioural Public Policy, 5*(1), 2–49. https://doi.org/10.2139/ssrn.3478066; and List, J.A. (2022). *The voltage effect.* Currency.

51 Klein, R.A., Vianello, M., Hasselman, F., Adams, B.G., Adams, R.B., Alper, S., Aveyard, M., Axt, J.R., Babalola, M.T., Bahník, Š., Batra, R., Berkics, M., Bernstein, M.J., Berry, D.R., Bialobrzeska, O., Binan, E.D., Bocian, K., Brandt, M.J., Busching, R., … Nosek, B. A. (2018). Many labs 2: Investigating variation in replicability across samples and settings. *Advances in Methods and Practices in Psychological Science, 1*(4), 443–90. https://doi.org/10.1177/2515245918810225.

52 See Brauer & Er-rafiy (2011); Er-rafiy & Brauer (2012); and Er-rafiy & Brauer (2013).

53 See Bauman, L.J., Stein, R.E.K., & Ireys, H.T. (1991). Reinventing fidelity: The transfer of social technology among settings. *American Journal of Community Psychology, 19*(4), 619–39. https://doi.org/10.1007/BF00937995; Burrow-Sánchez, J.J., Minami, T., & Hops, H. (2015). Cultural diversity

and ethnic minority psychology cultural accommodation of group substance abuse treatment for Latino adolescents: Results of an RCT. *Cultural Diversity and Ethnic Minority Psychology, 21*(4), 571–83. https://doi .org/10.1037/cdp0000023; Chambers, D.A., Glasgow, R.E., & Stange, K.C. (2013). The dynamic sustainability framework: Addressing the paradox of sustainment amid ongoing change. *Implementation Science, 8*(1), 1–11. https://doi.org/10.1186/1748-5908-8-117; Durlak, J.A., & DuPre, E.P. (2008). Implementation matters: A review of research on the influence of implementation on program outcomes and the factors affecting implementation. *American Journal of Community Psychology, 41*(3–4), 327–50. https://doi.org/10.1007/s10464-008-9165-0; Hawe, P., Shiell, A., & Riley, T. (2004). Complex interventions: How "out of control" can a randomised controlled trial be? *BMJ, 328*, 1561. https://doi.org/10.1136 /bmj.328.7455.1561; and Sundell, K., Beelmann, A., Hasson, H., & von Thiele Schwarz, U. (2016). Novel programs, international adoptions, or contextual adaptations? Meta-analytical results from German and Swedish intervention research. *Journal of Clinical Child and Adolescent Psychology, 45*(6), 784–96. https://doi.org/10.1080/15374416.2015.1020540.

54 See Durlak & DuPre. (2008); Kelly, B. (2013). Implementing implementation science: Reviewing the quest to develop methods and frameworks for effective implementation. *Journal of Neurology and Psychology, 1*(1), 1–5. https://www.avensonline.org/wp-content/uploads/JNP-2332-3469- 01-0003.pdf; Meyers, D.C., Durlak, J.A., & Wandersman, A. (2012). The quality implementation framework: A synthesis of critical steps in the implementation process. *American Journal of Community Psychology, 50*(3–4), 462–80. https://doi.org/10.1007/s10464-012-9522-x; and Nordstrum, L.E., LeMahieu, P.G., & Berrena, E. (2017). Implementation science: Understanding and finding solutions to variation in program implementation. *Quality Assurance in Education, 25*(1), 58–73. https://doi .org/10.1108/QAE-12-2016-0080.

55 Eccles, M.P., & Mittman, B.S. (2006). Welcome to implementation science. *Implementation Science, 1*(1), 1–3. https://doi.org/10.1186/1748-5908-1-1.

56 See Armstrong, K., & Kendall, E. (2010). Translating knowledge into practice and policy: The role of knowledge networks in primary health care. *Health Information Management Journal, 39*(2), 9–17. https://doi.org /10.1177/183335831003900203; Grimshaw, J.M., Eccles, M.P., Lavis, J.N., Hill, S.J., & Squires, J.E. (2012). Knowledge translation of research findings. *Implementation Science, 7*(1), 1. https://doi.org/10.1186/1748-5908-7-50; Lynch, E.A., Mudge, A., Knowles, S., Kitson, A.L., Hunter, S.C., & Harvey, G. (2018). "There is nothing so practical as a good theory": A pragmatic guide for selecting theoretical approaches for implementation projects. *BMC Health Services Research, 18*, 857. https://doi.org/10.1186/s12913

-018-3671-z; Mitton, C., Adair, C.E., McKenzie, E., Patten, S., & Perry, B.W. (2007). Knowledge transfer and exchange: Review and synthesis of the literature. *The Millbank Quarterly, 85*(4), 729–68. https://doi.org/10.1111 /j.1468-0009.2007.00506.x; and Straus, S.E., Tetroe, J., & Graham, I. (2009). Defining knowledge translation. *Canadian Medical Association Journal, 181*(3–4), 165–8. https://doi.org/10.1503/cmaj.081229.

57 See Barker, P.M., Reid, A., & Schall, M.W. (2016). A framework for scaling up health interventions: Lessons from large-scale improvement initiatives in Africa. *Implementation Science, 11*(1), 1–11. https://doi.org/10.1186 /s13012-016-0374-x; Damschroder, L.J., Aron, D. C., Keith, R.E., Kirsh, S.R., Alexander, J.A., & Lowery, J.C. (2009). Fostering implementation of health services research findings into practice: A consolidated framework for advancing implementation science. *Implementation Science, 4*(1), 1–15. https://doi.org/10.1186/1748-5908-4-50; Milat, A.J., Bauman, A., & Redman, S. (2015). Narrative review of models and success factors for scaling up public health interventions. *Implementation Science, 10*(1), 1–12. https://doi.org/10.1186/s13012-015-0301-6; Milat, A.J., King, L., Bauman, A.E., & Redman, S. (2013). The concept of scalability: Increasing the scale and potential adoption of health promotion interventions into policy and practice. *Health Promotion International, 28*(3), 285–98. https:// doi.org/10.1093/heapro/dar097; Milat, A.J., Newson, R., King, L., Rissel, C., Wolfenden, A.B., Redman, S., & Giffin, M. (2016). A guide to scaling up population health interventions. *Public Health Research & Practice, 26*(1), 1–5. https://doi.org/10.17061/phrp2611604; and Zamboni, K., Schellenberg, J., Hanson, C., Betran, A.P., & Dumont, A. (2019). Assessing scalability of an intervention: Why, how and who? *Health Policy and Planning, 34*(7), 544–52. https://doi.org/10.1093/heapol/czz068.

58 See Bauman et al. (1991); Burrow-Sánchez et al. (2015); Chambers et al. (2013); Durlak & DuPre (2008); Hawe et al. (2004); and Sundell et al. (2016).

59 See Bauman et al. (1991); and Hawe et al. (2004).

60 Pfadenhauer, L.M., Gerhardus, A., Mozygemba, K., Lysdahl, K.B., Booth, A., Hofmann, B., Wahlster, P., Polus, S., Burns, J., Brereton, L., & Rehfuess, E. (2017). Making sense of complexity in context and implementation: The Context and Implementation of Complex Interventions (CICI) framework. *Implementation Science, 12*(1), 1–17. https://doi.org/10.1186/s13012-017 -0552-5.

61 Ghate, D. (2016). From programs to systems: Deploying implementation science and practice for sustained real world effectiveness in services for children and families. *Journal of Clinical Child and Adolescent Psychology, 45*(6), 812–26. https://doi.org/10.1080/15374416.2015.1077449.

62 See Er-rafiy & Brauer (2013); and Hsieh, Wickes, et al. (2022).

63 Trafimow, D. (2014). Editorial. *Basic and Applied Social Psychology, 36*(1), 1–2. https://doi.org/10.1080/01973533.2014.865505.
64 Trafimow, D., & Osman, M. (2022). Barriers to converting applied social psychology to bettering the human condition. *Basic and Applied Social Psychology, 44*(1), 1–11. https://doi.org/10.1080/01973533.2022.2051327.
65 While the initial studies using the perceived variability approach by Er-rafiy and Brauer reported significant reductions in prejudice, when combined in a meta-anlysis with the results of our new perceived variability intervention, much more modest average effects for perceived variability were indicated. The average effect of perceived variability field interventions was $d = 0.12$, with a 95 percent confidence interval of –1.84 to 2.08 when our study results were pooled with previous studies. This compares to $d = 0.91$, with a 95 percent confidence interval of 0.78 to 1.04 based on just the earlier studies as reported in Hsieh et al. (2021). Hsieh, W., Faulkner, N., & Wickes, R. (2021). What reduces prejudice in the real world? A meta-analysis of prejudice reduction field experiments. *British Journal of Social Psychology, 61*(3), 689–710. https://doi.org/10.1111/bjso.12509. The addition of two more treatment groups from our studies to the previous perceived variability studies showed that, overall, the results changed notably. This casts some doubt on the usefulness of perceived variability as a prejudice reduction approach in the field – although a caveat must be noted here, as these results are based on a small sample, even with the addition of these new studies.

CHAPTER FIFTEEN

Horizontal Scaling of Reminders to Encourage COVID-19 Vaccination among the Elderly in Latvia

Andris Saulītis

AT A GLANCE

- **Our Goal:** To increase COVID-19 vaccination uptake by nudging seniors with behaviorally informed reminders.
- **The Intervention:** Personalized regular mail letters sent to seniors who are unvaccinated or eligible for a booster shot.
- **The Results:** Reminders effectively increase the rate of vaccination to a larger extent than the original study. The messages are likely to produce only a modest change among vaccine-hesitant individuals, while among those who do not strictly oppose vaccination, personalized reminders on vaccine availability effectively deliver behavioral change.
- **Lesson Learned:** Reminders are most effective when delivered early on in the vaccination efforts, and their cost-effectiveness decreases as the illness season progresses.

Motivation and Objective

What is the most effective way to address the complex phenomenon of vaccine hesitancy, which is influenced by various factors such as personal beliefs, social context, and vaccine type?[1] Reminders have been shown to increase the rate of vaccination uptake.[2] Others have found that reminders work best for the senior population.[3] This chapter reports on attempts to horizontally scale a study that effectively increased vaccine uptake among the senior population in Louisiana, USA. I will report on two randomized controlled trials (i.e., field experiments) carried out in Latvia. The objective of the study is to examine the effect of personalized reminders on COVID-19 vaccination uptake among the elderly and its costs at different stages of the vaccination campaign. In November 2021, the behaviorally informed messages were sent via regular mail to 51,520 unvaccinated seniors. In December 2021, similar messages, also via regular mail, were sent to 14,707 seniors eligible for a booster shot.

Inspiration

The intervention was a horizontal scaling (application of the intervention in a different domain) of a study carried out during the 2017–18 influenza season in Louisiana, USA.[4] I will refer to this trial in the chapter as the Louisiana postcard study. Researchers successfully increased the vaccination uptake by sending postcard reminders to seniors aged sixty-five to seventy. The postcard mentioned four vaccines that the Center for Disease Control and Prevention recommended for this US population subgroup: influenza, tetanus, pneumococcal pneumonia, and herpes zoster (shingles). Individuals were selected to receive the postcard if they were (over)due with at least one of the vaccines mentioned. Random assignment was done on the basis of the month when the postcard was sent – either in October or in any of the three following months.

Only postcards sent early in the influenza season (i.e., October) increased the vaccination uptake. Moreover, the positive effect was driven mostly by the influenza vaccines. Researchers of the study believe that the reason was the heightened public awareness based on various outreach campaigns to get a seasonal flu vaccine carried out in October. As the authors note, "vaccination campaigns may have a 'the sum is greater than the whole of its parts' quality, with different pieces of a campaign reinforcing each other to create and maintain the salience of vaccination among the public."[5] On the other hand, the effect was fairly modest. For the flu vaccine, it was 0.71 percentage points higher among those who received postcards in October compared to the control group, which did not receive the postcard.

In this study, the horizontal scaling of the findings consisted of two trials that likewise examined the effect of a behaviorally-informed direct mail letter relative to not receiving a message (control group) for a vaccine against COVID-19. There are three important differences with the Louisiana postcard study, however. First, the messages were sent to a larger population than just individuals aged sixty-five to seventy. Second, even though the COVID-19 pandemic was still high on the public agenda in November with various public campaigns ongoing, vaccine uptake lost its momentum in June, and the number of daily doses administered fell sharply. Third, reminders were highly personalized and used various text templates instead of a single message. The letter was signed personally by the head of the National Health Service, referred personally to the receiver, and provided personal information, including the name of the family doctor and the COVID-19 infection rate in the county. It also referred to the vaccine as something that the individual possessed and had not used yet. A side-by-side comparison of our two trials with the original study can be found later in the chapter (Table 15.3).

Trial 1: Unvaccinated Seniors

Seven months after the vaccines against COVID-19 were freely available to anyone in Latvia, the vaccination rate was the fifth lowest in the European Union. Only around 60 percent of the population had completed the primary course at the beginning of November 2021. Along with the other Eastern European countries, the major problem was vaccination hesitancy among the elderly. In Latvia, the uptake among those over sixty did not exceed 61 percent, far below the EU average of 85 percent, even though they were the first ones who could get the shot. At this point, the government authorized the National Health Service of Latvia to send out reminders by regular post to those seniors who could not be reached through other means (emails and text messages) due to lack of contact information.

There was a total of 126,414 such individuals in Latvia. The reminders were sent in two waves, with the first one carried out in the last week of November 2021. Whether to receive the message in the first or second wave was assigned randomly. As such, a randomized controlled trial was set up to assess the effectiveness of the activity.

Before the random assignment, some exclusion criteria were adopted to avoid so-called spillover effects when a single individual is exposed to several messages (see Figure 15.1). One risk to avoid was to send several messages to a single household with more than one unvaccinated senior. For this reason, the sample for the trial was restricted to postal addresses that had a maximum of two

Figure 15.1. Design of Trial 1

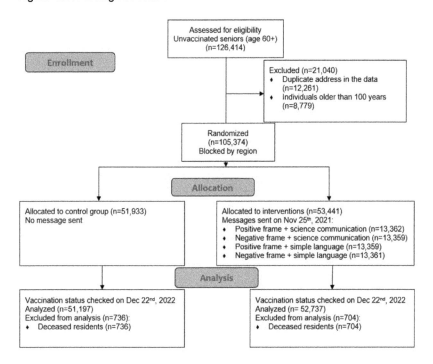

unvaccinated individuals. If two individuals were not vaccinated in the same household, only the first one on the list was assigned to the trial. As a result, the trial included a sample of 105,374 unvaccinated individuals aged 65–100 years, with around half of them randomly assigned to the control group that did not receive the message. The other half was randomly split into four groups to receive one of the four text templates.

The differences between the text templates were in the framing and the writing style. The gain frame stated the benefits of getting vaccinated. The loss frame emphasized the risks of being unvaccinated. Regarding the writing style, the text was designed either as in the Louisiana postcard study in so-called simple language (using simple and short sentences and bullet points) or in style reflecting science communication language (see Table 15.1 for the treatment texts varied in the letters). On the other side of the letter, an infographic (framed as either a gain or a loss) was placed (see Figure 15.2).

Table 15.1. Reminder texts in Trial 1 (translated to English; see the online Appendix for Latvian version)

Treatments	Gain Frame	Loss Frame
Science Communication		
Language	**Reminder: Your vaccine against Covid-19 is still waiting for you!**	**Reminder: Your vaccine against Covid-19 is still waiting for you!**
	Dear John Smith!	Dear John Smith!
	I am writing you this letter with a kind reminder that you have not yet received your vaccine against Covid-19, according to the data by the National Health Service. You can get your vaccine at any vaccination point in Latvia or request a home visit. Your family doctor Jane Brown also does the vaccination. You can book the most convenient place and time by calling 8989. You do not have to pay for the vaccine. Unvaccinated people are not protected against the Covid-19 infection. In October, four were not vaccinated out of every five people in Latvia who were diagnosed with Covid-19 infection. Unvaccinated people are more likely to be hospitalized if infected with Covid-19: in October, nine out of ten Covid-19 hospitalized patients were not vaccinated. Unvaccinated seniors are the ones most often admitted to the hospital. Nine out of ten deaths from this dangerous disease occur among those over sixty. If you do not get vaccinated against Covid-19, it will be difficult to avoid infection and serious illness, and you will not be able to see your relatives without worry.	I am writing you this letter with a kind reminder that you have not yet received your vaccine against Covid-19, according to the data by the National Health Service. You can get your vaccine at any vaccination point in Latvia or request a home visit. Your family doctor Jane Brown also does the vaccination. You can book the most convenient place and time by calling 8989. You do not have to pay for the vaccine. Vaccinated people are protected against the Covid-19 infection. In October, only one was fully vaccinated out of every five people in Latvia who were diagnosed with Covid-19 infection. Vaccinated people are less likely to be hospitalized, even if they are infected with Covid-19: in October, only one in ten Covid-19 hospitalized patients were fully vaccinated. Nine out of ten deaths from this dangerous disease occur among those over sixty. If you are vaccinated against Covid-19, it will be simple to avoid infection and serious illness, and you will be able to meet your relatives without any worries.

(Continued)

Table 15.1. (Continued)

Treatments	Gain Frame	Loss Frame
	The Covid-19 infection is still spreading. At the time that I am writing you this letter, the Covid-19 infection has been diagnosed in more than 4675 individuals in Riga during the last two weeks alone. Therefore, I urge you not to postpone the vaccination: call 8989 or book the place and time for receiving your vaccine on the website manavakcina.lv! If you have already been vaccinated, I thank you for your collaboration! I would like to remind you that after vaccination, every senior citizen receives a benefit of 20 euros per month until March next year.	The Covid-19 infection is still spreading. At the time that I am writing you this letter, the Covid-19 infection has been diagnosed in more than 4675 individuals in Riga during the last two weeks alone. Therefore, I urge you not to postpone the vaccination: call 8989 or book the place and time for receiving your vaccine on the website manavakcina.lv! If you have already been vaccinated, thank you for your collaboration! I would like to remind you that after vaccination, every senior citizen receives a benefit of 20 euros per month until March next year.
Simple Language	**Your vaccine against Covid-19 is still waiting for you!** Dear John Smith! Reminder: you have not yet received your vaccine against Covid-19, according to the data by the National Health Service! **How to receive the vaccine?** You can get your vaccine at any vaccination point in Latvia or request a home visit. Your family doctor Jane Brown also administers the vaccination. You can book the most convenient place and time by calling 8989. You do not have to pay for the vaccine. **Why do you need the vaccine?** • **Unvaccinated seniors** are most likely to get Covid-19. • Without the vaccine, the risk of severe Covid-19 disease increases	**Your vaccine against Covid-19 is still waiting for you!** Dear John Smith! Reminder: you have not yet received your vaccine against Covid-19, according to the data by the National Health Service! **How to receive the vaccine?** You can get your vaccine at any vaccination point in Latvia or request a home visit. Your family doctor Jane Brown also administers the vaccination. You can book the most convenient place and time by calling 8989. You do not have to pay for the vaccine. **Why do you need the vaccine?** • **Vaccinated seniors** less often get Covid-19. • The vaccine reduces the risk of severe Covid-19 disease.

Treatments	Gain Frame	Loss Frame
	A large proportion of Covid-19 patients in Latvian hospitals are **unvaccinated seniors**	A very small proportion of Covid-19 patients in Latvian hospitals are **vaccinated seniors**
	• Nine out of ten deaths from Covid-19 are over sixty years of age	• Nine out of ten deaths from Covid-19 are over sixty years of age
	• We will not be able to return to normal life without the vaccine!	• The vaccine will allow us all to return to normal life!
	• The Covid-19 infection **is still spreading.**	• The Covid-19 infection **is still spreading.**
	The Covid-19 infection has been diagnosed in more than 4675 individuals in Riga during the last two weeks.	The Covid-19 infection has been diagnosed in more than 4675 individuals in Riga during the last two weeks.
	Where can you get your free vaccine?	**Where can you get your free vaccine?**
	• You can get your vaccine at any vaccination point in Latvia or request a home visit.	• You can get your vaccine at any vaccination point in Latvia or request a home visit.
	• Your family doctor Jane Brown also does the vaccination.	• Your family doctor Jane Brown also does the vaccination.
	• Book your vaccine by calling 8989 or manavakcina.lv!	• Book your vaccine by calling 8989 or manavakcina.lv!
	Thank you if you have already been vaccinated! After vaccination, every senior citizen receives **a benefit of 20 euros per month** until March next year.	Thank you if you have already been vaccinated! After vaccination, every senior citizen receives **a benefit of 20 euros per month** until March next year.

Figure 15.2. Infographics on the back side of the reminder letter (left: positive frame; right: negative frame). Source: The National Health Service of Latvia.

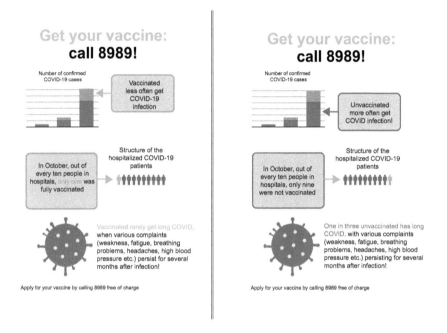

When the updated information on vaccination uptake was collected one month later, results showed that reminders effectively increased the rate of vaccination. Figure 15.4 compares the vaccination rates. In the control group, which did not receive the reminder, only 9.8 percent of seniors took a vaccine. Reminders, on average, increased vaccination by 1.4 percentage points (a 14 percent lift; unadjusted $P<0.001$).

The most effective letter was the one that stated the benefits of getting vaccinated in the style of science communication. This reminder increased the vaccination uptake by 1.86 percentage points compared to the control group (a 19 percent lift; unadjusted $P<0.001$). By contrast, the least effective message explained the risks of not being vaccinated, which increased the vaccination rate only by 0.95 percentage points relative to the control group (a 10 percent lift; unadjusted $P<0.002$). The differences between various messages were not statistically significant; therefore it cannot be ruled out that the messages are equally effective relative to not sending a reminder.

Figure 15.3. Vaccination uptake in Trial 1

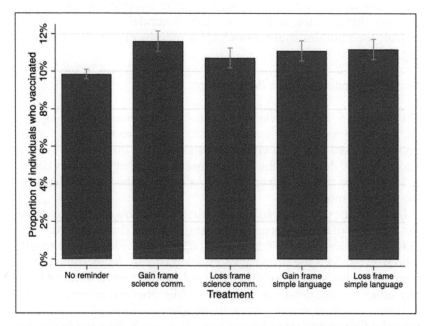

Notes: Coefficients controlled for age, gender, ethnicity, region, and being registered with a family doctor. Confidence intervals at 95 percent. Full regression models can be found in the online Appendix.

Soon after the end of the trial, the control group received the positively framed reminders. Thanks to the reminders, it can be estimated that around an extra two thousand seniors were immunized against COVID-19. A back-of-the-envelope calculation shows that the incremental cost per additional vaccine delivered was €55. The total expenses of this reminder campaign did not exceed the costs that would have occurred in the case of eight COVID-19 hospitalizations. It significantly reduced the risk of severe illness and suffering in society's most vulnerable group.

The effect of a reminder in this study is larger than the one found in the Louisiana postcard study. In this trial, the effect of a reminder is nearly double the size – even though the baseline uptake for the COVID-19 vaccine was much lower than for the flu shot in Louisiana. On the other hand, a 2 percentage point increase is still a modest result. Could it be that an even larger effect can be achieved by sending reminders even earlier – like in the Louisiana postcard study, in which reminders were sent when the flu season was about to start? It was possible to examine this question in the second trial: reminders were sent to those eligible for a booster shot two and a half months prior to them becoming eligible.

Trial 2: Reminding to Get a Booster Shot

On October 6, 2021, Latvia started to offer the booster shot against COVID-19 to individuals over sixty-five. Seniors were eligible for the booster if there had been eight weeks since their dose of the Janssen vaccine or 180 days since the second dose of any other vaccine available in Latvia. Less than 20 percent of seniors received the booster shot over the next two months.

Based on the positive results of the first trial, it was decided to examine the effect of reminders on booster shot uptake. The second trial was launched on December 17, 2021, with 63,052 individuals aged 65–101 who had received the primary vaccination course. As in Trial 1, these were individuals for whom the National Health Service did not have any other contact details (email and mobile phone number), and the trial was restricted to addresses with no more than two eligible seniors, with the first one selected for the trial. As a result, the sample size for Trial 2 was 51,462 individuals. The National Health Service could send a maximum of 15,000 letters due to financial constraints. Therefore, 14,701 individuals were randomly assigned to receive one of the four reminders, while 36,761 did not receive the letter and were featured as a control group (see Figure 15.4).

Considering the suggestive evidence from Trial 1 that positive messages work best, the four treatment texts used in the trial stated only the benefits of the booster shot: either personal or societal. Like in Trial 1, these messages employed either simple or science communication language (see Table 15.2). The other side of the letter had the same infographic as in Trial 1, except that the lower bottom figure (effects of long COVID-19) was replaced with information on which booster vaccine will be administered. The control group did not receive any message.

After a month, the vaccination status was updated to measure the effect of the reminder campaign. The analysis excluded 213 individuals that died during the trial. The final sample for the analysis consists of 51,249 individuals. Same as in Trial 1, reminders increased the vaccine uptake. Figure 15.5 depicts the share of individuals who took a booster shot. In the control group, the uptake of the booster shot was less than

Figure 15.4. Design of Trial 2

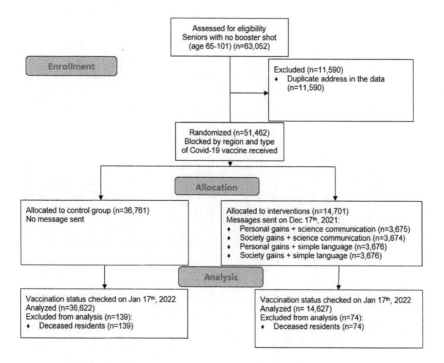

half (48 percent). Reminders increased the uptake by 5.4 percentage points (an 11 percent lift; unadjusted $P<0.001$).

All four versions of the reminder text deliver nearly the same effect; the difference between the treatment groups is around one percentage point. Figure 15.5 shows that the baseline booster uptake varies depending on the vaccine used for the primary vaccination course. For individuals who previously took the Janssen (Johnson & Johnson) vaccine, a message that states personal benefits is superior not only to the control group by 4.7 percentage points (a 17 percent lift; unadjusted $P<0.001$) but also to the message of the social benefits by additional 3.1 percentage points (a 10 percent lift; unadjusted $P<0.05$). There are no significant differences between treatment texts among individuals who took any other vaccine.

The effect of the reminder did not change depending on how long an individual had been eligible for the booster shot. On the one hand, the further the vaccination date, the higher the booster uptake. On the other

Table 15.2. Texts in Trial 2 (translated to English; see the online Appendix for Latvian version)

	Personal Benefits	Societal Benefits
Science Communication Language	**Invitation: Your booster shot is already available!** Dear John Smith! I am writing you this letter with a kind invitation to receive your booster vaccine against Covid-19. It is already available for you. You can get your booster vaccine at any vaccination point in Latvia or request a home visit. Your family doctor Jane Brown also does the vaccination. You can book the most convenient place and time by **calling 8989.** Please do not delay receiving your booster vaccine! It has been more than three months since you completed your first vaccination course. So far, the vaccine you received has effectively reduced your risk of developing a severe illness of Covid-19. However, as predicted, the effectiveness of your vaccine gradually decreases over time. The time has come to strengthen your immune system with a booster dose. It will effectively increase your personal protection against Covid-19. The Covid-19 infection is still spreading. At the time that I am writing you this letter, the Covid-19 infection has been diagnosed in more than 4675 individuals in Riga during the last two weeks alone. Therefore, I urge you not to postpone the booster vaccination: call 8989 or book the place and time for receiving your booster vaccine on the website manavakcina.lv! If you have already received booster vaccine, I thank you for your collaboration!	**Invitation: Your booster shot is already available!** Dear John Smith! I am writing you this letter with a kind invitation to receive your booster vaccine against Covid-19. It is already available for you. You can get your booster vaccine at any vaccination point in Latvia or request a home visit. Your family doctor Jane Brown also does the vaccination. You can book the most convenient place and time by **calling 8989.** Please do not delay receiving your booster vaccine! It has been more than three months since you completed your first vaccination course. The sooner everyone receives the booster dose, the more effectively we will protect each other from Covid-19, collectively reducing the risk of another outbreak this winter and making it easier for doctors to work. The Covid-19 infection is still spreading. At the time that I am writing you this letter, the Covid-19 infection has been diagnosed in more than 4675 individuals in Riga during the last two weeks alone. Therefore, I urge you not to postpone the booster vaccination: call 8989 or book the place and time for receiving your booster vaccine on the website manavakcina.lv! If you have already received booster vaccine, I thank you for your collaboration!

Simple language

Invitation: Your booster shot is already available!

Dear John Smith!

I invite you to receive your booster vaccine against Covid-19. It is already available for you. Please do not delay receiving your booster vaccine!

How to receive the booster vaccine?

You can get your booster vaccine at any vaccination point in Latvia or request a home visit. Your family doctor Jane Brown also does the vaccination. You can book the most convenient place and time by **calling 8989**.

Why do you need a vaccine?

- **Vaccinated seniors** less often get Covid-19.
- The vaccine reduces the risk of severe Covid-19 disease.

A very small proportion of Covid-19 patients in Latvian hospitals are **vaccinated seniors**

- Nine out of ten deaths from COVID-19 are over sixty years of age
- The vaccine will allow us all to return to normal life!

Where can you get your free booster vaccine?

- You can get your vaccine at any vaccination point in Latvia or request a home visit.
- Your family doctor Jane Brown also does the vaccination.
- Book your vaccine by calling 8989 or manavakcina.lv!

If you have already received booster vaccine, I thank you for your collaboration!

Invitation: Your booster shot is already available!

Dear John Smith!

I invite you to receive your booster vaccine against Covid-19. It is already available for you. Please do not delay receiving your booster vaccine!

How to receive the booster vaccine?

You can get your booster vaccine at any vaccination point in Latvia or request a home visit. Your family doctor Jane Brown also does the vaccination. You can book the most convenient place and time by **calling 8989.**

Why do you need a vaccine?

- **Unvaccinated seniors** are most likely to get COVID-19.
- Without the vaccine, the risk of severe COVID-19 disease increases

A large proportion of COVID-19 patients in Latvian hospitals are **unvaccinated seniors**

- Nine out of ten deaths from COVID-19 are over sixty years of age
- We will not be able to return to normal life without the vaccine!

Where can you get your free booster vaccine?

- You can get your vaccine at any vaccination point in Latvia or request a home visit.
- Your family doctor Jane Brown also does the vaccination.
- Book your vaccine by calling 8989 or manavakcina.lv!

If you have already received booster vaccine, I thank you for your collaboration!

Figure 15.5. Booster shot uptake in Trial 2

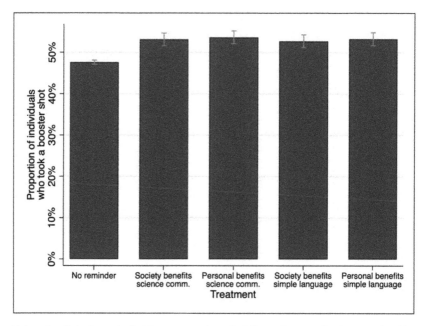

Notes: Coefficients controlled for age, gender, ethnicity, region, vaccine type received for the primary course, and being registered with a family doctor. Confidence intervals at 95 percent. Full regression models can be found in the online Appendix.

hand, the reminders were as effective as when sent a week or three months after the eligibility date.

Overall, Trial 2 shows that sending reminders early in the vaccination campaign (no later than three months after the booster shot becomes available) significantly increases the vaccination uptake among seniors. In this case, the back-of-the-envelope calculation shows that the incremental cost per additional vaccine delivered was €10. The trial also shows that the behavior differs for individuals who got the Janssen vaccine for the primary vaccination course compared to those administered with any other available vaccine in the past. It might be that individuals who chose to be vaccinated with Janssen for the primary course requiring a single shot were more hesitant toward immunization programs than those who had a primary vaccination course with two required doses. The baseline rate for the booster shot is much lower among the group of seniors that received the Janssen vaccine. Emphasizing to this

Figure 15.6. Booster shot uptake in different groups of the primary vaccination course

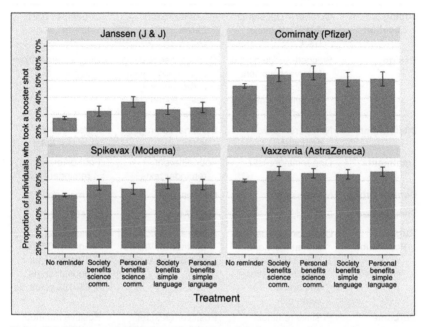

Notes: Coefficients controlled for age, gender, ethnicity, region, being registered with a family doctor, and time since the booster is available. Confidence intervals at 95 percent. Full regression models can be found in the online Appendix.

group the personal benefits of a booster shot was the most effective way to convince these individuals to revaccinate. It was more effective than emphasizing the benefits for broader society.

Discussion: In Search of the Best Reminder

The results from the two trials confirmed previous findings that regular mail letters increase vaccination against COVID-19, and hence our horizontal scaling effort was successful. The effect ranges from 1.4 percentage points for the primary vaccination course to 5.4 percentage points for the booster shot (see Table 15.3). The results exceed the positive effect of the Louisiana postcard study, where the effect of the postcard reminder on vaccination uptake was no larger than 0.71 percentage points, only for flu vaccines, and only when sent out early in the influenza season.

Table 15.3. Overview of the three experimental trials

	Louisiana Study	Trial 1	Trial 2
Timing & Location	October – December 2017; Louisiana, USA	November 2021; Latvia	December 2021; Latvia
Design	Stepped-wedge design (interventions sent in four randomly assigned monthly waves)	Stepped-wedge design (interventions sent in two randomly assigned monthly waves)	Single intervention in one wave
Intervention	Non-personalized postcard	Personalized regular letter	Personalized regular letter
Treatments	One reminder text	Four different reminder texts	Four different reminder texts
Control Group	No message	No message	No message
Sample Size	208,511	105,374	51,462
Target Population	Unvaccinated seniors with at least one of four vaccines mentioned (over) due and 65–70 years old	Seniors unvaccinated against COVID-19 and 60+ years old	Seniors vaccinated against COVID-19 eligible for booster shots 65–101 years old
Outcome	Positive reminder effect for the first wave only and for flu vaccine only	Positive reminder effect; no significant differences among messages	Positive reminder effect; no significant differences among messages
Effect Size	+0.71 pp (first wave & flu vaccine only; a 2% lift from the baseline of 29.8%)	+1.4 pp (a 14% lift from the baseline of 9.8%)	+5.4 pp (a 11% lift from the baseline of 47.5%)

Overall, the replication with horizontal scaling confirms the Louisiana postcard study finding that reminders work best early in vaccination efforts. Sending a reminder within the four months after an individual becomes eligible – at least for a booster shot, as in this case – is relatively efficient and cost-effective. It is rather late to send a reminder for the primary vaccination course more than half a year after the vaccine has become available, delivering modest results and bearing high costs. Note that in both trials of this study, the uplift from the baseline is similar, around 11–14 percent. The main variation between the two trials' outcomes is in the baseline uptake, which significantly changed the total number of individuals that altered their behavior after the intervention. Evidently, it is crucial to send vaccination reminders as early as possible to boost the effectiveness of the vaccination campaign.

Reminders can help overcome cognitive biases, such as procrastination and forgetfulness.[6] They are less effective in persuading behavioral change for those who do not trust that vaccines are safe, effective, and needed. The effect of a reminder in the trials reported in this chapter is higher than in the Louisiana postcard study because of the successful efforts and investments in communication with the public. Information on COVID-19 and the risks associated with not being vaccinated were intensively communicated by government officials, health experts, and various public campaigns throughout 2021. Hence, the size of the effect for reminders also indicates the performance of the efforts to convince the public to be vaccinated. When those who do not believe in vaccine efficiency are the majority remaining in the target group, reminding them that the vaccine is still available is very unlikely to change their behavior.

On a more general note, the goal of a reminder should be broader than just getting attention and reminding pro-vaccine individuals to get a shot. Regular mail letters are not limited in length like mobile text messages and are not delivered in countless numbers every day as emails. For these reasons, a regular mail letter is very likely to stand out. That should be used as an opportunity to provide individuals with facts and figures on vaccine efficiency, as one of the primary drivers of low vaccine take-up is the inability to make an informed decision.[7] Also, the vaccination history of an individual is important when choosing the exact wording for the letter.

Personalization of a reminder is another way to increase the vaccination uptake. Customized reminders support personalized healthcare that is adapted to the specific needs of individuals.[8] In the Louisiana postcard study, the reminder did not include any personalization. In the two trials of this chapter, letters included the name of the recipient, the name of the recipient's family doctor (who could administer the vaccination), and the number of registered infections in the recipient's county as part of the overall personal tone of the letter. It might be another reason why interventions were more effective than in the Louisiana postcard study. The best way to communicate the need to be vaccinated and deliver positive behavioral change is to implement a shared decision-making process which is based on a personal interaction between the users and the provider of healthcare.[9] The results probably would have been even larger if the letter had been signed by the receiver's family doctor instead of the director of the National Health

Center. As this chapter shows, engaging with seniors in personalized communication early enough with clear and comprehensive information on vaccines against COVID-19 can effectively support the efforts to improve vaccine uptake.

NOTES

1 See Cascini, F., Pantovic, A., Al-Ajlouni, Y., Failla, G., & Ricciardi, W. (2021). Attitudes, acceptance and hesitancy among the general population worldwide to receive the COVID-19 vaccines and their contributing factors: A systematic review. *EClinicalMedicine, 40*. https://doi.org/10.1016/j.eclinm.2021.101113; and MacDonald, N.E. (2015). Vaccine hesitancy: Definition, scope and determinants. *Vaccine, 33*(34), 4161–4. https://doi.org/10.1016/j.vaccine.2015.04.036.

2 See Regan, A.K., Bloomfield, L., Peters, I., & Effler, P.V. (2017). Randomized controlled trial of text message reminders for increasing influenza vaccination. *Annals of Family Medicine, 15*(6), 507–14. https://doi.org/10.1370/afm.2120; Milkman, K.L., Patel, M.S., Gandhi, L., Graci, H.N., Gromet, D.M., Ho, H., Kay, J.S., Lee, T.W., Akinola, M., Beshears, J., Bogard, J.E., Buttenheim, A., Chabris, C.F., Chapman, G.B., Choi, J.J., Dai, H., Fox, C.R., Goren, A., Hilchey, M.D., ... Duckworth, A.L. (2021). A megastudy of text-based nudges encouraging patients to get vaccinated at an upcoming doctor's appointment. *Proceedings of the National Academy of Sciences, 118*(20). https://doi.org/10.1073/pnas.2101165118; Milkman, K.L., Gandhi, L., Patel, M.S., Graci, H.N., Gromet, D.M., Ho, H., Kay, J.S., Lee, T.W., Rothschild, J., Bogard, J.E., Brody, I., Chabris, C.F., Chang, E., Chapman, G.B., Dannals, J.E., Goldstein, N.J., Goren, A., Hershfield, H., Hirsch, A., ... Duckworth, A.L. (2022). A 680,000-person megastudy of nudges to encourage vaccination in pharmacies. *Proceedings of the National Academy of Sciences, 119*(6). https://doi.org/10.1073/pnas.2115126119; and Murphy, R.P., Taaffe, C., Ahern, E., McMahon, G., & Muldoon, O. (2021). A meta-analysis of influenza vaccination following correspondence: Considerations for COVID-19. *Vaccine, 39*(52), 7606–24. https://doi.org/10.1016/j.vaccine.2021.11.025.

3 Hurley, L.P., Beaty, B., Lockhart, S., Gurfinkel, D., Breslin, K., Dickinson, M., Whittington, M.D., Roth, H., & Kempe, A. (2018). RCT of centralized vaccine reminder/recall for adults. *American Journal of Preventive Medicine, 55*(2), 231–9. https://doi.org/10.1016/j.amepre.2018.04.022.

4 Chen, N., Trump, K.-S., Hall, S., & Le, Q. (2023). The effect of postcard reminders on vaccinations among the elderly: A block-randomized experiment. *Behavioural Public Policy, 7*(2), 240–65. https://doi.org/10.1017/bpp.2020.34.

5 Chen et al. (2022).
6 Gravert, C. (2022). Reminders: Their value and hidden costs. In N. Mažar & D. Soman (Eds.), *Behavioral science in the wild* (pp. 120–32). University of Toronto Press.
7 Bronchetti, E.T., Huffman, D.B., & Magenheim, E. (2015). Attention, intentions, and follow-through in preventive health behavior: Field experimental evidence on flu vaccination. *Journal of Economic Behavior & Organization, 116*, 270–91. https://doi.org/10.1016/j.jebo.2015.04.003.
8 Ramaswami, R., Bayer, R., & Galea, S. (2018). Precision medicine from a public health perspective. *Annual Review of Public Health, 39*(1), 153–68. https://doi.org/10.1146/annurev-publhealth-040617-014158.
9 Sanftenberg, L., Kuehne, F., Anraad, C., Jung-Sievers, C., Dreischulte, T., & Gensichen, J. (2021). Assessing the impact of shared decision making processes on influenza vaccination rates in adult patients in outpatient care: A systematic review and *meta*-analysis. *Vaccine, 39*(2), 185–96. https://doi.org/10.1016/j.vaccine.2020.12.014.

CHAPTER SIXTEEN

Reducing Student Absenteeism at Scale: Translating Social Norms and Attention Interventions

Todd Rogers and Avi Feller

AT A GLANCE

- **Our Goal:** To reduce student absenteeism nationwide through a social enterprise that implements replicated absence-reduction research for school districts.
- **The Intervention:** Repeatedly-delivered, mail-based, accessibly-written information interventions with dynamic content that focuses parent attention on absenteeism, while correcting parent misbeliefs about their student's total absences and how it compares to that of their classmates.
- **The Results:** Increased attendance, at-scale, and fifty times more cost effective than next best intervention.
- **Lesson Learned:** Student absenteeism can be reduced cost-effectively, districtwide, in a continuously improving way, especially for the most vulnerable students.

Motivation and Objective

We are delighted to contribute the story of EveryDay Labs as a chapter in this impressive book. EveryDay Labs (EDL) is a social enterprise that scales the absence-reduction interventions we initially developed, tested, and published. Mounting evidence suggests that absenteeism from school contributes to students not achieving their potential and even dropping out of school. Each year EDL administers millions of interventions throughout the United States. These interventions are based on dozens of randomized controlled trials involving hundreds of thousands of K-12 students and families. We estimate that EDL has recovered more than 1.4 million net days of student attendance, disproportionately among the most disadvantaged students. Moreover, we estimate that it has generated $1 billion of future lifetime earnings for the students it has treated.

In this chapter, we first outline the origins and academic research underlying the intervention itself. We then discuss founding EDL and the many trade-offs and challenges in delivering this type of intervention at scale. We end with some reflections and possible future directions.

Developing the Intervention

Intervention's Origin

The two of us first met in 2007 while working to increase civic engagement: Rogers focused on using the tools and insights of behavioral science[1] and Feller focused on using statistics and other quantitative tools. We reconnected in 2012, both interested in applying similar ideas to challenges in education.

By then Rogers had founded a research lab searching for scalable interventions to empower and mobilize families to support students. Two figures loom large in the research the S3 R&D Lab pursued, and they continue to be important mentors and friends today: Karen Mapp and Hedy Chang.

Karen Mapp is one of the foremost thinkers and researchers on family engagement. She is a senior lecturer at Harvard Graduate School of Education. Her writing, research, and trainings focus on the tremendous benefits that arise when schools view families as assets and partners for the joint project of educating children.[2] This perspective stands in contrast to the too common (often implicit) view that when students fail to thrive in school, families are the problem, and the best solutions circumvent families.[3] Dr. Mapp provided insights, inspiration, and counsel as we searched for behaviorally informed, light-touch, scalable interventions to help schools help families help students succeed. She continues today as an advisor to EDL.

Hedy Chang has been America's most important advocate for reducing student absenteeism. Chang founded an organization, Attendance

Works, which is widely credited with leading educators, administrators, and policymakers to focus on absenteeism, culminating in absence reduction being an important part of the *Every Student Succeeds Act* in 2015. As the S3 R&D Lab was beginning, Chang highlighted the importance of reducing absenteeism to achieve equity in education[4] and the extensive research documenting that absences robustly predict academic performance,[5] high school graduation,[6] drug and alcohol use,[7] criminality,[8] and risk of adverse outcomes later in life.[9]

Taken together, the input from Hedy Chang and Karen Mapp prompted a search for existing proven interventions that increase student success by supporting families. We discovered work from Bergman, Burzstyn, and Coffman, and Kraft and Dougherty. Several practitioners also offered invaluable advice at this early stage, particularly Michael Goldstein (founder of MATCH Education), Ross Wilson (principal of a Boston Public School), and Tonya Wolford (director of research at the School District of Philadelphia).

It became clear that student absenteeism would be a relatively easy outcome measure to study since it is collected costlessly and comprehensively. Moreover, parents would be the ideal recipients of the interventions. However, we faced a challenge: what interventions could we develop and administer that would reduce student absenteeism and empower parents?

Inspiration

The S3 R&D Lab began interviewing families, conducting parent surveys, and talking with educators and researchers. This led to the discovery of two consistent misbeliefs:

1. *Total Absences*: Parents tended to underestimate their own student's absences by around 50 percent.
2. *Relative Absences*: Parents of the most highly absent students tend to think their student is average or better compared to their classmates.

These misbeliefs are understandable because of the cognitive challenge of keeping track of the accumulation of one-day absences over time. Like all people, parents have limited attention, limited memory, and self-serving biases that could help explain why these misbeliefs arise.

This exploration also found that educators rarely tell families social comparison information: parents have little way of knowing what constitutes "normal attendance." Reluctance to share this information is completely sensible to protect students from unhelpful competition or discouragement. However, social psychological research suggests that such information can sometimes be conveyed in ways that are helpful and motivating.

In particular, people tend to change their behaviors in the direction of what they think is normal. This is called the "descriptive social norm."[10] Conveying that most people vote makes others more motivated to vote.[11] Conveying that most people pay their taxes makes others more likely to pay their taxes.[12] Conveying that most people reuse their towels in a hotel makes others more likely to reuse their own towels.[13] Conveying that most people use less water makes others decrease their water use.[14] Conveying that most people use less home energy makes others decrease their home energy use.[15]

The finding regarding home energy use has proven to be especially valuable in practice. The company Opower built a sizable clean energy business out of mailing households social comparison information about their home energy use. Figure 16.1 shows an example.

Mailing this intervention to households on a monthly or quarterly basis reduced home energy use by around 2 percent, equivalent to a short-term price increase of 20 percent.[16] Subsequent research found that repeatedly delivering this intervention did not lead to habituation and disappearing incremental effects. Rather, the impact sustained and grew over.[17]

Power utilities paid Opower to motivate customers to reduce energy consumption. This is confusing at first since power utilities generate revenue when their customers use and even increase their energy consumption. However, most states in the United States have created incentives through regulatory processes for power utilities to reduce their customers' energy use. Reducing energy consumption has environmental benefits, consumer bill benefits, and can reduce the need to build new power plants. These regulations allow power utilities to make incremental profit if they can demonstrably reduce how much energy their customers consume. Similar profitable niches exist outside the United States, and Opower successfully served these niches, entering the public stock market in an initial public offering that valued the company at nearly one billion dollars in 2014.

The company WaterSmart applies a similar business model to water use. As cited above, people tend to reduce water use after learning they consume more water than their neighbors do.[18] WaterSmart delivers

Figure 16.1. Example Opower home energy report[19]

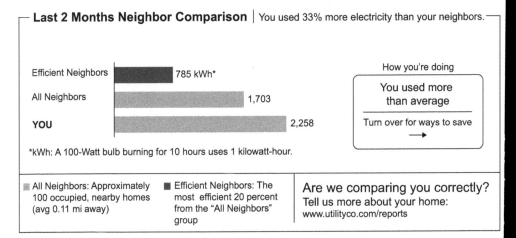

this information to water consumers in drought-stricken regions on behalf of their water utility, often through snail mail.

Initial Academic Study

Setup and Intervention

The intervention we developed and tested flows naturally from the prevalence of the *Total Absences* and *Relative Absences* misbeliefs among parents, and the successful scaleup of the Opower and WaterSmart businesses. We tested the effectiveness of an intervention delivered to parents through snail mail that conveyed different kinds of student absenteeism information.[20]

We delivered and evaluated this intervention in partnership with the School District of Philadelphia (SDP), and particularly their director of research, Tonya Wolford. SDP is a large school district of over 130,000 students, 53 percent of whom are Black/African American, 19 percent are Hispanic/Latino, and 14 percent are White/Caucasian. About three-quarters of all SDP students qualify for Free or Reduced-Price Lunch, and a third of all students in Philadelphia live in households below the Federal Poverty Line, making it among the poorest major cities in the United States. We began with a pilot randomized control

Table 16.1. Key similarities and differences between the pilot study and main study

	Pilot Study	Main Study
Design	Randomized controlled trial	Randomized controlled trial, clustered at household level
Conditions	3: Control, Total Absences, Relative Absences	4: Control, Reminder, Total Absences, Relative Absences
Timing	Spring semester-only	Full academic year
Intervention	2 rounds of mail-based treatment	Average of 4.2 rounds of mail-based treatment
Sample Size	3,007	28,080
Population	High-absence students	Moderate- and high-absence students

trial (N=3,007) in spring 2014, which showed significant and promising results. For academic year 2014–15, we replicated and extended the pilot study with qualifying families across the district (N=28,080). The experimental universe included all families meeting a range of criteria, the most important of which was that their students missed many days of school the previous year.

We randomly assigned each family to one of four conditions (see Figure 16.2 for a flow chart showing the study procedure). Households assigned to the control group received no additional contact beyond normal school communications. Households assigned to treatment received up to five rounds of treatment mail throughout the school year. The treatments differed only in their content, with treatments associated with each condition adding an additional piece of information; see Figure 16.3:

- *Reminder* treatments reminded parents of the importance of absences and of their ability to influence them.
- *Total Absences* treatments added information about students' total absences.
- *Relative Absences* treatments further added information about the modal number of absences among focal students' classmates.

Data reported in the first treatment, mailed in October, reflected absences from the previous school year. Data reported in the remaining treatments, mailed January to May, reflected current-year absences.

Figure 16.2. Flow chart illustrating procedure

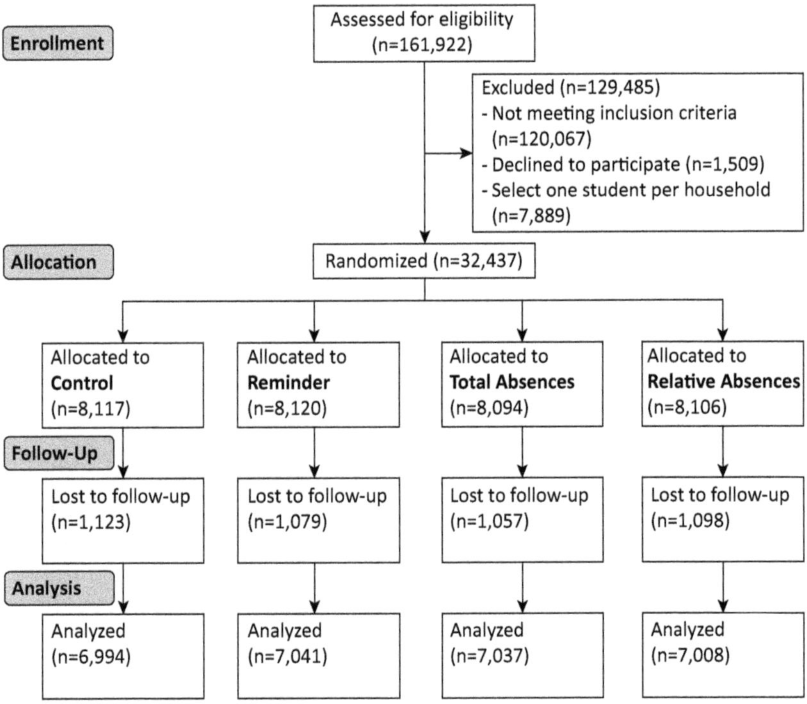

Results

Students in the control group were absent 17.0 days on average, and 36.0 percent were chronically absent. Those assigned to the *Reminder* condition were absent 0.6 days less than those assigned to control and were 3.0 percentage points less likely to be chronically absent (8 percent reduction). Those assigned to the *Total Absences* condition were absent 1.1 days less than those assigned to control and were 3.6 percentage points less likely to be chronically absent (10 percent reduction). In addition, those assigned to the *Relative Absences* condition were absent 1.1 days less than those assigned to control and were 4.1 percentage points less likely to be chronically absent (11 percent reduction).

Further analyses revealed several other relevant findings. First, the treatment effects meaningfully spilled over to other untreated students in the treated households (Basse & Feller, 2018).[21] Second, the daily attendance data showed that the treatment effect was strongest the

Figure 16.3. Samples from each condition from Rogers & Feller (2018)

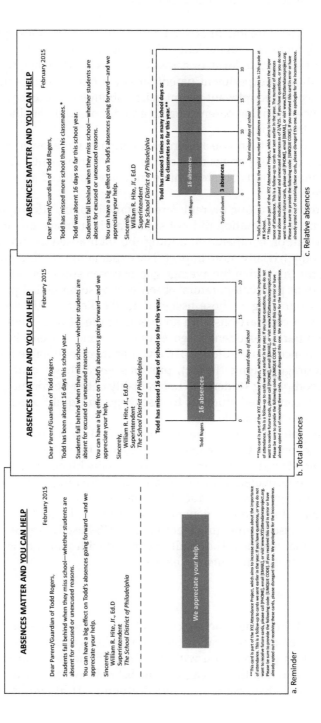

a. Reminder

b. Total absences

c. Relative absences

week after a treatment arrived and decayed in the subsequent weeks. Third, there was no evidence of meaningful treatment effect variation by student grade-level, or across other observed demographic groups. Fourth, post-experiment parent surveys confirmed that the interventions corrected relevant parent beliefs about total absences and relative absences, and that parents shared and discussed the mailings with others in their homes.

Finally, we found no evidence that impacts were lower in subsequent rounds; that is, parents did not habituate to treatments. This suggested that more rounds of intervention may have reduced absenteeism even more.

Contrary to our preregistered analysis plan, adding the relative absences information did not significantly increase the impact of the intervention compared to adding the total absences information – it had only trivially more impact. The explanation we find most compelling for this is that the average gap between students' actual absences and their peer comparators' absences was so large that parents found it discouraging.[22] Those assigned to the *Relative Absences* condition received comparisons with an average ratio of own-student absences to comparison-student absences of five to one. It seems likely that this attendance gap would be perceived as insurmountable and so might discourage parents. In fact, previous research we conducted found that comparing students to unattainably better performing peers in an online course led students to disengage and quit.[23] A similar mechanism seems plausible here.

The intervention we studied cost around $6 per incremental school day generated. One common best practice for reducing absenteeism – absence-focused mentors – has substantially higher cost per net day of absence recovered. A randomized trial evaluating that absence-reduction strategy found it reduced absenteeism at a cost of around $500 per net day of attendance generated for students in grades 5 through 7.[24] There is also an emerging literature on SMS-based absence communications interventions. The results are mixed with some finding no effect,[25] and others finding outsized effects.[26]

Replications

Around the same time we conducted the first studies in SDP, the S3 R&D Lab began replicating the main findings at other sites.

First, in collaboration with the Urban Education Lab at University of Chicago and the Chicago Public Schools, we conducted a randomized controlled trial that included around 20,000 families focused on reducing absenteeism. The intervention was a version of the intervention studied above and included multiple mail-based rounds with absence-focused messaging conveying total absences information. That study is unpublished, though the official report to the school district reported 10 percent reductions in chronic absenteeism at a cost effectiveness similar to the SDP study.

The lab conducted another replication in a randomized controlled trial across nine districts (N=10,504). In collaboration with the San Mateo County Office of Education, we studied a multi-round, mail-based absence-reduction intervention that included total absences information.[27] Students in the control group were absent 6.9 days on average, and 5.5 percent were chronically absent. Those in the treatment condition were absent 0.5 fewer days (7.7 percent reduction) than those assigned to control and were 0.9 percentage points less likely to be chronically absent (15 percent reduction).

EveryDay Labs

Moving beyond Academic Research

Following the initial research and subsequent replications, we began exploring how best to speed adoption of this new intervention in districts across the country. This was driven in part by requests from several school districts to continue implementing the absence-reduction intervention – but as a vendor rather than a research partner.

Since the principal goal was no longer scholarly research, Harvard University informed us that the S3 R&D Lab could not continue as the primary implementation partner. We needed an alternative structure. Before founding EveryDay Labs, we first explored two main alternatives: a hands-off approach and founding a nonprofit.

Hands-off approach. The simplest option was to develop templates and related materials, and to ensure that these materials were widely available for school districts to adapt themselves. Two unsuccessful efforts dissuaded us from this approach.

First, we worked with a large school district to implement the intervention themselves. Several months later, we learned that the district had spent substantial resources building a functionality into their learning management system to print reports with personalized total and relative absences information. The reports were to be printed by school sites on an as-needed basis and handed to students to deliver to their parents. There are several concerning aspects of this implementation. First, it appears to have been very expensive to develop. Second, if a school site decided to use it, they would have to use it repeatedly for each student who had missed many days. The logistics get complicated: a large high school would need to print and hand out several thousand personalized reports over the course of the year. Third, relying on students to deliver reports that are potentially unfavorable to parents can cause friction.[28] For example, the S3 R&D Lab ran an unpublished study in which 25 percent of high school students actually paid researchers $5 to prevent their parents from hearing about their performance on a future test. Fourth, and most importantly, it appears zero school sites ever used the feature, and therefore it appears to have generated zero additional days of attendance.

The second effort involved another large school district that decided to "test" the intervention itself. We helped leaders from this district understand the findings and the key elements of the intervention and hoped they would implement it with fidelity. We later learned that the district research office ran a randomized controlled trial evaluating one round of the intervention with 69 total students across both the treatment and control groups combined. This is roughly four hundred times smaller than our other replication efforts (which also involved stronger treatments in the form of at least four rounds of treatment) and statistically extremely underpowered. Unsurprisingly, they found no meaningful differences between conditions. The leaders decided this intervention "does not work" in their district. They did not continue implementing it, and they reported their underpowered results to other districts as if the information was informative.

Launching a nonprofit. When it became clear that a hands-off approach was insufficient, we instead explored starting a nonprofit organization to deliver the intervention. Philanthropic foundations were excited about the intervention, and a philanthropist hired a consultant to help us develop a plan for launching a nonprofit. Despite initial enthusiasm, however, there was little appetite among foundations to fund this organization directly, including by the foundation that funded the plan development. Their rationale was that given the importance of student attendance, school districts should pay for this service directly so that the organization and the implementation would be sustainable year-over-year. One major challenge was that a nonprofit would be difficult to sustain, requiring continual fundraising.

Transitioning to a For-Profit Structure

Our natural next step was then to launch a for-profit social enterprise, now called EveryDay Labs. This seemed especially promising after the success of Opower and WaterSmart, which were for-profit companies that succeeded at delivering similar behavioral interventions at scale for social impact.

A for-profit social enterprise offered many advantages over a non-profit. First, a social enterprise could be more stable since it would not depend on sustained philanthropic interest and continual fundraising. In fact, we saw this immediately when several foundations that declined to fund a nonprofit were enthusiastic about investing in EveryDay Labs. They saw the for-profit structure as aligning with the service EveryDay Labs would deliver to districts, and an investment in it as aligning with their philanthropic missions. The enterprise structure also meant we could raise capital more easily and with fewer restrictions, allowing for much faster growth. Similarly, the enterprise structure enabled more competitive wages for recruiting top talent, which similarly enabled rapid growth. Taken together, these advantages have allowed it to serve far more families in an accelerated timeframe than would have been possible via a nonprofit.

The case for why school districts should hire EveryDay Labs had several elements. First, many states (including California and Texas) disburse funds to their school districts based on daily attendance. This means that increasing attendance often generates additional revenue for districts; the exact amount of revenue varies, but it is typically $25–$65 per student per day. (Recall that this intervention costs around $6 per net day of attendance generated.) Thus, in addition to increasing student attendance – and the academic benefits that attendance generates for students – this intervention also generates substantial net revenue for school districts in many states.

Second, the intervention has many advantages over the most common absence-reduction interventions. For example, since it can be produced and delivered by EveryDay Labs, it can be implemented with perfect fidelity, districtwide without requiring school-level staff to change their behavior. These advantages help to overcome several of the limitations we experienced with the "hands-off" approach. Implementing with fidelity at scale is a major challenge for many social policy interventions.[29] More subtly, the intervention's reliance on snail mail is a feature and not a bug. Most federal, state, and local governmental communications of consequence (e.g., tax information, benefit eligibility, etc.) come through the mail. This results in families keeping the US Postal Service updated on forwarding addresses. Typically, school districts have valid mailing addresses for 90 percent or more of their families, even in school districts with high rates of families experiencing homelessness.[30]

And so with that, the enterprise now called EveryDay Labs was born to implement the intervention in partner districts. Officially launched in 2016, its first two clients were the research partners for the original two published papers: the School District of Philadelphia and the San Mateo County Office of Education.

As of September 2022, EveryDay Labs has over forty full-time employees and ten part-time employees. It delivers millions of interventions each year and has recovered an estimated 1.4 million net days of student attendance. Three leaders were central to growing EveryDay Labs from its first two clients to now serving dozens of districts around the United States, including many of the largest like LAUSD and Dallas ISD. Johannes Demarzi led the organization from its earliest days and passed the reins to Marc Laitin. Marc, who had formerly led Opower's product research and development, secured initial angel investment, and found the current CEO, Emily Bailard.

Bailard took over in 2018 when EveryDay Labs had only three full-time employees and scaled the organization to what it is today. Her professional experience and goals suited the needs of the organization: she is a former management consultant, leader at Opower, and advisor and coach to more than a dozen other social enterprises formed at Stanford Graduate School of Business. She has led EveryLabs through Seed and Series A investment rounds anchored by Reach Capital and Rethink Capital, and through the COVID-19 pandemic when schools shifted to remote learning (more on this below).

Goals

When we decided to cofound EveryDay Labs, we laid out three goals, in order of priority.

First, we wanted EveryDay Labs to serve as many students and families as possible by recovering as many days of absenteeism as possible with this proven and replicated intervention. EveryDay Labs could not pivot to more profitable but unproven products; its core business must be built around increasing student attendance using proven interventions.

Second, we wanted EveryDay Labs to have a culture and ethic of continuous testing and transparency about causality and impact. New products and services had to have strong causal evidence that they were good for students and families, and if they did not, EveryDay Labs must try to generate it. We hoped this culture and ethic could be a model for other education enterprises.

Finally, we wanted EveryDay Labs to be a sustainable, profitable social enterprise. We intentionally listed profitability as the least among these three goals – if the organization could not succeed in selling the proven intervention while also being transparent about causality, effect sizes, and impact, then we were fine with it not being viable.

Experimentation

As stated in the goals above, a culture of randomized controlled trials and learning is core to EveryDay Labs. These are broadly of two types: (1) comparing an active intervention against an untreated control; and (2) comparing variations of the treatment (e.g., message A to message B or timing 1 to timing 2). While limited in what results school districts permit it to publicly disclose, EveryDay Labs has conducted dozens of randomized trials. This was only possible because of the stewardship and capability of Jessica Lasky-Fink, EveryDay Labs's original research director.

To date, randomized trials have evaluated the impact of the intervention against an untreated control group with more than fourteen school districts involving a total sample of several hundred thousand students; the Los Angeles Unified School District, the School District of Philadelphia, and San Mateo County Office of Education have made the findings of some of these public. For all of these evaluations, the intervention continues to effectively reduce absenteeism districtwide, across diverse demographic and grade-level segments. Consistent with that, the EveryDay Labs intervention is the only absence-reduction program that qualifies as having Level 1 evidence standard for the *Every Student Succeeds Act* evidence portal hosted at Johns Hopkins University.

Randomized trials have also been invaluable in improving the intervention itself. The original papers make the intervention look straightforward and static: it is just a series of mailings with behaviorally-informed messaging, right? But maximizing the impact is nuanced and dynamic. Delivering the right message to the right student and family at the right time is critical to maximizing the intervention's effectiveness.

As of September 2022, there are roughly ten thousand versions of the absence report delivered to families. In particular, the written content of the report depends on attributes of the student, the student's classmates, the student's grade-level, and the time of year, among other features. Three dimensions of note are:

- *Language.* The reports vary the language based on what language is spoken at home. Robinson et al. found that sending absence reports in Spanish to Spanish speakers generated particularly large effects, so the absence reports sent by EveryDay Labs are sent in eight different languages, depending on what language is spoken at home.[31]

- *Comparisons.* Another important factor is whether the intervention includes absence information related to a students' classmates. For example, if the student's median classmate has accumulated just a couple absences fewer than the student (e.g., the student has accumulated twenty absences and the classmate comparator has accumulated eighteen absences) then the social comparison bar is included in the report, in line with *Relative Absences* condition in Figure 16.2 above. However, if the student's median classmate has accumulated unattainably fewer absences than the student (e.g., the student has accumulated twenty absences and the classmate comparator has accumulated eight absences) then the social comparison bar is excluded, in line with *Total Absences* condition in Figure 16.2. This reflects what we have learned about the impact of social comparisons that are attainable and unattainable.[32]
- *Timing and frequency.* The intervention is also more effective due to EveryDay Labs' research on timing and frequency. For example, sending absence reports before breaks and holidays are less effective than sending them after breaks and holidays. Additionally, recall that each successive round of intervention appears to be at least as effective as the previous. Add to that that the treatment effect decays at a predictable rate over time, and one can see why EveryDay Labs has moved from an average of about four rounds of treatment per academic year in the original studies to now about seven rounds.[33]

Randomized evaluations are also important for creating a predictive model for reporting to school districts the estimated number of absences that were recovered resulting from their collaborations with EveryDay Labs. This is useful because most school districts are either too small or uninterested in conducting a program evaluation randomized controlled trial in their districts.[34]

Finally, the findings of these trials have been valuable through sharing them with other practitioners and vendors. EveryDay Labs contributes to norms of collaboration and openness among those who work to reduce absenteeism. It also aims to elevate the field's causal inference standards. An example of an experimental result it has shared involves how to talk about absence data. EveryDay Labs found that saying "your child has missed fifteen days of school" was 20 percent more effective at reducing absenteeism in the subsequent week than "your child has missed more than fourteen days of school." Subsequent survey experiments suggest that parents are more likely to believe the precise number ("fifteen days") than the imprecise number ("more than fourteen days"), leading to more behavioral change. Two other scholars are developing this further and plan to include this trial in a future scholarly paper.

Absenteeism during the Pandemic

The COVID-19 pandemic upended education around the world. As schools quickly pivoted to remote learning, EveryDay Labs's focus on in-person student attendance seemed no longer necessary. As time passed, however, it became increasingly clear that student attendance in remote learning was still important, and more of a challenge than it had been for in-person attendance. As the pandemic continued, student absenteeism spiked.

CEO Emily Bailard saw this as an opportunity for EveryDay Labs to contribute to national policy discussions about absenteeism in remote learning. EveryDay Labs was uniquely situated for this since it had up-to-date absenteeism data for districts across the United States. Every-Day Labs published a white paper with Phylis Jordan of FutureEd called "Present Danger: Solving the Deepening Student Absenteeism Crisis," which presented the most up-to-date snapshot of attendance at the time from across multiple districts.[35] It was cited in the *Washington Post* and *USA Today*, among other outlets. EveryDay Labs hosted and participated in webinars viewed by thousands on attendance trends and strategies at this time as well.

In addition to advocating for absence-reducing practices, EveryDay Labs shifted its services to increasing attendance in remote learning. Since its interventions were optimized for increasing in-person attendance in the prepandemic context, it developed and tested new messages and tactics – a key area where Jessica Lasky-Fink's expertise was so valuable. It conducted nineteen randomized controlled trials with absenteeism as the outcome measure during the first year and a half of the pandemic. To our knowledge these were the only randomized controlled trials conducted in the US during this period examining how to increase student attendance.

Several of the tactics and strategies EDL tested proved to be effective, and several did not. For example, despite the mixed results prepandemic on using text messaging to deliver attendance interventions, EveryDay Labs conducted a series of studies on them. They found (and shared publicly) that generic text message encouragements to attend school had no effect, but adding personalized total absences data to the text messages could increase attendance. This increase was modest, though, accounting for 35 percent of the total attendance effect when added to the mail-based interventions. Since cell phone coverage for the most disadvantaged families tends to be relatively poor, text-message alone is not especially effective. But it proved to be a cost-effective addition to the mail-based intervention, and so is now a component of the full intervention program even when students are in-person.

Another pandemic innovation that districts and families found valuable was using the back of the absence reports to add timely and personalized information for families. A randomized controlled trial conducted prepandemic found that adding content to the back of the absence report had no detectable effect on student absenteeism relative to not adding content to the back. This was good news, since we expressed concern that adding content to the back of the report could distract recipients from the potent and proven attendance-reducing content on the front. Since it did not, the back of the report became a space for districts to add content families needed. These included digital login information, confirmation of cell phone and email contact info, information to connect families with food, health, and computer resources, and more.

EveryDay Lab's Impact and Future

The development and growth of EveryDay Labs has taught us more than we can report in this chapter. We note just a few here.

First, in our experience, it is important to treat absenteeism as a challenge that requires repeated, regular intervention – rather than a one-off treatment. This is consistent with a theory of parents having limited time and attention budgets to direct toward their children's schooling. Repeated absence report interventions redirect this time and attention to a consequential educational activity over which parents appear to have substantial agency.[36]

Second, as discussed above, the paramount goal of EveryDay Labs is to recover as many days of attendance as possible using proven interventions. Initially, we thought the key to this was developing increasingly potent interventions and publishing them in excellent scholarly journals. We evolved to see that school districts benefit most from partnering with an organization that specializes in implementing and improving on the proven intervention. Recently, we have come to understand what is obvious to everyone who is not an academic – successfully *selling* the intervention is key to scaling it. This is a dramatic departure from our starting position, but it has been edifying.

Finally, a brief note about the impact of the intervention. EveryDay Labs estimates that it has reduced student absenteeism by around 1.4

million days. As we note above, this has immediate value to school districts, many of which receive funding based on average daily attendance. What is this worth to students? One approach is to quantify the impact of additional attendance on students' lifetime earnings. While necessarily speculative, a plausible range of estimates from scholarship in labor economics is that an additional day of attendance is worth $500 to $1,000 in additional lifetime earnings per student. With 1.4 million additional days of attendance generated by EveryDay Labs, this suggests that it has increased total lifetime earnings of students it serves by $1 billion – a truly large impact.[37]

At the same time, reducing chronic absenteeism by 10 percent means that 90 percent of the chronically absent students are still chronically absent. Same with 1.4 million recovered absences: there are nearly a billion student absences to be recovered in the US each year. This intervention is not a panacea but rather a complement to more labor-intensive, student-focused absenteeism interventions; it's an implementable at-scale with fidelity, cost-effective complement to those other interventions.

Taken together, the impact to date exceeds our aspirations for this social enterprise. Early on in this journey we considered naming the enterprise *One Million Days* because we thought recovering one million total absences from at-risk students would be an audacious aspirational goal. Our friend and advisor Louis Harrison talked us out of it. He expected that we might exceed that number of recovered days. He was the only one to consider that possibility. If EveryDay Labs considers changing its name, we might propose *One Billion Days*.

NOTES

1 See Issenberg, S. (2012). *The victory lab: The secret science of winning campaigns.* Crown; Nickerson, D.W., & Rogers, T. (2014). Political campaigns and big data. *Journal of Economic Perspectives, 28*(2), 51–74. https://doi.org/10.1257/jep.28.2.51; and Nickerson, D.W., & Rogers, T. (2020). Campaigns influence election outcomes less than you think. *Science, 369*(6508), 1181–2. https://doi.org/10.1126/science.abb2437.

2 See Henderson, A.T., & Mapp, K.L. (2002). *A New wave of evidence: The impact of school, family, and community connections on student achievement. Annual synthesis, 2002.* National Center for Family & Community Connections with Schools. https://files.eric.ed.gov/fulltext/ED474521.pdf; and Mapp, K.L., & Bergman, E. (2021). *Embracing a new normal: Toward a more liberatory approach to family engagement.* Carnegie Corporation.

https://www.carnegie.org/publications/embracing-new-normal-toward
-more-liberatory-approach-family-engagement/.

3 Valencia, R.R., & Solórzano, D.G. (1997). Contemporary deficit thinking. *The evolution of deficit thinking: Educational thought and practice* (pp. 160–210). Routledge.

4 Gottfried, M.A. & Hutt, E.L. (Eds.). (2018). *Absent from school: Understanding and addressing student absenteeism.* Harvard Education Press.

5 See Gershenson, S., Jacknowitz, A., & Brannegan, A. (2017). Are student absences worth the worry in US primary schools? *Education Finance and Policy, 12*(2), 137–65. https://doi.org/10.1162/EDFP_a_00207; Liu, J., & Loeb, S. (2021). Engaging teachers: Measuring the impact of teachers on student attendance in secondary school. *Journal of Human Resources, 56*(2), 343–79. http://jhr.uwpress.org/content/early/2019/07/02/jhr.56.2.1216 -8430R3; and Ansari, A., & Gottfried, M.A. (2021). The grade-level and cumulative outcomes of absenteeism. *Child Development, 92*(4), e548–e564. https://doi.org/10.1111/cdev.13555.

6 See Byrnes, V., & Reyna, R. (2012). *Summary of state level analysis of early warning indicators.* Everyone Graduates Center; and Schoeneberger, J.A. (2012). Longitudinal attendance patterns: Developing high school dropouts. *The Clearing House: A Journal of Educational Strategies, Issues and Ideas, 85*(1), 7–14. https://www.jstor.org/stable/23212842.

7 Henry, K.L., & Thornberry, T.P. (2010). Truancy and escalation of substance use during adolescence. *Journal of Studies on Alcohol and Drugs, 71*(1), 115–24. https://doi.org/10.15288/jsad.2010.71.115.

8 See Baker, M.L., Sigmon, J.N., & Nugent, M.E. (2001). Truancy reduction: Keeping students in school. Juvenile Justice Bulletin, Office of Juvenile Justice and Delinquency Prevention. https://www.ojp .gov/pdffiles1/ojjdp/188947.pdf; and Jacob, B.A., & Lefgren, L. (2003). Are idle hands the devil's workshop? Incapacitation, concentration, and juvenile crime. *American Economic Review, 93*(5), 1560–77. https:// doi.org/10.1257/000282803322655446.

9 Rohrman, D. (1993). Combating truancy in our schools – A community effort. *NASSP Bulletin, 77*(549), 40–5. https://doi. org/10.1177/019263659307754906.

10 Rogers, T., Goldstein, N.J., & Fox, C.R. (2018). Social mobilization. *Annual Review of Psychology, 69*, 357–81. https://doi.org/10.1146/annurev-psych -122414-033718.

11 Gerber, A.S., & Rogers, T. (2009). Descriptive social norms and motivation to vote: Everybody's voting and so should you. *The Journal of Politics, 71*(1), 178–91. https://doi.org/10.1017/S0022381608090117.

12 Hallsworth, M., List, J.A., Metcalfe, R.D., & Vlaev, I. (2017). The behavioralist as tax collector: Using natural field experiments to enhance

tax compliance. *Journal of Public Economics, 148*, 14–31. https://doi.org
/10.3386/w20007.

13 Goldstein, N.J., Cialdini, R.B., & Griskevicius, V. (2008). A room with a
viewpoint: Using social norms to motivate environmental conservation in
hotels. *Journal of Consumer Research, 35*(3), 472–82. https://doi.org/10.1086
/586910.

14 Ferraro, P.J., Miranda, J.J., & Price, M.K. (2011). The persistence of
treatment effects with norm-based policy instruments: Evidence from a
randomized environmental policy experiment. *American Economic Review,
101*(3), 318–22. https://doi.org/10.1257/aer.101.3.318.

15 Schultz, P.W., Nolan, J.M., Cialdini, R.B., Goldstein, N.J., & Griskevicius,
V. (2007). The constructive, destructive, and reconstructive power of social
norms. *Psychological Science, 18*(5), 429–34. https://doi.org/10.1111/j.1467
-9280.2007.01917.x.

16 Allcott, H. (2011). Social norms and energy conservation. *Journal of Public
Economics, 95*(9–10), 1082–95. https://doi.org/10.1016/j.jpubeco.2011.03.003.

17 See Allcott & Rogers. (2014); and Rogers, T., & Frey, E. (2015). Changing
behavior beyond the here and now. In Keren, G., & Wu, G. (Eds.). *The
Wiley Blackwell Handbook of Judgment and Decision Making* (pp. 723–48).
John Wiley & Sons.

18 Ferraro et al. (2011).

19 Image from Allcott, H., & Rogers, T. (2014). The short-run and long-run
effects of behavioral interventions: Experimental evidence from energy
conservation. *American Economic Review, 104*(10), 3003–37. https://doi.org
/10.1257/aer.104.10.3003.

20 Rogers, T., & Feller, A. (2018). Reducing student absences at scale by
targeting parents' misbeliefs. *Nature Human Behaviour, 2*(5), 335–42.
https://doi.org/10.1038/s41562-018-0328-1.

21 Basse, G., & Feller, A. (2018). Analyzing two-stage experiments in the
presence of interference. *Journal of the American Statistical Association,
113*(521), 41–55. https://doi.org/10.1080/01621459.2017.1323641.

22 See, for example, Rogers, T., & Feller, A. (2016). Discouraged by peer excellence:
Exposure to exemplary peer performance causes quitting. *Psychological Science,
27*(3), 365–74. https://doi.org/10.1177/0956797615623770; and Beshears, J.,
Choi, J.J., Laibson, D., Madrian, B.C., & Milkman, K.L. (2015). The effect of
providing peer information on retirement savings decisions. *The Journal of
Finance, 70*(3), 1161–201. https://doi.org/10.3386/w17345.

23 Rogers & Feller (2016).

24 See Guryan, J., Christenson, S., Cureton, A., Lai, I., Ludwig, J., Schwarz,
C., Shirey, E., & Turner, M.C. (2021). The effect of mentoring on school
attendance and academic outcomes: A randomized evaluation of the
Check & Connect Program. *Journal of Policy Analysis and Management, 40(3),*

841–82. https://doi.org/10.1002/pam.22264; and for a quasi-experimental evaluation of absence-focused mentors targeting a population that also includes students with more extreme absenteeism, see Balfanz, R., & Byrnes, V. (2013). *Meeting the challenge of combating chronic absenteeism: Impact of the NYC mayor's Interagency Task Force on Chronic Absenteeism and School Attendance and its implications for other cities.* Johns Hopkins School of Education.

25 See Balu, R., Porter, K., & Gunton, B. (2016). *Can informing parents help high school students show up for school?* MDRC Policy Brief. https://www.mdrc .org/sites/default/files/NewVisionsRCT_2016_Brief.pdf

26 Musaddiq, T., Pretyman, A., & Smith, J. (2020). Using existing school messaging platforms to inform parents about their child's attendance. *Metro Atlanta Policy Lab for Education.* https://files.osf.io/v1/resources /f8mvg/providers/osfstorage/5f22c1359c90940057484e4b?action=download &direct&version=1.

27 Robinson, C.D., Lee, M.G., Dearing, E., & Rogers, T. (2018). Reducing student absenteeism in the early grades by targeting parental beliefs. *American Educational Research Journal, 55*(6), 1163–92. https://doi.org/10.3102 /0002831218772274.

28 Bergman, P. (2021). Parent-child information frictions and human capital investment: Evidence from a field experiment. *Journal of Political Economy, 129*(1), 286–322. https://doi.org/10.1086/711410.

29 Bhatt, M.P., Guryan, J., Ludwig, J., & Shah, A.K. (2021). *Scope challenges to social impact* (No. w28406). National Bureau of Economic Research. https://www.nber.org/system/files/working_papers/w28406/w28406 .pdf.

30 People are often surprised when they first learn about the high coverage by mail. Contrast this with text messages: just as COVID-19 arrived in 2020 many districts did not have *valid* cell phone or email contact information for many of their families, especially their most disadvantaged families (Rogers and Lasky-Fink, 2020; Musaddiq et al., 2020). This was especially true for the families of students with the highest rates of absenteeism. Schools often have digital contact information on file for their students, according to Hester Tinti-Kane; see Bray, J. (Host). (2022, March 22). Understanding the digital learning pulse survey with Cengage and Bay View Analytics. In *In the Know with ACCT.* https://www.audacy.com /podcast/in-the-know-with-acct-03f93/episodes/understanding-the -digital-learning-pulse-survey-with-cengage-and-bay-view-analytics-f7561. However, many families are no longer reachable through those cell phone numbers or email addresses. They may have changed the email and cell phone numbers they use, or the person associated with the contact information is no longer the primary guardian. Even when the

cell phone is deemed "valid" by a cellular service provider, it may have been reassigned to a subscriber other than the guardian who originally shared the number with the district. This helps explain the low response rates typical to these modalities (between 1.5 percent and 8.1 percent). Again, valid digital contact information is likely even lower for the most disadvantaged families (Musaddiq et al., 2020).

31 Robinson et al. (2018).

32 See Rogers & Feller (2016); and Rogers & Feller (2018).

33 FutureEd. (2019, December 16). *A researcher's take on reducing chronic absenteeism*. Future-ed.org. https://www.future-ed.org/a-researchers-take-on-reducing-chronic-absenteeism/

34 Interestingly, school districts appear to find this kind of impact reporting unconvincing. They seem to prefer the kind of reporting typical of education vendors: reporting all inputs, or comparing pre-treatment to post-treatment outcomes during a cherry-picked time period or for a cherry-picked subgroup. Since attendance data has substantial variation between years, within year, and across schools and demographics, these estimates are not very reliable or accurate reflections of causal impact. It appears that since they use actual data from within a given school district they are more credible to districts, though. To say this concisely: the data we believe is most credible (a predictive model based on many randomized controlled trials across districts and demographics) school districts do not believe; the data we do not believe (noisy and cherry-picked observational data) districts seem to believe.

35 Jordan, P.W. (2021). *Present danger: Solving the deepening student absentee crisis*. Future-ed.org. https://www.future-ed.org/wp-content/uploads/2021/05/REPORT_Present_Danger_Final.pdf.

36 Robinson, C.D., Chande, R., Burgess, S., & Rogers, T. (2022). Parent engagement interventions are not costless: Opportunity cost and crowd out of parental investment. *Educational Evaluation and Policy Analysis, 44*(1), 170–7. https://doi.org/10.3102/01623737211030492.

37 This approach to estimating lifetime earnings increases necessarily rests on many simplifying assumptions. First, we take estimates of total lifetime earnings from Carnevale et al. (2013), who use Census data, and Tamborini et al. (2015), who use Social Security Administration data. Estimated lifetime earnings in undiscounted 2022 dollars range from $1.5M to $1.8M for high school graduates and $1.7M to $2.4M for those with some college or an associates degree. To approximate the impact of an additional day of attendance on lifetime earnings, we begin with the widely accepted estimate that an additional year of schooling increases future earnings by 10 percent (see Kolesnikova, 2010). Thus, for a population that predominantly has a high school degree or has attended some college,

an additional year of school increases undiscounted lifetime earnings by roughly $150,000 to $200,000. A simple linear extrapolation implies that the value of an additional day (out of 180 school days) is roughly $800 to $1,000 per day. Following the discussion in Carnevale et al. (2013), we can also compute the net present value using a 2.5 percent real discount rate, which yields discounted estimates of roughly $500 to $600 per day. As one benchmark, Chetty et al. (2014) estimate that replacing a teacher who is substantially below-average (in terms of estimated value-added scores) with an average teacher increases a child's undiscounted lifetime earnings by $50,000. Following the rough calculations above, this is equivalent to attending an additional one-third of the school year for a typical student. Finally, our estimate of 1.4 million additional days is based on an assumption that the impact in districts without a randomized controlled trial is roughly the same as the impact in the districts in which randomized control trials were conducted (for counterexamples, see Allcott [2015]). Carnevale, A.P. (2013, July 1). *Recovery: Job growth and education requirements through 2020.* DigitalGeorgetown. https://repository.library.georgetown. edu/handle/10822/559311; Tamborini, C.R., Kim, C.H., & Sakamoto, A. (2015). Education and lifetime earnings in the United States. *Demography,* 52(4), 1383–1407. https://doi.org/10.1007/s13524-015-0407-0;Kolesnikova, N. (2010, January 1). *The return to education isn't calculated easily.* Federal Reserve Bank of St. Louis. https://www.stlouisfed.org/publications /regional-economist/january-2010/the-return-to-education-isnt-calculated -easily; Chetty, R., Friedman, J.N., & Rockoff, J.E. (2014). Measuring the impacts of teachers I: Evaluating bias in teacher Value-Added estimates. *The American Economic Review, 104*(9), 2593–632. https://doi.org/10.1257 /aer.104.9.2593; and Allcott, H. (2015). Site selection bias in program evaluation. *Quarterly Journal of Economics, 130*(3), 1117–65. https://doi.org /10.1093/qje/qjv015.

CHAPTER SEVENTEEN

Replicating, Adapting, and Scaling Rule of Thumb–Based Business Management Training to Help Entrepreneurs across the Developing World

Lois Aryee, Manasee Desai, and Mukta Joshi

AT A GLANCE

- **Our Goal:** To increase the accessibility and digestibility of training using financial heuristics for micro and small business entrepreneurs globally in order to help them adopt vital skills to grow their businesses.
- **The Intervention:** A behaviorally designed, short (three to four minute) digital business training program that provides simplified business lessons to entrepreneurs at their convenience.
- **The Results:** The intervention resulted in (a) high take-up rates and (b) increases in the adoption of business practices across multiple countries, as well as (c) improved business outcomes in the Dominican Republic.
- **Lesson Learned:** In order to successfully scale interventions and ensure that they feel relevant and applicable to recipients, it is critical to leverage qualitative research tools, user testing, and piloting to ensure that the voices and practices of target users are incorporated.

Motivation and Objective

Our chapter is different from other chapters in this volume. Most other chapters describe attempts to replicate, translate, or scale a laboratory study (or a pilot) in the field. In contrast, we describe our efforts at replicating and scaling one of our own successful field-based interventions across geographies and populations. We also discuss our learnings and offer advice for others looking to similarly scale successful interventions horizontally and vertically.

Have you ever sat through a long training course and struggled to pay attention? Do you find it harder to learn new ideas after a long day? Are there times of the day when you are more productive than others? Have you ever heard strategies that seem ideal in theory, but that you know won't work for you? These are the types of issues that we sought to design for in ideas42's Financial Heuristics Training.

Many people around the world depend on micro, small, and medium enterprises (MSMEs) for their livelihoods. Small and medium-sized enterprises (SMEs) make up more than 90 percent of businesses worldwide, and account for over 50 percent of the world's employment.[1] They also contribute substantially to the GDP of many nations, especially in developing and emerging economies across Africa, Asia, and Latin America.[2] Despite the prominence of small businesses, many small business owners lack essential skills for growing their businesses and managing their finances effectively. In an attempt to address these skill gaps, millions of dollars have been invested into numerous traditional classroom-based training programs that teach business management and financial education. Yet, several studies show that many of them are unsuccessful at changing financial behaviors and business outcomes.[3] Even when they do, such programs have a very modest impact.[4] Given the hassles often involved in attending in person, many programs also experience low attendance, diminishing their impact even further.[5]

The Case for Behavioral Design

The practice of behavioral design enables us to examine different features of an individual's environment to understand how and why they act in the ways that they do. This is particularly useful when working across multiple contexts where cultures, norms, values, and access to resources may be different. Applying a behavioral lens also helps program designers strip themselves of assumptions and limit biases that could lead to flawed hypotheses and ultimately ineffective designs. It involves conducting qualitative and quantitative research to understand key problems, user testing for relevance and feasibility, and rigorous evaluation to understand if the designed solutions work.

Behavioral science offers some insight into why business and financial education training programs, though carefully designed, may not achieve intended outcomes. Such programs require a significant time commitment from already busy microentrepreneurs who often juggle many responsibilities. To participate, trainees may need to find some-one to attend to their business, organize childcare, and figure out trans-portation logistics, which could be burdensome. This is particularly challenging for women entrepreneurs who tend to wear multiple hats and have more domestic responsibilities than men. In the midst of long workdays and household responsibilities, participating in training may not be top of mind. Even when business owners attend training ses-sions, lessons are often not designed in a way that is engaging and eas-ily digestible. Materials are often unnecessarily complex and not easily applicable to trainees' day-to-day realities, particularly for small busi-ness owners in the developing world. All of these issues can greatly affect attendance, engagement, and the subsequent application of les-sons in the real world, leading to decreased impact.

ideas42 used a behavioral approach to seek a more actionable and effective way of helping microentrepreneurs (owners of micro, small, and medium-sized enterprises) to obtain the important skills that they need to manage their businesses. We partnered with Antoinette Schoar, pro-fessor of finance and entrepreneurship at the Massachusetts Institute of Technology Sloan School of Management, and Shawn Cole, professor of business administration at the Harvard Business School, to develop a rule of thumb-based training which we called the Financial Heuristics Train-ing. The Financial Heuristics Training is a scalable program that simplifies financial management lessons into easy-to-adopt rules of thumb delivered to small business owners over mobile phones. Unlike traditional training programs that aim for a more comprehensive understanding of finance, accounting, and business management, the heuristics training focuses on distilling important business and financial management practices into simple insights, making the lessons easier to learn, remember, and apply.

We have tested the Financial Heuristics Training in three disparate parts of the world – Latin America, South Asia, and Southeast Asia – with an ongoing study in Sub-Saharan Africa. We first tested the concept of leveraging heuristics to improve the financial management practices of business owners in the Dominican Republic and found encouraging impacts on both business practices and business outcomes. Recipients of the heuristics-based training were 10 percentage points more likely to keep accounting records, calculate revenues, and separate business from household accounts. The training also helped business owners increase sales during bad weeks by almost 19 percent and to improve weekly revenues. Once we had evidence that it worked, we tested a similar heuristics-based training in India. We focused on the successful "cash separation" rules of thumb from the training in the Dominican Republic and added lessons on other topics that would be helpful for microenterprises. Here, we saw mixed results on impact and gathered

feedback that allowed us to improve on the product and delivery channel. We tested the refined prototype again in India and scaled it to the
Philippines. This time, we saw positive effects on business practices.
The Financial Heuristics Training is currently being evaluated in Ethiopia and so far shows promising engagement rates, especially relative to
other training programs offered to that group of entrepreneurs.

Inspiration

As financial literacy is (arguably too often) seen as the main barrier
to low-income populations engaging in financial services and improving business practices, many countries have government-mandated
requirements that financial service providers offer some form of financial education or business training. As a result, an enormous amount of
money has been spent on these programs.[6] Yet the impact of such programs is mixed. Many do not achieve the effects they expect or the magnitude of impact hoped for.[7] Recent studies have found some impact
from financial education training programs,[8] but the majority show low
to no impact. A meta-analysis of over two hundred studies showed that
most financial education training programs do not lead to changes in
financial behaviors, and only 0.1 percent of the changes observed in
financial practices were attributed to such training.[9] Other studies conducted in developing countries could not detect statistically significant
improvements in business sales or profits.[10] Also, the burden of traditional classroom-based training programs on providers and recipients
alike can negatively impact whether they are offered and the take-up
and engagement with these programs. ideas42 and our research partners sought more effective ways to help business owners build useful
skills and enable them to maximize the benefits of entrepreneurship.

We designed the Financial Heuristics Training based on other studies that show the benefits of simplification in improving social outcomes
like enrollment rates in retirement savings plans,[11] Medicare drug plans,[12]
weight loss,[13] and student loan applications.[14] Other research conducted
by psychologists and behavioral scientists helps explain why simplified
approaches to training like rule of thumb-based lessons are more likely to
lead to action and better outcomes than traditional trainings:

- Improves recall: It is easier for people to absorb and recall information when it is presented simply.[15]
- Cuts through the noise: How information is provided impacts our
  ability to process it. When important information is surrounded by
  a lot of less important or nonactionable details, it may be difficult

for people to identify the most useful takeaways, reducing the likelihood that people will absorb the key messages.[16]

- Quicker application: When complex information is simplified into heuristics, it requires less time to implement. People are less likely to procrastinate and more likely to follow through on steps that are more actionable because they are not overwhelmed with too much information.[17]

Original Rules of Thumb Training: Dominican Republic (2006–8)

To address the barriers described above, our first intervention focused on evaluating whether a simplified, rule of thumb-based training will improve how entrepreneurs engage with the program, apply the concepts, improve business practices, and experience business outcomes like increased profits and sales. We partnered with ADOPEM, a microfinance institution in the Dominican Republic, to redesign and simplify their financial education curriculum by distilling key financial management best practices into lessons that were easy to learn and act on. The Financial Heuristics Training sought to provide entrepreneurs with the most useful and actionable insights on managing business finances rather than providing comprehensive accounting knowledge (as traditional training typically does).

For instance, the curriculum included a focus on the importance of separating personal or household accounts from business accounts. Separating personal finances from business accounts is important because it allows firms to gauge their profitability and sustainability, and it acts as a commitment device to mitigate the risk of business owners overconsuming the working capital of their businesses. In developing countries, the tax and legal incentives to keep these accounts separate are relatively weaker, and many business owners cross-spend. The Financial Heuristics Training provided simple recommendations like keeping cash in two separate physical locations and only transferring money from one location to the other with a clear intention to pay back. Participants were also taught to pay themselves a fixed salary each week or month, and to determine their profits at the end of the month by counting the money that was left in the location where they stored business funds. Additionally, they were given simple lessons on savings and debt management.

In conjunction with our research partners, we tested the intervention in a classroom setting between November 2006 and July 2008 using a randomized controlled trial. Classes were offered once a week for five weeks, with each class lasting three hours, and ADOPEM clients were randomly assigned to receive the rules of thumb training, standard accounting training, or no training at all.

Figure 17.1. Excerpt from training manual: Classroom-based heuristics training in the Dominican Republic

MODULE 4 SESSION 4: LOANS FROM HOUSEHOLD TO BUSINESS AND FROM BUSINESS TO HOUSEHOLD

REGISTER OF LOANS FROM BUSINESS TO HOUSEHOLD AND FROM HOUSEHOLD TO BUSINESS			
Date	Details	Loans from business to household	Loans from household to business
20/10	Spare part		1,200

- Explain to pupils that all money lent by the household to the business must be recorded in the column for loans from the household to the business, and that all loans from the business to the household must be recorded in the column for loans from the business to the household. In order to explain this you may wish to use the following diagram.

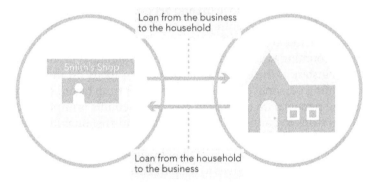

We were excited to find that the Financial Heuristics Training was uniquely effective at improving both the adoption of the suggested business practices by entrepreneurs and the profitability of their businesses. A year after the training, microentrepreneurs who received the heuristics-based training were 10 percentage points more likely to adopt positive business practices, like keeping accounting records and separating their business and personal finances. These benefits extended to business outcomes: entrepreneurs who received the Financial Heuristics Training experienced improved weekly revenues and experienced a nearly 19 percent increase in sales during reported bad weeks, self-defined by entrepreneurs as periods in the business when "things are not going well."[18]

Not only did the Financial Heuristics Training lead to a positive impact on business management behaviors and business outcomes, we recognized from our past work that the challenges it addressed were common to microentrepreneurs across the developing world. However, the fact that lessons were delivered in a classroom setting limited the scalability of the intervention. These results and insights motivated us to think about making the program scalable and adapting it for new contexts.

Piloting a New Curriculum and Delivery Channel: India (2014–16)

The encouraging results from the Dominican Republic led us to explore new frontiers and better ways of delivering the training. Classroom-based training programs lacked scalability – beyond the significant time commitment required, they're expensive to set up and difficult to standardize across trainers. With this in mind, we developed a second prototype of the Financial Heuristics Training. We maintained the rules of thumb-based approach but expanded on the curriculum, targeting a wider range of business management skills. We also used an Interactive Voice Response (IVR) service that enabled people to listen to prerecorded messages delivered via phone call, with the goal of reaching as many people with the training as possible.

The IVR channel enabled us to reach more business owners irrespective of their location, standardize the delivery of the content, and ensure the same level of quality for all participants. It also allowed individuals to access the program independent of their literacy levels – a critical feature, especially for women who may not have had as much access to educational opportunities.[19] Delivering the training digitally also enabled us to offer content in small digestive chunks, addressing the challenge of limited attention that all humans face, given our limited cognitive capacity which makes learning over long periods of time (as is typical for classroom-based training programs) more difficult.

Lessons were narrated in an instructional manner from the perspective of a business owner. There was a callback feature which allowed participants to access all the previous lessons, in case they missed any or wanted to relisten, and we allowed participants to select the time of day that they wanted to receive the calls. Led by the Institute for Financial Management and Research (IFMR LEAD), our research partner, participants were guided through an onboarding process, focusing on how to engage in the training digitally.

We learned from our initial pilot of this prototype that mobile phones could serve as an effective delivery channel for the Financial Heuristics Training. However, the pilot also revealed that the training had several opportunities for improvement. We recorded low engagement rates – while 83 percent of participants picked up the calls, they only listened to 48 percent of the message on average, and there was no impact found on business practices or outcomes two to three months after the end of the program. Although the delivery channel was improved, the training had to be further refined to meet the needs of listeners.

To do this refinement, we conducted qualitative interviews with study participants who had been highly engaged with the training, and with those who weren't. We also conducted multiple rounds of user testing to understand how we could increase engagement. Our investigations revealed that listeners wanted shorter, more concise, and relatable messages, and a smoother technology experience. This feedback helped us to further refine and replicate the intervention in India, and then to test it in the Philippines.

Refining and Scaling the Heuristics Training in India and the Philippines (2016–17)

In our next interventions in India and the Philippines, we made the following changes to the Financial Heuristics Training:

- **More engaging content:** We brought on voice actors from India and the Philippines to narrate the lessons, to make them more relatable and engaging for listeners.
- **Relatable narrative:** The voice actors narrated the lessons in a story-telling manner as anecdotes from a business owner who was similar to the recipients, sharing experiences and advice on business management that she had learned over the years in the same context. We ensured that the narrator used names, expressions, and terms that were familiar to the target audience. The tone was conversational, and training was delivered in the local language that participants were comfortable with. This personalized approach was also informed by research that shows that people are more likely to remember information that is presented to them in a way that feels relevant.[20]
- **Pre-scheduling:** We encouraged participants to think about the time of day when they were less likely to be busy, and scheduled lessons for those time slots. This framing enabled them to request the training call at a time when they were more likely to be able to listen and engage with it.
- **Call back feature:** If participants missed a session, or wanted to re-listen to past lessons, they were able to call back to listen to the last two training sessions. We limited the retrievable lessons to the last two lessons rather than all the past sessions based on findings

from India which showed that participants were overwhelmed when they had access to all previous lessons, and rarely used the feature. Limiting it to the past two lessons made it more manageable for clients to engage.

- **MFI-led in-person orientation:** Our microfinance partner, which had established a relationship of trust with the business owners, led the orientation activity before the training began. Orientation was either conducted in fifteen-to-twenty-minute one-on-one sessions with business owners, or in thirty-minute sessions with groups of about twenty-five entrepreneurs who were in the same community. Group orientation sessions were held at the office of the microfinance institution (MFI) or at other central locations where other group meetings were held with entrepreneurs. Orientation was primarily aimed at (1) showing participants how to respond to and engage with the program, (2) enabling participants to share the times when they were less busy for receiving the training calls, (3) setting expectations about the training – when to expect calls, the training duration, and reminders to be available for the calls, and (4) teaching the concept of separation of cash between household and business. Orientation was conducted with clear infographics and visuals that participants could take home.
- **Real-time engagement tracking:** We selected an IVR platform that provided us with real-time engagement statistics to enable us make changes and course-correct during training implementation. The technology platform enabled automated delivery of messages and therefore was less prone to human error.
- **Targeted delivery:** We focused on retail business owners for whom the key lessons on inventory and supplier management were most relevant. Retail businesses are present in large numbers across the developing world, highlighting the potential for scale.

We launched and tested the refined prototype in the Philippines, exploring whether the curriculum would be relevant in a new context. There, we conducted interviews with microentrepreneurs to understand whether their business practices were similar to what we found in India. We learned that financial and business management challenges were largely common across the two very different countries, especially with regards to key business practices like cash separation, credit management, inventory management, and supplier management, and that the curriculum was relevant for multiple contexts. We also observed from past work that these challenges may be relatively universal for retail microentrepreneurs. We only found one difference in business practices between India and the Philippines: business owners in the

Figure 17.2. Visual used to explain lesson on cash separation during entrepreneur orientation in India, entitled "Cash Separation for My Business and Household"

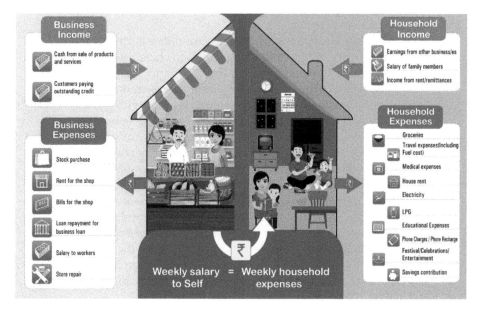

Table 17.1. Main topics

Cash Separation	Customer Credit	Inventory Management	Supplier Management
- Cash separation between household and business - Business salary setting - Business profit measurement	- Identifying when to give customer credit - Recording customer credit - Tracking and updating decisions on customer credit	- How to choose items to stock - Frequency of stocking items - Visiting and tracking competitors	- Comparing options - Negotiating prices - How to finance supply purchases

Philippines did not take goods to sell on credit while business owners in India did. We refined the curriculum to reflect this difference.

Further testing in India and the Philippines yielded more promising results:

- **Engagement:** On average, across both countries, 76 percent of clients answered the training calls and listened to at least 70 percent of the message.

- **Business practices:** In India, The Financial Heuristics Training increased by 8 percent the likelihood that clients separated business and personal cash (which aids in identifying profitability) and increased by 2 percent their likelihood of not running out of stock. In the Philippines, entrepreneurs who received heuristics training were 8 percent more likely to separate business and personal cash, 5 percent more likely to keep customer credit records, and 4.4 percent more likely to visit competitors to compare prices, stock, etc. These results were more modest than those found in the Dominican Republic, but still encouraging given that we were only able to measure effects three months after the training (vs. twelve months in the Dominican Republic when there would have been more time to implement the best practices), and that the training happened during demonetization, which had catastrophic negative effects on small businesses in India.
- **Cost-effectiveness:** In India, delivering the Financial Heuristics Training via mobile phone was significantly cheaper than doing so through a classroom – it cost about 67 percent less than the institution's in-person financial education training. In the Philippines, where the cost of airtime was higher than in India, the digital Financial Heuristics Training was slightly more expensive than in-person training. Despite this expense, the Filipino partner MFI still decided to invest in scaling it to more of their clients because of the convenience it provided entrepreneurs, along with the proven positive impact on their behaviors. They hired someone specifically to scale the program further and rolled it out to larger communities until mobile airtime costs increased and became too expensive to sustain.

Scaling to a New Context: Ethiopia (2021–2)

Encouraged by these results, we partnered with the World Bank to scale the Financial Heuristics Training to Ethiopia. This training was offered to women who were beneficiaries of the World Bank–funded Women's Entrepreneurship Development Project (WEDP) as part of an effort to specifically help female microentrepreneurs grow their businesses. Because women entrepreneurs tend to have disproportionately high levels of domestic responsibilities on top of their businesses and are therefore less likely to travel and more likely to be bandwidth depleted during traditional training hours, the Financial Heuristics Training could provide the flexibility and convenience critical to their being able to participate. Also, movement was restricted during the COVID-19 pandemic, but the Financial Heuristics Training enabled women entrepreneurs to participate from the safety of their homes.

We tested a few new features of the program in Ethiopia. First, entrepreneurs received text messages before each lesson reminding them about it, as well as text messages after each lesson summarizing the key takeaways. We included a quiz at the end of each lesson to gauge how well participants remembered and understood the key insights. Also, due to restrictions on movement imposed by COVID-19, orientation sessions were done over the phone by enumerators hired by a local research firm.

We were uncertain about how successfully the training would scale to the Ethiopian context because both the population and the delivery of the training were very different than in past interventions:

- **Education Levels:** Entrepreneurs in WEDP had considerably higher education levels compared to those we worked with in India. This made us wonder if some parts of the lessons – like how to calculate profit – were too basic for them.
- **Business Sizes:** Entrepreneurs had larger businesses than in India and the Philippines. We wondered if these businesses had the same types of challenges that we found with smaller businesses.
- **Training Providers:** The training could not be offered by a lender or alongside a loan. We suspected that the relationship with lenders could have been driving listenership and the likelihood of applying business practices in past pilots. Without this connection, we worried that there would be less engagement or incentive to apply lessons in this context.
- **Remote Onboarding:** Due to COVID-19, no physical contact was made with entrepreneurs and all orientation sessions were conducted over the phone instead of in person. We wondered if the in-person orientation was critical to ensuring trust and engagement in the training.

We were pleased to find through interviews and user testing that female entrepreneurs in Ethiopia still stood to benefit from the existing Financial Heuristics Training curriculum. For example, half of the business owners that we interviewed did not have separate locations for business and household earnings, almost half of them did not know how much they spent on their household, and close to 90 percent did not pay themselves a salary – all core to business profitability, and important skills for growing a successful business. Similarly, ideas42 observed suboptimal credit practices among a large proportion of the sample. For example, 69 percent of respondents said they did nothing if customers did not pay them back, 73 percent had no maximum credit limit for customers, and 31 percent of respondents kept track of credit on memory only. The result was that 64 percent said that customers with outstanding credit affected their ability to stock inventory.

Preliminary engagement statistics from Ethiopia were highly encouraging. On average across the program, 82.1 percent of the calls were answered, compared to 73 percent in the Philippines and 79 percent in India. Furthermore, entrepreneurs listened to 87.3 percent of the messages on average, with 84.2 percent completing the key lesson and 68.3 percent listening to the entire message. This surpassed our expectations based on past results: in the Philippines recipients listened to 83 percent of each message on average, and in India the figure was 59 percent. Beyond the initial engagement, for each lesson nearly 20 percent of entrepreneurs on average called back to listen again, with 81.7 percent of entrepreneurs using the callback feature at least once throughout the program. These results are particularly remarkable because the training was implemented at a time when the country was dealing with the effects of COVID-19, as well as the effects of political unrest, all of which (in addition to technical issues faced by our technology partner) led to interruptions in the training schedule. Preliminary results from a randomized controlled trial around the impact and effectiveness of this program show that the intervention led to a 24 percent increase in a financial practice score comprised of business practices like separating business and household expenses, calculating profits, and knowing which items are making more money and which items are incurring losses. These preliminary findings along with high engagement numbers imply that the scaling of this program was successful in Ethiopia. It also affirms our strategy for scaling this program on the path to growing businesses around the world.

Once orientation was complete, the training began. It consisted of twenty-one or twenty-two weekly lessons covering the four main thematic areas of cash separation, credit management, inventory management, and supplier management (see examples of topics covered in Table 17.1 above, and an example script in Table 17.2 above).

Iterative Training Design

Our first study in the Dominican Republic explored whether rules of thumb training could lead to improved business practices and outcomes, and the pilots in India focused on updating the curriculum, refining the delivery channel, and optimizing on other design features to improve the impact of the interventions. In the Philippines, we explored whether the curriculum developed in India was relevant to new contexts. In Ethiopia, we are testing the relevance of the training curriculum to a new region of the world, Africa, and exploring its relevance to a different profile of clients.

Table 17.2. Sample lesson from Ethiopia

Lesson:	Keep a credit notebook and each day call the customers whose credit is due.
Reminder Pre-SMS	You will receive a new message this [morning/afternoon/evening] from the WEDP Mobile Business Training. Please expect the call from XXX XXX XXX
Episode Structure	**Script**
Introduction	Hello, this is Samrawit. Welcome back to the WEDP business training program.
	Last week, my tip to you was to give credit only to customers who promise to pay you back within seven days. Today, I'm going to teach you how to make sure that the customers who you gave credit to actually pay you back within seven days.
Lesson Outcome	We are all humans – even if your neighbor Tsehaye told you that she will pay you back within seven days for the injera and sweets she bought from you last week, she might forget to do it when the time comes. Or you yourself might lose track of when Tsehaye's credit is due.
	For the seven-day credit rule to work well, you need to stay on top of when your customers' credit is due and ask them to pay back. But how can you do that?
Key Lesson	It's simple. The first step you need to take is to start using a credit notebook for your business. Right after you sell on credit to a customer, go to your notebook, and set up a page where you keep track of the credit you give to this customer. Use a separate page for each of your credit customers, writing their name on the top. Then under the name, write down the date and credit amount for that customer. All credit given to this customer should be on this same page. Once the customer pays you back the full amount of the credit they took, you can cross out that entry. But keep the page, as you will record any new credit for that same customer there.
	The next thing you do is to check the notebook each morning to find out who of your customers have their credit due on that day. Sometimes people forget, so if they haven't paid you, politely remind them to pay you back that day. To contact them, you can call them on their phone, send an employee, or reach out through one of their neighbors. When you talk to them, remind them that not getting your money back on time hurts your business. This is not about you being greedy, it is about you running your business well and being able to serve your customers well.
Comprehension Question	Let's see if you understand how to use this strategy. What will you do if your customer needs to make a purchase on credit? On your phone, press the number 1 if you would write down in your notebook how much credit you gave this customer and when it is due, and press 2 if you would only ask them to remember to pay you back as soon as they can.

If 1 => Great work, you are right! If a customer needs to make a purchase on credit, you should write down in your notebook how much credit you gave this customer and when it is due.

If 2 => Thank you for your response, but the right answer is that if a customer needs to make a purchase on credit, you should write down in your notebook how much credit you gave this customer and when it is due.

Over this next week, please spend five minutes each morning going through your credit notebook to identify who has not paid you back in seven days, and then contact them to remind them to pay you back.

Conclusion   Thank you for listening. We'll call you again next week with more tips for how to manage customer credit. If you'd like to hear this message again, please give me a call at the same number. And remember, keep listening and keep succeeding.

Summary Post-SMS   This is Samrawit. Remember to check your credit notebook each day and ask anyone who has not paid you back for a purchase within seven days to do so.

Figure 17.3. Higher engagement rates in Ethiopia suggest that the content may have become more engaging and useful to participants.

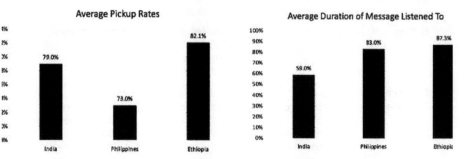

Figure 17.4. Experiment design (based on our work in India, the Philippines, and Ethiopia)[21]

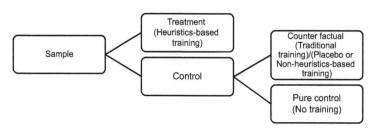

Table 17.3. Key differences in interventions

	Dominican Republic	India and the Philippines	Ethiopia
Objective	- Explore whether rule of thumb-based training works.	- Investigate relevance for new contexts, assess if mobile phone channel and improved features work. *Design changes here were based on an initial pilot conducted in India.*	- Further explore whether the mobile-based heuristics training is scalable to new regions of the world. - Explore relevance for entrepreneurs with different characteristics. - Test new training features – Interactive Voice Response (IVR), quiz. - Explore effectiveness of remote/phone-based orientation.
Sample Size	1,193	- India: 3,849 - Philippines: 2,096	6,000
Setting	Urban	- India: Urban and Peri-urban - Philippines: Urban and Rural	Urban and semi-urban
Participant Profile	Clients of the microfinance institution, ADOPEM, who expressed interest in financial education training	India: Individual business loan clients of Janalakshmi speaking Hindi/Kannada/Urdu, with access to phone, owning a retail business Philippines: Active group loan clients of the Negros Women for Tomorrow Foundation (NWTF) microfinance institution, speaking Hiligaynon, having access to mobile phone, and managing retail business	Members of the Women's Entrepreneurship Development Program – a World Bank initiative dedicated to supporting female entrepreneurs through the provision of loans and training, with access to phone, and owning a retail business

	Dominican Republic	India and the Philippines	Ethiopia
Type of Evaluation	Randomized controlled trial; baseline and endline (twelve months after intervention)	Randomized controlled trial; baseline and endline at least three months after intervention completed	Randomized controlled trial; Baseline, midline (halfway through) and endline (after ~sixteen months)
Training Features	- Classroom-based Financial Heuristics Training	- In-person orientation - Phone-based heuristics training - Professional voice actors[22] - Prescheduling feature - Callback feature	- Phone-based orientation - Phone-based heuristics training - Professional voice actors - Prescheduling feature - Call back feature - Reminder pre-lesson SMS and summary post-lesson SMS - Post-lesson quiz
Duration	forty-one weeks	twenty-two weeks (India); twenty-one weeks (Philippines)	twenty-one weeks
Delivery channel	Classroom based	Mobile phone (IVR)	Mobile phone (IVR)
Content and Narrative Style	Formal training using rules of thumb; Instructional tone	Story-like narrative using culturally relevant examples	Story-like narrative using culturally relevant examples
Trainer	Microfinance institution trainers	Professional voice actors	Professional voice actors
Tied to Loans?	Yes	Yes	No
Timing of Delivery	Not tailored to individual entrepreneurs' availability	Messages delivered at prescheduled times according to entrepreneurs' stated availability (time when they are less busy)	Messages delivered at prescheduled timing windows according to entrepreneurs' stated availability
Technology	Delivered in person by trainers	- Automated functionalities for scheduling calls - Real-time user-activity dashboard	- Automated functionalities for scheduling calls - Real-time user-activity dashboard

Table 17.4. The iterative process

	Iterative Design Steps	Actions Undertaken
1)	**Develop curriculum** (Dominican Republic)	- Identify key business principles - Distill them into simple rules of thumb - Test curriculum (classroom-based delivery)
2)	**Refine channel: add new training features** (India and the Philippines)	- Expand curriculum - Test mobile phone delivery - Use voice actors - Pre-schedule calls at time of day when entrepreneurs indicated that they would be less busy - Conduct orientation to onboard trainees - Enable and refine call back feature
3)	**Test scalability to new context with different population characteristics, partner type, onboarding process, business type and training features** (Ethiopia)	- Test the relevance of curriculum to a population with different entrepreneur profiles (education, levels, ages, business size, etc.) - Test intervention with nonmicrofinance institution partner - Test phone-based orientation - Test with new business type (service in addition to retail) - Test reminder and summary SMS messages before and after lessons, and a quiz at the end of each lesson

Reconciliation, Discussion, and Advice

Conducting this study in so many different parts of the world has given us many valuable insights about what works in the delivery of financial and business management training to small business owners. We highlight a few of these lessons below:

- **Check Assumptions about Universality and Tailor Intentionally:** The positive results that we found from testing the Financial Heuristics Training in multiple regions of the world point to two ideas: (1) that leveraging a rules of thumb-based training approach can be uniquely effective at improving business practices and outcomes, and (2) that entrepreneurs across the developing world struggle with a core set of common challenges to growing their businesses. As a result, we have been able to replicate many of the core elements of the Financial Heuristics Training across contexts.

That said, we believe that many of the features of these trainings that made them successful required a notable amount of preliminary investigation and user testing to ensure relevance and applicability, in order to drive engagement. The training modules always had to be adapted to reflect each population's local context. Business practices, resources, and terminology might differ from place to place and should be seen as equally valuable aspects of the design of the curriculum and delivery channel as is adherence to the application of behavioral tools and rigorous testing methodologies.

Sample lessons should always be initially user-tested with the target population to gauge relatability, relevance, and enjoyability so that appropriate refinements can be made based on findings. Also, keywords that describe business practices, like profit and revenues, places where money is stored, names of people and places, etc., should be run by the target audience and adapted according to what they are used to.

- **Adapt the Delivery Channel to the Population's Accessibility:** Heuristics training programs can be provided in traditional classroom-based settings or digitally if key lessons are distilled into simple, actionable rules of thumb. Each channel has its benefits and challenges. Classroom-based training provides valuable facetime for establishing rapport with participants but can be burdensome on trainers and recipients alike. IVR services, on the other hand, provide easier access to clients and are scalable, yet they rely on participants having access to phones and reliable network connections.
  - There may be differential ownership practices around mobile phones by different populations. Women may not have access to smartphones or may share a phone with other family members, which limits when and how they can be used.
  - For any SMS-related feature enhancements, participants need to have basic literacy skills to engage in any SMS-based interventions like quizzes or reminders.
  - Civil unrests, inadequate infrastructure, limited tech capacities, or high airtime costs can affect the delivery or affordability of digital training programs. These factors must be considered and adequately prepared for when planning digital training interventions.

- **Don't Run a Rigorous Evaluation on a Poorly Designed Intervention:** Even when we feel that certain design features might be effective at improving outcomes across contexts, it is important to pilot or test these assumptions before scaling to large audiences. Testing can be complex and rigorous, or simple and rapid. For example, qualitative interviews can be conducted to understand the wants, needs, and constraints of the target audience. Also, early prototypes can be user-tested to collect feedback on demand, interest, and relevance. Such data is critical to ensuring that when a program is eventually scaled, the likelihood of success is high. Even if certain designs and interventions have been proven to work in similar contexts, we recommend testing and piloting in each new context, as there may be hidden idiosyncrasies to a place that may not be obvious until further investigation is done. For example, our technology partner in Ethiopia strongly recommended that we include comprehension questions in our intervention to test retention of key lesson takeaways. They had successfully used this feature in multiple countries across Sub-Saharan Africa. However, we found that although this feature had worked in other contexts, engagement with it was very low in Ethiopia. Most listeners dropped off the call without waiting to answer the comprehension question. Testing new features will save program implementers from investing resources into designs that do not work.
- **Be Flexible in Your Approach while Maintaining a Feedback Loop with Recipients:** In Ethiopia, the COVID-19 pandemic significantly changed our approach for tailoring training to a new context. Typically, our team of behavioral experts would have spent time in Ethiopia to conduct in-person interviews with entrepreneurs and observe the contexts in which they live and work. Travel restrictions caused us to adapt to a completely phone-based process for exploring the Ethiopian context and adapting the curriculum to suit the target audience. We hired a local consultant who helped us understand the context better and conducted all interviews in a culturally appropriate manner. We also relied on our local partners at the World Bank to share previously collected data and insights on the populations. To account for the lack of in-person time, we did an extra round of user testing and ran a small pilot on the tailored program before launching to the full population, enabling us to gain multiple rounds of feedback and helping us to identify issues during larger implementation efforts. Being flexible with these constraints enabled us to successfully adapt and implement the training, completely remotely.

- **Communicate Proactively to Build Trust and Maintain Engagement:** Beyond the pandemic, we experienced frequent network disruptions, and sometimes politically related interruptions (e.g., elections, protests) to the phone network in Ethiopia. These issues led to delays and disruptions to program delivery. Sometimes, participants did not receive calls at the expected time or on the expected day. However, by communicating proactively and providing open lines of communication to participants, engagement was not hurt too badly. Having a contingency plan and responding in a timely manner were also critical to gaining and maintaining the trust of participants. For example, due to anticipated disruptions to the phone network during elections, we paused the delivery of messages for a week. Right after elections, we sent SMSs to apologize for the disruptions and inform participants about when to expect the next message. Setting expectations proactively where disruptions could be anticipated and responding promptly where disruptions could not be anticipated or mitigated helped manage frustration with changes in the program schedule.

Recommendations for Future Work

Even though the Financial Heuristics Training has worked in multiple contexts, there are still many opportunities for further program expansion and testing:

- **Expanding the Heuristics Training Model to Other Topics:** The current training curriculum focuses on four key business practices – cash separation, inventory management, credit management, and supplier management. However, entrepreneurs and financial service providers alike have asked for training on new topics such as savings, debt management, investment, digitization, customer management, etc. Further research and funding will be needed to understand whether a heuristics-based approach will lead to similarly positive outcomes for such topics.
- **Expanding the Financial Heuristics Training to Other Populations:** Our studies so far have focused mainly on retail businesses and businesses that are on the smaller end of the Small and Medium-Sized Enterprise (SME) spectrum. We have done some preliminary exploration to determine which of the current lessons could be applied to different business types, but we believe that there would be benefits in developing new heuristics-based content

for other business types, sizes, and geographies. For example, a curriculum tailored to the needs of larger businesses, in partnership with potential lenders, could help to close information and financing gaps.

- **Expanding the Interactivity of the Training:** The Interactive Voice Response-based Financial Heuristics Training, in its current form, does not allow for much interaction by training participants with one another or with trainers. Apart from the initial orientation that they receive, an ability to call back in to review old lessons, and access to a call center to report complaints, participants are limited to receiving and responding to automated messages. It would be interesting to explore more interactive components of the training where participants can share insights and comments and learn more from each other and the program implementers. For example, groups could be created on messaging platforms such as WhatsApp and Telegram, or other social media applications like Facebook to share local insights, or to provide reminders or social proof of applying lessons learned from the training. Further tests are necessary to understand whether such features would be used, and whether they would positively impact entrepreneur outcomes.

- **Exploring funding options for scaling the training further:** We have explored the possibility of partnering with various organizations to develop curricula for many of these topics and have been surprised and encouraged by the amount of incoming demand. However, adapting, translating, and expanding the curriculum to new populations requires a sizable financial investment that may be challenging for a single financial service provider to cover. We are currently exploring more lean scaling strategies while evaluating our options for funding. We are also considering the possibility of turning the Financial Heuristics Training into a stand-alone business venture.

Simple, actionable information improves recall and applicability of key lessons, and delivering these sessions digitally at participants' preferred time improves the likelihood of participation and engagement, especially for busy business owners. The Financial Heuristics Training holds significant promise as a scalable solution for helping owners of small- and medium-sized businesses to learn and adopt critical skills for running their enterprises. Better business management skills will help people build flourishing businesses, leading to greater employment opportunities and stronger economies. Ultimately, these benefits will produce improvements in the quality of life of people across the world, especially in emerging economies where the majority of small businesses can be found.

NOTES

1 World Bank. (n.d.). *Small and Medium Enterprises (SMEs) finance*. Understanding Poverty. https://www.worldbank.org/en/topic/smefinance.
2 World Bank (n.d.).
3 Fernandes, D., Lynch, J.G., & Netemeyer, R.G. (2014). Financial literacy, financial education, and downstream financial behaviors. *Management Science, 60*(8), 1861–83. https://doi.org/10.1287/mnsc.2013.1849.
4 McKenzie, D., & Woodruff, C. (2014). What are we learning from business training and entrepreneurship evaluations around the developing world? *The World Bank Research Observer, 29*(1), 48–82. https://doi.org/10.1093/wbro/lkt007.
5 McKenzie, D. (2022). *Do financial literacy interventions actually work better than I think they do? (And thoughts about meta-analyses)*. World Bank Blogs. https://blogs.worldbank.org/impactevaluations/do-financial-literacy-interventions-actually-work-better-i-think-they-do-and.
6 McKenzie, D. (2020). *Small business training to improve management practices in developing countries: Reassessing the evidence for "training doesn't work."* Policy Research Working Paper 9408. World Bank Group. https://documents1.worldbank.org/curated/en/593081600709463800/pdf/Small-Business-Training-to-Improve-Management-Practices-in-Developing-Countries-Reassessing-the-Evidence-for-Training-Doesn-t-Work.pdf.
7 McKenzie & Woodruff (2014).
8 Kaiser, T., Lusardi, A., Menkhoff, L., & Urban, C.J. (2020). *Financial education affects financial knowledge and downstream behaviors*. Working Paper No. 27057. https://www.nber.org/system/files/working_papers/w27057/w27057.pdf.
9 Fernandes et al. (2014).
10 McKenzie (2020).
11 Beshears, J., Choi, J.J., Laibson, D., & Madrian, B.C. (2013). Simplification and saving. *Journal of Economic Behavior & Organization, 95*, 130–45. https://doi.org/10.1016/j.jebo.2012.03.007.
12 Mullainathan, S., & Shafir, E. (2009). Savings policy and decisionmaking in low-income households. In R.M. Blank & M.S. Barr (Eds.), *Insufficient funds: Savings, assets, credit, and banking among low-income households* (pp. 121–45). Russell Sage Foundation.

13 Mata, J., Todd, P.M., & Lippke, S. (2010). When weight management lasts. Lower perceived rule complexity increases adherence. *Appetite, 54*(1), 37–43. https://doi.org/10.1016/j.appet.2009.09.004.

14 Bettinger, E.P., Long, B., Oreopoulos, P., & Sanbonmatsu, L. (2012). The role of application assistance and information in college decisions: Results from the H&R Block FAFSA experiment. *Quarterly Journal of Economics, 127*(3), 1205–42. https://doi.org/10.1093/qje/qjs017.

15 Kahneman, D. (2013). *Thinking, Fast and Slow* (1st ed.). Farrar, Straus and Giroux.

16 Townsend, C., & Shu, S.B. (2010). When and how aesthetics influences financial decisions. *Journal of Consumer Psychology, 20*(4), 452–8. https://doi.org/10.1016/j.jcps.2010.06.013.

17 Bettinger et al. (2012).

18 Drexler, A., Fischer, G., & Schoar, A. (2014). Keeping it simple: Financial literacy and rules of thumb. *American Economic Journal: Applied Economics, 6*(2), 1–31. https://doi.org/10.1257/app.6.2.1.

19 The initial pilot in India was conducted in partnership with the Institute for Financial Management and Research (IFMR LEAD).

20 He, L., Han, W., & Shi, Z. (2021). Self-reference effect induced by self-cues presented during retrieval. *Frontiers in Psychology, 12*(562359). https://www.frontiersin.org/articles/10.3389/fpsyg.2021.562359.

21 The placebo/non-heuristics-based training control group was only included in the study in Ethiopia. In India and the Philippines, we only tested a pure control group which did not receive any training.

22 Professional voice actors were not used in the initial pilot in India but were used in the subsequent interventions in India and the Philippines based on lessons from the initial work in India.

Lessons Learned and the Way Forward

Dilip Soman

Each chapter in this volume is an instance of practitioners taking an intervention that has been demonstrated to be efficacious in the lab or in a pilot and translating and scaling it into an applied field setting. As the reader would have noticed, the scope of translation and scaling increased from chapter 1 to chapter 17. For instance, chapters 1 and 2 represented a simple translation attempt where the researcher took an intervention that had been successfully tested in the lab and used it in a field setting. Chapter 3 provided an example of a slightly more complex translation setting. Here the researchers took interventions from prior studies, but rather than simply replicating them as they were, they adapted them to suit the needs of the field study. Later on in chapter 12, we read not just about translation but also scaling (i.e., applying the intervention to sample sizes that were significantly larger than the original settings). We next saw instances of horizontal scaling (taking an intervention that has been successfully implemented in one domain and applying it to a new one). Finally, in chapter 17, we saw a situation that involved replication, translation, and iterative scaling across multiple countries.

Each chapter not only described the interventions and showcased their results but also provided rationale on why they chose the interventions that they did, and more importantly what lessons they learned as a result of conducting the field translation or scaling. This epilogue attempts to summarize some of the lessons learned into a checklist of principles for practitioners as they attempt to use behavioral science for welfare or business impact.

One major lesson from these cases is the importance of providing real-world evidence to inform policy, welfare programs, going-to-market approaches, and management practices. I have often been in situations where practitioners are tempted to simply use interventions tested only in the lab. As the chapters in this book illustrate, this can be a costly mistake. Given the fact that behavioral results are typically not portable due to changes in situation as well as heterogeneity in how respondents react to our interventions, a result that might appear robust in the laboratory (or a given field setting) might end up appearing quite fragile in the field (in a different setting). As Sah (chapter 1) emphasizes, it is critically important to have some evidence from field demonstrations before making any changes to practice.

The Laboratory Is a Sterile Environment

The setup and operation of behavioral labs usually dictates how interventions are delivered, when they are delivered, how many times they are delivered, and the incentives that respondents have in responding to them. For instance, most behavioral laboratories have a participant pool drawn from a student population from the university in which it is housed. By definition this is often a very homogeneous participant pool, and it might be difficult to detect heterogeneous treatment effects. Likewise, many behavior laboratories are set up as a series of cubicles with a computer terminal at which participants are seated and respond to questions. This setup usually dictates how stimuli are generated and how interventions are delivered. Researchers design studies that can be administered using the setup rather than designing studies that attempt to mimic what happens in the real world.[1] Similarly, laboratories might incentivize participants by offering cash compensation or course credit. This influences the attention that participants pay to the task. There is also no distraction for participants – no internet, no TV shows, no smartphones, no children, and no other tasks that people usually encounter in life while making decisions. Finally, most laboratory experiments are run in sessions of thirty to sixty minutes, at the end of which the experimental world "comes to a close." This limits the number of times that any interventions that can be delivered. Indeed, in many laboratory studies, interventions are delivered typically just once, and the short-term effects are captured while the participant is still in the lab. Therefore, as Singh and Wendel (chapter 6) emphasize, we need to be extremely careful to not overgeneralize from the lab to the field, and indeed from one field setting to another one.

Ten Principles for Translation and Scaling

The learnings across the seventeen chapters can be condensed into a series of ten prescriptive principles, as well as four broader ideas for the field going forward.

Principle 1: Do a careful and thorough analysis of the situation. As was evident across all chapters, practitioners need to better understand the situation in which the intervention would be delivered, the situation in which the target behavior happens, and the situation facing the respondent. In understanding the situation, it is important to figure out who the different actors are. What does their day look like? What other competing activities might they be engaged in? What are the considerations that might drive their decision-making? Are there other social influences in the environment that might change the effectiveness of the intervention? An analysis of the situation and of variations that might happen in the situation would allow the choice architect to make decisions about how a message should be delivered, when it should be delivered, and how many times. Whether it be an intervention to improve the conservation of heating energy in buildings (chapter 5) or an intervention to reduce the over-prescription of antibiotics by physicians (chapter 12), a contextual analysis is critically important and perhaps the starting point for the translation process. As O'Flaherty et al. (chapter 7) and Aryee et al. (chapter 17) emphasize, it is important not just to do an analysis of the situation and be "done with it," but to also keep the proverbial "ear to the ground" so as to be aware of any changes in the situation.

Principle 2: Adapt your delivery channels to suit the context. The delivery of interventions in the laboratory is dictated (constrained) by the medium available in the laboratory (i.e., a computer). It is now critical for the practitioner to determine which channel to use and decide how best to adapt the intervention in order to get the same traction in the field.[2] In chapter 3, the message had to be adapted for delivery on a smartphone as opposed to a paper and pencil intervention. O'Flaherty et al. (chapter 7) also emphasized the importance of having the right medium and the right format of the message. Pe'er (chapter 9) acknowledged that implementation details were key, while Robitaille et al. (chapter 13) acknowledged that the design of the message was key in ensuring the success. Likewise, Saulītis (chapter 15) reported that reminders had to be adapted to better suit the context after an analysis of what worked and what didn't. In particular, both for encouraging the take up of COVID-19 vaccinations and for reducing student absenteeism in schools (chapter 16), generic messages did not work very well, but personalized messages had a significant effect. Recipients of messages were clearly dealing with other issues in life, and hence the messages needed to attract more attention than a generic message would usually get.

Principle 3: Analyze heterogeneous treatment effects. In many behavioral experiments, we often compare two (or more) conditions – a controlled condition in which no intervention is delivered and a treatment condition(s) in which it is. We often deem an intervention to be a success if on average, people in the treatment condition respond more favorably than in the control condition. However, as we have argued elsewhere, the average response in the treatment condition could actually mask heterogeneous treatment effects.[3] In some of the chapters in this book, this principle was clear. In chapter 4, for example, gamification worked on average to improve savings, but it did so more for people who were inherently playful relative to those that were not. Likewise, chapter 9 emphasizes the importance of understanding heterogeneous treatment effects because they allow us to potentially customize interventions. Successfully scaled interventions need not be homogenous.[4]

Principle 4: Go beyond the end user . Much of the published research in the behavioral sciences focuses on changing the behavior of the end user. This makes sense – after all, a lab experiment usually involves a researcher delivering an intervention to a participant (end user) with no intermediary agents. However, the chapters in this volume show that sometimes it is equally important (perhaps if not more) to influence the behavior of other agents in the system while translating. For example, Hahnel et al. (chapter 5) show that success in improving the conservation of heating energy in buildings was contingent on changing the behavior of professional heating technicians. While analyzing the context and situation (*Principle 1*), it is equally important to think through different actors in the system and to determine the role that each one of them might play in influencing the behavior of the end user.

Principle 5: Go beyond psychology. While most published laboratory interventions are psychological in nature (i.e., they employ theories and phenomena from psychology to help change individuals' behavior), it is often critically important to also focus on improvements in processes or practices that are not psychological in nature in order to enable the success of interventions. As an example, the ability of the practitioner to reduce fair evasion in Santiago Public Transit was enhanced by an improvement in the payment process itself. Likewise, the importance of adaptation of processes was highlighted in the example of reducing prejudice against immigrants and in encouraging female entrepreneurs in the global south.

Principle 6: Not all interventions scale equally. As Kim and Soman (chapter 3) suggest, attention and engagement with the intervention and stimulus are often guaranteed in the lab because of the nature of the operations of behavioral labs and the incentives for participants to be there. As a result, interventions that require a great deal of attention and engagement to potentially change cognitive processes might be successful in the lab. These same interventions might not translate well to the field with individuals who have limited attention. On the other hand, interventions that are more perceptual in nature might have a better shot at succeeding in the field. Therefore, I encourage practitioners to ask themselves the following question – does the nature of my intervention require the same level of attention/engagement that is typically available in the lab? If yes, is it possible for me to recreate that same level of attention/engagement in the field? If not, it is likely that the intervention will not translate successfully in the field. Therefore, it might be incumbent on the practitioner to create the mechanisms for generating attention.

Principle 7: Track data over time. As discussed earlier, laboratory studies usually involve a short span of time. In chapter 3, we learned that there was a lot of heterogeneity across the eight weeks of the study in terms of how people responded to behaviorally informed reminders. Is it possible that interventions work initially but then that effectiveness declines over time? Is it also possible that interventions do not work at the beginning but increase in effectiveness over time? Unless we continue to measure and track outcome variables as a function of time, we will not have the answers to questions like these. It is therefore important for the practitioner to ensure that data is collected over a period of time. This point was driven home by Robitaille et al. (chapter 13) when they advocated for the importance of tracking outcome variables over an extended period of time.

Principle 8: The best interventions needn't be the ones that are delivered just once. Rogers and Feller (chapter 16) suggest that the important ingredient for the success of their interventions was the fact that they could deliver regular, repeated interventions rather than a one-off intervention. Unlike the lab, the field allows for the delivery of repeated and frequent interventions. Robitaille et al. specifically take this opportunity to test the effects of repeating an intervention across time. In the same vein, I advocate that when testing for the efficacy of the intervention, practitioners also test the effectiveness of repeating the same intervention over time, as well as the effects of changing the length of time between the delivery of the intervention as a function of the kind of behavior change that is sought.

Principle 9: Multiple interventions. The field also allows the practitioner to take interventions from different studies and different theories/phenomena and to use them simultaneously in the field. This can take many forms. For example, in chapter 3, Kim and Soman built an intervention entirely anew but based on the nature of interventions from multiple laboratory studies. Robitaille et al. (chapter 13) caution against a kitchen sink approach in which multiple interventions are offered simultaneously (perhaps a situation in which the control condition has no intervention, and the treatment condition has multiple interventions). In situations like these, it is impossible to determine which of the interventions, if any, had a positive effect. Alternatively, it is also possible that while each of interventions on their own might be efficacious, their interaction effects might conspire to reduce the overall efficacy. Conway et al. (chapter 8) also advocate for using multiple interventions – but not simultaneously. These authors advocate for a "horse racing approach" in which different interventions are pitted against each other in different arms of a randomized trial to determine which might be the most efficacious under a given context. This approach is important. In much of our research, we focus on one intervention at a given point in time, but our research is unable to answer questions such as "which one of these two interventions should be prioritized?"

Principle 10: Avoid solution-mindedness. Oftentimes, organizations are enamored by a particular solution that they believe might be the best way to translate and scale an intervention. This might occur if the organization has invested resources in developing that form of solution, or if a similar solution has worked elsewhere in the organization. Kim and Soman (chapter 3) lamented the fact that they were too solution minded – they had determined that a smartphone app was the best way to deliver an intervention, and hence their design efforts were dictated by the capability of the delivery mechanism (much like how the intervention in the lab is dictated by the "computer in a cubicle" delivery mechanism). This constrained their thinking and narrowed it down to quickly eliminate solutions that did not fit the delivery mechanism. They caution against solution mindedness and advocate the discipline of a thorough behavioral diagnosis before even thinking of solutions. This point that is echoed by several other authors.

Looking Forward: Best Practices and New Initiatives for the Field

I next spotlight four initiatives that the authors of this volume have collectively suggested for improving translation and scaling in our field going forward.

Initiative 1: The need for implementation science. Hsieh et al. (chapter 14) write that the field of medical sciences has developed a companion science called implementation science and call for an equivalent in behavioral science. This is a science that relates to how learnings from the laboratory and from clinical trials can best be used in practice. In essence, it calls for the adaptation of interventions to the local context even while maintaining causal relationships. This science prescribes how an analysis of the context/situation can be done. It also prescribes ways in which reporting of lab results can be standardized for practitioners to best understand them at a glance. This is a practice that we have employed in this book. Other commentators have also called for developing a science of using behavioral science.[5] This is definitely something that our field needs to establish and develop for successful translation and scaling.

Initiative 2: Triangulation. Haris Khan et al. (chapter 11) believe that there is a lot of value in triangulating research approaches. Triangulation involves the use of multiple methods, multiple samples, and multiple approaches for data collection as well as for intervention design to assess the generalizability of findings. The term triangulation is borrowed from civil engineering techniques to survey land or to determine navigation routes that determine a single point in space with the convergence of measurements taken from two other distinct points.[6] I encourage all practitioners to adopt the notion of triangulation and to design multiple field studies to assess the robustness of the intervention that they are hoping to scale.

Initiative 3 : Preregistration and piloting. Whillans (chapter 2) writes about her experiences with piloting and preregistering studies. The discipline associated with running a pilot trial, doing the due diligence in the field, then preregistering a field study (identifying the process and the analysis plan for the study prior to even collecting the data) imposes discipline on practitioners to identify the underlying causal mechanism that they were hoping to test. I hope that our field can make preregistration a habit and indeed the norm going forward. The added benefit of preregistration is that it encourages and celebrates null results. This is because interventions that we believe to be a success end up not being so, and as a result, we have learned about something in the situation as a consequence.

Initiative 4: An iterative process. Singh and Wendel (chapter 6) advocate for an iterative process of translating results from the lab to the field. This process includes the steps of gathering the literature and synthesizing it, using iterative fieldwork to locate the interventions in the context of the field, using a hybrid of laboratory and field studies to generate evidence and whittle away non-portable findings, using a larger scale field replication of robust effects, and using ongoing measurements and testing. The road map provided by these authors is an excellent path for all future translators and scalers of behavioral results to follow.

Translation and scaling is not easy. As a field, we could easily become slave to the belief that our results are not portable, and that the success of interventions is akin to a lottery. However, with some of the lessons learned in this volume, the prescriptive advice, principles, and initiatives that the contributors encourage our field to adopt, translation and scaling will hopefully become more of a science and less of a lottery going forward.

NOTES

1 Note that in translating a lab study into the field, the practitioner needs to make a number of decisions about the mechanics of the translation process. For instance, when (what time) should the intervention be delivered? What medium should be used to deliver it? What should the content and nature of any relevant message be? To whom should it be delivered and under what circumstance? Should the intervention be delivered just once or repeatedly?

2 See also Wu, S.J., & Paluck, E.L. (2021). Designing nudges for the context: Golden coin decals nudge workplace behavior in China. *Organizational Behavior and Human Decision Processes, 163*, 43–50. https://doi.org/10.1016/j.obhdp.2018.10.002

3 See Mažar, N. & Soman, D. (Eds.). (2022). *Behavioral science in the wild*. University of Toronto Press; and Soman, D., & Hossain, T. (2020). *Successfully scaled solutions need not be homogenous* (SSRN Scholarly Paper No. 3624305). https://doi.org/10.2139/ssrn.3624305.

4 Soman & Hossain (2020).

5 See Mažar & Soman (2022); List, J.A. (2022). *The voltage effect: How to make good ideas great and great ideas scale*. Currency.

6 Rothbauer, P. (2008). "Triangulation." In L. Given (Ed.), *The SAGE encyclopedia of qualitative research methods* (pp. 892–4). Sage Publications.

Contributors

Lois Aryee is a senior behavioral designer at ideas42. Her work focuses on the design and implementation of behavioral interventions aimed at boosting financial inclusion, social protection, and health outcomes across Sub-Saharan Africa and the USA. Lois holds an MPA from New York University and a BA in Economics from DePauw University. Prior to enrolling at NYU, she worked as an evaluation coordinator for Innovations for Poverty Action (IPA) where she helped run a randomized control trial that studied the effectiveness of a government-run apprenticeship program aimed at enhancing the employment opportunities of Ghanaian youth.

Tobias Brosch holds the chair for Sustainability Psychology at the University of Geneva. His research is focused on understanding how emotions, values, heuristics, and automatic affective processes help us understand our complex environment and influence our choices, and how this knowledge can be used to promote sustainable decisions and behaviors. He is an associate editor for the *Journal of Cognition and Emotion* and a member of the editorial advisory board of the *Journal of Environmental Psychology*.

Juan Camilo Salcedo is regional director LATAM at BEworks, where he is responsible for business development and project execution in Latin America. He has degrees in business administration (BSBA) and psychology (PhD). His research is in the area of costly signaling theory and moral reasoning. In his spare time, Juan enjoys running, traveling, and cooking.

Lauryn Conway (PhD, University of Toronto) is the senior lead of behavioral science at Impact Canada, housed centrally at the head of the Canadian Federal Public Service within the Privy Council Office. In this role, she oversees the design and execution of multiyear programs of research that seek to apply and integrate insights and methodologies from the behavioral sciences to high-priority policy areas for the Government of Canada. Previously, Lauryn was a behavioral science fellow at the Public Health Agency of Canada, working on chronic disease prevention and health equity. She enjoys espresso, historical fiction, and super long walks.

Tessa Dent Ferrel is a lecturer in organizational psychology and sustainability at the University of Geneva. Her work focuses on how leadership development, employee motivation, and organizational culture can influence sustainability within organizations and how they can be leveraged to drive transformation. She is also the head of learning and development within a Swiss private company.

Manasee Desai is a vice president at ideas42, where she co-leads the organization's financial health work, which applies tools from behavioral science to the design of financial products and programs for underserved and underrepresented populations. Over the past seventeen years, she has advised a variety of banks, fintechs, governments, nonprofits, and insurance companies in the US, Africa, and Asia on behavioral and data-driven strategies for product refinement and growth. She has also conducted research on financial inclusion, entrepreneurship, and gender equity with academics at Harvard, MIT, and Yale. Manasee founded and leads the Behavioral Evidence Hub (Bhub.org), which serves as a global repository of proven applications of behavioral design tools to improving social impact outcomes. She is a lead author on multiple ideas42 publications relating to the application of behavioral science to financial services and gender equity. She has a BA in political science from Boston University and an MPA in international development policy and management from New York University.

Nicholas B. Diamond (PhD, University of Toronto) is a behavioral science fellow in the Impact and Innovation Unit (IIU) housed centrally at the head of the Canadian Federal Public Service within the Privy Council Office. He works on misinformation and related topics (e.g., trust and social media behavior), including survey and experiment design and data analysis, in the context of the IIU's longitudinal program of behavioral research on COVID-19. Previously, Nicholas was a postdoctoral fellow at the University of Pennsylvania, doing cognitive neuroscience research on human memory. He enjoys hiking and bagels.

Nicholas Faulkner (PhD, Monash) is an adjunct senior research fellow in applied behavioral science at Monash University, and senior data translator at the Victorian Department of Families, Fairness, and Housing. His research interests involve using methods from the applied behavioral sciences (social and political psychology, political science) to build more fair, inclusive, healthy, and sustainable societies. His work has been published in leading social, political, health, and multidisciplinary science journals.

Avi Feller is an associate professor at the University of California, Berkeley, where he works at the interface of statistics and data science and the social sciences. His research focuses on developing practical, transparent methods that can be applied at scale, and on deploying these tools in a range of policy domains, with a particular emphasis on education and criminal justice. Avi is a cofounder and equity holder at Everyday Labs. He received his PhD in statistics from Harvard.

Alex Gyani is the director of the Behavioural Insights Team's Australian office. Since joining the team in 2012, he has worked in a diverse set of fields, including antimicrobial resistance, domestic violence, mental health policy, energy usage, health system efficiency, obesity, financial regulation, employment services, and education. His PhD focused on encouraging people with anxiety and depression to seek treatment using a mobile phone app and encouraging psychological therapists to use evidence-based treatments. In 2018, he was named one of Apolitical's 100 Future Government Leaders. He holds a research fellowship at the University of Melbourne's School of Psychology.

Ulf J.J. Hahnel is a professor for psychology of sustainability and behavior change at the Faculty of Psychology of the University of Basel, Switzerland. He investigates human judgment and decision-making and the underlying cognitive and affective mechanisms in the context of global climate change and the energy transition. His research moreover aims to develop evidence-based behavioral interventions to promote more sustainable behavior. He is leading several international projects on these topics and is a member of the editorial advisory board of the *Journal of Environmental Psychology*.

Michael Hallsworth, PhD, is managing director (Americas) at the Behavioural Insights Team, where he has worked since its origins as the "nudge unit" of the UK government. Michael has been a leading figure in developing the field of applying behavioral science to government and coauthored the book *Behavioral Insights* (MIT Press, 2020). He has been an assistant professor (adjunct) at Columbia University and is a member of the editorial board of the *Journal Behavioural Public Policy*.

Elizabeth Hardy is the senior director of research and experimentation in the Office of the Chief Human Resources Officer, Treasury Board Secretariat, Government of Canada, responsible for leading research initiatives to improve people management outcomes. Previously, she was senior lead, behavioral science, at the Impact and Innovation Unit at the Privy Council Office, where she oversaw the application of behavioral science to public policy challenges. During her time working for the Government of Ontario, she led the Behavioural Insights Unit, where she was instrumental in creating and building Canada's first behavioral science team in government.

Nethal Hashim is a fellow in marketing at Bayes Business School, City, University of London. He holds a PhD in management from Bayes Business School. Nethal's research investigates the impact that gamification can have on consumer decision-making and motivation.

Julian House (PhD, Toronto) is a scientist in the Ontario government's Behavioural Insights Unit (BIU). He also teaches behavioral economics and marketing at the University of Toronto's Rotman School of Management, where he is a research fellow. His research into how behavioral science can be applied to advance public policy and social welfare aims appears in top academic journals, including the *Proceedings of the National Academy of Sciences and Management Science*. His favorite way to pass the long Canadian winter is with friends and family gathered around an ever-expanding collection of board games.

Wing Hsieh (PhD, Monash) is director, health, human services and behavioural economics at Deloitte Access Economics. She has a PhD in behavior change from Monash University for a thesis titled "Reducing prejudice in the real world – what works, what scales" and an LLM focused on behavioral law and economics from Harvard University. Her work and research interests center on helping public and private organizations to apply behavioral sciences to achieve positive social impact.

Mukta Joshi is a principal behavioral designer at ideas42, where she manages projects in the cash transfers domain and ideas42 Academy to enhance ideas42's capacity-building efforts at scale. A development economist by training, Mukta has over ten years of experience in leading projects across multiple disciplines (development finance, private sector development, and behavioral design) and geographies (Africa, Asia, and the Americas). Before joining ideas42, Mukta worked with the World Bank and International Finance Corporation (IFC) in Washington, DC. Mukta holds a PhD in development economics from the Ohio State University and a bachelor's and master's in economics from Mumbai University.

Haris Khan is a behavioral insights and policy lead in the Research and Experimentation Team in the Office of the Chief Human Resources Officer at the Government of Canada's Treasury Board Secretariat. In his current position, he leads research projects that apply evidence-based policy development techniques to the federal public service's people management agenda. He has previously worked in behavioral insights, innovation, and research at the Government of Canada's Privy Council Office and in the United Arab Emirates. He holds an honours bachelor of arts in economics and a master of public policy, both from the University of Toronto.

Joonkyung Kim (PhD, University of Toronto) is a data analyst at the *Globe and Mail*. Joonkyung has experience in data visualization, machine learning, and big data processing. Previously, she served as a visiting assistant professor at Tulane University and has been published in marketing journals.

Wardah Malik is the CEO of BEworks, the world's first consulting company dedicated to the application of behavioral science to real-world challenges. She joined the company as a founding team member and has since helped leaders develop innovative solutions in health, wealth, sustainability, and organizational behavior. She is passionate about charting a new path for the future of behavioral science, focused on multidisciplinary partnerships that bring powerful solutions to life. Prior to joining BEworks, Wardah worked for LoyaltyOne (Air Miles), where she specialized in conducting behaviorally informed consumer research to inform strategic corporate decisions.

Nina Mažar (Dr. rer. pol., University of Mainz) is a professor of marketing at Boston University's Questrom School of Business, and cofounder of

BEworks. With her focus on behavioral science, she examines ways to help individuals and organizations make better decisions and increase societal welfare. When not working, Nina enjoys randomly bursting into song and staging impromptu musicals with her daughter.

Christian Mumenthaler is an assistant professor in the Department of Information Science at the Geneva School of Business Administration of the University of Applied Sciences and Arts Western Switzerland. His research is at the intersection between computational and behavioral science, focused on exploiting new and emerging digital data sources, combined with an experimental approach to translating data into tangible actions.

Shibeal O' Flaherty is a PhD candidate in public policy at King's College London, an associate fellow at the Office of Evaluation Sciences, and a research fellow at Harvard Kennedy School. Her research focuses on behavioral science and public-sector employee well-being. She previously worked as a research associate at What Works for Children's Social Care (2019–22), and as a program manager at the Harvard Business Insights Group (2017–18). She received her MRes management at University College London (2019), and MA psychology at the University of Aberdeen (2015).

Shannon O'Malley is the head of client experience at BEworks, where she helps clients apply behavioral science by creating engaging and informative content through workshops, speaking events, reports, and other outlets. An experienced practitioner, she has led numerous complex and impactful behavior change initiatives in financial services, transit, marketing, and beyond. Prior to BEworks, Shannon earned her PhD in cognitive psychology at the University of Waterloo, where she studied the role of attention and visual processing, and has published her academic work in several top-tier scientific journals.

Meera Paleja (PhD, Toronto Metropolitan University) is program head of investor research and behavioral insights at the Ontario Securities Commission, leading the Commission's innovative investor research and behavioral insights portfolio, the first of its kind for a securities regulator in Canada. She is a sessional lecturer at Rotman School of Management, teaching MBA courses in behavioral economics. Dr. Paleja led early work in behavioral insights in the federal government including at the Public Health Agency of Canada, Privy Council Office, and Treasury Board of Canada, as well as in the Ontario government and in a management consultancy. She holds a postdoctoral fellowship and doctorate in cognitive neuroscience.

Eyal Pe'er is an associate professor at the Federmann School of Public Policy and Governance, Hebrew University of Jerusalem, Israel. His research focuses on the psychology of judgment and decision-making and its applications to behavioral public policy in domains such as consumer protection, energy consumption, pro-environmental behavior, and compliance. In his spare time, he likes to play beach volleyball and the drums (when his family is out of the house).

Kelly Peters is a renowned behavioral scientist, innovation expert, and entrepreneur. She cofounded BEworks in 2010 with esteemed academics Dan Ariely and Nina Mažar. She pioneered the BEworks Method to build a bridge between cutting-edge science and real-world application. The Method has been applied to over three hundred projects in the financial services, energy, healthcare, retail, and sustainability domains. She led the sale of the company to kyu in 2017, a Japanese-owned creative services firm. She served as the firm's CEO until 2022. Her new venture, Trial Run, is dedicated to solving sustainability challenges with the science of behavior and the power of blockchain technology.

David A. Pizarro is a professor from Cornell University, and chief science officer at BEworks. David is renowned for his work in understanding the impact of emotions on decision-making, particularly the impact the emotion of disgust has on moral judgments. He is also interested in the influence of emotional states on thinking and deciding – more specifically on how emotions (anger, disgust, fear, etc.) impact how people process information, how they remember events, and how these emotions impact their judgments of others. David is a featured TED Talk presenter and hosts a podcast on the nature of human morality called Very Bad Wizards.

Nicole Robitaille is an assistant professor of marketing at the Smith School of Business, Queen's University. Her research broadly studies how to apply behavioral science to improve consumer welfare, marketing, and public policy. Her work has been published in journals such as the *Journal of Marketing, Management Science*, and the *Harvard Business Review*. In addition to her academic work, Nicole has worked as an adviser to the Government of Canada's and the Ontario Government's Behavioural Insights Units. Her work on increasing organ donation with the Ontario government was honored as an H. Paul Root Award Finalist.

Olga E. Rodriguez-Sierra is a director of behavioral science at Innovative Research Group. She received a BSc in psychology from the National University of Mexico and a PhD in neural and behavioral sciences from Rutgers University. Her doctoral thesis focused on how emotions affect decision-making and brain function. Her work has spanned the USA, Mexico, Canada, Brazil, and Germany, where she has collaborated with interdisciplinary teams and led projects in the private and public sectors. In her spare time, Olga enjoys reading novels, learning about different cultures, and being outside in nature.

Todd Rogers is a professor of public policy at the Harvard Kennedy School of Government. He is senior scientist at ideas42, and academic advisor at the Behavioural Insights Team. Todd cofounded two social enterprises. First is the Analyst Institute, which uses data and behavioral science to improve voter communications. He serves on Analyst Institute's board. Second is EveryDay Labs, which partners with school districts to reduce student absenteeism. He is chief scientist (unpaid), cofounder, and equity holder at Everyday Labs. Todd received his PhD jointly from Harvard's Department of Psychology and Harvard Business School.

Renante Rondina is a behavioral scientist in the Office of Chief Human Resources Officer, Treasury Board of Canada Secretariat, where he leads projects on hybrid work experimentation and digital skills strategy transformation. Previously, he was a postdoctoral fellow at BEAR and Western University, where he studied the ethics of choice architecture, the application of behavioral insights in mental health initiatives, and the cost-effectiveness of financial health incentives in a smartphone application. He completed his PhD in cognitive neuroscience at the University of Toronto and the Rotman Research Institute, where he used eye tracking and MEG to study how memory changes with healthy aging.

Sunita Sah, MD, PhD, MBA is director of Cornell University's Academic Leadership Institute and a professor in the management and organizations group at Cornell University's College of Business. A physician turned organizational psychologist, she has published widely on conflicts of interest, disclosure, trust, ethics, and how we respond to outside influence.

Michael T. Sanders is a professor of public policy at King's College London, where he is director of the Experimental Government Team, which focuses on the use of behavioral and data sciences and experimental methods to improve outcomes in governments. He was previously the founding chief executive of What Works for Children's Social Care, and the first chief scientist of the Behavioural Insights Team.

Andris Saulītis is a senior researcher at the Institute of Philosophy and Sociology (University of Latvia). He has an MA degree in social anthropology (The New School, USA) and a PhD in sociology (European University Institute, Italy). Andris's interdisciplinary background has given him the ability to deliver broad insights on human behavior from healthcare to debt collection and tax compliance. He has carried out several field experiments to evaluate and examine various business activities and public policies in the Baltics. In his free time, he walks his two greyhounds in the forest and collects mushrooms if they're in season.

Irene Scopelliti is a professor of marketing and behavioral science at Bayes Business School, City, University of London, where she is also codirector of the L@B. She holds a PhD in management from Bocconi University and was previously a postdoctoral research fellow at Carnegie Mellon University. Irene's research interests are in the field of judgment and decision-making, and her work has been published in leading management, marketing, and psychology journals.

Anisha Singh is the director for research and innovation at Busara, where she leads Busara's research portfolio focused on creating new knowledge and testing behavioral interventions for poverty alleviation. She is a practitioner-in-residence at MIT GOV/LAB, putting together a guide on running behavioral lab experiments for development. Occasionally, she teaches behavioral experiments for international development at the University of Chicago. Anisha's research focuses on gender equality in workspaces in the developing world. If not working, Anisha is photographing wildlife, decorating her home, or enjoying a new city.

Dilip Soman is a Canada research chair in behavioral science and economics at the Rotman School of Management, University of Toronto, and the project director of the "Behaviourally Informed Organizations" initiative. He has degrees in behavioral science, management, and engineering, and is interested in the applications of behavioral science to welfare and policy. He is the author of *The Last Mile* (2015), coeditor of *The Behaviorally Informed Organization* (2021), and coeditor of *Behavioral Science in the Wild* (2022), all with University of Toronto Press. His nonacademic interests include procrastination, cricket, travel, and taking weekends seriously.

Janina Steinmetz is an associate professor of marketing at Bayes Business School, City, University of London. She holds a PhD in social psychology from the University of Cologne and has since worked at the University of Chicago's Booth School of Business and at Utrecht University. Janina's research investigates how the social context affects consumer motivation and self-control. Furthermore, she studies how consumers engage in impression management.

Chiara Varazzani (PhD, Sorbonne) is lead behavioral scientist at the Organisation for Economic Co-operation and Development (OECD) in Paris. She also serves as a member of the World Health Organization (WHO) Technical Advisory Group on Behavioural Insights. Previously, she held several positions in government: principal advisor of the Behavioural Insights Unit of the Victorian Government in Australia, senior advisor in behavioral economics to the Australian Federal Government, and research fellow at the Behavioural Insights Team in London. She holds a PhD in behavioral neuroscience from Sorbonne University, an MSc from the School for Advanced Studies in Social Sciences and an MSc in cognitive sciences from the École Normale Supérieure.

Steve Wendel currently serves as a vice president at the Busara Center for Behavioral Economics, where he is responsible for technical excellence, growing Busara's presence in Latin America, and overseeing the inclusive finance portfolio. Previously, he founded and led behavioral science teams at Morningstar and HelloWallet, developing and field-testing hundreds of interventions to improve financial behavior. He has had the opportunity to publish dozens of pieces, including three books on applied behavioral science, including *Designing for Behavior Change*. To help himself and others learn about behavioral science, he founded BehavioralTeams.com and the nonprofit Action Design Network. Steve has two wonderful kids and a wife, who don't care about this behavioral science stuff at all.

Ashley Whillans is an assistant professor at the Harvard Business School, where her research focuses on understanding how decisions about time and money shape happiness. She has a PhD in social psychology from the University of British Columbia. Previously, she cofounded the Behavioural Science Division of the British Columbia Public Service Agency. She is the author of the trade book *Time Smart: How to Reclaim Your Time and Live a Happier Life*. In her spare time, you can find Ashley writing popular press articles, going for long walks, and hanging out with her kitty, daughter, and husband.

Rebecca Wickes (PhD, Griffith) is a professor at the School of Criminology and Criminal Justice, Griffith University. Her research focuses on neighborhood social processes and their effects on crime and other social problems in Australia, and she is the lead investigator on the Australian Community Capacity Study (ACCS) – a multimillion-dollar, internationally leading longitudinal study of the concentration of social problems in residential communities. Prior to joining Griffith, Rebecca was the founding director of the Monash Migration and Inclusion Centre (MMIC), established in 2018 at Monash University, where she worked with local governments, nongovernmental organizations, and state governments to identify programs and pathways that enhance social, economic, and cultural inclusion in urban and regional communities.